Security, LLC

The Entrepreneur's Comprehensive Blueprint for Launching and Running a Thriving Consulting Business

Meb West, CPP, CCM, CHS-III

To Jenny:

The consummate partner in life and business and more than I can deserve to ask for. You took a chance by buying a ticket on this wild ride, and you've taken us places I never dreamed we could go. You are the spirit, dedication, motivation, and darn hard work behind our brand. The only person I've met who consistently outworks, outperforms, and outshines me. I'm lucky to have such a strategic partner.

Endorsements

"Launching your own security consulting company can be daunting. In his book, Meb has bridged the gap between theory and practice. It is an indispensable guide packed with actionable insights, strategic advice, and real-world experiences. Simply put, this is a must-read for anyone looking to make an impact in the security industry." - James Rusk, Director of Risk Management, Gates Family Office

"Meb has a brilliant mind and an artful way of communicating. The distinction is he's one of the few who's both 'been there and done that' but can also communicate the lesson learned in a digestible way. Recommended." – Elijah Shaw Elijah, CEO, ICON

"Security, LLC is a must-read for anyone serious about launching and scaling a successful consulting business in the security industry. Meb has delivered a comprehensive, clear, and actionable blueprint to help readers navigate common pitfalls and accelerate their path to success. Whether you are just starting or looking to refine your existing business, this book provides invaluable insights from real-world experience. It is not just a guide; it is a roadmap to building a thriving security consultancy." –

Gerard Boniello, CPP, PSP, CCAP, President, Omnium Protection Group.

"In the world of security-related how-to books (there are many), Security, LLC stands out and is a gold standard. This is a comprehensive guide and blueprint for you to ingest on the varying complexities of starting and succeeding in today's modern and ever-changing world of international security consulting. I wish a book like this existed when I entered the business so many years ago, as this one is thorough and compelling. There is information contained within the pages that will take years to learn on your own, through trial and error, and lost revenue. This book is highly recommended on many levels and should be an integral part of your reading and reference material for years to come. For those of you who would like to start swimming in the right direction and not just treading water, then this is the book for you. As said in the book, 'Learn to play chess while others are playing checkers.'" – Charles (Chuck) A. Mauldin, CPS.

This Book should be in the library of every Executive Protection & Consulting practitioner. Meb effectively combines an easy, humorous writing style with comprehensive, well-organized information. His depth of knowledge, research, and experience produced a highly detailed, level-headed guidance tool. The result is a step-by-step, understandable manual for building a great company and establishing a fine career. I wish I had had this when starting my company. It would have saved countless hours of trial & error, stress, and concerns while improving the company's performance, stability, and growth. Barry Wilson, President, Anlance Protection Ltd.

"In "Security LLC," Meb West masterfully guides aspiring consultants through the transition from employee to entrepreneur with a refreshing blend of practical strategies and candid insights. This essential roadmap demystifies the complexities of starting a consulting business and empowers readers to embrace the journey with confidence and humor. I wish this book was around when I started my security consulting firm. A

MUST READ for security professionals." - Nate Romero C.P.S, M.A, Security Consultant.

From senior leadership in a Tier 1 Military Unit to founding a trusted and successful security business, Meb's experience spans the Globe. As a servant leader who provides guidance built upon decades of experience, Meb is a humble titan in the security industry that anybody at any level of experience can emulate. Meb is an adroit security professional and, most importantly, a man of character who leads with intellectual humor and wit and will leave an impact for years to come. Chris W. | Former SOT-A and a Trusted Cybersecurity Advisor, 360 Privacy

Contents

Introduction

Let's start this book off with a face-slapping reality check. If you're reading this, you're probably teetering on the edge of a monumental decision: stepping out of the warm, fluorescent glow of employee security work and into the exhilarating (and sometimes terrifying) world of independent consulting. Maybe you've been dreaming about setting your own schedule, choosing your clients, and finally becoming the captain of your own security ship. Or you're sick of writing incident reports under flickering office lights while surviving on lukewarm coffee. Either way, you're in the right place.

The Odds, The Opportunities, and The Plan to Beat Them

Here's the thing: the leap from security practitioner to independent consultant is more common than you might think. In fact, according to recent industry statistics, nearly 20% of security professionals consider starting their own consulting businesses at some point in their careers. You're not alone in this journey. Yet, out of those brave souls, only a fraction make the jump, and even fewer land safely. Why? Because, as the saying goes, 'Failing to plan is planning to fail.' (And let's face it, winging it doesn't work well when you're in the business of preventing chaos.)

Now, let's talk about small businesses in general. Did you know that 20% of small businesses fail in their first year? And by year five, that number climbs to a sobering 50%? I don't share these stats to scare you off. I share them because the other side of that statistic is this: half of small businesses succeed. And the ones that thrive don't do so by accident. They do it through meticulous planning, strategic execution, and yes, a touch of stubborn resilience – which is precisely what this book is here to help you achieve.

Unlike other guides that leave you guessing, Security LLC is your safety net, game plan, and secret weapon all rolled into one. Think of it as your friendly co-pilot for navigating the uncharted airspace of entrepreneurship (trust me, turbulence IS included at no charge!).

Why Listen to Me?

Fair question. My name is Meb West, and I've spent over two decades knee–deep in the trenches of security consulting, compliance management, and global risk mitigation. As the owner of Seven Spears Security International, I've advised Fortune 500 companies, worked with ultra-high–net–worth individuals, and directed security operations in some of the most complex and volatile environments on the planet. I've been there, done that, and got the t–shirt (and it's stained and no longer form–fitting).

But beyond the war stories and the jargon, what sets me apart is my passion for helping others succeed. I know the hurdles you're facing because I've faced them, too: the fear of financial instability, the steep learning curve of business fundamentals, and the challenge of carving out a niche in a crowded market. And let's not forget the soul-crushing existential dread of trying to craft a LinkedIn bio that doesn't sound like a robot wrote it. (Spoiler alert: that's covered in this book too.) I have had to take the leap from the safety of the corporate employee nest into the wide-open air of the freedom (and outright terror) of running my own company.

And I have to be brutally honest, straight from the jump. With all my background and experience in a wide array of public and private sector challenges, I've never worked harder in my life than as an entrepreneur. First, being your own boss is a dual-edged sword. Yes, time off requests are approved more quickly, but 9 times out of 10, my boss is a bigger jerk than anyone I've ever worked for! Every morning when my feet hit the floor, my thoughts immediately go to, "How am I keeping the lights on today?" "Are my clients happy?" "Do I have enough cash on hand to make payroll?" "Is today the day it all explodes in a glorious explosion of insecurities and fear of failure?" That and more makes me crack the whip and keep myself in line.

There are many security experts out there who have tried to write a book like this before. Some of them aren't half–bad, either. But I've found that most (if not all) of them miss the final ingredient that you'll get from me. Yes, I have the training, certifications, education, and experience to be considered a subject matter expert in security consulting, but I also have post-graduate certificates from some of the nation's leading business schools. What sets this book apart is its unique blend of security expertise and business acumen. I'm honored to be a graduate of programs from some of the most elite business schools in the world: Harvard Business School, the Wharton School of Business, and IE Business in Madrid, Spain. So, I can talk to you about customer acquisition costs, free cash flow, international risk, quality management processes, and other subjects that will make your eyes roll back in your head. Bottom line, you can rest assured that you are in uniquely qualified hands to guide you on this journey.

What This Book Will Do for You

Now, let's get down to brass tacks. Security LLC isn't just a guide – it's a comprehensive blueprint that equips you with the knowledge and tools to navigate every step of launching, marketing, and scaling your security consulting business. Here's what you can expect:

The Mindset Shift: Let's not sugarcoat it – entrepreneurship is a mental game as much as it is a business one. That's why we'll explore personal growth strategies to help you build resilience, manage stress, and embrace your new role as a business owner.

The Business Fundamentals: Ever wonder how to write a business plan that doesn't just gather dust on a shelf? Or how to navigate legal requirements without needing a law degree? I've got you covered.

The Marketing Machine: Marketing isn't just for influencers and coffee shops. I'll show you how to build a killer brand, network like a pro, and position yourself as the go-to expert in your niche.

The Tech Toolbox: Scared of all the tech talk? Don't be. I'll break down the latest security technologies in plain English and show you how to integrate them into your services without breaking a sweat (or your budget).

The Client Playbook: Finding clients is one thing; keeping them is another. We'll explore strategies for building lasting relationships that turn one-off gigs into ongoing contracts.

The Survival Kit: Remember those statistics about business failure? I'll arm you with risk management frameworks, time management techniques, and pricing strategies to ensure your business stays in the success column.

Why Have Humor in a Serious Business Book

As you read this book, you'll notice that I don't take myself too seriously. Why? Because humor makes the hard stuff easier. Starting a business is serious work, but we can still have some fun along the way. Whether it's poking fun at my missteps (yes, I've made a few) or sharing a laugh about the absurdities of the industry, my goal is to keep you engaged, entertained, and, most importantly, empowered.

A Few Words of Encouragement (and a Gentle Kick in the Pants)

Here's the deal: You already have the skills, the expertise, and the drive to succeed. You need a roadmap – and maybe a little nudge to take the first step. That's where this book comes in. By the time you turn the last page, you'll have everything you need to build a thriving consulting business that pays the bills and fulfills your passion for making the world a safer place.

So, what are you waiting for? Let's get to work. Together, we'll turn your vision into a reality, one step (and one chuckle) at a time.

1

So, you want to be an Independent Security Consultant? Let's Get Your Head Examined!

"Entrepreneurship is living a few years of your life like most people won't, so you can spend the rest of your life like most people can't."

— Unknown

Did you know? According to the Small Business Administration, over 60% of small businesses in the U.S. are launched by individuals transitioning from traditional employment to entrepreneurship.

Traits of the Successful Security Entrepreneur

Being a successful entrepreneur in the security consulting space is about something more than owning a fancy suit or knowing how to install the latest camera system (though, hey, that doesn't hurt). It's about embodying specific traits that allow you to thrive in an ever-changing, high–stakes environment. Here are the Top 25 traits of a successful security entrepreneur, each tailored to the unique demands of this industry.

Visionary Thinking – The best security entrepreneurs don't just see the world as it is – they see it as it *could be.* They anticipate trends, foresee threats, and develop solutions before their clients even realize they need them. Being a step ahead in security isn't just smart – it's lifesaving.

Resilience – Let's face it: Clients cancel, contracts fall through, and sometimes, you run out of energy drinks at about hour 2 of a 48–hour deadline push. Resilience is the ability to bounce back stronger and keep your cool when the unexpected happens (which is basically every Tuesday in this business).

Attention to Detail – In security consulting, the devil is *literally* in the details. Miss one minor vulnerability and the consequences could be enormous. Successful entrepreneurs notice the things others overlook – and then fix them.

Strong Communication Skills – You could be a security wizard, but you're sunk if you can't explain your plan to a client without using 37 acronyms. Great entrepreneurs speak clearly and persuasively, whether addressing a boardroom or training a team.

Adaptability – The security landscape changes fast. Today's challenge might be cybersecurity; tomorrow's might be drones; the next day anti–drones. Flexibility ensures you stay relevant, no matter what comes next. Think of it as professional yoga – minus the spandex.

Empathy – Security isn't just about locks and alarms; it's about people. Empathy allows you to understand your clients' fears and the culture of their family or company and provide solutions that truly address their needs. Plus, a little kindness goes a long way in building trust.

Problem–Solving Skills – The security world is full of puzzles, from designing access controls to mitigating risks. Successful entrepreneurs thrive on solving these challenges and don't rest until every piece fits.

Confidence – Clients want to feel safe, and nothing says "I've got this" like a consultant who exudes confidence. Just ensure it's backed by competence and humility; overconfidence without substance will sink you faster than a leaky boat.

Integrity – Trust is your most valuable currency in this field. Without integrity, your reputation will crumble faster than a house of cards in a hurricane. Consistently deliver on your promises, even when it's tough.

Strategic Thinking – Great entrepreneurs think several steps ahead. Whether designing a security system or planning a business expansion, they play chess while others are playing checkers.

Risk Tolerance – Starting any business is risky, but security consulting has its own challenges. Whether it's navigating regulatory issues, legal liabilities, or handling high–stakes situations, successful entrepreneurs know how to take calculated risks.

Creativity – Security solutions aren't one–size–fits–all. The best entrepreneurs think outside the box, designing innovative strategies that address unique challenges. Remember: it's not just about thinking *big* – it's about thinking *smart*.

Leadership – From managing a team to guiding clients, leadership is non-negotiable. And no, barking orders like a drill sergeant doesn't count. Authentic leadership inspires confidence and motivates everyone to work toward a common goal.

Networking Savvy – In the security industry, who you know can be as important as what you know. Building relationships with other professionals, vendors, and clients can open doors you didn't even know existed.

Financial Acumen – If you can't balance a budget, your business will be in trouble faster than you can say "overhead." Successful entrepreneurs understand cash flow, pricing strategies, and the importance of financial planning.

Passion for Learning – The security industry evolves constantly. Staying on top means committing to lifelong learning. Whether it's new technology or regulatory updates, successful entrepreneurs never stop sharpening their skills.

Patience – Not every client will be easy, and not every project will go smoothly. Patience keeps you calm, collected, and professional, even when the going gets tough.

Marketing Know–How – You might have the best services in the world, but if no one knows about them, it doesn't matter. Successful entrepreneurs understand how to market themselves effectively, both online and offline.

Decisiveness – When faced with a tough choice, hesitation can be costly. Successful security entrepreneurs make informed decisions quickly and confidently, knowing when to act and when to hold.

Tech–Savviness – From surveillance systems to cybersecurity, technology is at the heart of modern security. The conflux of physical and technical security happened over a decade ago, and we must stop pretending that this is an emerging concept. Entrepreneurs who embrace technology will always have the edge over those who resist it.

Time Management Skills – Managing your time effectively is crucial in a field where emergencies can happen at any time. Successful entrepreneurs prioritize wisely and know when to delegate.

Customer Focus – Your clients are your lifeline. Putting their needs first, delivering exceptional service, exceeding expectations (even in areas outside your area of responsibility), and following up consistently are essential for building a loyal client base.

Self–motivation – No boss is looking over your shoulder when you're an entrepreneur. Successful individuals set their own goals, hold themselves accountable, and keep pushing forward – even on the tough days.

Cultural Sensitivity – Understanding different cultures is vital in a globalized world. This trait ensures you can work effectively with diverse clients and teams, building trust across cultural lines wherever the job takes you.

Sense of Humor – If we're serious for a second, we must acknowledge that sometimes things will go hilariously wrong. A good laugh can diffuse tension, foster connections, and remind you why you love what you do.

These traits aren't just admirable – they're your toolkit for success. As you grow your business, revisit this list often. Think of it as your entrepreneurial compass, guiding you toward the skills and habits that will set you apart in the security consulting world. You should constantly be assessing where you stand in relation to each of these traits and looking for ways to level–up your game. Now, which of these traits will you focus on cultivating today?

Entrepreneur Self–Assessment Questionnaire: Are You Ready?

Embarking on the journey of becoming a security entrepreneur is no small feat. It's like preparing for a marathon – only this one involves managing clients, juggling responsibilities, and dodging the occasional curveball. To help you gauge your readiness, grab a scrap sheet of paper and take this questionnaire based on the Top 25 traits of a successful security entrepreneur we just discussed. Answer honestly (there's no judgment here), and at the end, we'll tally your score and see where you stand.

The Entrepreneurial Readiness Questionnaire

In each category, rate yourself on a scale from 1 to 5:

1 = Not my strength at all.

2 = I have some experience but need growth.

3 = Average – working on it!

4 = Above Average – feeling good here.

5 = This is my superpower!

1. Visionary Thinking: I can see opportunities and anticipate trends before they happen.

2. Resilience: I bounce back quickly from setbacks and keep moving forward.

3. Attention to Detail: I notice the small stuff others overlook and know it makes a big difference.

4. Strong Communication Skills: I explain ideas clearly and persuasively to clients or my team.

5. Adaptability: I stay flexible and thrive in changing circumstances.

6. Empathy: I understand others' perspectives and use this to build trust and relationships.

7. Problem–Solving Skills: I enjoy tackling challenges and finding creative solutions.

8. Confidence: I project assurance in my abilities while staying grounded in reality.

9. Integrity: I always deliver on my promises and prioritize honesty and trust.

10. Strategic Thinking: I can plan ahead and see the bigger picture while managing the details.

11. Risk Tolerance: I can take calculated risks without losing sleep (most of the time).

12. Creativity: I approach challenges with fresh, innovative ideas.

13. Leadership: I inspire and guide others to achieve common goals.

14. Networking Savvy: I actively build and maintain professional relationships.

15. Financial Acumen: I understand the basics of budgets, cash flow, and financial planning.

16. Passion for Learning: I am eager to learn new skills and stay updated in my field.

17. Patience: I stay calm and composed, even when things don't go as planned.

18. Marketing Know–How: I understand how to promote my business and attract clients.

19. Decisiveness: I make informed decisions quickly and confidently.

20. Tech–Savviness: I embrace technology and use it to enhance my business.

21. Time Management Skills: I prioritize tasks effectively and avoid wasting time.

22. Customer Focus: I put my client's needs first and deliver exceptional service.

23. Self–motivation: I set goals and stay disciplined to achieve them.

24. Cultural Sensitivity: I respect and understand different cultures in professional settings.

25. Sense of Humor: I can laugh at myself and find humor in tough situations.

Grading System – How'd You Do?

Add up your total score. Max score: 125 (you're basically an entrepreneurial superhero).

Evaluate your score using the guide below:

- **100 – 125**: Great Job! You've got what it takes to rock the entrepreneurial world! Your readiness level is high, but there's always room to fine-tune your skills.
- **75 – 99:** Solid start! You have many strengths and a few areas to focus on. Consider this your checklist for growth.
- **50 – 74:** You're on your way, but there's room to develop key traits. With effort and commitment, you can absolutely get there!
- **Below 50**: Don't fret! Remember, entrepreneurship isn't a sprint; it's a marathon. Focus on one or two traits at a time to build your foundation.

A Word of Encouragement: No matter your score, take this assessment as a tool for growth, not a final verdict. The best entrepreneurs aren't born ready – they *become* ready through learning, persistence, and action. If you scored lower in some areas, don't sweat it. Each step you take to improve brings you closer to success. And if you're already flying high, keep sharpening your skills.

Remember: every entrepreneur starts somewhere, and every journey is unique. Now, grab that energy drink (or kombucha, you culturally sensitive ninja!) and start planning how you're going to level up your entrepreneurial acumen. Your security consulting dream is waiting!

Skills Inventory: Bridging Gaps for Business Launch

So, you've taken the Entrepreneur Self–Assessment. Maybe you scored like a champ in some areas, while others need a bit of TLC. That's perfectly normal – nobody starts their journey with every skill polished to perfection. The key is identifying those gaps and building an action plan that works for *you*. Think of this as your personal entrepreneurial boot camp: targeted, achievable, and (yes) even a little fun.

Step 1: Tackling the Traits Assessment Gaps

Let's start with your results from the self–assessment. Did a few traits land closer to a "1" or "2" than you'd like? Don't worry; we're not here to judge – we're here to grow.

Here's how to build a realistic, milestone-driven action plan:

Pick One Trait to Focus on at a Time: Trying to master everything simultaneously is a recipe for burnout. Instead, start with the trait that will make the most significant and immediate impact on your business. Maybe it's improving your financial acumen or boosting your networking savvy.

Set a Specific Goal: Vague goals like "get better at marketing" aren't helpful. Instead, define what success looks like. For example: "Learn three digital marketing strategies and apply them to my business within two months."

Break It Down: Divide your goal into smaller, bite-sized steps. If you're working on your tech-savviness, your steps might look like this:

- Week 1: Watch a free tutorial on basic cybersecurity tools.
- Week 2: Sign up for a free trial of a project management app like Trello or Asana.
- Week 3: Research affordable tech certifications and set a budget for training.

Add Milestones and Deadlines: Motivation loves a deadline. On your journey, create checkpoints to track your progress. For example, "By the end of this month, I'll have attended one webinar and implemented two marketing strategies."

Celebrate Small Wins: Learning a new skill is hard work – reward yourself for progress. Crushed that public speaking workshop? Treat yourself to your favorite dessert (or a nap – naps are underrated; Jesus took naps!).

Step 2: Reviewing the Table of Contents for Business Gaps

Next, flip back to the Table of Contents for this book. It's more than a list; it's the plan for your entrepreneurial journey. As you scan the chapters, ask yourself these questions:

What chapters feel like familiar territory? Maybe you're already confident about "Building a Unique Business Model" or "Establishing Credibility."

What chapters make you think, "Uh–oh"? Perhaps "Financial Management for a Security Consulting Business" or "The Importance of Professional Associations" feels like an alien language.

Action Plan for Business Knowledge Gaps

Highlight Chapters That Need Extra Attention: Grab a pen (or digital highlighter) and mark the chapters or subsections that feel intimidating or unfamiliar.

Pinpoint Specific Areas Within Those Chapters: For example, if "Marketing Your Security Consulting Services" is daunting, narrow it down: Are you nervous about social media, speaking at industry events, or SEO? The more specific you can be, the easier it will be to tackle.

Pair Learning with Action: Learning isn't about reading endless books or watching endless videos – it's about applying what you learn. If you're studying "Developing an Online Presence," build your LinkedIn profile as you go.

Create a Timeline for Mastery: Assign time frames to each chapter or subsection. For example:

- Week 1: Review "Essential Certifications for Security Consultants" and decide which certifications align with my goals.
- Week 2: Research certification programs and register for one.

Seek Out Support and Resources: Remember, you're not alone. Join professional groups, take online courses, or find a mentor to guide you through tricky topics.

Step 3: Build Your Action Plan

Here's a template to get you started (the **bold** is just an example for clarity):

- Skill or Knowledge Gap: (**Marketing Strategies**)
- Why It's Important: (**Attracting clients and building my brand.**)
- Action Steps:
    - (**Watch a webinar on LinkedIn marketing.**)
    - (**Write and publish three LinkedIn posts this month.**)
    - (**Network with five professionals in my niche**.)
- Timeline: (**Complete all steps within four weeks.**)
- Milestones:
    - Week 1: (**Finish the webinar.**)
    - Week 2: (**Draft LinkedIn posts.**)
    - Week 3: (**Publish posts and network**.)
- Reward: (**An energy drink for each milestone achieved!**)

Remember, bridging gaps is not about fixing what's "wrong" with you; it's about building on your strengths and creating a solid foundation for your business. Every entrepreneur starts with areas of uncertainty – it's what you *do* with those uncertainties that counts.

So, roll up your sleeves, get excited about the challenge, and take it one step at a time. Rome wasn't built in a day, and neither is a thriving security consulting business. But with focus, determination, and maybe a little humor along the way, you'll get there.

Ready? Let's start closing those gaps – because your entrepreneurial dream is closer than you think!

Transitioning from Employee to Entrepreneur

If you're still reading, it means that I haven't been able to convince you NOT to set out and become you're the business owner you've always known you had in you. Congrats! You're about to trade in that 9–to–5 grind for the glorious freedom of being your own boss – where the hours are technically 24/7, and the energy drinks will flow like mana from heaven. But before you march into your boss's office with a mic–drop–worthy resignation speech, let's talk about how to make this transition smooth, ethical, and – most importantly – successful.

Preparing for Takeoff: Your Employee–to–Entrepreneur Inventory

The best time to prepare for entrepreneurship is <u>*before*</u> you quit your job. Think of your current employment as the training ground where you can quietly (and ethically) get your ducks in a row. Here's your transition checklist:

Accrue a Financial Buffer (6 – 12 Months of Expenses): Let's be real: starting a business can be financially unpredictable at first. Save enough to cover personal and business expenses for at least six months, ideally a year. This safety net will let you focus on growing your business instead of panicking over your next grocery run. Bonus tip: Start living lean now – your future self (and future boss) will thank you!

Design and Register Your Brand: While you're still employed, brainstorm your business name, design a logo, and register your brand legally. This ensures your business identity is ready to shine the moment you step out on your own. Plus, it's way more fun than spreadsheets (no offense, financial buffer).

Earn Relevant Certifications: If your dream business requires certifications (and in the security world, it often does), now's the time to get them. Use your evenings or weekends to study for and earn credentials like Certified Protection Professional (CPP) or FEMA Incident Command System (ICS) certifications.

Create a Basic Business Plan: Outline your vision, target market, and initial service offerings. This doesn't have to be a novel – just a clear path to guide your launch. If the idea of a business plan sounds daunting, remind yourself that it's basically your entrepreneurial GPS.

Network Like a Pro: Start building relationships in your industry now. Attend events, join online forums, and engage with professional associations. Networking while employed shows initiative, and it's a great way to get your name out there (without raising any office eyebrows).

Test the Waters with a Side Hustle: If possible, start your business on the side. This lets you experiment, learn, and build a small client base before going full-time. Just be mindful of your employer's policies – more on that in the ethics section below.

Develop Key Skills: Use your current role to strengthen transferable skills. Negotiation, project management, and client communication – these are gold for entrepreneurs. Treat every task at work as a chance to prep for your business.

Set Up Systems: Research tools and software you'll need, such as accounting platforms (QuickBooks, anyone?) or project management tools. Setting up systems while you still have a paycheck cushions the initial investment.

Finding Your "Decision Point"

Knowing when to make the leap is critical. Quitting too soon could leave you unprepared; waiting too long might mean missing opportunities. Here's how to identify your "decision point":

Establish Clear Criteria: Create a list of conditions to meet before resigning. For example:

- Financial buffer secured.
- The business plan is finalized.
- At least one certification is completed.
- Side hustle generating consistent income.

Set a Realistic Timeline: Assign dates to your criteria. This keeps you accountable and prevents endless delays caused by the "I'll do it next month" syndrome.

Conduct a Gut Check: Are you emotionally and mentally ready for uncertainty? You don't have to feel 100% confident (nobody does), but you should feel prepared to embrace the journey with all its ups and downs.

Seek Input: Talk to mentors, friends, or other entrepreneurs. Sometimes, an outside perspective can confirm you're ready – or point out an area you've overlooked.

Staying Ethical During the Transition

Let's talk ethics. Building your own business doesn't mean burning bridges. In fact, you'll want to leave your current role with your integrity – and reputation – intact.

Don't Poach Clients: It's tempting to reach out to your employer's clients, especially if you have great relationships with them. Don't. It's not only unethical but could land you in legal hot water. Plus, this industry is smaller than you think. Word gets around.

Avoid Plagiarism: Sure, your current company's policies and templates look handy, but resist the urge to "borrow" them. Instead, create original documents or invest in industry-standard templates to keep everything above board.

Respect Confidentiality: If you signed a non-disclosure agreement (NDA), honor it. Trust and professionalism are indispensable in the security industry, and breaking them could ruin your reputation.

Give Proper Notice: When the time comes, provide a respectful notice period – two weeks is standard, but longer may be appropriate depending on your role.

Leave on Good Terms: Even if you didn't love your job, thank your employer for the experience and keep communication cordial. You never know when your paths might cross again.

Pep Talk Time: Transitioning from employee to entrepreneur is exciting, nerve-wracking, and deeply rewarding. It's okay to feel scared – that just means you're stepping out of your comfort zone. With preparation, a clear decision point, and an ethical approach, you'll set yourself up for success.

So, go tackle your checklist, and remember: every great entrepreneur once faced the same choice you're making now. The difference? They took the leap. And you can, too.

Chapter 1 Wrap–Up: Are You Ready to Take the Leap?

Congratulations! You've just completed Chapter 1 and are officially on the first step of your journey toward becoming a successful security entrepreneur. Let's take a moment to recap the tools, insights, and strategies we've covered. Think of this as your entrepreneurial toolkit – polished, sharpened, and ready to go.

Traits of a Successful Security Entrepreneur

We kicked things off by diving into the Top 25 traits of a successful security entrepreneur. From resilience (because, let's face it, stuff *will* go wrong) to visionary thinking (turning problems into opportunities), you explored the qualities that set great entrepreneurs apart. These traits aren't about perfection – they're about growth. The good news? You can cultivate every single one of these traits, one step at a time.

Entrepreneur Self–Assessment: Are You Ready?

Next, you held up the proverbial mirror with a self–assessment questionnaire. Sure, some traits might have landed squarely in the "needs improvement" category, but that's just part of the process. You can't fix what you don't acknowledge, right? With your honest answers in hand, you now have a clear picture of where you shine and where you need to level up. Remember, this isn't about being perfect from day one – it's about progress.

Skills Inventory: Bridging Gaps for Business Launch

Keeping your assessment results in mind, we created an action plan to bridge gaps. Whether tackling marketing strategies, earning certifications, or mastering time management, you learned to break big goals into manageable milestones. Even better, you paired each step with a realistic timeline and some well–earned rewards. (Go ahead, plan that celebratory pizza night!)

We also encouraged you to take a peek at the Table of Contents of this book, identifying areas that might require extra attention. Whether it's certifications, finances, or building your online presence, you now have a process to tackle those challenges head-on.

Transitioning from Employee to Entrepreneur

Finally, we tackled the big one: making the leap from employee to entrepreneur. You learned how to prepare while still employed, from building a financial buffer (hello, six months of breathing room!) to earning certifications and testing the waters with a side hustle.

We also covered the importance of setting a clear "decision point" – knowing when it's time to make your move. And, of course, we couldn't skip over the ethical considerations. Leaving your current role with integrity ensures you walk into entrepreneurship with your reputation – and opportunities – intact.

The Big Takeaway

Starting your own security consulting business isn't about being fearless or flawless. It's about being prepared, adaptable, and persistent. If you've made it through this chapter, you've already proven you've got what it takes to build a strong foundation for success.

So, what's next? Revisit your action plans and remember that every successful entrepreneur started exactly where you are now. The difference? They didn't let fear stop them. They took the leap – and so will you.

Here's to your journey ahead! You've got this. Let's move on to Chapter 2 and explore the fascinating world of security consulting.

2

Introduction to the Security Consulting Industry

"Security is not a product, but a process."

— Bruce Schneier

Global security services is projected to surpass $300 billion by 2027, driven by rising concerns about safety, technology advancements, and increasingly complex risks.

The security consulting industry plays a vital role in today's fast-changing world. From advising corporations on physical and cyber threats to protecting ultra-high–net–worth individuals, security consultants are the unsung heroes behind the scenes. In this chapter, we'll examine the industry's role, explore its many advantages, and address the challenges you'll likely face. By the end, you'll clearly understand what it means to be a security consultant and why this career path is as rewarding as it is essential.

The Role of Security Consulting in Today's World

Security consulting isn't just about cameras, locks, or the occasional bodyguard – it's a multifaceted industry that touches nearly every sector on the planet. Public or private, large or small, every organization faces risks that require tailored solutions. And that's where you come in as a security consultant. Your job isn't just to react to threats; it's to foresee them, prevent them, and, when necessary, manage them effectively.

The Ubiquity of Security Consulting

Think of any industry, and chances are, security consulting is involved. There's no shortage of need, from retail stores needing loss prevention strategies to financial institutions safeguarding against cyberattacks, educational campuses requiring physical security assessments, and government agencies addressing national security concerns.

Here's a staggering figure: the global private security market, which includes consulting, is projected to grow at a compound annual growth rate (CAGR) of 6.9%, reaching over $300 billion by 2027. Why? Because threats evolve, regulations tighten, and organizations are more aware than ever of the risks they face.

Countless Niches to Explore

The beauty of security consulting is its versatility. You're not locked into one area – you can specialize, pivot, and grow as your interests and the industry evolve. We'll cover niches in detail in the next chapter, but here are just a few to get the brain juices flowing:

Cybersecurity Consulting: With cyberattacks increasing in frequency and sophistication, consultants who can safeguard digital assets are in high demand.

Corporate Security: Helping businesses protect physical assets, employees, and sensitive information.

Ultra-high Net Worth (UHNW) Security: Advising affluent individuals and families on estate security, travel safety, and personal protection.

Event Security: Planning and managing security for high–profile gatherings, concerts, or sporting events.

Government Contracting: Working with local, state, or federal agencies to enhance public safety and compliance.

Physical Security Assessments: Analyzing vulnerabilities in buildings, facilities, and infrastructure.

Crisis Management and Disaster Recovery: Assisting organizations in preparing for and responding to natural disasters or emergencies.

Drone and Anti–Drone Operations: A fast-growing field focused on both utilizing and countering drone technologies.

Cyber-Physical Security Integration: Merging traditional security measures with advanced technology for comprehensive solutions.

These are just the tip of the iceberg. The field's adaptability means you can pivot to a new area if one niche feels stale or oversaturated.

A Dynamic Career Path

The security consulting industry is not just vast – it's dynamic. Unlike static careers where you're confined to the same role for decades, security consulting offers endless opportunities for reinvention.

Consider this: 95% of businesses believe they are at risk of a security breach, yet only a fraction have the expertise to handle it internally. That's where consultants step in, bridging the gap with specialized knowledge. And as industries evolve – whether through advancements in technology, shifts in geopolitics, or changes in societal norms – new niches emerge, creating fresh opportunities for consultants to innovate.

A Global Need

Security isn't just a local concern – it's a global one. Whether you're advising a small nonprofit on protecting donor data, helping a multinational corporation comply with international regulations, or supporting an executive who is a global jetsetter, the scope of security consulting knows no borders.

For example:

In the United States, private security spending exceeds $50 billion annually – more than many countries allocate to their military budgets.

In emerging markets, businesses are investing heavily in security to support economic growth and protect their assets.

The rise of remote work has created new challenges, making cybersecurity and home–office security prime consulting opportunities worldwide.

Artificial Intelligence (AI), The Internet of Things (IoT), drones, and anti-drone aspects are creating a nuanced layer of complexity that allows global threat actors to impact your clients' assets at a local level. While the reality of this is concerning, the opportunity to counter global risks at a regional level is making the world much smaller.

The Role You Play

As a security consultant, you're more than just a problem–solver. You're a strategist, an innovator, and a trusted partner to your clients. Your work ensures safety and peace of mind – a priceless asset in today's uncertain world.

With an industry so expansive and adaptable, the only limits are the ones you set for yourself. Whether you're drawn to technology, logistics, or the human side of risk management, there's a niche waiting for your unique expertise.

Security consulting isn't just a career – it's a calling. And as the world grows more complex, your role in shaping safer environments becomes ever more critical.

Advantages of Starting a Security Consulting Business

Starting your own security consulting business is a little like jumping out of a plane – but don't worry, you've got a parachute that you {{ahem}} packed yourself! There's excitement, nervous anticipation, and, yes, a little fear of the unknown. But when you land, the freedom, opportunity, and sense of accomplishment are worth every bit of the initial adrenaline rush. Let's explore why launching your own security consulting business is one of the most rewarding paths you can take.

You're the Boss

No more middle managers who think "synergy" is an actual skill. When you're running your own business, you call the shots. Want to focus on cybersecurity for small businesses this year and pivot to drone security next year? You can. Your business is your playground, and the freedom to shape it to your vision is exhilarating.

Contrast this with being an employee: your job role, pay scale, and career trajectory are often at the mercy of someone else's decisions. As a business owner, you're in control of your destiny. Sure, the responsibility can feel heavy at times, but it's also empowering.

Building and Growing Your Own Brand

Starting your security consulting business is like raising a child – but without the diaper changes and the pesky teenager phase. You create the name, design the logo, and decide how your brand will appear in the world. Watching that brand grow, evolve, and gain recognition is deeply satisfying.

As your business gains traction, you'll start seeing your hard work pay off in tangible ways: glowing client reviews, a growing roster of clients, and a reputation for excellence in your niche. Each milestone – your first logo design, your first client, your first "we crushed it!" moment – feels like a celebration.

Compare this to working for someone else's company, where you're building their brand, not your own. Sure, you might play a role in their success, but the satisfaction of seeing your name on the door? Priceless.

Limitless Opportunities to Pivot and Innovate

The security industry is massive and ever-changing, and as a consultant, you're perfectly positioned to adapt. If you spot a new trend – say, the rise of anti-drone technologies – you can pivot to meet the demand.

This flexibility is one of the biggest perks of running your own business. You're not confined to a rigid job description; you can evolve as the industry does. And if one niche starts to feel stale, you can reinvent your business to keep things fresh. Try telling your boss at a corporate job that you're bored and want to switch gears – you might get a polite smile, but probably not much else.

Financial Upside

Let's talk money. As an employee, your income is capped by your salary, regardless of how much value you bring to the company. But as a business owner, the sky's the limit. Sure, it takes time and effort to build a steady income, but the rewards can far exceed what you'd earn as an employee.

Plus, you have control over how you structure your pricing – hourly rates, retainers, project-based fees, or even subscription models. The more you grow your expertise and reputation, the more you can charge.

Freedom to Work Your Way

Fancy a late start so you can have cereal on the porch? Want to work from the beach (Wifi permitting)? Want to take an impromptu vacation? As the owner of your own business, you get to design a work-life balance that works for you.

Contrast that with a typical 9–to–5, where your schedule is dictated by someone else's needs. As a business owner, you have the flexibility to prioritize what matters to you – whether that's family time, travel, or simply taking a random Wednesday off because you can.

The Joy of Solving Problems That Matter

Security consulting is more than a business – it's a calling. You're helping clients safeguard what's most important to them, whether that's their people, data, or assets. The satisfaction of knowing your work makes a real difference is hard to beat.

Sure, as an employee, you might still solve problems, but the personal fulfillment of building a solution for *your* clients under *your* brand is next level.

Challenges = Growth

Okay, running your own business isn't all sunshine and rainbows. There will be challenges – demanding clients, tight deadlines, and the occasional "What was I thinking?!" moment. But here's the thing: every challenge is an opportunity to grow.

As an entrepreneur, you'll develop resilience, adaptability, and resourcefulness in ways you never imagined. And unlike working for someone else, where your mistakes might earn you a slap on the wrist, your challenges as a business owner become part of your success story.

Why Start Now?

Starting your own security consulting business isn't just about financial independence or career growth – it's about creating something that's truly yours. It's about waking up every day excited to tackle new challenges and knowing that every ounce of effort you put in is building _your_ dream, not someone else's.

Yes, it's a leap of faith. Yes, it's hard work. But the rewards – freedom, fulfillment, and the joy of growing something from the ground up – are worth every moment. So, why wait? Your security consulting empire is waiting to be built. So, start planning, and get ready to make your mark. You've got this!

Common Challenges in the Security Industry

To be sure, it's not all rainbows and unicorns. And it's important to be frank about this from the outset. While it's a rewarding field with endless opportunities, it also comes with its fair share of challenges. The good news? Each challenge is a hidden opportunity to set yourself apart and thrive in a highly competitive industry. So, grab your favorite beverage (energy drink, tea, or something stronger – we won't judge), and let's break down the hurdles you might face – and how to overcome them.

The Competitive Marketplace

The security consulting industry is crowded, with consultants offering everything from cybersecurity assessments to physical security plans. Standing out can feel like trying to yell over a crowd at a rock concert.

Reframe It as an Opportunity: Competition is proof of demand. The key is to carve out your niche. Instead of being a generalist, focus on a specific area where you can shine, like drone security or corporate risk assessments. Your unique expertise will make you the go-to expert, turning the competitive landscape into a stage where you can shine.

Regulatory and Compliance Headaches

Security consulting is a maze of laws, regulations, and standards that vary by location, industry, and even client type. For example, the licensing requirements in California might be completely different from those in Florida. Worse yet, the licensing requirements in Colorado are different in Denver, which are different than in Colorado Springs, which are different than in Fort Collins (and don't even get us started on international clients).

Reframe It as an Opportunity: This complexity can feel daunting, but it's also a chance to become the expert your clients need. You position yourself as an indispensable resource by mastering these regulations and staying current. Plus, building strong relationships with legal and compliance professionals can give you an edge – and maybe even save you a few headaches. It also allows you to develop strategic alliances with vetted and trusted peer vendors licensed in areas where you are not.

Lack of a Central Governing Body

Unlike other professions with standardized certifications and governing boards, security consulting is a bit like the Wild West. While organizations like ASIS International provide certifications, there is no universal governing body to set industry standards.

Reframe It as an Opportunity: This lack of uniformity means you have the freedom to shape your practice and define your standards. To build credibility, focus on earning respected certifications (like CPP, PSP, or CISSP). Then, go a step further by educating your clients about why these certifications matter. You'll stand out as a trusted, informed professional in an industry where not everyone is playing by the same rules.

Disparate Licensing Requirements

Depending on where you operate, you might need to navigate a patchwork of licensing requirements. Some states demand specific security consultant licenses, while others don't. Internationally, the rules can be even more convoluted.

Reframe It as an Opportunity: While it is tempting to see this as red tape, meeting licensing requirements can be a differentiator. Many consultants overlook this step, but clients value compliance. Take the time to understand and meet these requirements. It's an investment in your business and reputation – and a great way to avoid the awkwardness of explaining to a client why you're not licensed to work in their state.

Balancing Technology and Human Expertise

Technology is advancing at breakneck speed, with AI, drones, and biometrics transforming the security landscape. But here's the rub: no matter how advanced the tech, it can't replace human judgment. Clients often need a consultant who can integrate both.

Reframe It as an Opportunity: Embrace technology as a tool, not a replacement. Stay ahead of the curve by learning about emerging tech and understanding how to apply it effectively. By positioning yourself as someone who blends cutting–edge tools with critical human insight, you offer clients the best of both worlds.

Building Trust in a Skeptical Market

Clients aren't just buying services – they're buying peace of mind. But in an industry with no shortage of over–promisers and under–deliverers, earning trust can be an uphill battle.

Reframe It as an Opportunity: Transparency is your best friend. Be upfront about what you can deliver and let your results speak for themselves. Build a portfolio of case studies, testimonials, and certifications that showcase your expertise. When clients see your authenticity, they'll return and bring their friends.

Staying Relevant in a Rapidly Changing World

The security challenges of today might not be the challenges of tomorrow. Adapting to new threats, technologies, and client needs is part of the job, and staying relevant requires constant learning.

Reframe It as an Opportunity: A dynamic industry means endless learning and growth opportunities. Invest in continuing education, attend industry conferences, and join professional associations. By staying ahead of the curve, you'll not only remain relevant but also establish yourself as a thought leader.

The Solo Entrepreneur Juggling Act

As an independent consultant, you're not just the expert but also the marketer, accountant, and receptionist. Wearing all these hats can feel overwhelming, especially in the early stages.

Reframe It as an Opportunity: This is your chance to build systems and processes that work for *you*. Use tools like CRM software, project management apps, and financial planners to streamline your workflow. Over time, you can outsource tasks you don't enjoy (looking at you, bookkeeping) and focus on what you love: solving problems and helping clients.

The Bottom Line

Every challenge in the security consulting industry is a chance to grow, innovate, and set yourself apart. By reframing obstacles as opportunities, you'll build a resilient business primed for success.

Remember, you're not just navigating a tricky industry – you're becoming a trusted partner to your clients, helping them protect what matters most. That's not just a job; it's a calling. Challenges? Sure. But with the right mindset, they're just stepping stones to your next big win.

So, ready to tackle these hurdles and turn them into triumphs? We think you are! Let's keep going – there's much more to explore on this exciting journey.

Developing the Mindset of a Security Consultant

Becoming an independent security consultant is like balancing on a tightrope while juggling chainsaws – and occasionally dodging unexpected curveballs. It's a thrilling, rewarding act, but one that requires a specific mindset to pull off successfully.

In Chapter 1, we explored the traits of a successful entrepreneur, and in this chapter, we've discussed the opportunities and challenges of the security consulting industry. Now, it's time to discuss the glue that holds it together: your mindset. To thrive in this field, you need a determined, flexible, and steadfast mental framework – one that keeps you grounded while adapting to ever-changing circumstances. Let's break it down.

Determination with a Dash of Stubborn Optimism

Determination is the backbone of a security consultant's mindset. When faced with a seemingly impossible task, a determined mindset doesn't say, "I can't." It says, "How can I?" Whether securing a high-stakes client or navigating a tricky regulatory environment, determination keeps you moving forward, even when the going gets tough.

Think of it as a mix of grit and stubborn optimism. Yes, there will be setbacks – late-paying clients, last-minute demands, or tech that refuses to cooperate. But with a determined mindset, you'll see each challenge as a stepping towards your dream, not a stumbling block.

Pro Tip: When frustration strikes, breathe and remind yourself why you started this journey. Then, get back to solving the problem. I have a sign on the wall of my desk at eye level that reminds me, "Listen, Breath, Think, Respond." Bonus points if you have a motivational playlist handy.

Flexibility Without Losing Focus

In the security consulting world, the only constant is change. Threats evolve, client needs shift, and technology races ahead. A flexible mindset allows you to pivot gracefully, whether that means learning new skills, updating your service offerings, or reworking a plan mid-project.

But here's the trick: flexibility doesn't mean losing sight of your goals. It's about adjusting your approach while keeping your destination in view. Think of it like navigating a GPS route – sometimes you hit a detour, but the end goal remains the same.

Pro Tip: Embrace the mantra, "Adapt or be left behind." And remember: even the best plans might need a little tweaking. That's not failure – it's growth.

Decisiveness with a Side of Thoughtfulness

As a security consultant, you'll face moments where indecision isn't an option. Clients will look to you for clear, confident answers, often under tight timelines. A decisive mindset is critical – not because you'll always have perfect information, but because the ability to make informed, timely decisions builds trust and keeps projects moving.

At the same time, rash decisions can be as damaging as no decision. Balancing decisiveness with thoughtfulness is key. Take the time to weigh options, but don't let "analysis paralysis" slow you down.

Pro Tip: Use the 80/20 rule: Make the call if you have 80% of the information you need. The other 20% often becomes apparent as you move forward.

Resilience: Your Secret Weapon

Truth be told, setbacks are inevitable. Whether it's a failed pitch, a missed opportunity, or an unexpected hiccup, resilience helps you bounce back stronger. It's the ability to shake off disappointment, learn from mistakes, and keep moving forward with renewed energy.

Resilience also means maintaining perspective. Sure, losing a client might sting, but it's not the end of the world – or your career. As a good friend likes to remind me, "Nobody died...this time." A resilient mindset looks at the big picture and finds silver linings (or at least a good story to tell at industry events).

Pro Tip: Cultivate resilience by practicing self-care. Yes, that might sound cliché, but burnout doesn't serve you or your clients. Take breaks, celebrate wins, and occasionally unplug – your mental health matters.

Confidence Built on Competence

Confidence is essential in this field – clients need to trust that you know your stuff. However, confidence without competence is a recipe for disaster (and possibly some very unhappy clients). We've all seen "that guy" with the "crap don't stink" ego and the ILS (Inflated Lat Syndrome). Don't be that guy.

Developing the right mindset means building confidence on a foundation of expertise. Stay sharp by continually investing in your knowledge and skills through certifications, industry events, or good old-fashioned reading.

Pro Tip: "Fake it 'till you make it." confidence can only take you so far. True confidence comes from preparation and experience. So, if you feel unsure, don't bluff – double down on learning instead.

Integrity: Your Non-Negotiable Compass

A successful security consultant operates with unwavering integrity. Your reputation is your most valuable asset in an industry built on trust. Whether it's being honest about your capabilities, respecting client confidentiality, or admitting when you've made a mistake, integrity will set you apart from the pack.

Pro Tip: Remember that every decision – big or small – strengthens or weakens your reputation. Always choose the high road, even when it's the harder path. I'd take it a step further. Constantly be on the lookout for the good-better-best option. When it comes to integrity, always choose the 'best right' over the 'better right'.

Humor as a Survival Tool

Let's not underestimate the power of humor. Yes, the security industry is serious business, but that doesn't mean you have to take yourself too seriously. A good laugh can diffuse tension, build rapport with clients, and remind you to enjoy the journey.

Pro Tip: When things go sideways (and they will), find the humor in the situation. It's incredible how a well-timed joke can lighten the load. Self-deprecating humor is my secret de-escalation weapon.

The Bottom Line

Developing the mindset of a successful security consultant isn't about perfection – it's about progress. By cultivating determination, flexibility, decisiveness, resilience, confidence, and humor, you'll be ready to tackle the challenges of this dynamic industry. The exception to this is integrity. You need to be all-in with an integrity mindset from the jump. It's non-negotiable.

Remember, your mindset isn't fixed – it's a muscle that grows stronger with practice. So, trust in your abilities and embrace the upcoming ride. You've got what it takes to thrive in this exciting field. Now, let's get to work!

Chapter 2 Wrap-Up: Welcome to the World of Security Consulting

Congratulations! You've just completed Chapter 2, and you're officially equipped with a full understanding of what it takes to thrive in the dynamic world of security consulting. Let's take a quick stroll through the highlights of what we've covered – and get ready to carry this momentum forward as you build your dream business.

The Role of Security Consulting in Today's World

We started by exploring the security consultant's vital role across every industry. Whether designing cybersecurity solutions for tech companies, assessing physical risks for corporate campuses, or safeguarding personal estates, your expertise will make a tangible difference. The security industry's incredible diversity offers endless niches to explore, so if you ever feel like switching gears, the opportunities are there. Remember: as a security consultant, you're not just reacting to threats but proactively shaping safer, more secure environments.

The Advantages of Starting a Security Consulting Business

Why settle for working on someone else's dream when you can build your own? Starting your own security consulting business gives you the freedom to craft a brand that's uniquely yours, pivot into exciting new areas, and watch your hard work pay off in real-time. From the joy of being your own boss to the financial upside of running your own company, this career path is as rewarding as it is empowering. Sure, it comes with its challenges, but as we pointed out, being an employee has its own set of limitations. Here, you're holding the reins – and that's a powerful place to be.

Common Challenges in the Security Industry

We took a frank look at some hurdles you might face, from navigating a competitive marketplace to dealing with regulatory headaches. But for every challenge, there's an opportunity. Competition drives you to stand out; licensing requirements build credibility, and staying on top of an ever-changing industry keeps you sharp and ahead of the curve. Challenges aren't roadblocks but stepping stones to growth, innovation, and success. With the right mindset (spoiler alert: that's next), you'll tackle these head-on and become stronger.

Developing the Mindset of a Security Consultant

Finally, we dove into the mindset required to thrive as an independent security consultant. Determination, flexibility, decisiveness, and resilience form the foundation of this mindset, while integrity and humor keep you grounded and sane. This isn't just about solving problems – it's about becoming the confident, capable entrepreneur you're meant to be. And yes, you'll stumble occasionally (who doesn't?), but time you do, you get a chance to recover, learn, adapt, and come back stronger.

The Big Picture

Chapter 2 was about equipping you with the knowledge and mindset to confidently enter the security consulting industry. Yes, it's a field with challenges, but also bursting with opportunities for those bold enough to seize them.

Remember, every successful consultant once stood where you are now: at the beginning. What set them apart wasn't perfection – it was the courage to start, the determination to keep going, and the mindset to grow through every experience.

So, trust in your abilities, and keep moving forward. You're on the path to building something amazing. Now, let's move on to Chapter 3 and start shaping the unique business model that will set you apart in this exciting industry. You've got this!

3

Building a Unique Business Model: Specialized Services and Expertise

"The man who chases two rabbits catches neither."

— Confucious

Businesses with a clearly defined niche are 2.1 times more likely to achieve long-term growth compared to those that try to be everything to everyone.

In a world filled with generic service providers, the most successful security consultants stand out by specializing. Chapter 3 is about building a business model that reflects your expertise, passions, and unique value proposition. Whether you're drawn to cutting-edge drone operations or the nuanced world of cybersecurity, this chapter will help you define your niche, differentiate yourself in the marketplace, and create a thriving business.

The Value of Choosing a Niche in Security Consulting

There's an old saying in the security industry: "Jack of all trades, master of none." Yet, the idea persists that security consultants should be good at *everything* – from cybersecurity to event security to drone operations. Let's get real for a moment. Trying to master every area of security consulting is like trying to win a decathlon after spending all your time training for the high jump. You'll spread yourself thin, burn out, and miss the opportunity to truly excel. A much better option is specialization and strategic partnerships with areas in which you are weak.

Choosing a niche is not about limiting yourself; it's about focusing your energy, building deep expertise, and positioning yourself as the go-to person in a specific area. Let's explore how specialization can transform every facet of your business – and why it's the smartest move you can make as a security entrepreneur.

Training: Depth Over Breadth

When you pick a niche, you can concentrate your training efforts on the skills that matter most. Instead of spending hours learning everything from biometric systems to perimeter fencing techniques, you can focus on mastering the tools and strategies relevant to your chosen specialty. For example, if you're diving into cybersecurity, you'll invest your time in certifications like CISSP or ethical hacking courses, not first responder training.

Specialized training makes you a true expert in your field, and clients will pay a premium for expertise. Plus, it's way less stressful than trying to memorize everything under the security sun.

Budgeting: Spending Smart, Not Broad

When you know your niche, you can direct your budget toward tools, certifications, and resources that enhance your specific offerings. No more splurging on gear or software you'll never actually use.

Example: If you specialize in drone security, you'll allocate funds for high-quality drones, anti-drone tech, and related software – not an arsenal of unrelated equipment that collects dust.

So What: A focused budget saves you money and ensures every dollar spent contributes to your expertise and growth.

Marketing: Speaking Your Clients' Language

Specialization makes your marketing sharper, clearer, and far more effective. Instead of vague messaging like "We do it all," you can confidently say, "We're the leading experts in natural disaster preparedness for small businesses" or "We help ultra-high-net-worth families secure their estates with discreet, cutting-edge solutions."

So What: Specificity resonates with clients. It shows them you understand their unique needs and makes you memorable in a sea of generalists.

Branding: Building a Distinct Identity

Your brand is your identity, and specializing gives it a clear personality. Instead of being "just another security consultant," your niche helps define what you stand for and why clients should choose you.

Example: A consultant specializing in cybersecurity might brand themselves as tech-savvy, forward-thinking, and innovative, while a consultant focused on physical security assessments might emphasize reliability, precision, and trustworthiness.

So What: A strong, niche-focused brand builds trust and recognition. It sets you apart in the market and helps you attract your ideal clients.

Certifications: Targeted Expertise

Let's face it – there are *a lot* of certifications in the security world. Without a niche, you might feel pressured to collect them like baseball cards, which is exhausting and unnecessary. A niche lets you focus on the certifications that matter most for your field.

So What: Targeted certifications boost your credibility and competence without overwhelming your schedule (or your wallet).

Competency: Becoming the Go-To Expert

When you specialize, you can dive deep into your chosen field, developing skills and insights that generalists can't match. You become "known" as 'the guy' (or 'the gal'). Over time, this expertise makes you the go-to person for clients who need your specific services.

So What: Clients want specialists because they value precision and knowledge. By honing your niche, you make yourself indispensable.

Time Management: Focusing Your Efforts

Specialization helps you streamline your time. Instead of juggling a million unrelated tasks, you can focus on projects, training, and opportunities that align with your niche.

Example: A consultant specializing in houses of worship security won't waste time learning cybersecurity strategies – they'll focus on physical security, crowd management, and threat assessment specific to those environments.

So What: Your time is your most valuable resource. Specialization ensures you're using it wisely.

Why "Good at Everything" Doesn't Work

The idea that security consultants should be good at everything might sound noble, but it's wildly impractical. Here's why:

The Field Is Too Broad: Security consulting spans physical security, cybersecurity, emergency planning, personal protection, and more. No single person can master it all.

Clients Value Expertise: Clients seek specialists who can solve their unique problems, not generalists who dabble in everything.

Burnout Is Real: Trying to do it all leads to exhaustion, frustration, and – ironically – lower-quality work.

Niche Your Way to Success

Choosing a niche isn't a limitation – it's a difference-maker. It lets you focus your efforts, build unmatched expertise, and stand out in a competitive industry. Yes, it might feel counterintuitive to narrow your focus. Still, the results speak for themselves: clearer messaging, stronger branding, targeted training, and, most importantly, happy clients who see you as the expert they need.

So, reflect on your passions and strengths, and find your niche. It's the first step toward building a security consulting business that's successful and uniquely yours. And hey, who doesn't want to be the best at *something*? Go on – claim your spot!

Specializing in a niche allows you to be known as an expert in a particular area, attracting clients who value your targeted skills. Below, we explore a sampling of security niches, describing what they entail, the industries they support, and examples of tasks a consultant might handle.

Corporate Security

What It Is: Protecting businesses from physical and digital threats to assets, personnel, and operations. It can also include C-Suite Leadership Executive Protection, Travel Security Program Management, Security Operations Cell (SOC) activities, etc., depending on the size and scope of the client supported. As an independent consultant, you would often be brought in as an external advisor, Red Team coordinator, policy/procedure reviewer, trainer, or augmentee.

Industries Supported: Any business sector with corporations large enough to afford a security apparatus.

Example Task: Conducting a security audit for a corporate office, identifying vulnerabilities such as poorly secured access points, outdated camera systems, or a lack of employee training on emergency procedures. Recommending upgrades like biometric access controls, modern surveillance technology, and a corporate security policy.

Unique Characteristics: Requires balancing preventative measures with strategies for real-time response while maintaining employee morale and operational flow. Requires balancing industry best practices and solutions with an accurate assessment of the supported corporation's strategic vision and culture. The independent security consultant is often considered an 'outsider', brought in because something went wrong. In those cases, the independent consultant must navigate a delicate landscape so they are not perceived as threatening to an existing Chief Security Officer or Director of Security.

Ultra-High Net Worth (UHNW) Family/Estate Management Security Consulting

What It Is: Safeguarding the safety, privacy, and assets of affluent individuals and their families. This can include conducting Security Advance work in support of a travel plan for an existing EP team or an external audit of existing plans, policies, or procedures.

Industries Supported: High-profile clients in entertainment, finance, tech, and more.

Example Task: Designing a multi-layered estate security system, including perimeter cameras, motion detectors, and discreet security patrols. Providing travel risk assessments for international vacations or business trips.

Unique Characteristics: Requires discretion and customization, ensuring security measures blend seamlessly with the client's lifestyle, as well as the lifestyle of the client's family.

Security Operations Center (SOC) Consulting Support

What It Is: Setting up or optimizing a centralized hub for monitoring and responding to security threats.

Industries Supported: Large corporations, government agencies, and cybersecurity firms.

Example Task: Designing a SOC for a regional bank, integrating threat detection software, real-time monitoring dashboards, and a team workflow for responding to cyber and physical breaches and monitoring the travel of the bank's key leaders. Training the SOC team to handle alerts efficiently.

Unique Characteristics: High reliance on technology, requiring an understanding of both software systems and human decision-making processes. It also requires access to intelligence databases and a mastery of Open-Source Intelligence (OSINT) research techniques.

Surveillance and Private Investigations

What It Is: Gathering intelligence through surveillance and investigative techniques.

Industries Supported: Corporate investigations, insurance claims, legal firms, and private individuals.

Example Task: Conducting covert surveillance to gather evidence in an employee theft case. Conducting an investigation against an employee suspected of making a fraudulent workman's compensation injury claim. Monitoring activity around a client's property to identify suspicious behavior.

Unique Characteristics: Requires patience, attention to detail, and a knack for blending into environments unnoticed. Bonus points if you've got the stamina for stakeouts.

Drone and Anti-Drone Operations

What It Is: Using drones for surveillance, mapping, or enforcing security and countering unauthorized drone activity.

Industries Supported: Critical infrastructure, oil field and pipeline security, large corporate campuses, events, agriculture, corporate facilities, and private estates.

Example Task: Deploying drones to monitor a construction site for unauthorized access or theft. Implementing anti-drone systems to protect a high-profile event from potential surveillance or disruption.

Unique Characteristics: Combines cutting-edge tech with problem-solving, making it ideal for tech enthusiasts.

Natural Disaster/Emergency Relief Consulting

What It Is: Preparing organizations to respond to natural disasters and emergencies.

Industries Supported: Corporations, schools, healthcare facilities, communities, and government agencies.

Example Task: Developing a disaster preparedness plan for a regional hospital, including evacuation routes, backup power systems, and staff training. Conducting a drill to test the plan's effectiveness.

Unique Characteristics: High-pressure but highly impactful work that directly contributes to saving lives and minimizing damage.

Security Consulting Support to Local, State, and Federal Government Agencies

What It Is: Providing expertise to government agencies on security policy, compliance, and operational support.

Industries Supported: Public safety, law enforcement, regulatory bodies, town/city councils, town/city office of emergency management.

Example Task: Assisting a state government in implementing new cybersecurity protocols to comply with updated federal regulations. Conducting training for law enforcement personnel on threat assessment. Counseling a city council on how to implement public-private security partnerships to support a newly adopted community policing policy.

Unique Characteristics: Requires navigating complex legal and bureaucratic frameworks while addressing real-world security needs.

Security Consulting to Houses of Worship

What It Is: Protecting religious institutions from threats while preserving an atmosphere of openness and community.

Industries Supported: Churches, synagogues, mosques, and other religious organizations.

Example Task: Developing a safety plan for a large church, including training volunteers on emergency response, installing discreet cameras, and coordinating with local law enforcement.

Unique Characteristics: Balances sensitivity to cultural and spiritual values with practical security measures. Consideration of faith-based security policies. There is much more focus on discrete, proactive techniques based on protective intelligence.

Augmenting an Existing Security Apparatus

What It Is: Enhancing and improving a client's existing security systems and processes.

Industries Supported: Any organization with a security presence, such as corporations or educational institutions.

Example Task: Upgrading the surveillance system of a retail chain to include facial recognition and real-time alerts. Training the in-house security team on the new system's operation. Augmenting an existing Executive Protection (EP) team by conducting Security Advance Operations.

Unique Characteristics: Focuses on improving what's already in place rather than starting from scratch. Many existing organizations prefer to handle nearly every task "in-house", so securing these types of opportunities takes a lot of networking and trust/confidence.

Cybersecurity

What It Is: Protecting digital assets and systems from cyber threats like hacking, ransomware, and phishing attacks.

Industries Supported: Technology, finance, healthcare, and any data-driven organization.

Example Task: Conducting a vulnerability assessment for a law firm, identifying weak points in their network, and implementing firewalls, intrusion detection systems, and employee cybersecurity training.

Unique Characteristics: Rapidly evolving, requiring constant learning and adaptability.

Physical Security Assessments

What It Is: Evaluating buildings and facilities to identify vulnerabilities and recommend protective measures.

Industries Supported: Corporate offices, schools, retail stores, hotels, and government buildings.

Example Task: Conducting a walkthrough of a high-rise office building to assess risks like unsecured entrances or inadequate lighting. Recommending solutions like keycard access systems and security personnel placement.

Unique Characteristics: Requires a keen eye for detail, a mastery of physical security best practices, a knowledge of Criminal Prevention Through Environmental Design (CPTED), and a thorough understanding of threat scenarios.

Risk Management and Threat Assessment

What It Is: Identifying risks and developing strategies to mitigate them before they become crises.

Industries Supported: Corporations, events, and public institutions.

Example Task: Assessing the security risks for a global company expanding into a politically unstable region. Recommending travel safety protocols and hiring local security personnel.

Unique Characteristics: Requires a strategic mindset and the ability to foresee potential issues before they arise.

Security Driver

What It Is: Providing secure transportation services for individuals or goods, ensuring safe *and comfortable* travel.

Industries Supported: Executive protection, logistics, ultra-high-networth individuals, and corporate clients.

Example Task: Safely transporting a corporate executive to a high-profile event, using advanced route planning to avoid potential risks, and employing defensive driving techniques to ensure safety in an emergency.

Unique Characteristics: Security driving goes beyond chauffeuring – it requires advanced training in defensive and evasive driving, risk assessment, and often maintaining discretion while protecting the client. This niche might get your motor running if you're a skilled driver who thrives under pressure.

Event Security

What It Is: Planning and managing security for large-scale events like concerts, festivals, and conferences.

Industries Supported: Entertainment, corporate, and sports sectors.

Example Task: Coordinating security for a high-profile awards show, including crowd control, backstage access monitoring, and emergency response planning.

Unique Characteristics: Fast-paced and dynamic, with the need to handle high-pressure situations with multiple high-profile figures gracefully.

Security Training

What It Is: Teaching individuals or teams skills like threat response, situational awareness, and emergency protocols.

Industries Supported: Law enforcement, corporate teams, security training institutions, schools, and nonprofits.

Example Task: Conducting an active shooter preparedness workshop for school staff, including scenario-based drills and de-escalation techniques.

Unique Characteristics: Focuses on empowering others to handle security challenges effectively. Requires the ability to develop curriculums, instruct, and manage deliverables.

The Power of Specialization

Each of these niches offers unique opportunities to specialize, differentiate, and make a meaningful impact. Whether you're drawn to high-tech drone operations, the fast-paced world of event security, or the precision of cybersecurity, there's a niche for your skills and passions.

So, where will you plant your flag? Your niche is waiting, and so are the clients who need you. It's time to claim your space and make it your own!

Standing Out in a Competitive Industry

In the world of security consulting, being "good" at what you do isn't enough to thrive. Good gets you hired once; being *great* – or better yet, becoming an *industry leader* – makes you the go-to consultant everyone remembers and recommends. Success in this competitive field doesn't just come from mastering your niche; it requires a deliberate strategy to differentiate yourself in the marketplace and position your business as the gold standard.

Let's break down what it takes to stand out, carve your space, and create a reputation that gets clients knocking on your door.

The Roadmap to Becoming an Industry Leader

Standing out starts with setting your sights on excellence. But excellence isn't just a mindset; it's a journey. Here are the key steps to get you there:

Master Your Craft

Invest in continuous learning. Certifications, workshops, and industry events aren't just resume fillers – they're ways to stay sharp and ahead of the curve.

Don't just keep up with trends; anticipate them. Be the person who knows what's next before anyone else.

Pro Tip: Think of learning as fuel for your business. Without it, you're just idling in the driveway while others speed past.

Build a Strong Brand

Your brand is your business's identity. It's more than a logo or a catchy tagline – it's how you make clients feel.

Define your unique value proposition (UVP). What makes you different? Are you the tech-savvy cybersecurity guru? The ultra-reliable event security expert? Own it.

Example: If you specialize in UHNW family security, your UVP could be: "Discreet, personalized security solutions that fit seamlessly into your lifestyle."

Deliver Beyond Expectations

Good consultants solve problems. Great consultants anticipate them, solve them, and make it look effortless, if it is even noticed at all.

Always ask, "What more can I do for this client?" Whether it's a follow-up report or an additional consultation, those extras build loyalty.

Pro Tip: Overdelivering doesn't have to mean overspending. Small touches – like a detailed debrief, timely communication, or a handwritten 'thank you' card at the end of a project – leave big impressions.

Focus on Client Relationships

Security consulting is built on trust. Strong relationships aren't just about getting the job done; they're about making clients feel safe, heard, and valued.

Stay in touch with past clients. Even if they don't need your services immediately, they'll remember you when they do – and they'll recommend you to others.

What is Market Differentiation?

Here's the big secret: standing out in a competitive industry isn't about being the loudest; it's about being the most memorable. That's where market differentiation comes in.

Market Differentiation is the art of defining what sets you apart from competitors in a way that resonates with your target audience. It's about answering the question: *Why should clients choose you over someone else?*

How to Differentiate Yourself

Specialization: A niche isn't just something you're good at; it's your calling card. Specializing allows you to focus your efforts and build unmatched expertise.

Example: Instead of being "a security consultant," you become "the premier consultant for drone and anti-drone operations." Specificity creates clarity – and clarity wins clients.

Service Excellence: How you deliver your services matters as much as what you deliver. Exceptional customer service, clear communication, and consistent reliability can set you apart in a field where many consultants drop the ball.

Pro Tip: A client should never wonder if you're on top of things. Keep them informed and engaged every step of the way.

Innovation: Stay ahead by offering solutions no one else does. Whether you integrate AI into physical security or pioneer new risk assessment techniques, innovation makes you unforgettable.

Emotional Connection: People don't just buy services – they buy trust, confidence, and peace of mind. By understanding your clients' fears and goals, you build emotional connections that go beyond a contract.

The Secret to Success: Be Memorable

Here's the thing: clients aren't just looking for a security consultant. They're looking for *their* security consultant – the one who gets them, their industry, their company, their employees, their family, their strategic vision, and their unique challenges. Becoming that person means going the extra mile to create an experience they won't forget.

Example: Imagine you're a consultant for a small business and, after completing their risk assessment, you also provide a simple emergency response checklist for their employees. It's thoughtful and practical and ensures you're the first name they think of for future projects.

Aim to Lead, Not Blend

Standing out in a competitive industry isn't about shouting louder than everyone else – it's about being so good, unique, and reliable that people can't help but notice you. Others shout your praise because you're too busy providing best-in-class service. By mastering your craft, delivering excellence, and differentiating your business, you're not just building a brand – you're building a legacy.

Remember, security consulting isn't just a job; it's a responsibility. Clients entrust you with what they value most, and your ability to lead in your niche ensures they're always in good hands.

So, set your sights high, craft your differentiation strategy, and prepare to own your space in the industry. You're not here to blend in – you're here to stand out. And trust us, the view from the top is worth it!

By now, you know that specialization is key to building a thriving security consulting business. You've explored the many niches in the industry and understand the need to be not just good but *best-in-class* in your chosen field. Now comes the exciting part – charting your unique path to becoming the go-to expert in your niche.

Crafting your path isn't just about dreaming big; it's about creating a step-by-step plan with actionable goals, measurable milestones, and realistic timelines. Let's break it down.

Step 1: Define What "Best-in-Class" Means in Your Niche

To excel, you need a clear picture of what excellence looks like. Ask yourself:

- *Who are the top players in your chosen niche?*
- *What services do they offer that make them stand out?*
- *What skills, certifications, or technologies are must-haves in your field?*

Action Step: Conduct a competitive analysis:

- Research 3–5 successful consultants or firms in your niche.
- Identify their strengths, service offerings, and differentiators.
- Note gaps or opportunities they may be overlooking – these could be your way to stand out.

Milestone: Complete your competitive analysis within two weeks.

Step 2: Conduct a Personal Skills Assessment

Compare your current skills, certifications, and experience with your identified benchmarks. Be honest with yourself – this is about growth, not self-criticism.

Action Step: Create a "Skills Gap Chart."

- List the skills, education, experience, and certifications needed in your niche.
- Mark those you already have and those you need to develop.
- Prioritize the top 2–3 gaps to address first.

Milestone: Finish your chart within one week and create a plan for closing those gaps.

Step 3: Set Tangible, Measurable Goals

Greatness doesn't happen by accident. Break your vision into clear, achievable goals.

Examples of Goals:

- Earn a specific certification (e.g., CPP, CISSP) within six months.
- Gain three new clients in your niche within the next quarter.
- Develop and implement a new service offering within the next year.

Pro Tip: Use the SMART framework – make your goals Specific, Measurable, Achievable, Relevant, and Time-bound.

Step 4: Create a Learning and Development Plan

To be best-in-class, you need to be a lifelong learner.

Action Steps:

- Identify Learning Resources: Find courses, workshops, books, or mentors specific to your niche.
- Set a Schedule: Dedicate consistent time each week for learning – whether earning a certification, attending webinars, or shadowing a seasoned professional.

Milestone: Complete one learning activity every month.

Step 5: Build a Brand That Reflects Excellence

Your brand should communicate your expertise, values, and commitment to best-in-class service.

Action Steps:

- Develop a Professional Online Presence:
    - Create a polished website showcasing your niche services, case studies, and client testimonials.
    - Stay active on LinkedIn, sharing industry insights to establish yourself as a thought leader.
- Refine Your Messaging: Clearly articulate your unique value proposition in all your marketing materials.

Milestone: Launch or update your website and social media profiles within three months.

Step 6: Network Strategically

Success in consulting is as much about who you know as what you know.

Action Steps:

- Join industry associations and attend relevant events (e.g., ASIS International or ISSA).
- Build relationships with complementary professionals –

lawyers, tech experts, or HR consultants – who can refer clients to you.

Milestone: Attend one industry event and make five new professional connections each quarter.

Step 7: Measure and Adjust

Your path to best-in-class isn't static – it's a process. Regularly evaluate your progress and adjust as needed.

Action Steps:

- Review your goals and milestones quarterly. Are you hitting them? If not, why?
- Gather feedback from clients, peers, and mentors to identify areas for improvement.

Milestone: Conduct quarterly reviews and make necessary adjustments to your plan.

A Sample Timeline for Becoming Best-in-Class

Months 1–3:

- Research and define what best-in-class means for your niche.
- Complete your competitive analysis and skills gap chart.
- Begin studying for a key certification.
- Update your website and social media presence.

Months 4–6:

- Earn your first certification or complete a critical training course.
- Secure your first new client within your niche.
- Begin publishing thought leadership content online.

<u>Months 7–9:</u>

- Attend an industry event and grow your professional network.
- Expand your service offerings based on client feedback.
- Gain two additional clients in your niche.

<u>Months 10–12:</u>

- Conduct a full review of your progress and recalibrate your goals.
- Begin planning a long-term growth strategy, such as scaling your business or adding team members.

Your Path, Your Success

Crafting your path in security consulting isn't about following someone else's footsteps – it's about forging a way forward that reflects your strengths, passions, and goals. With focus, determination, and the steps outlined here, you can position yourself as the best-in-class provider in your niche.

Remember, greatness doesn't happen overnight, but it does happen with consistent effort. Stay the course, celebrate your milestones, and keep pushing forward. The industry is waiting for someone like you to lead – so why not get started today?

Chapter 3 Wrap-Up: Crafting Your Unique Path to Success

Congratulations! You've made it through Chapter 3, where we explored the building blocks of a unique and successful security consulting business. Let's recap the highlights, solidify what you've learned, and send you forward with the confidence that you're ready to carve out your space in this exciting industry.

The Value of Choosing a Niche in Security Consulting

We started by hammering home the importance of specialization. You can't be everything to everyone – nor should you try! Defining a niche isn't about limiting yourself; it's about sharpening your focus and becoming the *go-to* expert in your chosen field. Whether it's cybersecurity, UHNW family security, or drone operations, a niche allows you to direct your efforts, maximize your skills, and attract clients who truly need your expertise.

Overview of Security Consulting Niches

Next, we took a closer look at the many niches in the security industry. From corporate security to physical security assessments, event security to risk management, the opportunities are as diverse as the threats they address. Each niche has its unique challenges, rewards, and client needs. The beauty of this industry is that there's room for everyone – whether you're a tech enthusiast, a strategic thinker, or a people person.

Pro Tip: If one niche doesn't fit, don't worry. The security industry is dynamic, and there's always room to pivot. It's like trying on shoes – keep going until you find the perfect fit.

Standing Out in a Competitive Industry

Here's the truth: good isn't good enough if you want to thrive in a crowded marketplace. Standing out requires deliberate effort, from mastering your craft to delivering exceptional service and building a strong brand. We introduced the concept of market differentiation – defining what makes you unique – and emphasized the importance of becoming a thought leader in your field.

The key takeaway? Clients don't want a jack-of-all-trades; they want someone who's *the best* at solving their specific problem. That someone is *you* – provided you're willing to put in the work to make your business memorable.

Crafting Your Path in Security Consulting

Finally, we tackled the nuts and bolts of turning your vision into reality. Crafting your path means setting clear goals, identifying the necessary skills and certifications, and building a plan to get there. With actionable steps, milestones, and timelines, you have a template for becoming best-in-class in your niche.

Pro Tip: Progress doesn't happen overnight, but it *does* happen when you consistently put in the effort. Celebrate every milestone, no matter how small – it's proof you're on the right track.

Closing Thoughts: You've Got This!

Chapter 3 was about laying the foundation for a business that reflects your strengths, passions, and expertise. By choosing a niche, understanding the opportunities within the security industry, and committing to standing out, you've taken the first steps toward building something truly remarkable.

Remember, the journey will not always be easy, but it will be worth it. The key is to keep learning, growing, and focused on your goals. You're not just starting a business – you're creating a legacy.

So, pat yourself on the back and prepare for the next chapter. The future of your security consulting career is bright, and it's yours to shape. What do you say we get to starting this business already?

4

Building Your Security Brand

"A brand is not just a logo, a website, or a business card – it's an experience."

— Unknown

Businesses with strong branding are 20% more likely to retain clients and attract new ones than those without a clear brand identity.

In the security consulting industry, your brand is your promise to your clients. It communicates who you are, what you stand for, and the value you bring. Chapter 4 is about crafting that identity – from choosing the proper legal structure to establishing an online presence that tells your story and builds trust. Let's study the essential components of building a brand that reflects your expertise and sets you apart.

Choosing the Right Legal Structure

When starting your security consulting business, one of the first – and most important – decisions you'll make is choosing the legal structure for your company. It's not just a bureaucratic box to check; it's the foundation of how your business will operate, how you'll pay taxes, and how much liability you'll bear if things go sideways (and let's face it, in security consulting, the unexpected is part of the job).

The options are as varied as the niches we've discussed, but don't worry – we'll break them down together so you can make an informed decision. And, as always, when it comes to taxes or complex legal questions, consult a certified tax professional or attorney. Let's cover the big four: sole proprietorship, LLC, S-Corporation, and C-Corporation.

Sole Proprietorship: The One-Person Show

A sole proprietorship is the easiest path if you start small and fly solo. After all, there's no formal registration, board meetings, or complex paperwork – just you and your dream of making it big.

Advantages:

- Simplicity is the name of the game. You can get up and running quickly with minimal setup.
- The costs are low. You don't have to worry about filing incorporation documents or paying annual state fees.
- Taxes are straightforward. Your business income is reported on your personal tax return, which keeps things simple at tax time.

Disadvantages:

- Unlimited liability. If something goes wrong (e.g., a lawsuit or a debt you can't repay), your personal assets – your car, house, or savings – are fair game.

- Limited credibility. Larger clients might hesitate to work with a sole proprietor because it can seem less "official."
- Growth constraints. Raising capital or bringing on partners is tricky without a formal business entity.

Best for: Hobbyists, freelancers, or those dipping their toes into the security consulting waters before diving all the way in.

Limited Liability Company (LLC): The Best of Both Worlds

The LLC is the darling of small businesses, and for good reason. It offers the liability protection of a corporation while maintaining the simplicity of a sole proprietorship. It's like having your cake and eating it, too – just with fewer calories and more paperwork.

Advantages:

- Liability protection. Your personal assets are shielded from business debts and legal claims. If a client sues your business, they can't come after your house.
- Tax flexibility. By default, LLCs are taxed as pass-through entities, meaning profits and losses flow to your personal tax return. But you can also elect to be taxed as an S-Corp or C-Corp, depending on your financial situation.
- Ease of management. While there are more formalities than a sole proprietorship, LLCs are much simpler to operate than corporations.

Disadvantages:

- Costs. There are filing fees and ongoing state fees, which can vary depending on where you live.
- Self-employment taxes. As an LLC owner, you'll pay self-

employment taxes on your share of the profits. This can add up, though there are ways to mitigate it with tax elections.

- Limited lifespan. In some states, an LLC dissolves if a member leaves or passes away (though operating agreements can address this).

Best for: Small-to-medium security consulting businesses looking for liability protection without diving into the complexity of a corporation.

S-Corporation: The Tax-Savvy Option

An S-corporation isn't actually a type of corporation; it's a tax election that LLCs or corporations can make. It's designed to help business owners avoid the dreaded double taxation that can plague C-corporations.

Advantages:

- Tax savings. S-Corps allow you to pay yourself a reasonable salary and take the remaining profits as distributions, which aren't subject to self-employment taxes. This can save you money if your business is profitable.
- Liability protection. Like LLCs, S-Corps shield your personal assets from business liabilities.
- Pass-through taxation. Business income flows to your personal tax return, avoiding corporate-level taxes.

Disadvantages:

- Ownership limits. S-Corps are limited to 100 shareholders, all of whom must be U.S. citizens or residents.
- More formalities. You'll need to hold board meetings, keep detailed minutes, and file more paperwork than an LLC.
- Salary requirements. The IRS requires you to pay yourself a "reasonable" salary, and trust me, they'll be watching.

Best for: Security consultants with steady profits who want to optimize their tax situation while maintaining liability protection.

C-Corporation: The Heavyweight Champion

The C-corporation is the big leagues. It's the most formal business structure, designed for companies that want unlimited growth potential and are willing to jump through a few hoops to achieve it.

Advantages:

- Unlimited growth. C-Corps can have unlimited shareholders, making them ideal for businesses planning to scale or attract investors.
- Separate taxation. The company pays corporate taxes, and shareholders pay taxes on dividends. While this can result in double taxation, it also separates personal and business income.
- Credibility. The C-Corp structure carries weight with clients, investors, and lenders, signaling you're serious about your business.

Disadvantages:

- Double taxation. Yes, it's worth mentioning twice because it can be a significant drawback.
- Complexity. C-corps require detailed record-keeping, annual meetings, and compliance with corporate formalities.
- Higher costs. Filing fees, legal fees, and accounting expenses can add up quickly.

Best for: Large-scale operations, security firms planning to go public, or those seeking significant investment.

Which Structure is Right for You?

Far and away, the most common legal structure for independent security consultants is an LLC taxed as an S-Corp. However, choosing your business's legal structure isn't a one-size-fits-all decision. It depends on your goals, financial situation, and tolerance for complexity. A sole proprietorship or LLC might be the easiest path if you're starting out. As you grow, transitioning to an S-Corp or C-Corp could offer more significant advantages.

Pro Tip: Start with the end in mind. Consider where you want your business to be in five or ten years, and choose a structure that aligns with that vision.

Consult the Experts

While this overview gives you the essentials, consult with a tax professional or attorney. They'll help you navigate the nuances of your state's laws, financial picture, and long-term goals.

Building your security brand starts with a strong foundation. Choose wisely, and you'll be well on your way to establishing a business that's not only successful but also built to last.

Naming and Registering Your Business – Making it Official

Well done! You've decided to start your security consulting business. Now, it's time to make it official by registering your business with the necessary authorities. This step can feel bureaucratic, but it's vital to laying a solid foundation for your company. Let's walk through the process step-by-step so you can navigate it with confidence (and maybe a little less stress).

What's In a Name? Best Practices in Naming Your Company

Naming your company is one of the most exciting – and daunting – tasks in launching your security consulting business. Your name is the first thing potential clients will notice, setting the tone for how they perceive you. No pressure, right? But don't worry – naming your company is more science than magic, and with some guidance, you'll find the perfect moniker that reflects your brand, resonates with clients, and stands out in the marketplace.

Let's talk about some best practices for crafting a name that's memorable, meaningful, and uniquely yours.

Be Clear, Not Cryptic: Your name should immediately convey what you do. This is not the time to channel your inner poet or get overly clever. While names like "Titan Shield" sound impressive, they leave potential clients scratching their heads about what you actually provide.

Pro Tip: Add a descriptor to clarify your services, such as "Titan Shield Security Consulting." It's clear, professional, and leaves no room for doubt.

Keep It Simple (and Spelled Correctly): Simplicity is your best friend. A name that's easy to spell, pronounce, and remember will work wonders for your branding. Avoid unusual spellings, obscure acronyms, or overly long phrases that make people question whether you've been hacking into a Scrabble game.

Example: Instead of "Phynix Protektion Strategiez," stick to "Phoenix Protection Strategies." Your clients – and their autocorrect – will thank you.

Make It Timeless: Trendy names might seem cool today, but trends fade. Avoid references to current fads, buzzwords, or technology that could age poorly. Remember, your company's name is a long-term investment.

Example: "Drone Defenders 2024" might sound cutting-edge now, but what happens when drone technology evolves? Choose a name that grows with your business.

Reflect Your Values: Your name should hint at what you stand for. Are you dependable? Innovative? Client-focused? Choose words that resonate with your company's mission and values.

Example: Names like "Integrity Security Consulting" or "Fortress Solutions" evoke strength, trust, and reliability – qualities every client seeks in a security partner.

Consider Your Target Audience: Consider who your clients are and what will resonate with them. A corporate audience might prefer a formal, polished name, while a more niche market (like creative startups) might appreciate something with personality.

Example: "Summit Risk Advisory" might appeal to Fortune 500 companies, while "Guardian Edge Security" could work for tech-savvy startups.

Check for Availability: Before falling in love with a name, make sure it's available:

Website Domains: Check if the .com version of your name is available. Clients often equate a .com domain with credibility.

Social Media Handles: Secure consistent handles across platforms to make it easy for clients to find you.

Trademarks: Use the USPTO's Trademark Electronic Search System (TESS) to ensure your name isn't already in use (we'll get more in-depth on this later in this section).

Pro Tip: Consider how much competition exists even if the name is legally available. If there are already five "Sentinel Security" companies, yours could get lost in the mix.

Test It Out: Say the name out loud. Say it again. And again. How does it sound? Does it roll off the tongue, or does it make you stumble? Ask friends, family, or trusted colleagues for their honest reactions.

Example: A name might look great on paper but sound awkward when spoken. "Aegis Risk Solutions" might seem sleek until someone mispronounces it as "Egg-is."

Think Beyond the Present: What happens if your business grows or pivots into new areas? What happens if you sell your company? A name that's too specific could box you in. Worse, a buyer named Dave would hesitate to purchase "Brian's Security Solutions."

Example: "Church Security Solutions" works well if you only serve houses of worship. But if you expand into corporate security, the name could limit your appeal. A broader name like "Faith & Fortress Consulting" might allow for growth while staying true to your original mission.

Infuse Creativity, But Don't Go Overboard

While clarity is critical, creativity can make your name memorable. Use metaphors, strong imagery, or unique pairings to stand out – avoid anything too abstract or hard to decipher.

Example: "Iron Wall Security" conveys strength and protection with a touch of creativity. It's straightforward yet memorable.

Sleep on It: Finally, give yourself time to reflect. Naming your business isn't a decision to rush. Sleep on your options, say them in different contexts, and imagine them on business cards, websites, and signage. The correct name will feel like it fits naturally.

The Power of a Name

Choosing a name for your security consulting business is critical in defining your brand. It's your first impression, calling card, and opportunity to set the tone for your company's mission. By keeping it simple, meaningful, and timeless, you'll create a name that resonates with clients and stands the test of time. So, take your time, have fun with the process, and remember: the perfect name is out there, just waiting for you to claim it. Now, go make your mark!

Checking for Trademarks: Avoiding the Name Game Drama

Your business name is more than just a label – it's your identity. Before printing business cards or launching a website, you must ensure your name doesn't infringe on someone else's trademark. This is where the U.S. Patent and Trademark Office (USPTO) comes in.

To check for trademarks, visit the USPTO's Trademark Electronic Search System (TESS). You'll search not just for your exact business name but also for similar names, symbols, and services that might cause confusion. Here's how:

Search for Exact Matches: Type in your proposed business name to see if anyone's already registered it.

Search for Similar Names: Look for variations in spelling or phrasing that might be too close for comfort.

Search by Class: Trademarks are categorized into different classes based on industries and services. Two companies can have the same name if they operate in unrelated fields (e.g., "Guardian Security" for physical security and "Guardian Consulting" for financial services).

Analyze the Results: If your name or a similar one is registered in the same class as your services, it's time to reconsider.

Pro Tip: If the results are unclear, consider consulting a trademark attorney to ensure you're not setting yourself up for a legal headache. It's better to invest time now than face rebranding costs later. Or just go to your next favorite name on the list.

Registering with Your State: Location, Location, Location

Once your name is cleared, the next step is to register your business with the state. This process varies depending on where you choose to register, so let's break it down.

Choosing the Right State:

Most business owners register in the state where they plan to operate. However, some entrepreneurs choose states like Delaware or Nevada for their favorable tax laws, lower fees, or privacy protections. Consider these factors:

Taxation: Some states have no corporate income tax, which can save you money.

Filing Costs: Registration fees and ongoing compliance costs greatly vary by state.

Privacy Protections: Some states, like Wyoming, offer better privacy for business owners, protecting your personal information.

State legal Requirements: To operate in some states, the state will require you to be a registered entity in their state. Know the rules and your expected area of operations before you make a final call.

Registered Agent – What's That?

Every state requires businesses to have a registered agent, the person or entity designated to receive legal documents and official notices on behalf of the company.

Should You Be Your Own Registered Agent? If you're comfortable listing your name and address publicly and are available during business hours, you can save money by being your own agent.

Hiring a Registered Agent Service: If you value privacy or don't want the hassle of managing correspondence, you can hire a service for a small annual fee. These services ensure compliance and give you peace of mind.

Registering with the IRS: Getting Your EIN

An Employer Identification Number (EIN) is like a Social Security number for your business. It's a unique identifier that the IRS uses to track your business's tax obligations. Even if you don't plan to hire employees immediately, you'll need an EIN to open a business bank account, file taxes, and apply for licenses.

Here's how to get your EIN:

Visit the IRS Website: Go to the EIN Assistant on the IRS website (it's free!).

Complete the Online Application: You'll answer questions about your business type, structure, and purpose. Make sure you know what type of legal entity you want because they will ask you in this step!

Receive Your EIN Instantly: Once you complete the form, your EIN is issued immediately.

Pro Tip: Keep your EIN secure. It's a critical piece of your business's identity and will be used frequently.

Registering with Dun & Bradstreet: Giving Your Business Its Own Identity

Imagine your business as its own person – a professional, buttoned-up individual with a firm handshake and an impeccable resume. Legally speaking, once your business is registered, it becomes a separate entity capable of making decisions, entering into contracts, and even building its own credit. But like any person trying to establish themselves, your business needs credentials, and that's where Dun & Bradstreet (D&B) comes in.

Registering with Dun & Bradstreet is like getting your business its first report card – but instead of grades, you get a credit profile that tells lenders, partners, and vendors how trustworthy your company is. Let's explain why this step is important and how it can set your security consulting business up for success.

Why Register with Dun & Bradstreet?

Dun & Bradstreet is a global business analytics company that helps businesses establish credibility and manage financial relationships. When you register with D&B, your business is assigned a unique D-U-N-S Number (Data Universal Numbering System). Think of it as your business's Social Security number for the financial world.

Here's why it's important:

Establishing Business Credit: A business needs its own credit history to borrow money, lease office space, or secure vendor terms. Your D-U-N-S Number is the key to building that credit. With good business credit, you can secure lower interest rates on loans and better payment terms with suppliers.

Partner and Vendor Trust: Many companies, especially large organizations, check a potential partner's D&B profile before doing business. A solid credit history signals that your company is reliable and professional.

Government Contracts and Grants: If you're eyeing federal contracts or grants, having a D-U-N-S Number is often a requirement. Uncle Sam likes to know he's working with a legitimate business.

Separating Personal and Business Finances: Registering with D&B reinforces the separation between you and your business. This is critical for financial reasons and for protecting your personal assets.

When you register with Dun & Bradstreet, you're creating a financial profile for your business. This profile includes:

Business Details: Name, address, industry, and structure.

Financial History: Payments made to vendors, loans taken out, and repayment history.

Risk Indicators: D&B assigns a "PAYDEX" score, which reflects your business's payment habits. Scores range from 0 (terrible) to 100 (excellent).

Pro Tip: Always pay your business bills on time – or early. Vendors report payment activity to D&B, and that information directly impacts your creditworthiness.

How to Register with Dun & Bradstreet

Gather Your Information:

- Business name and address.
- Employer Identification Number (EIN).
- Industry classification code (NAICS or SIC code).

Visit the D&B Website: Go to the Dun & Bradstreet D-U-N-S Number application page. The process is free for most businesses.

Complete the Registration: Fill out the required forms with your business details. Provide any additional information about your company's structure and operations.

Wait for Your D-U-N-S Number: Once submitted, your D-U-N-S Number will be issued, typically within 30 days. Expedited services are available for a fee.

What Happens After Registration?

Once your business is registered, it's time to start building a positive financial reputation. Here's how:

Open Business Credit Accounts: Work with vendors who report payments to D&B to build your credit history.

Monitor Your Profile: Use Dun & Bradstreet's tools to check your PAYDEX score and ensure your profile accurately reflects your business.

Keep Personal and Business Finances Separate: Open a business bank account and use it for all company transactions.

The Big Picture: Empowering Your Business

Registering with Dun & Bradstreet is about more than just a number – it's about giving your business the tools to thrive independently. Whether securing funding, negotiating with suppliers, or pursuing government contracts, a strong D&B profile sets you apart as a trustworthy, professional company.

So, take the time to register, build that credit history, and watch your security consulting business grow. After all, a well-armed credit profile is one of the best tools in your entrepreneurial arsenal. Now, go out there and make your business shine – financially and beyond!

Writing Your Articles of Incorporation

The Articles of Incorporation (or Articles of Organization for LLCs) are legal documents filed with the state to create your business entity officially. Think of them as the birth certificate of your business.

Key Sections of Articles of Incorporation:

Business Name and Address: Include your official name and primary business location.

Purpose: A broad statement about your services (e.g., "to offer security consulting services").

Registered Agent: Name and address of the person or service receiving legal notices.

Ownership and Management Structure: Define who owns the business and how it will be managed.

Duration: Most businesses are set up to exist perpetually, but you can specify a finite term if desired.

Where to Find Templates:

- State websites often provide free templates.
- Platforms like LegalZoom and Rocket Lawyer offer customizable forms.

Writing Your Operating Agreement

While Articles of Incorporation are filed with the state, an Operating Agreement is an internal document that outlines how your business will run. It's not required in all states but is highly recommended, especially for LLCs.

What's in an Operating Agreement?

Ownership Structure: Who owns the business, and in what proportions?

Management Roles: Who controls day-to-day operations, and how are decisions made?

Profit Distribution: How will profits (and losses) be divided among owners?

Shareholder Distribution: How many shares are in the company? What kinds of shares? How much is each share of each type worth? Who owns certificate shares?

Voting Rights: Define how decisions are made and how voting power is allocated.

Buyout or Dissolution Plan: Procedures for adding or removing members or dissolving the business.

An Operating Agreement minimizes disputes by clearly defining roles, responsibilities, and expectations. Even if you're the sole owner, it's a great way to think through critical business decisions.

Where to Find Templates:

- Websites like Nolo, LawDepot, and SCORE offer free or low-cost templates.
- State business resources often provide downloadable examples.

Your Business, Officially Born

Registering your business might not be the most glamorous part of launching your security consulting firm, but it's one of the most important. Securing your name, filing the proper paperwork, and creating foundational documents set you up for long-term success.

Take it one step at a time, and don't hesitate to seek expert advice when needed. After all, you're building something that represents your expertise, values, and ambitions – so it's worth doing right. Now, let's move on to the next step of bringing your brand to life!

Creating a Professional Logo

Your logo is the face of your brand. It's the first impression your security consulting business will make on potential clients, so it's essential to get it right. A well-designed logo conveys professionalism, builds trust, and sets you apart in a crowded market. But creating one is more complex than slapping your initials into a fancy font and calling it a day. Let's discuss the components of logo design, explore third-party services, and understand how colors influence your brand's message.

Logo Design Best Practices

A great logo is the cornerstone of your brand identity. Here's what separates a forgettable logo from one that makes an impact:

Simplicity Rules the Day: The best logos are clean and uncluttered. Think of brands like Apple or Nike – there's no confusion about what you're looking at. Simple logos are easier to recognize, scale, and reproduce across different mediums.

Make It Memorable: Your logo should stick in people's minds. Use unique shapes, clever symbolism, or distinctive typography to make it stand out. Avoid clichés like shields or lock icons unless you're using them in a fresh, unexpected way.

Scalability is Key: A logo must look just as good on a business card as it does on a billboard. Test your design at different sizes to ensure it's legible and visually appealing.

Timeless, Not Trendy: Avoid falling into design fads. A trendy logo might look cool now, but it can quickly become outdated. Aim for a design that will still feel relevant in 10 years.

Versatility is a Must: Your logo should work in full color, black and white, and grayscale. It should also look good on digital and physical materials, from websites to promotional swag.

Third-Party Logo Design Services

Creating a logo doesn't mean you have to go it alone. Whether you use artificial intelligence tools or hire a professional graphic designer, here's how to make the most of the process.

Using AI for Logo Design: AI-powered logo generators are a fast, cost-effective way to create a logo. These platforms use algorithms to design logos based on your preferences, such as industry, color, and style.

Top AI Logo Design Tools:

- Canva: User-friendly with a library of customizable templates.
- Looka: Uses AI to generate professional designs tailored to your inputs.
- Tailor Brands: Offers branding packages, including logo design and marketing materials.
- Hatchful by Shopify: Free and geared toward small businesses.

Pros of AI Tools:

- Budget-friendly or free options.
- Instant results and infinite revisions.
- Great for experimenting with ideas before committing to a final design.

Hiring a Graphic Designer

Hiring a designer is the way to go if you want a unique and professional logo. But not all designers are created equal – choose carefully.

What to Consider When Hiring:

Portfolio: Look for designers with experience in creating logos for your industry.

Communication: A designer who listens and responds promptly is invaluable.

Process: Ask about their workflow and whether they'll provide initial concepts and revisions.

Deliverables: Ensure you'll receive the following file formats:

- Vector files (.AI, .EPS): Scalable without losing quality.
- Raster files (.PNG, .JPG): Ideal for web use.
- PDF: Versatile for both digital and print applications.

Where to Find Designers:

- Fiverr: Affordable, with a wide range of talent.
- 99designs: Run a contest to receive multiple design options.
- Upwork: Hire freelancers with specific expertise.
- Local Designers: Consider supporting local talent for a more personalized experience.

The Specific Meaning of Colors in Logo and Brand Design

Colors speak volumes. They evoke emotions, influence perception, and can even shape buying decisions. Choosing the right color palette is critical for conveying your brand's personality and values.

The Meaning of Individual Colors:

Blue: Trust, professionalism, and calm. Prevalent in the security and tech industries.

Black: Power, sophistication, and elegance. It's a classic choice for a high-end feel.

Green: Growth, stability, and environmental consciousness. Great for sustainability-focused brands.

Red: Energy, passion, and urgency. Attention-grabbing but best used sparingly.

Yellow: Optimism, warmth, and clarity. Often paired with darker tones for balance.

Orange: Creativity, friendliness, and enthusiasm. Ideal for approachable brands.

Purple: Luxury, wisdom, and creativity. Works well for premium services.

Gray: Neutrality, balance, and professionalism. It's a reliable supporting color.

Color Combinations

The way colors are paired can amplify their meaning and create visual harmony. Look up a color wheel so these definitions make more sense for all of you reading this in black-and-white:

Complementary Colors: Opposites on the color wheel (e.g., blue and orange) create high contrast and vibrant energy.

Analogous Colors: Neighbors on the wheel (e.g., green, blue-green, and blue) convey harmony and sophistication.

Monochromatic Colors: Variations of a single hue create a clean, minimalist look.

Pro Tip: Test your color palette on multiple platforms (digital screens, print, and merchandise) to ensure it works consistently.

Your Logo, Your Legacy

Your logo is more than a design – it's the visual representation of your security consulting business. By following best practices, leveraging the right tools or talent, and selecting a thoughtful color palette, you'll create a logo that leaves a lasting impression.

Remember, this is an investment in your brand's future. Take your time, have fun with the process, and don't settle for anything less than a design you're proud to put on everything – from your business cards, to your building, to a billboard in Times Square. You've got this!

Creating a Vision Statement and Tagline

Every great business starts with a compelling vision – a guiding star that illuminates where you're going and why you're in the game. Pair that vision with a snappy, memorable tagline, and you've got the verbal foundation for your brand. Together, these elements communicate your purpose, inspire your team, and attract clients who align with your mission. Let's break them down and create a vision statement and tagline that genuinely reflects your security consulting business.

What Is a Vision Statement?

A vision statement is your business's long-term aspiration. It defines your ultimate goal and the impact you aim to have on the world. Think of it as your "why" – the deeper purpose behind your business that inspires you to keep going, even when you're knee-deep in paperwork or troubleshooting a website glitch.

Example: "To be the trusted global leader in innovative security solutions, safeguarding what matters most to our clients and communities."

Key Components of a Vision Statement

Aspirational: Your vision statement should reach beyond the present, painting a picture of what success looks like in the future. Aim high – this is your chance to dream big.

Client-Focused: Emphasize the value you bring to your clients. How will your services improve their lives or businesses?

Impact-Oriented: Highlight the difference your business will make in the world. What legacy are you building?

Concise and Clear: You're not writing a novel. Keep it short – one or two sentences are enough to inspire and resonate.

Pro Tip: Read your draft aloud. Keep tweaking if it doesn't give you a tiny spark of pride or excitement.

Best Practices for Writing a Vision Statement

Be Authentic: Your vision statement should reflect your core values and the true essence of your business. Skip the jargon – this is about heart, not buzzwords.

Involve Your Team: If you have employees, include them in the process. A shared vision fosters unity and motivation.

Think Long-Term: Your vision statement should stand the test of time. Avoid referencing fleeting trends or current events.

Make It Actionable: Even though it's aspirational, it should feel attainable with hard work and dedication. "Attainable, yet strain-able" was a quote I heard somewhere before.

What Is a Tagline?

A tagline is your brand's elevator pitch in five words or less. The short, catchy phrase sums up your business's unique value and sticks in your clients' minds like a great chorus in a pop song. If your vision statement is the novel, your tagline is the Twitter post.

Example: "Securing Your Future, Today."

Key Components of a Tagline

Memorable: A good tagline sticks. Use rhythm, rhyme, or clever phrasing to make it catchy and quickly recalled.

Unique: Your tagline should highlight what sets you apart. Avoid clichés and overused phrases like "Safety First" or "We've Got Your Back."

Emotive: Tap into emotions like trust, safety, or empowerment. Clients should feel something when they read or hear it.

Short and Sweet: The best taglines are concise. Aim for a maximum of seven words – and if you can do it in three, even better.

Best Practices for Writing a Tagline

Reflect Your Core Services: Your tagline should instantly give people a sense of what your business does.

Keep It Client-Focused: Speak directly to your target audience and their needs.

Test It Out: Run your tagline by friends, family, or colleagues. If it doesn't make sense or stick with them, it's back to the drawing board.

Avoid Being Too Generic: Phrases like "Excellence in Security" might sound good, but don't differentiate your business.

Crafting Your Vision Statement and Tagline Together

Your vision statement and tagline should complement each other. The vision statement captures the big picture, while the tagline distills it into a bite-sized, impactful message. Together, they create a cohesive narrative for your brand.

Example Pairing:

- Vision Statement: "To revolutionize the security consulting industry by delivering personalized, innovative solutions that empower our clients and build safer communities."
- Tagline: "Your Safety. Our Mission."

Inspiration Meets Clarity

Your vision statement and tagline are more than just words – they're your business's identity boiled down to its essence. They tell the world who you are, what you stand for, and why clients should trust you. Take the time to craft them thoughtfully because these are the messages you'll carry forward as your brand grows and evolves.

And remember: an outstanding vision statement inspires, and a great tagline sticks. Together, they make your business unforgettable. Now grab that pen (or keyboard) and start creating!

Developing an Online Presence: Websites and Social Media

In today's world, having a strong online presence is as essential as having a business card used to be. If potential clients can't find you online – or worse, they find an outdated, clunky website – they're likely to look elsewhere. The good news is that building a professional, engaging online presence is easier (and often more affordable) than you might think. We begin with how you can master social media and websites to grow your security consulting business.

The Importance of Social Media in Today's Business Environment

Social media isn't just for selfies and cat videos anymore – it's a powerful tool for businesses to connect with clients, showcase expertise, and build a reputation. For security consultants, social media provides a platform to:

Build Credibility: Sharing industry insights, success stories, and educational content establishes you as a thought leader.

Engage Directly with Clients: Social media allows you to interact with your audience in real time, whether through comments, messages, or live sessions.

Reach a Wider Audience: Platforms like LinkedIn and Facebook can expand your reach beyond your local network to national or international markets.

Pro Tip: You don't need to be on *every* platform. Focus on the ones where your target clients spend their time.

Crafting Your Online Presence – Holistic Strategies and a Solid Foundation

A holistic approach means ensuring your online presence is cohesive and reflects your brand consistently across platforms. Think of your website as your home base and social media as the satellites driving traffic.

How to Establish a Strong Foundation:

Define Your Brand Voice: Are you formal and professional or approachable and conversational? Maintain this tone across all platforms.

Invest in Quality Visuals: Professional logos, consistent color schemes and fonts, and high-quality images make a great first impression.

Content is King: Offer value through posts, blogs, or videos. Whether it's security tips, case studies, or industry trends, give your audience a reason to follow and trust you.

Engage Regularly: Post consistently and interact with your followers. An inactive profile is almost as bad as no profile at all.

Website Design and Functionality

Your website is your digital storefront – it's where potential clients learn who you are, what you do, and why they should hire you. A great website should be professional, user-friendly, and functional.

Key Functions of a Security Consultant's Website:

Advertising: Prominently showcase your services with clear calls to action (e.g., "Contact Us for a Free Consultation").

Educating: Include blogs, case studies, or white papers to demonstrate your expertise.

Customer Engagement: Make it easy for clients to get in touch through contact forms or chat features.

Scheduling: Offer an online booking system for consultations or appointments.

Merchandising: If you sell related products (like security equipment or branded merchandise), set up an e-commerce section.

DIY Website Design Services: DIY website builders are an excellent option if you're starting out and watching your budget.

Top DIY Platforms:

- Wix: Drag-and-drop functionality and customizable templates.
- Squarespace: Sleek designs and strong e-commerce capabilities.

- WordPress: Highly customizable and scalable for growing businesses.

Pros:

- Cost-effective.
- No coding knowledge is required.
- Quick setup with professional results.

Cons:

- Limited flexibility compared to custom-built websites.
- It may require upgrades for advanced features.

Third-Party Design Services: Consider hiring a professional designer or agency for a more polished, customizable, unique look.

What to Look for in a Designer:

Experience: Check their portfolio for past work with service-based businesses.

Communication: Choose someone who listens to your ideas and provides clear feedback.

Deliverables: Ensure they provide all necessary files, including scalable formats like .AI or .EPS, and optimize the site for mobile devices.

Top Freelance Platforms to Find Designers:

- Fiverr: Affordable, but quality varies.
- Upwork: Great for mid-range budgets.
- Local Designers: Personal interaction can lead to better collaboration.

Social Media Platforms and Their Specific Uses for Security Consultants

Not all social media platforms are created equal, and each has unique strengths. Here's how to leverage them for your business:

Facebook

Audience: Broad, ranging from individuals to small businesses.

Best For: Community engagement, sharing security tips, and showcasing success stories.

Example Post: A video on "5 Ways to Secure Your Home This Holiday Season."

Pro Tip: Create a professional Facebook Business Page to appear more credible.

LinkedIn

Audience: Professionals, corporate clients, and decision-makers.

Best For: Networking, sharing thought leadership, and connecting with potential B2B clients.

Example Post: A case study on how you improved corporate security for a client.

Pro Tip: Regularly engage in industry groups to expand your reach. Join industry- and niche-specific groups.

Twitter

Audience: Fast-paced, news-oriented users.

Best For: Sharing industry news, quick tips, and joining relevant conversations.

Example Post: "Did you know 90% of breaches are due to human error? Train your team to stay secure. #CyberSecurity #RiskManagement."

Pro Tip: Use trending hashtags to increase visibility.

Instagram

Audience: Visual learners and younger demographics.

Best For: Sharing images or short videos, such as behind-the-scenes looks at your work or infographics.

Example Post: A carousel showing a step-by-step home security checklist.

Pro Tip: Use Stories and Reels to increase engagement.

YouTube

Audience: Video enthusiasts seeking detailed information or tutorials.

Best For: Educational content, such as training videos, webinars, or case studies.

Example Post: "The Top 3 Security Tips for Small Businesses: Watch Now!"

Pro Tip: Optimize your videos with keywords to improve search rankings.

Your Online Presence is Your Digital Handshake

Developing an online presence isn't just about being seen – it's about being remembered. Your website and social media platforms are your chance to showcase your expertise, connect with clients, and establish your security consulting business as a trusted authority.

With a solid website, thoughtful social media strategy, and consistent engagement, you'll create a digital presence that attracts clients and builds lasting relationships. So, get out there, get online, and let your brand shine – because in today's world, your business's first impression often starts with a click.

The Importance of Professional Associations and Accreditation

In the security consulting industry, credibility and connections go hand in hand. Joining professional associations and earning accreditations isn't just about stacking initials after your name (though, let's admit, they look impressive). These memberships give you access to a wealth of resources, networking opportunities, and industry recognition that sets you apart as a trusted professional. Let's look at some of the most influential organizations in the security consulting world and explore the benefits they bring to the table.

ASIS International

ASIS International is the gold standard for security professionals worldwide. Founded in 1955, this organization caters to every corner of the security industry globally, from physical security to cybersecurity and beyond.

Who They Cater To: Security consultants, risk management experts, executive protection professionals, and corporate security officers.

Benefits of Membership:

Certifications: ASIS offers highly respected certifications, including the Certified Protection Professional (CPP), Physical Security Professional (PSP), and Professional Certified Investigator (PCI).

Networking: ASIS is a networking powerhouse with over 34,000 members in more than 250 chapters globally.

Resources: Access to industry research, webinars, and their magazine, *Security Management*.

Events: The organization's annual GSX (Global Security Exchange) conference is a must-attend for anyone in the industry. They also hold regional yearly conferences around the globe if that aligns with your operations.

International Association of Professional Security Consultants (IAPSC)

IAPSC is the leading association for independent security consultants. They focus on promoting high ethical standards and providing resources for consultants to thrive.

Who They Cater To: Independent security consultants across all specialties, from physical security to risk assessment.

Benefits of Membership:

Networking: Connect with fellow consultants to share insights and opportunities.

Resources: Access to technical guides, white papers, and marketing tools.

Visibility: Members are listed in the IAPSC consultant directory, making it easier for potential clients to find you.

Pro Tip: If you're going solo as a consultant, IAPSC membership is like having a professional safety net.

International Protective Security Board (IPSB)

IPSB is the premier organization for executive protection (EP) professionals. They focus on advancing the standards and practices of protective services globally.

Who They Cater To: Executive protection specialists, security drivers, and UHNW (Ultra-High-Net-Worth) family security consultants.

Benefits of Membership:

Education: Offers specialized training and workshops tailored to EP professionals.

Networking: Connect with top-tier professionals in the protective services field.

Conferences: Their annual EP Forum is a hotbed of innovation and collaboration in the field of personal protection.

Pro Tip: If you're working in executive protection or aspire to, IPSB membership is an excellent way to connect with the movers and shakers in the industry.

Board of Executive Protection Professionals (BEPP)

BEPP is dedicated to setting the bar for excellence in the executive protection field. They focus on professional development and certification.

Who They Cater To: Executive protection professionals aiming to elevate their credentials and skill sets.

Benefits of Membership:

Certification: BEPP offers the Certified Executive Protection Professional (CEPP) designation, a mark of credibility in the EP space.

Standards: Access to best practices and operational guidelines that set the benchmark for EP services.

Community: Join a network of like-minded professionals committed to excellence in protection.

BEPP membership shows clients you mean business in a niche where reputation is everything.

Overseas Security Advisory Council (OSAC)

OSAC is a U.S. State Department initiative that fosters cooperation between private-sector security professionals and the government to enhance overseas security.

Who They Cater To: Security professionals working with international businesses, NGOs, or U.S. government contractors.

Benefits of Membership:

Intel: Gain access to critical security information and reports about global threats.

Networking: Connect with both government and private-sector security experts.

Events: Attend briefings and conferences that focus on international security trends.

If you work internationally, OSAC is your go-to resource for staying ahead of global threats and integrating with regional and country leadership.

American Board for Certification in Homeland Security (ABCHS)

ABCHS provides certifications and training for homeland security, disaster response, and emergency management professionals.

Who They Cater To: Homeland security professionals, emergency managers, and security consultants focused on crisis preparedness.

Benefits of Membership:

Certifications: Earn credentials like Certified in Homeland Security (CHS) and Certified National Threat Analyst (CNTA).

Training: Access specialized courses in disaster response and homeland security.

Recognition: Being certified by ABCHS signals a commitment to protecting national interests.

Pro Tip: If your focus is on disaster preparedness or counterterrorism, ABCHS is a great fit.

Association of International Risk Intelligence Professionals (AIRIP)

AIRIP serves professionals specializing in risk intelligence, providing resources and a community for those managing threats to organizations.

Who They Cater To: Risk intelligence analysts, corporate security teams, and consultants specializing in threat management.

Benefits of Membership:

Education: Offers webinars and resources on cutting-edge risk management techniques.

Networking: Build connections with peers in the risk intelligence space.

Insights: Access to research and case studies that enhance your knowledge base.

AIRIP membership is perfect for those who live by the motto, "Know the risk before it knows you."

International Association for Counterterrorism and Security Professionals (IACSP)

IACSP focuses on counterterrorism education and networking, supporting professionals dedicated to mitigating terrorist threats.

Who They Cater To: Counterterrorism consultants, security trainers, and professionals in high-risk security environments.

Benefits of Membership:

Training: Access to workshops and resources on counterterrorism strategies.

Publications: Stay informed with their magazine, *Counterterrorism and Homeland Security International.*

Networking: Join a global community of professionals tackling the most demanding security challenges.

Pro Tip: If counterterrorism is your passion, IACSP membership is a badge of honor.

The Security Executive Council (SEC)

The Security Executive Council (SEC) is the leading research and advisory firm specializing in corporate security risk mitigation solutions.

Who They Cater To: Chief Security Officers (CSOs) and any practitioner in the corporate security space. Although not an organization you can "join," per se, SEC is a tremendous resource.

Benefits of Membership:

Regular email updates: Their email updates are timely and do not reach the spam level that most mailing lists rise to.

Industry trends and projections: SEC's research is data-driven, objective, and proactive in its viewpoint.

Leadership Focused: One of SEC's main goals is to inform, empower, and train the current and next generation of leaders in the corporate security space. Their offerings are always focused on the development of those leaders through informed risk mitigation processes.

Pro Tip: You don't have to be some big wig to get on the SEC's mailing list. Just register on their website. They don't spam you, and when an article comes in from SEC, _read it._ You'll sound like an informed rockstar in your following conversations with clients or peers!

Membership Has Its Privileges

Joining professional associations and earning accreditations isn't just about adding lines to your resume. It's about growing your expertise, building valuable connections, and showing clients you're committed to excellence. Whether you're focusing on executive protection, risk intelligence, or counterterrorism, there's a community waiting to support you.

So, don't hesitate – join the ranks of these organizations, and let your membership open doors to new opportunities, knowledge, and success. After all, in security consulting, being part of the right network can be as important as your skills.

Chapter 4 Wrap-Up: Your Brand, Your Business, Your Success

Congratulations! You've just tackled one of the most exciting and foundational aspects of launching your security consulting business – building your brand. Boy, we covered a lot of material! In Chapter 4, we explored everything from legal structures to logos, all designed to help you craft a business identity that's not only professional but also uniquely yours. Let's recap what we've covered and celebrate how far you've come.

Choosing the Right Legal Structure

We started by discussing the legal nuts and bolts of your business. Whether you're leaning toward the simplicity of a sole proprietorship, the flexibility of an LLC, or the growth potential of an S-Corp or C-Corp, you now understand the advantages and disadvantages of each structure. And let's not forget the registered agent – whether you're stepping into that role yourself or outsourcing, you're set up to keep everything compliant and running smoothly.

Takeaway: Your business's legal foundation is set, and you're ready to move forward confidently.

Registering Your Business – Making it Official

From clearing trademarks with the USPTO to securing your EIN with the IRS, we walked through the steps to officially register your business. You also learned about crafting Articles of Incorporation and Operating Agreements to create a framework for your company's operations. These documents might not be glamorous, but they're the bedrock of a legitimate, professional enterprise.

Takeaway: Your business now has an official identity. You've gone from "thinking about it" to "owning it."

Creating a Professional Logo

Next, we dove into the art of logo design because, let's face it, your logo is the face of your brand. From best practices like simplicity and scalability to exploring AI tools and third-party design services, you have the tools to create a logo that makes a lasting impression. And we can't forget the psychology of colors – choosing the perfect palette is like giving your brand its personality.

Takeaway: You're equipped to create a logo that's memorable, professional, and true to your vision.

Creating a Vision Statement and Tagline

With your logo ready to shine, we turned to your business's verbal identity. A compelling vision statement captures the heart of your brand and inspires clients and team members alike. Pair that with a catchy tagline, and you have a combination that sticks in people's minds. Remember, your vision statement is the "why," and your tagline is the "wow."

Takeaway: Your business now speaks with purpose and clarity, setting you apart in the crowded security consulting field.

Developing an Online Presence: Websites and Social Media

In the digital age, you're invisible if you're not online. You learned how to build a functional and professional website, with features like customer engagement tools, blogs, and even e-commerce options. On social media, we explored how platforms like Facebook, LinkedIn, Twitter, Instagram, and YouTube can amplify your reach and establish you as a thought leader in your niche.

Takeaway: Your online presence is no longer a question of "if," but "how soon can I launch?"

The Importance of Professional Associations and Accreditation

Finally, we looked at the power of community and credibility. From ASIS International to the IAPSC, joining professional associations connects you with industry leaders, resources, and opportunities. Add accreditations, and you're signaling to clients that you're not just good – you're the best.

Takeaway: You're now plugged into the networks and certifications that give your business authority and respect.

What's Next?

You've built a strong foundation and crafted a brand that's ready to shine. But even the best brand needs trust to thrive. In Chapter 5, "Establishing Credibility and Trust in Security Consulting," we'll explore how to prove your worth to clients through continuing education, thought leadership, and certifications. We'll also discuss how to position yourself as your field's go-to expert and build lasting relationships.

You've got the tools. You've got the vision. Now, let's show the world why your security consulting business is the one they can count on. Let's get started!

5

Establishing Credibility and Trust in Security Consulting

"Trust is the glue of life. It's the most essential ingredient in effective communication. It's the foundational principle that holds all relationships."

— Stephen Covey

A 2023 survey found that 85% of clients choose security consultants based on perceived credibility and trustworthiness.

Credibility and trust are the cornerstones of success in the security consulting industry. In a field where your expertise can make the difference between safety and vulnerability, clients need to know they're in capable hands. This chapter explores the steps you can take to build that trust, from advancing your education and sharing your knowledge to obtaining essential certifications and adhering to industry standards. By the end of this chapter, you'll be equipped with the tools to establish yourself as a respected authority in your field.

The Importance of Continuing Education

In the security consulting world, one truth remains constant: change. The threats evolve, the technology advances, and client expectations grow more sophisticated. A successful security consultant must embrace a lifelong commitment to learning to stay ahead of the curve. Think of it as your perpetual edge – a tool that ensures you're relevant and indispensable.

The Rapidly Changing Threat Landscape

Gone are the days when a sturdy lock and a well-positioned camera were enough to secure an office or home. Today, threats range from cyberattacks and drone surveillance to AI-enabled security breaches.

If you rely on techniques or tools you learned a decade ago; you might as well be handing your client a rotary phone in a smartphone world. Continuous education ensures you remain an expert in identifying and mitigating these modern threats.

Pro Tip: Stay current by following industry publications, joining webinars, and attending conferences. Organizations like ASIS International or the International Association for Counterterrorism and Security Professionals (IACSP) regularly update members on emerging threats.

Advancements in Technology

Technology isn't just advancing – it's sprinting. From facial recognition systems and biometric access controls to predictive analytics and machine learning in surveillance, the tools of the trade are transforming rapidly. Clients expect you to not only understand these technologies but also to know how to implement them effectively.

Advice: Take online courses on LinkedIn Learning or Udemy to keep up with tech trends. These platforms often offer affordable courses tailored to professionals.

Being More Valuable to Clients

Clients don't just hire consultants for what they know – they hire them for what they *can do*. Expanding your expertise allows you to offer more value by adding new services, solving unique problems, or simply bringing fresh ideas to the table.

For example:

Traditional Knowledge: Locks, cameras, firearms, and access control.

Emerging Skills: Cybersecurity, risk assessment for smart devices, and advanced threat modeling.

Soft Skills: Communication, leadership, and emotional intelligence – because how you interact with clients is just as important as the solutions you provide.

The Importance of Business Acumen

Let's face it: being an expert in security alone won't make your consulting business thrive. Understanding the fundamentals of marketing, branding, and sales can be the difference between a struggling shop and a booming enterprise. Continuous learning in these areas equips you to:

Attract Clients: Build a brand that resonates with your target audience.

Close Deals: Learn persuasive sales techniques to win contracts.

Expand Services: Discover ways to grow your business and adapt to market demands.

Pro Tip: Subscribe to business podcasts, follow thought leaders on LinkedIn, and read books about entrepreneurship and marketing (including this one!).

Education Beyond Security

Here's a surprising truth: some of the most valuable lessons for a security consultant don't come from textbooks about locks, cameras, or guns. They come from understanding people.

Courses or resources on emotional intelligence, conflict resolution, and leadership can elevate your consulting practice to new heights. Why? Because understanding your client's pain points – and communicating solutions effectively – is just as critical as solving the technical problem.

Consider the concept of "Connection" Knowledge. Do you want to take your continuing education game to the next level? Study a bit about those interests and hobbies that your clients are interested in. If your client is a fan of World War I history, take a weekend to brush up on the rise and fall of the Ottoman Empire. Does he have an interest in fine cigars? Brush up a little bit on the topic. Connecting with your client on subjects other than security and on a deeper level than "How are you doing today?" will build that human connection they want to have around. A bonus is that you become a more well-rounded human being who may have a chance of a winning streak on Jeopardy!

The Role of College Degrees

Earning a college degree can open doors and provide credibility in certain circles. Degrees in fields like security management, international relations, criminal justice, cybersecurity, or business administration offer foundational knowledge and networking opportunities. However, formal education isn't the only way to learn. Some of the most effective continuous education happens outside the walls of a university.

Affordable (and Free) Learning Resources

If the thought of tuition fees makes you cringe, you're not alone. Fortunately, continuous education has never been more accessible. Here are some affordable or free options to expand your expertise:

LinkedIn Learning: Short, focused courses on topics ranging from cybersecurity to soft skills.

Udemy: Affordable courses on niche topics like drone security, marketing strategies, and leadership.

Coursera: Offers free or low-cost classes from top universities on a wide range of subjects.

Khan Academy: Great for brushing up on foundational topics like math, statistics, and data analysis.

Books: Focus on industry-relevant titles (like this one!) or explore other business and self-development books.

Pro Tip: Dedicate 15-30 minutes a day to learning – whether reading a chapter of a book, watching a course module, or listening to a podcast during your commute. Small, consistent efforts add up over time.

Pro Tip 2: Look into apps that will summarize a book and give you the audio 15-minute CliffsNotes version. There's quite a few of them out there. I can't tell you how smart I sound to my clients because I can speak intelligently about some great classic American Literature novel or the latest leadership book from Simon Sinek. I'm not saying I've never read anything; I'm just saying I sound like I've read A LOT more than I actually have.

Learning Is Your Key to Success

Continuous education is not a burden – it's an investment. It's the key to staying ahead of threats, technology, and market trends. It's what makes you a better consultant, entrepreneur, and leader. Remember, your clients aren't looking for someone who was the best five years ago – they're looking for someone who's the best *today*. They're also looking to add people they trust to their inner circle. You build that trust by having knowledge about common interests.

So, embrace the journey of lifelong learning. Stay curious, stay adaptable, and never stop sharpening your skills. Because in the world of security consulting, the only constant is change – and you're here to master it.

Becoming a Thought Leader in Security Consulting

If there's one universal truth in today's information-driven world, it's this: people automatically assume that if you publish something that looks polished, professional, and even mildly authoritative, you must be an expert. Is it fair? Maybe not. But it's reality – and a powerful opportunity. Becoming a thought leader in security consulting doesn't require reinventing the wheel. It requires being visible, offering well-researched insights, and consistently sharing relevant content demonstrating your expertise.

The Power of Public Presence

The best way to earn trust and establish legitimacy in your niche is to show up with timely, valuable content consistently. Whether through blogs, social media posts, or speaking engagements, being in the public space makes you visible – and visibility breeds credibility.

Here's the kicker: your impact grows exponentially when others discuss and share your work. When industry peers or professionals reference your insights, you're no longer just a voice; you're _the_ voice. That's why collaboration and building a platform that serves others is so vital. Now, let's review the tools that can help you achieve this.

Blogs: Your Industry Soapbox

Blogs are one of the simplest and most effective ways to establish thought leadership. Why? They allow you to share your expertise in a casual, conversational tone while targeting specific issues within your niche.

What to Write About:

Emerging trends (e.g., "The Role of AI in Risk Management").

Practical how-to's (e.g., "5 Steps to Conduct a Comprehensive Physical Security Audit" or "10 Ways to Stay Safe During This Holiday Shopping Season").

Industry myths or misconceptions (e.g., "Why Security Cameras Alone Aren't Enough to Protect Your Business").

Pro Tip: Consistency is key. Publishing one excellent blog post every three months won't build momentum. Aim for at least one post per month, even if it's shorter.

Why It Works:

Blogs can be shared across your website and social media, expanding your reach.

They establish you as someone who knows their stuff, but it can be delivered in an easy-going manner that doesn't come across as a know-it-all.

Articles Posted to Industry Social Media Pages

If blogs are your soapbox, social media is your megaphone. Platforms like LinkedIn allow you to post articles and updates that reach decision-makers and industry peers.

How to Make an Impact:

Keep your posts concise and visually appealing. Use bullet points, subheadings, or infographics.

Include actionable takeaways (e.g., "Three quick ways to evaluate your company's cybersecurity protocols").

Interact with readers. Respond to comments or start conversations in the thread.

Pro Tip: Use LinkedIn's publishing feature to post articles directly to your profile. This will make your content visible to your network and establish you as an active contributor in your field.

Peer-Reviewed Articles on Industry Websites/Periodicals

Want to impress? Get published in respected industry journals or on trusted websites. Peer-reviewed articles signal that your work has been vetted by experts, elevating your reputation as a subject matter authority.

Why Peer Review Should be Considered:

It adds a layer of credibility that's hard to match.

Your name becomes associated with quality, research-backed content.

Where to Publish:

Journals like *Security Management* or *Counterterrorism and Homeland Security International*.

Websites like ASIS International's resource library.

Pro Tip: Invest the time to ensure your submissions are meticulously researched and flawlessly written. These pieces will live online (or in print) for a long time and can significantly influence how others perceive your expertise.

Books: The Ultimate Credibility Booster

Writing a book may sound daunting, but it's one of the most powerful ways to position yourself as a thought leader. A published book demonstrates deep knowledge and commitment to your field, setting you apart from competitors. Plus, seeing your work on a shelf for someone to buy is pretty cool.

What to Write About:

Your niche expertise (e.g., "Mastering Corporate Security Consulting" or "How to Start a Security Consulting Business").

A comprehensive guide for clients (e.g., "The Business Owner's Handbook to Threat Assessment").

Trends shaping the industry (e.g., "The Future of Drone Security Operations").

Pro Tip: Self-publishing platforms like Amazon Kindle Direct Publishing make getting your work in front of readers easier than ever. With a bit of self-education (see a theme here?), you can use AI to streamline the process and create quality content that you can edit and publish in a fraction of the time it used to take.

Why It Works: People assume authors are experts. Having "Author of..." in your bio instantly boosts credibility.

Podcasts: Your Voice, Your Platform

Podcasts are booming, and for good reason – they're a personal, engaging way to connect with an audience. Whether you start your own or guest on someone else's, podcasts allow you to share your insights conversationally.

Ideas for Episodes:

- Interviews with other industry experts.
- Case studies of successful security strategies.
- Deep dives into niche topics, like counter-drone measures or cybersecurity protocols.

Pro Tip: You don't need expensive equipment to start a podcast. A good microphone and free editing software like Audacity are all you need to begin.

Discussion Panels: Collaboration in Action

Participating in (or moderating) a discussion panel is a fantastic way to showcase your expertise while networking with other leaders in the field.

Why:

- You're viewed as part of a collective of trusted experts.
- The format allows for real-time knowledge sharing and Q&A, which clients value.

Pro Tip: Volunteer to moderate panels at industry conferences – it positions you as both a facilitator and a thought leader.

Speaking at Industry Events

Few things reduce men to shivering, scared kittens more than public speaking. Having said that, few things establish authority faster than standing on stage and delivering a compelling talk. Whether at a conference or a local business meeting, speaking engagements put you in front of an audience that wants to hear what you have to say.

How to Succeed as a Speaker:

Share actionable, current, relevant insights rather than vague platitudes.

Use storytelling to make your points memorable.

Leave time for audience questions – it shows confidence and expertise.

Collaboration Projects with Industry Peers

Thought leadership isn't a solo endeavor. Collaborating with other professionals can amplify your reach and credibility.

Ideas for Collaboration:

- Co-authoring a white paper or research report.

- Hosting a joint webinar or training session.
- Partnering on a case study or project that highlights complementary expertise.

Why It Works:

When peers share your work or endorse your efforts, it validates your expertise in ways that self-promotion can't. Plus, you can exponentially expand your audience.

Thought Leadership is Visibility + Credibility

Becoming a thought leader in security consulting is more than being the loudest voice but the most consistent, valuable, and respected one. You position yourself as a trusted authority by sharing high-quality, relevant content and engaging with industry peers. And when your work gets shared by others, your credibility multiplies.

So, get out there, write that blog, join that panel, and record that podcast. The more you contribute to the conversation, the more the industry will look to you for leadership. Because in the end, trust isn't just earned – it's built, one piece of content at a time.

Essential Certifications for Security Consultants

In security consulting, your knowledge and expertise are your most valuable assets. But how do you communicate your competence to clients who may not yet know you? This is where industry certifications come in. Certifications serve as a professional handshake, signaling to clients, peers, and industry leaders that you have the skills and have met rigorous standards to validate them.

For the security consultant entrepreneur, certifications are more than just a line on a resume – they're a ticket to trust. They show that you're not simply winging it; you've put in the work to master your craft. Certifications announce to the world that you can stand up to the rigorous standards the industry has set to define an expert in the field. They also open doors to lucrative contracts, partnerships, and industry recognition.

However, not all certifications are created equal. With countless options available, focusing on those that align with your chosen niche is crucial. Whether specializing in executive protection, cybersecurity, physical security, or risk management, tailoring your certifications to your expertise ensures maximum impact.

Before diving into specific organizations and their certifications, let's emphasize that certifications are investments, not expenses. They require time, effort, and sometimes a financial commitment. But the return on this investment is credibility, authority, and trustworthiness that can transform your business.

Now, let's explore the major organizations in security and the certifications they offer.

ASIS International

Founded in 1955, ASIS International (originally the American Society for Industrial Security) is the gold standard for professional development in the security industry. What began as a U.S.-based organization for security managers has grown into a global powerhouse with over 34,000 members in over 250 chapters worldwide. ASIS is the hub for education, certification, and networking across virtually every security discipline, from private corporations to public-sector agencies.

ASIS's reach extends far beyond its membership numbers. Its influence is felt in boardrooms, government offices, and on the ground where security operations take place. Members include leading figures in cybersecurity, physical security, risk management, and crisis response. Among its ranks are government leaders, pioneers in security innovation, and some of the most respected subject matter experts in the field.

ASIS's contributions to the industry include setting global standards, producing comprehensive research, and hosting the Global Security

Exchange (GSX). This annual event brings together thousands of professionals to discuss the latest trends and technologies.

For the security consultant entrepreneur, aligning with ASIS is a sign of credibility, signaling to clients and peers that you are serious about maintaining the highest industry standards.

ASIS Certifications

ASIS offers several certifications that cater to different specialties within the security field. These credentials are globally recognized and reflect rigorous testing and adherence to high professional standards. Let's look at each certification.

Certified Protection Professional (CPP)

What It Is: The CPP certification is ASIS's flagship credential, designed for security managers and consultants who oversee entire security programs. This is the gold standard for individuals responsible for identifying and mitigating security risks while developing comprehensive protection strategies.

Who It's For: Experienced security professionals who manage large-scale security operations, including physical and personnel security, risk assessment, and crisis management.

Requirements to Obtain the Certification:

Experience:

- Nine years of security experience, with three in a management role, OR
- A bachelor's degree (or higher) and seven years of security experience, with three in a management role.

Exam: Candidates must pass a 225-question multiple-choice exam covering seven domains, including security principles, investigations, personnel security, and more.

Application Fee:

- ASIS members: $450
- Non-members: $650

Requirements to Maintain the Certification:

- Earn 60 Continuing Professional Education (CPE) credits every three years by attending seminars, webinars, or contributing to the industry through writing and speaking.
- Submit proof of CPE activities and pay a renewal fee.

Physical Security Professional (PSP)

The PSP certification is tailored for professionals focused on physical security assessments, system design, and implementation. This certification validates expertise in identifying vulnerabilities and designing systems to mitigate physical threats.

Who It's For: Security consultants, engineers, and managers specializing in physical security technologies and solutions.

Requirements to Obtain the Certification:

Experience:

- Six years of physical security experience OR
- A bachelor's degree (or higher) and four years of physical security experience.

Exam: Candidates must pass a 140-question exam covering three domains: Physical Security Assessment, Application, and Implementation.

Application Fee:

- ASIS members: $350
- Non-members: $550

Requirements to Maintain the Certification:

- Earn 60 CPE credits every three years.
- Renewal involves submitting proof of credits and a renewal fee.

Professional Certified Investigator (PCI)

The PCI certification is designed for professionals investigating incidents like fraud, employee misconduct, and criminal cases. It emphasizes knowledge of investigative techniques, legal considerations, and case management.

Who It's For: Investigators, security consultants, and professionals managing and conducting investigations for businesses, governments, or law enforcement agencies.

Requirements to Obtain the Certification:

Experience: Five years of investigations experience, with two years in case management or supervision.

Exam: A 125-question multiple-choice exam covering three domains: Case Management, Investigative Techniques, and Case Presentation.

Application Fee:

- ASIS members: $350
- Non-members: $550

Requirements to Maintain the Certification:

- Earn 60 CPE credits every three years.

- Submit renewal documentation and pay the required fee.

Associate Protection Professional (APP)

The APP is ASIS's entry-level certification, ideal for individuals newer to the security field. It demonstrates foundational knowledge in security management, risk assessments, and physical security.

Who It's For: Early-career security professionals looking to validate their expertise and establish credibility.

Requirements to Obtain the Certification:

Experience: One to four years of security experience, depending on educational background.

Exam: Candidates must pass a 100-question exam covering four domains: Security Fundamentals, Business Operations, Risk Management, and Response Management.

Application Fee:

- ASIS members: $200
- Non-members: $300

Requirements to Maintain the Certification:

- Earn 60 CPE credits every three years.
- Renewal requires proof of credits and a renewal fee.

For security consultant entrepreneurs, ASIS certifications are more than credentials – they are professional game-changers. Here's why:

Global Recognition: Clients, peers, and employers worldwide recognize ASIS certifications as the benchmark of excellence in security.

Enhanced Credibility: Having "CPP," "PSP," or "PCI" after your name signals that you've met rigorous industry standards. This trust can directly translate to winning more clients and larger contracts.

Expanded Knowledge: Preparing for these certifications forces you to master industry best practices and stay current with evolving threats and solutions.

Networking Opportunities: ASIS membership and certification connect you to a global community of professionals who can offer advice, partnerships, and career opportunities.

Competitive Edge: Certifications differentiate you from competitors who may lack formal credentials, giving you an edge in a crowded marketplace.

For the security consultant entrepreneur, ASIS certifications represent an investment in expertise, credibility, and long-term success. They are a decisive step forward if you want to stand out, align with an industry leader, and gain tools to build your business.

American Board for the Certification in Homeland Security (ABCHS)

The American Board for the Certification in Homeland Security (ABCHS) is a leading organization dedicated to advancing the knowledge and skills of professionals in homeland security, disaster preparedness, and emergency management. Established to address the growing complexities of domestic and international security challenges, ABCHS provides rigorous certification programs designed to validate expertise and commitment to excellence in this critical field.

Over the years, ABCHS has built a reputation as a trusted security and disaster management authority. Its certifications are widely recognized across government agencies, private corporations, and nonprofit organizations involved in emergency response and counterterrorism. ABCHS members include industry pioneers, government leaders, and private-sector professionals who share a commitment to safeguarding communities and critical infrastructure.

Today, ABCHS is a vital resource for professionals navigating the ever-evolving landscape of security threats. Its certifications are designed to keep members abreast of industry standards, technological advancements, and effective practices in homeland security.

ABCHS Certifications

ABCHS offers a robust lineup of certifications covering various aspects of homeland security, disaster preparedness, and threat analysis. Let's explore each certification in detail.

Certified in Homeland Security (CHS) Levels 1–5

The CHS certification series is a tiered program that progressively validates expertise in homeland security operations, policies, and strategies. Each level builds on the previous, offering a comprehensive pathway to mastery.

Who It's For: Professionals in homeland security, law enforcement, emergency management, or related fields. The certification is ideal for individuals at all career stages, from entry-level to senior leadership.

Requirements to Obtain the Certification:

CHS Level I: Designed for entry-level professionals. Requires completion of a training course and passing an online exam.

CHS Levels II-V: Each successive level requires proof of experience, completion of advanced coursework, and passing a proctored exam.

Higher levels often require prior certification in CHS Level 1 or lower levels.

Requirements to Maintain the Certification:

- Earn Continuing Education Units (CEUs) through ABCHS-approved activities, such as attending conferences or completing training.
- Submit renewal fees every three years.

Certified Homeland Security Training (CHST)

The CHST certification focuses on practical, hands-on training in homeland security techniques and strategies. It emphasizes actionable skills for field operations.

Who It's For: Professionals seeking tactical training to complement their theoretical understanding of homeland security.

Requirements to Obtain the Certification:

- Attend a multi-day training course covering topics like threat mitigation, crisis management, and incident response.
- Pass a skills assessment test at the end of the course.

Requirements to Maintain the Certification:

- Complete refresher courses every two years.
- Participate in field exercises or related professional development activities.

Certified National Threat Analyst (CNTA)

The CNTA certification is tailored for professionals specializing in threat analysis, including terrorism, cyber threats, and domestic security risks.

Who It's For: Intelligence analysts, law enforcement officers, and consultants focusing on identifying and mitigating national and international threats.

Requirements to Obtain the Certification:

- Complete a rigorous training program focused on threat analysis methodologies.
- Pass a comprehensive exam that tests knowledge of risk assessment, data analysis, and predictive modeling.

Requirements to Maintain the Certification:

- Submit proof of ongoing education in threat analysis or related fields every three years.
- Earn CEUs through ABCHS-approved activities.

Certified in Disaster Preparedness (CDP) Levels 1–3

The CDP certification series validates disaster preparedness, emergency response, and recovery planning expertise. Like the CHS series, it offers progressive levels of certification.

Who It's For: Emergency managers, disaster response professionals, and consultants specializing in business continuity and recovery planning.

Requirements to Obtain the Certification:

CDP Level 1: Requires completion of an introductory disaster preparedness course and passing an online exam.

CDP Levels 2–3: Advanced levels require evidence of experience in disaster response, completion of specialized training, and passing a proctored exam.

Requirements to Maintain the Certification:

- Earn CEUs through participation in disaster simulations, attending relevant conferences, or completing advanced training courses.
- Submit renewal fees every three years.

Why ABCHS Certifications Matter

For security consultant entrepreneurs, ABCHS certifications offer a unique blend of credibility, specialization, and practical knowledge. Here's why they're a valuable investment:

Credibility with Clients: ABCHS certifications signal to clients that you've met high professional standards in homeland security and disaster management.

Comprehensive Expertise: The tiered structure of certifications like CHS and CDP ensures that you can progressively build and demonstrate mastery in key areas of homeland security.

Relevance Across Niches: ABCHS certifications cover a wide range of security consulting specialties, from disaster preparedness to threat analysis, making them versatile and impactful.

Networking Opportunities: Joining the ABCHS community connects you with a network of professionals dedicated to homeland security and emergency response, offering collaboration and learning opportunities.

Differentiation in a Competitive Market: ABCHS certifications serve as a differentiator for entrepreneurs, demonstrating your commitment to staying current and offering best-in-class service.

In a world where security threats constantly evolve, ABCHS certifications equip security consultants with the tools and knowledge needed to stay ahead. These credentials aren't just a professional milestone for entrepreneurs – they're a competitive advantage.

Federal Emergency Management Agency (FEMA)

The Federal Emergency Management Agency (FEMA) was established in 1979 to coordinate disaster response efforts in the United States. Over the decades, FEMA has evolved into a critical entity for managing and mitigating emergencies, from natural disasters like hurricanes and wildfires to complex crises like cyberattacks and terrorism. FEMA operates under the Department of Homeland Security (DHS) and collaborates with state, local, tribal, and territorial governments, as well as private-sector partners.

FEMA's influence extends well beyond disaster response. Its training programs, standards, and certifications set the benchmark for emergency management professionals, ensuring they are prepared to handle crises effectively. FEMA has developed a suite of frameworks, such as the National Incident Management System (NIMS), that have become worldwide cornerstones of emergency preparedness and response planning.

For the security consultant entrepreneur, FEMA certifications are invaluable. They not only demonstrate expertise in managing emergencies but also signal a commitment to best practices recognized across industries. Whether your niche is corporate security, natural disaster consulting, or risk management, FEMA's credentials enhance your ability to win contracts, build credibility, and protect your clients. What's more, most of FEMA's certifications are _free_ and take just some effort and interest online to obtain.

Now, let's explore FEMA's certifications in detail.

FEMA Incident Command System (ICS) -100 and -200

The ICS -100 and -200 courses provide foundational knowledge of the Incident Command System (ICS), a standardized approach to managing emergencies.

Who It's For: Entry-level professionals, team members in emergency response roles, and individuals who need a basic understanding of ICS principles.

Requirements to Obtain the Certification:

ICS-100: Complete an online course covering ICS basics, including organizational structure, roles, and responsibilities.

ICS-200: Builds on ICS-100, introducing more advanced concepts such as delegation of authority and planning.

Both courses are free and available through FEMA's Emergency Management Institute (EMI) website.

Requirements to Maintain the Certification: No formal renewal is required, but professionals should consider periodic refreshers or advanced ICS courses.

FEMA Incident Command System (ICS) -300 and -400

ICS-300 and ICS-400 are advanced courses for professionals managing more extensive, complex incidents.

Who It's For: Mid-level managers, supervisors, and incident response leaders.

Requirements to Obtain the Certification:

ICS-300: Classroom or virtual training focused on expanding incidents, resource management, and operational planning.

ICS-400: Focuses on multi-agency coordination, incident complexity analysis, and advanced command structures.

Prerequisite: Completion of ICS-100 and ICS-200.

Requirements to Maintain the Certification: No mandatory renewal, but ongoing professional development is encouraged to stay current with evolving practices.

FEMA National Incident Management System (NIMS)

NIMS provides a comprehensive framework for managing emergencies at all levels of government and across all sectors.

Who It's For: Emergency management, security consulting, and risk assessment professionals.

Requirements to Obtain the Certification:

- Completion of NIMS introductory courses (often combined with ICS training).
- Courses are available for free on FEMA's EMI website.

Requirements to Maintain the Certification: No renewal is required, though additional training in NIMS updates is recommended.

FEMA Continuity of Operations Planning (COOP)

COOP training focuses on developing continuity plans to ensure critical operations can continue during emergencies.

Who It's For: Security consultants, business continuity planners, and emergency managers.

Requirements to Obtain the Certification:

- Attend a COOP workshop or complete online training.
- Topics include identifying essential functions, delegations of authority, and reconstitution planning.

Requirements to Maintain the Certification: Ongoing participation in COOP exercises or advanced continuity planning courses.

FEMA Professional Continuity Practitioner (PCP)

The PCP certification validates continuity planning and program management expertise.

Who It's For: Experienced professionals managing continuity programs for organizations or agencies.

Requirements to Obtain the Certification:

- Completion of multiple FEMA continuity courses, including IS-546 and IS-547.
- Participation in FEMA-sponsored continuity exercises.

Requirements to Maintain the Certification: Recertification every three years by earning CEUs through FEMA or related activities.

FEMA Master Continuity Practitioner (MCP)

The MCP certification is FEMA's highest level of continuity certification, showcasing advanced expertise in continuity planning and execution.

Who It's For: Senior professionals responsible for large-scale continuity programs or advising organizations on continuity strategy.

Requirements to Obtain the Certification:

- Successful completion of advanced FEMA continuity courses.
- Documented experience in continuity planning and participation in exercises.

Requirements to Maintain the Certification: Recertification every three years by earning CEUs and participating in ongoing continuity education.

International Association of Emergency Managers (IAEM) Certified Emergency Manager (CEM)

The CEM certification, offered in collaboration with IAEM, is a globally recognized credential for emergency management professionals.

Who It's For: Experienced emergency managers, security consultants, and disaster response coordinators.

Requirements to Obtain the Certification:

- At least three years of experience in emergency management.
- Completion of FEMA core training (ICS, NIMS, COOP).
- Submission of a comprehensive portfolio, including a management essay and supporting documentation.
- Passing a written exam.

Requirements to Maintain the Certification: Earn CEUs through professional development activities every five years.

Why FEMA Certifications Matter

Enhance Credibility: FEMA certifications are universally respected and demonstrate a commitment to excellence in emergency management.

Broaden Expertise: These credentials provide actionable skills for handling a wide range of emergencies, from natural disasters to cyber-attacks.

Align with Industry Standards: FEMA certifications ensure you operate within globally recognized frameworks like ICS and NIMS.

Open Doors: Many government contracts and private-sector opportunities require or prefer FEMA-certified professionals.

For the security consultant entrepreneur, FEMA certifications are more than badges – they're tools for building trust, expanding services, and staying ahead in an increasingly complex world.

Business Continuity and Disaster Recovery Certifications

Business Continuity and Disaster Recovery (BCDR) are vital components of modern organizational resilience. Whether it's a natural disaster, a cyberattack, or a supply chain disruption, businesses need robust plans to ensure they can maintain operations and recover swiftly. As organizations recognize crises' increasing frequency and complexity, demand for certified BCDR professionals continues to soar.

Certification in BCDR is more than an optional credential for the security consultant entrepreneur – it's a key differentiator. Certification signals that you have the expertise to help businesses plan for the unexpected, minimize downtime, and protect critical assets. With these credentials, you're not just providing services but peace of mind.

Now, let's delve into the organizations leading the charge in BCDR certification and explore the specific credentials they offer.

National Institute of Business Continuity Managers (NIBCM)

The National Institute of Business Continuity Managers (NIBCM) was founded to promote best practices in business continuity and disaster recovery. Focused on education, certification, and professional development, NIBCM supports individuals and organizations in navigating complex disruptions.

Certified Business Continuity Professional (CBCP)

Who It's For: Mid-level professionals responsible for developing, implementing, and managing business continuity plans.

Requirements to Obtain the Certification:

Experience: At least two years of hands-on experience in business continuity planning.

Training: Completion of a NIBCM-approved course or equivalent training.

Exam: A proctored exam that assesses knowledge in business impact analysis, continuity strategies, and recovery planning.

Requirements to Maintain the Certification:

- Earn 30 Continuing Education Units (CEUs) every two years through training, conferences, or related professional activities.
- Submit documentation of CEUs and pay a renewal fee.

Master Business Continuity Professional (MBCP)

Who It's For: Senior-level professionals who lead business continuity programs or serve as consultants for large organizations.

Requirements to Obtain the Certification:

Experience: Five years of experience in business continuity planning, with two years in a leadership role.

Training: Advanced coursework in continuity and disaster recovery.

Exam: A comprehensive exam covering advanced business continuity topics.

Portfolio: Submission of a portfolio documenting a completed business continuity project.

Requirements to Maintain the Certification:

- Earn 50 CEUs every two years.
- Participate in advanced training or contribute to the industry through publications or speaking engagements.

Disaster Recovery Institute International (DRII)

Founded in 1988, DRII is one of the most respected organizations in business continuity and disaster recovery. Known for its comprehensive certification programs and emphasis on global standards, DRII plays a pivotal role in shaping industry practices.

Associate Business Continuity Professional (ABCP)

Who It's For: Entry-level professionals looking to establish themselves in business continuity.

Requirements to Obtain the Certification:

- Completion of a DRII-approved introductory course.
- Passing a foundational exam covering BCDR basics.

Requirements to Maintain the Certification:

- Earn 20 CEUs every two years.
- Engage in continuing education activities or DRII-sponsored events.

Certified Business Continuity Professional (CBCP)

Who It's For: Mid-level professionals responsible for continuity planning and implementation.

Requirements to Obtain the Certification:

Experience: Two years of documented business continuity experience.

Exam: A rigorous exam testing intermediate knowledge in risk assessment, continuity planning, and recovery strategies.

Requirements to Maintain the Certification:

- Earn 40 CEUs every two years.
- Submit proof of CEUs and pay a renewal fee.

Master Business Continuity Professional (MBCP)

Who It's For: Seasoned professionals with extensive experience in continuity management and consulting.

Requirements to Obtain the Certification:

Experience: Five years in BCDR, with documented leadership experience.

Exam: A comprehensive test covering advanced topics like enterprise risk management and crisis communications.

Portfolio: Submission of case studies and completed projects.

Requirements to Maintain the Certification:

- Earn 50 CEUs every two years.
- Participate in leadership roles or contribute to the industry through speaking engagements or publications.

Business Continuity Institute (BCI)

The Business Continuity Institute (BCI), established in 1994, is a global leader in advancing business continuity. With members in over 100 countries, BCI sets the standard for resilience and continuity professionals worldwide.

Certificate of Business Continuity Institute (CBCI)

Who It's For: Professionals new to business continuity who want to build a foundational understanding.

Requirements to Obtain the Certification:

- Completion of a BCI introductory course.
- Passing an online exam covering the fundamentals of the BCI Good Practice Guidelines.

Requirements to Maintain the Certification: Although advanced certifications are recommended, no formal renewal is required.

Business Continuity Management (BCM) Practitioner

Who It's For: Professionals ready to take on greater responsibility in continuity planning and execution.

Requirements to Obtain the Certification:

- Completion of a BCM Practitioner course.
- Passing a detailed exam on BCM frameworks and strategies.

Requirements to Maintain the Certification: Earn CEUs through professional development activities or higher-level certifications.

Member of the Business Continuity Institute (MBCI)

Who It's For: Experienced professionals recognized as experts in business continuity.

Requirements to Obtain the Certification:

- Completion of advanced training.
- Submission of a professional portfolio and references.

Requirements to Maintain the Certification: Earn CEUs and actively contribute to the industry through publications, training, or leadership roles.

International Information Systems Security (ICS²) Certified Information Systems Security Professional (CISSP) with BCDR Specialization

Who It's For: Cybersecurity professionals integrating business continuity into IT security strategies.

Requirements to Obtain the Certification:

- Completion of CISSP coursework.

- Specialized training in BCDR practices.
- Passing a CISSP BCDR-specific exam.

Requirements to Maintain the Certification: Earn CEUs every three years through training and professional development activities.

National Institute for Business Continuity Management (NIBCM) Certified Continuity Manager (CCM)

Who It's For: Professionals managing continuity programs at the organizational level.

Requirements to Obtain the Certification:

- Completion of CCM-specific training.
- Passing an exam that tests comprehensive knowledge of continuity management principles.

Requirements to Maintain the Certification: Earn CEUs and participate in ongoing education.

FEMA Certifications: We've discussed FEMA certifications in-depth above. Suffice it to repeat here that FEMA has several BCDR certifications, including Professional Continuity Practitioner (PCP) and Master Continuity Practitioner (MCP)

Why BCDR Certifications Matter

Universal Application: Business continuity and disaster recovery are critical for organizations of all sizes and sectors, making these certifications highly versatile.

High Demand: With increasing disruptions, businesses prioritize continuity expertise, creating ample opportunities for certified professionals.

Enhanced Credibility: Certifications validate your expertise, making you a trusted client advisor.

Competitive Edge: In a crowded marketplace, certified BCDR professionals stand out for their proven ability to safeguard businesses.

For the security consultant entrepreneur, BCDR certifications are more than credentials – they're tools for building a resilient and respected consulting practice.

Workplace Violence Prevention Certifications

Workplace violence has become an unfortunate reality across industries, with incidents ranging from verbal threats to active shooter situations. According to the Occupational Safety and Health Administration (OSHA), nearly 2 million workers are victims of workplace violence each year, and the financial impact on organizations, including lost productivity, legal liabilities, and reputational damage, is staggering.

Creating safer environments is not just a legal obligation but a moral one for organizations. This demand places Workplace Violence Prevention (WVP) consultants in high demand. Certification in this sector ensures security professionals possess the knowledge and skills to address threats effectively, design prevention programs, and train employees.

For the security consultant entrepreneur, WVP certifications are indispensable. They signal expertise in handling sensitive, high-stakes situations and position you as a trusted advisor to organizations seeking to safeguard their employees.

Crisis Prevention Institute (CPI)

The Crisis Prevention Institute (CPI) was founded in 1980 to address the growing need for crisis prevention and de-escalation training. CPI is widely recognized as a leader in nonviolent conflict resolution, offering training programs emphasizing safety and dignity in workplace interactions.

Nonviolent Crisis Intervention (NCI) Certification

Who It's For: Professionals in healthcare, education, law enforcement, and corporate settings who need to de-escalate potentially violent situations.

Requirements to Obtain the Certification:

Training Course: Attend a 2-4 day in-person or virtual workshop covering de-escalation techniques, crisis prevention, and physical intervention methods (as a last resort).

Practical Application: Demonstrate proficiency in de-escalation strategies and nonviolent interventions during the course.

Requirements to Maintain the Certification:

Renewal Training: Complete a one-day refresher course annually.

Updated Materials: Stay current with CPI's updated techniques and guidelines.

The NCI certification provides actionable skills to defuse tense situations, making it essential for consultants specializing in workplace safety and training programs.

Occupational Safety and Health Administration (OSHA)

Established in 1970, OSHA is the U.S. government agency responsible for enforcing workplace safety standards. Its Workplace Violence Prevention Program (WVPP) is a critical component of its mission to ensure safe working conditions for all employees.

Workplace Violence Prevention Program (WVPP)

Who It's For: HR professionals, safety officers, and security consultants involved in creating and implementing workplace violence prevention strategies.

Requirements to Obtain the Certification:

Online Training: Completion of OSHA's WVPP training modules, which cover risk assessment, prevention program design, and incident response.

Implementation Plan: Develop and submit a sample workplace violence prevention plan.

Requirements to Maintain the Certification:

Ongoing Education: Participate in OSHA-approved courses or workshops every two years.

Updated Plans: Review and revise prevention plans regularly to align with OSHA's evolving guidelines.

WVPP certification ensures compliance with OSHA standards, crucial for legal and reputational risk mitigation.

The Association of Threat Assessment Professionals (ATAP)

Founded in 1992, ATAP is an international organization dedicated to advancing threat assessment as a profession. Its members include law enforcement officials, mental health professionals, and corporate security experts.

Certified Threat Manager (CTM)

Who It's For: Security consultants, threat assessment professionals, and organizational leaders responsible for identifying and mitigating risks of violence.

Requirements to Obtain the Certification:

Experience: At least three years of direct threat assessment experience.

Training: Completion of ATAP-approved courses on behavioral threat analysis, risk management, and mitigation strategies.

Exam: Pass a comprehensive test covering key concepts in threat management.

Requirements to Maintain the Certification: Earn Continuing Education Units (CEUs) every three years through ATAP webinars, conferences, or publications.

CTM certification validates expertise in assessing and managing workplace threats, a critical skill in high-risk industries.

The National Institute for the Prevention of Workplace Violence (NIPWV)

The NIPWV was created to address the need for proactive workplace violence prevention measures. The organization provides research, training, and certifications aimed at reducing workplace incidents and creating safer environments.

Workplace Violence Prevention Specialist (WVPS)

Who It's For: Security consultants, HR professionals, and safety officers tasked with developing and implementing comprehensive workplace violence programs.

Requirements to Obtain the Certification:

Training Course: Completion of a multi-day workshop or online training that covers prevention frameworks, employee training, and incident response.

Portfolio Submission: Create and submit a sample workplace violence prevention plan for evaluation.

Requirements to Maintain the Certification:

- Earn 20 CEUs every two years through NIPWV webinars, training sessions, or publications.
- Participate in workplace violence prevention exercises or case studies.

The WVPS certification equips professionals with the tools to create tailored violence prevention programs that protect employees and organizations.

Why Workplace Violence Prevention Certifications Matter

Workplace violence prevention isn't just about avoiding lawsuits – it's about creating environments where employees feel safe and supported. For the security consultant entrepreneur, these certifications:

Demonstrate Expertise: WVP certifications validate your ability to assess threats, design prevention programs, and effectively train employees.

Build Trust: Clients are more likely to hire professionals with formal credentials in this sensitive area.

Expand Services: Certifications open the door to additional services, such as employee training and incident response planning.

Mitigate Risks: Knowledge gained through WVP certification reduces liability and ensures compliance with legal standards.

As workplace violence remains a persistent challenge, certifications in this field empower security consultants to make a tangible impact, build trust with clients, and establish themselves as leaders in this critical sector.

Anti-Terrorism Accreditation Board (ATAB)

Established in 2001, the Anti-Terrorism Accreditation Board (ATAB) was created in collaboration with the International Society of Anti-Terrorism Professionals and leaders from government, military, private security, law enforcement, fire departments, emergency medical services, and other first responders. The goal was to define the education, training, and experience requirements for first responders to prepare for and respond to terrorist events effectively.

In the aftermath of the September 11 attacks, ATAB took a leading role in developing and implementing standardized anti-terrorism training and certification programs. By integrating resources from FEMA, the Department of Transportation, the U.S. Army, and the Federal Fire Academy, ATAB created comprehensive training modules that have become industry standards for terrorism response worldwide.

Today, ATAB's influence extends globally. It provides quality training and establishes industry standards utilized by responders worldwide. Its members include high-ranking officials such as four-star generals, deputy directors of homeland security, security directors of Fortune 500 companies, and university professors, underscoring its significant impact on the security industry.

ATAB Certifications

ATAB offers a range of certifications designed to equip professionals with the skills and knowledge necessary to combat terrorism effectively. Below is an overview of each certification, including target candidates and requirements for obtaining and maintaining it.

Certified Anti-Terrorism Specialist (CAS)

Who It's For: Professionals seeking to establish a foundational understanding of anti-terrorism strategies, including those in security management, law enforcement, and emergency response.

Requirements to Obtain the Certification:

Membership: Must be a member in good standing with ATAB.

Experience: Demonstrated knowledge, skills, and abilities acquired through education, training, and experience in anti-terrorism.

Examination: Achieve an 80% or higher score on the certification examination.

Requirements to Maintain the Certification:

Continuing Education: Engage in ongoing professional development to stay current with anti-terrorism practices.

Renewal: Comply with ATAB's recertification policies, which may include additional training or assessments.

The CAS certification sets the standard for personnel who meet the requisite knowledge, skills, and competencies to understand and combat the threat of global terrorism.

Certified Master Anti-Terrorism Specialist (CMAS)

Who It's For: Experienced professionals with a proven track record in terrorism response, typically holding leadership, management, or advisory positions.

Requirements to Obtain the Certification:

Prerequisite: Must hold the CAS credential.

Experience: Approximately seven years in the terrorism response field.

Examination: Achieve an 80% or higher score on the certification examination.

Portfolio Submission: Submit a comprehensive white paper, PowerPoint presentation, policy and procedure manual, standard operating procedures, or other relevant work authored by the candidate.

Requirements to Maintain the Certification:

Continuing Education: Participate in advanced training and contribute to the field through publications or instruction.

Renewal: Adhere to ATAB's recertification requirements, ensuring ongoing proficiency.

The CMAS credential signifies subject matter expertise and positions holders as preferred candidates for roles involving training, vulnerability assessments, security audits, and consulting services.

Certified Homeland Security Professional (CHSP)

Who It's For: Professionals involved in homeland security operations, policy-making, and strategic planning.

Requirements to Obtain the Certification:

Membership: Active membership with ATAB.

Experience: Relevant experience in homeland security or related fields.

Examination: Pass a comprehensive exam covering homeland security topics.

Requirements to Maintain the Certification:

Continuing Education: Engage in activities that enhance knowledge of homeland security.

Renewal: Meet ATAB's standards for recertification, including potential assessments.

The CHSP certification demonstrates a commitment to national security and equips professionals with the expertise to address complex security challenges.

ATAB Instructor Certified

Who It's For: Professionals aiming to train others in anti-terrorism strategies and response protocols.

Requirements to Obtain the Certification:

Prerequisite: Typically requires holding a CMAS credential.

Experience: Extensive experience in anti-terrorism and instructional roles.

Assessment: Demonstrate teaching proficiency and subject matter expertise.

Requirements to Maintain the Certification:

Teaching Engagements: Regularly conduct training sessions or workshops.

Professional Development: Stay updated with the latest anti-terrorism strategies and instructional methodologies.

Being an ATAB Certified Instructor enables professionals to disseminate critical knowledge, thereby enhancing the preparedness of organizations and individuals against terrorist threats.

The Importance of ATAB Certifications

Incorporating ATAB certifications into your professional portfolio elevates your standing in the security industry and equips you with actionable tools to meet client needs effectively. These certifications ensure you are prepared to:

Provide Specialized Expertise: The nuanced knowledge gained through ATAB certifications allows you to address specific client concerns, whether conducting a vulnerability assessment or developing anti-terrorism protocols.

Enhance Client Trust: Clients often seek professionals with credentials from trusted organizations. An ATAB certification assures them of your credibility and dedication to upholding industry standards.

Stay Ahead of Threat Trends: The ever-evolving nature of terrorism and security threats requires consultants to remain updated. Through continuing education and active involvement with ATAB, you stay informed of the latest methodologies, technologies, and global trends.

Expand Business Opportunities: Many government contracts and corporate engagements favor or require professionals with certifications

like CAS or CMAS, making these credentials a competitive edge for
securing high-value projects.

Establish Authority: Certifications like CMAS and CHSP position you
as an industry leader, opening doors to collaboration, speaking engagements, and advisory roles that further build your reputation.

For the security consultant entrepreneur, ATAB certifications are more
than badges – they are foundational tools that support credibility,
enhance skill sets, and ensure competitiveness in an ever-demanding
marketplace.

International Information Systems Security Certification Consortium (ISC²)

Founded in 1989, the International Information Systems Security Certification Consortium (ISC²) is a globally recognized cybersecurity education and certification leader. Headquartered in Clearwater, Florida,
ISC² was established to standardize practices and advance the skills of
professionals protecting critical information assets.

Today, ISC² is one of the most respected organizations in cybersecurity,
with over 168,000 members worldwide. Its certifications, such as the
Certified Information Systems Security Professional (CISSP), have
become industry benchmarks for excellence in information security.
ISC² plays a pivotal role in setting standards, publishing research, and
providing training to ensure that security professionals can meet the
challenges of an ever-evolving threat landscape.

ISC² certifications are recognized by governments, corporations, and
academic institutions globally. The organization's commitment to
advancing cybersecurity through certification, education, and collaboration has made it a cornerstone of the information security profession. For
the security consultant entrepreneur, ISC² credentials are invaluable in
demonstrating expertise, building credibility, and accessing a global
network of professionals.

ISC² Certifications

ISC² offers several certifications tailored to different aspects of cybersecurity. Each credential validates specific skills and knowledge, ensuring that professionals can meet diverse security challenges.

Certified Information Systems Security Professional (CISSP)

The CISSP certification is the gold standard in cybersecurity. It demonstrates advanced expertise in designing, implementing, and managing security programs to protect organizations from threats.

Who It's For: Senior-level security consultants, IT managers, and professionals responsible for enterprise-wide security.

Requirements to Obtain the Certification:

Experience: Five years of cumulative paid work experience in two or more domains of the CISSP Common Body of Knowledge (CBK). A four-year college degree can substitute for one year of experience.

Exam: A 3-hour, 125-question multiple-choice exam covering eight domains, including Security and Risk Management, Asset Security, and Software Development Security.

Endorsement: A certified ISC² professional must endorse your experience and application.

Requirements to Maintain the Certification:

- Earn 120 Continuing Professional Education (CPE) credits over three years.
- Pay an annual maintenance fee.

Systems Security Certified Practitioner (SSCP)

The SSCP certification validates practical technical skills in implementing, monitoring, and administering IT infrastructure using security best practices.

Who It's For: IT administrators, security analysts, and consultants managing operational security.

Requirements to Obtain the Certification:

Experience: One year of cumulative work experience in one or more of the SSCP CBK domains.

Exam: A 3-hour, 150-question multiple-choice exam covering domains such as Access Controls, Cryptography, and Incident Response.

Requirements to Maintain the Certification:

- Earn 60 CPE credits over three years.
- Pay an annual maintenance fee.

Certified Cloud Security Professional (CCSP)

The CCSP certification focuses on cloud security, covering best practices for securing cloud environments and ensuring compliance with regulations.

Who It's For: Security consultants, cloud architects, and IT professionals specializing in cloud technologies.

Requirements to Obtain the Certification:

Experience: Five years of work experience in IT, with three years in information security and one year in one or more of the CCSP CBK domains.

Exam: A 3-hour, 125-question multiple-choice exam covering six domains, including Cloud Data Security and Cloud Infrastructure.

Requirements to Maintain the Certification:

- Earn 90 CPE credits over three years.
- Pay an annual maintenance fee.

Certified Authorization Professional (CAP)

The CAP certification is tailored for professionals who manage risk and authorize systems to operate securely within compliance frameworks.

Who It's For: Security consultants, IT managers, and risk management professionals in government or regulated industries.

Requirements to Obtain the Certification:

Experience: Two years of cumulative work experience in one or more CAP CBK domains.

Exam: A 3-hour, 125-question multiple-choice exam covering domains like Security Assessment and Continuous Monitoring.

Requirements to Maintain the Certification:

- Earn 60 CPE credits over three years.
- Pay an annual maintenance fee.

Healthcare Information Security and Privacy Practitioner (HCISPP)

The HCISPP certification validates expertise in securing and managing sensitive healthcare information within a regulatory framework.

Who It's For: Professionals in healthcare security, risk management, and compliance roles.

Requirements to Obtain the Certification:

Experience: Two years of work experience in one or more HCISPP CBK domains, including at least one year in healthcare.

Exam: A 3-hour, 125-question multiple-choice exam covering six domains, such as Privacy and Risk Management.

Requirements to Maintain the Certification:

- Earn 60 CPE credits over three years.
- Pay an annual maintenance fee.

ISC^2 certifications are globally recognized credentials that offer unparalleled benefits to security consultant entrepreneurs:

Credibility and Authority: ISC^2 certifications demonstrate that you have met rigorous standards, which clients and employers value.

Comprehensive Expertise: From cloud security to healthcare compliance, ISC^2's diverse certifications cater to various niches, allowing you to align credentials with your consulting focus.

Networking Opportunities: Membership in ISC^2 connects you with a global community of security professionals, fostering opportunities for collaboration and learning.

Increased Marketability: Clients prefer certified professionals when choosing consultants for critical security projects. ISC^2 credentials make you stand out.

Staying Ahead: The cybersecurity landscape evolves rapidly, and ISC^2 certifications ensure you stay current with best practices and emerging threats.

For the security consultant entrepreneur, ISC^2 certifications are investments in knowledge, credibility, and success. They position you as a leader in your niche, opening doors to new opportunities and ensuring your clients receive top-tier expertise.

Government and Regulatory Requirements

The security consulting industry is a fascinating paradox: while security professionals are trusted to safeguard lives, assets, and sensitive information, the industry is not tightly regulated. Unlike fields such as medicine or law, where national standards are firmly established, security consulting operates under a patchwork of state, local, and sometimes federal regulations. Navigating these requirements can be complex, but understanding them for the security consultant entrepreneur is essential to building credibility and staying on the right side of the law.

State and Local Security Licensing

One of the defining challenges of the security consulting industry is the variability of licensing requirements. In the United States, each state – and often each municipality within a state – sets its own rules for licensing security professionals. For example:

State-Level Variability:

Some states, like California, require comprehensive licensing, background checks, and continuing education for private security consultants.

Others, such as Wyoming, have minimal or no statewide requirements, leaving regulatory oversight to local jurisdictions.

Municipality-Specific Rules:

Even within a state, cities and counties may impose their own regulations. For example, security consultants working in New York City face different requirements than those working upstate in Albany. There are no statewide licensing requirements for security practitioners in Colorado, but consultants working in Denver must be licensed there. That license, however, would not be valid in Fort Caron or Colorado Springs, both of which have unique licensing requirements.

This fragmented system means that a consultant licensed in one jurisdiction may not be legally recognized in another, even within the same state.

The Importance of Licensing:

While obtaining licenses for every jurisdiction where a consultant might work is nearly impossible, holding a license in at least one state or municipality demonstrates professionalism and commitment to industry standards.

Licensing often requires proof of competency, such as passing an exam or completing training, which reassures clients of your expertise.

Clients and regulatory bodies alike view unlicensed consultants with skepticism, making it critical to understand and comply with local rules where you operate.

Tips for Navigating State and Local Licensing:

Research Thoroughly: Before taking on a project, verify the licensing requirements for that specific jurisdiction. Local government websites and industry associations are excellent resources.

Leverage Reciprocity: Some states have reciprocity agreements that allow consultants licensed in one state to operate in another without additional licensing.

Engage Legal Counsel: Consider consulting an attorney specializing in licensing and compliance for multi-jurisdictional projects.

Federal Regulations for Security Providers

At the federal level, the regulation of the security consulting industry is less direct than state and local licensing, but there are still key frameworks and laws that impact operations:

General Federal Oversight: Although there are no federal licenses specifically for security consultants, specific federal laws influence how they conduct their work, particularly in sensitive areas like cybersecurity, data privacy, and anti-terrorism.

Applicable Federal Laws:

Homeland Security Directives: Consultants working with government entities or critical infrastructure may need to adhere to federal guidelines issued by the Department of Homeland Security (DHS).

Privacy Laws: The Gramm-Leach-Bliley Act (GLBA) and HIPAA govern how consultants handle sensitive financial and healthcare information, respectively.

FISMA Compliance: The Federal Information Security Management Act (FISMA) outlines requirements for managing information security risks for consultants working on federal contracts.

ITAR (International Traffic in Arms Regulations): Security consultants dealing with export-controlled technology or defense-related projects must comply with ITAR.

Government Contracting Requirements:

Consultants seeking government contracts must often meet additional criteria, such as obtaining a Federal Employer Identification Number (FEIN) or registering with the System for Award Management (SAM).

Some contracts may require specific certifications, such as those offered by FEMA, to demonstrate expertise in emergency management or continuity planning.

Industry-Specific Federal Oversight: Federal agencies like the Nuclear Regulatory Commission (NRC) or the Coast Guard may impose additional regulations on consultants operating in specialized areas like nuclear security or maritime protection.

Balancing the Patchwork

While the fragmented nature of security regulations can feel overwhelming, it also offers opportunities for differentiation. By staying informed and compliant, security consultants can position themselves as trusted professionals in a field where ambiguity is common.

Here's how to approach it:

Stay Proactive: Regularly review changes in licensing and regulations for jurisdictions where you work. Membership in professional associations, like ASIS International, can provide access to updates and resources.

Prioritize Training: Even in unregulated jurisdictions, obtaining certifications and attending training programs can fill gaps in formal oversight and reassure clients of your competency.

Focus on Niches: Some niches, like cybersecurity or anti-terrorism, align with federal standards and certifications, allowing you to side-step the variability of state and local rules.

Understanding and complying with government and regulatory requirements is about more than avoiding fines or penalties – it's about building trust and credibility. Clients are more likely to hire consultants who demonstrate professionalism by adhering to legal and ethical standards. By mastering the complexities of state, local, and federal regulations, security consultant entrepreneurs can confidently deliver services, expand their reach, and elevate their reputation in a competitive marketplace.

International Regulatory Requirements

Security consultants often work across borders as the world becomes increasingly interconnected. However, international security consulting comes with its own challenges, particularly when navigating diverse and often complex regulatory landscapes. Understanding these requirements is not just a professional courtesy for consultants considering global projects – it's a critical necessity for avoiding legal pitfalls and maintaining freedom and reputation.

Regulations Vary Widely – Thorough Research Is Key

Unlike in the United States, where state and local licensing govern much of the security industry, international regulations can vary dramatically from one country to the next. Some nations have rigorous licensing and certification requirements, while others may have little to no regulation at all. The consultant is responsible for investigating and complying with the legal framework of each country in which they operate.

Key Considerations for Researching International Regulations:

Work Permits: Many countries require a specific work visa or permit for foreign consultants. Make sure your immigration paperwork is in order before accepting a contract.

Local Licensing Requirements: Some countries require foreign security professionals to partner with local firms or obtain special licenses to operate legally.

Insurance and Liability: Verify whether your professional liability insurance extends to international operations and complies with local laws.

Where to Start Your Research:

U.S. Embassy (USEMB): The U.S. Embassy in your target country can be a valuable resource. They often provide information on local business regulations, licensing, and potential legal risks.

Overseas Security Advisory Council (OSAC): OSAC, an initiative of the U.S. Department of State, is a treasure trove of information for security consultants. It offers detailed country-specific reports, advisories, and networking opportunities with other professionals operating internationally.

ASIS CPP Network: If you hold a Certified Protection Professional (CPP) certification through ASIS International, leverage the organization's global network. CPP holders often share insights and experiences about operating in specific international markets, making it easier to navigate complex requirements.

Pro Tip: Researching international regulations isn't a one-time task. Rules can change rapidly, especially in politically unstable regions. Staying informed through continuous research and networking is critical to your success.

Some Countries Are Strictly Off-Limits for Foreign Consultants

While many countries welcome foreign expertise, others have stringent laws against foreign security consultants. Operating without explicit government approval in some nations is illegal and can lead to severe consequences.

Understanding the Risks:

"Persona Non-Grata" (PNG): In diplomatic terms, being declared PNG means you are no longer welcome in the country and must leave immediately. For security consultants, this status can result from failing to comply with local laws or offending government officials.

Imprisonment: In extreme cases, consultants operating without proper authorization may face fines, confiscation of equipment, or even imprisonment. Countries with strict national security laws, such as China or Russia, are particularly risky for unauthorized security operations.

Red Flags to Watch For:

National Security Sensitivities: Countries with histories of political instability or strong authoritarian governments often restrict foreign involvement in security matters.

Licensing Requirements Not Open to Foreigners: Some nations limit security consulting licenses to their citizens or require foreign firms to partner with a domestic entity.

Cultural or Political Considerations: Operating in regions with deeply ingrained cultural or political sensitivities requires additional caution and awareness.

Best Practices for International Security Consultants

Engage Local Experts: Partner with local consultants or legal advisors who understand the nuances of their country's regulatory landscape. Their guidance can prevent costly missteps and legal troubles.

Conduct Due Diligence: Before accepting an international contract, thoroughly vet the legal requirements for your services in that country. Document every step of your compliance process for your records.

Stay Within the Law:

If you encounter a jurisdiction where your services are restricted or prohibited, decline the contract. Reputation and personal safety are more valuable than any single project.

Build a Network: Associations like ASIS International or OSAC are invaluable for connecting with seasoned professionals who can share their experiences and insights about working abroad.

Operating internationally opens the door to exciting opportunities and lucrative contracts. However, it also introduces legal complexities and risks derailing even the most seasoned security consultants. You can ensure your global projects are successful and legally compliant by conducting thorough research, leveraging professional networks, and adhering to local laws.

Security consultant entrepreneurs who navigate international regulatory requirements with care and diligence not only expand their market reach but also reinforce their reputation as credible, professional, and trustworthy experts.

Industry Standards and Best Practices

Without unified regulations across local, state, and federal levels, the security industry has taken it upon itself to fill the void by developing comprehensive standards and guidelines. These standards serve as a form of self-regulation, creating a framework for professionalism, competency, and ethical practices. Understanding and aligning with these standards is voluntary but critical for security consultant entrepreneurs – providing high-quality services, demonstrating legitimacy, and building client trust.

Let's explore the landscape of industry standards and the organizations leading this charge, including ASIS International and the Board of Executive Protection Professionals (BEPP).

An Overview of the Standards and Guidelines Landscape

The security industry's standards and guidelines landscape is as vast and varied as the challenges it addresses. From physical security and cyber-security to executive protection and risk management, these guidelines aim to standardize best practices and ensure that professionals operate at the highest levels of competence and integrity.

Why Standards Matter

Consistency Across the Industry: Standards ensure that security practices are consistent and effective, regardless of where they are implemented.

Credibility and Trust: Adhering to established standards reassures clients that they are working with knowledgeable and reliable professionals.

Risk Mitigation: Following best practices reduces liability for consultants and their clients.

Professional Development: Standards serve as a benchmark for training and certifications, guiding professionals in their career growth.

Key ASIS Industry Standards and Guidelines

Enterprise Security Risk Management (ESRM):

What It Covers: ESRM is a strategic approach to managing security risks at the organizational level. It integrates security into core business operations and prioritizes risks based on their potential impact.

Why You Care: ESRM encourages a proactive, holistic approach to security, making it invaluable for consultants advising large corporations or multinational clients.

Physical Asset Protection Standards:

What It Covers: These standards detail the best practices for protecting physical assets, including buildings, equipment, and inventory. Topics include perimeter security, access control, and surveillance.

Why You Care: Adhering to these guidelines ensures the effectiveness and reliability of physical security measures, which is a cornerstone of many consulting engagements.

Investigations Standard:

What It Covers: This standard outlines protocols for conducting thorough, ethical, and legally compliant investigations.

Why You Care: Security consultants specializing in surveillance or private investigations can leverage this standard to enhance the credibility and quality of their work.

Using ASIS Standards

ASIS standards are freely available to members and widely referenced across the industry. Consultants can use them to guide operations, create training programs, and align their services with globally accepted practices. As you write reports, you can mention that you followed "ASIS Published Standard ####" to legitimize your reporting.

The Board of Executive Protection Professionals (BEPP)

BEPP was established to address the specialized needs of the executive protection sector. While this niche falls under the broader security industry, it demands unique expertise and an elevated level of professionalism. BEPP is dedicated to setting benchmarks that ensure the safety and security of high-net-worth individuals, corporate executives, and public figures.

Key BEPP Standards

Executive Protection Competency Framework:

What It Covers: A detailed breakdown of the knowledge, skills, and abilities required to succeed in executive protection, including risk assessment, protective driving, and Advance work.

Why You Care: This framework provides a system for consultants entering or advancing in the executive protection niche.

Ethical Guidelines for Executive Protection:

What It Covers: BEPP emphasizes ethics in all aspects of executive protection, from client confidentiality to conflict resolution.

Why You Care: In a field where discretion and trust are paramount, adhering to ethical standards is non-negotiable.

Training and Certification Standards:

What It Covers: BEPP outlines the training requirements and certifications for professionals to excel in executive protection.

Why You Care: These standards ensure practitioners are well-prepared to handle the unique challenges of protecting high-profile individuals.

By aligning with BEPP standards, consultants can position themselves as experts in executive protection, attract high-profile clients, and deliver services that meet the highest professional benchmarks.

Why Industry Standards Matter for Security Consultant Entrepreneurs

Filling the Regulatory Gap: In a fragmented regulatory environment, industry standards provide a consistent framework for professionalism.

Enhancing Credibility: Adhering to recognized standards signals to clients that you are committed to excellence and best practices.

Staying Competitive: As more clients demand adherence to established guidelines, following these standards becomes a competitive advantage.

Guiding Growth: Standards serve as a blueprint for professional development, helping consultants expand their knowledge and expertise.

By embracing industry standards and best practices, security consultant entrepreneurs not only elevate their operations but also contribute to raising the bar for the entire profession.

ISO Standards

The International Organization for Standardization (ISO) is an independent, non-governmental international organization that develops and publishes globally recognized standards. Founded in 1947 and headquartered in Geneva, Switzerland, ISO's mission is to create consistent guidelines that ensure quality, safety, efficiency, and interoperability across various industries. With over 24,000 standards and more than 165 member countries, ISO standards are foundational in shaping the global business landscape.

While adherence to ISO standards is not mandatory, compliance is often seen as a mark of quality and reliability. Many organizations voluntarily adopt these standards to gain a competitive edge, improve operational efficiency, or meet customer and stakeholder expectations. For security consultant entrepreneurs, understanding and aligning with ISO standards can significantly enhance credibility and open doors to new markets, particularly with large corporations and government entities.

ISO/TC 262 - Risk Management

What It Is: ISO/TC 262 is the technical committee responsible for developing risk management standards. Its flagship document, ISO 31000, provides principles and guidelines for effective risk management applicable to any organization, regardless of size or sector.

What Activities Does It Regulate?

Risk Identification and Assessment: Frameworks for identifying potential risks and evaluating their likelihood and impact.

Risk Treatment: Strategies for mitigating, transferring, accepting, or avoiding risks.

Monitoring and Review: Processes for regularly reviewing risk management practices to ensure ongoing effectiveness.

For security consultants, risk management is central to providing value to clients. Adopting ISO/TC 262 standards ensures your methodologies align with global best practices, making your services more attractive to clients prioritizing risk mitigation.

ISO/TC 292 - Security and Resilience

What It Is: ISO/TC 292 focuses on creating standards that enhance the security and resilience of organizations and communities. Its standards address a wide range of topics, including emergency management, business continuity, and protective security.

Key Standards Within ISO/TC 292:

ISO 22301: Business continuity management systems, outlining how organizations can prepare for, respond to, and recover from disruptions.

ISO 22320: Guidelines for incident response, covering everything from communication protocols to resource coordination.

What Activities Does It Regulate?

Crisis Management: Strategies for managing emergencies and ensuring operational continuity.

Resilience Planning: Frameworks for improving an organization's ability to withstand and recover from disruptions.

Protective Security Measures: Standards for safeguarding people, assets, and information.

Security consultants specializing in emergency preparedness, business continuity, or disaster recovery can leverage ISO/TC 292 standards to enhance service delivery and reassure clients of their expertise.

ISO 2700 - Information Security, Cyber Security, and Privacy Protection

What It Is: The ISO 2700 family of standards provides a framework for managing information security. Its flagship standard, ISO/IEC 27001, specifies requirements for establishing, implementing, maintaining, and continually improving an information security management system (ISMS).

What Activities Does It Regulate?

Data Protection: Ensuring the confidentiality, integrity, and availability of information.

Cybersecurity Protocols: Managing risks related to cyber threats and attacks.

Compliance: Aligning with legal and regulatory requirements related to information security and privacy.

In an era of increasing cyber threats, ISO 2700 standards are essential for cybersecurity or data protection consultants. Certification in ISO/IEC 27001 not only demonstrates expertise but also provides a structured approach to managing information security for clients.

ISO 9001:2015 - Quality Management Systems (QMS)

What It Is: ISO 9001:2015 is the world's most recognized quality management standard. It provides a framework for creating a Quality Management System (QMS) that ensures consistent delivery of products and services.

What Activities Does It Regulate?

Process Optimization: Identifying inefficiencies and implementing improvements to enhance productivity.

Customer Satisfaction: Ensuring that products and services meet or exceed client expectations.

Continuous Improvement: Establishing a culture of ongoing evaluation and enhancement.

For security consultant entrepreneurs, ISO 9001:2015 certification can set your business apart by demonstrating a commitment to quality and reliability. Clients often prefer or even require vendors to hold ISO 9001 certification, making it a valuable asset for attracting and retaining business.

Why ISO Standards Matter for Security Consultant Entrepreneurs

Global Credibility: Adopting ISO standards signals professionalism and adherence to best practices, making you a trusted advisor in the security industry.

Improved Service Delivery: ISO standards provide frameworks for enhancing efficiency, quality, and effectiveness, enabling you to deliver superior services.

Market Access: ISO certification is often a prerequisite for working with large corporations, government agencies, or international clients.

Competitive Edge: In a crowded marketplace, ISO compliance sets you apart as a consultant who goes above and beyond to meet industry benchmarks.

For the security consultant entrepreneur, ISO standards are not just guidelines but tools for success. By incorporating these standards into your practice, you can elevate your business, build client trust, and establish yourself as a leader in your niche.

Insurance Issues for the Private Contractor

There's a harsh reality in the world of security consulting: just as many drivers on the highway operate without insurance, so do numerous independent practitioners in the security industry. However, working uninsured carries tremendous risks for the consultant and the client. Without insurance, a security consultant is vulnerable to costly legal liabilities, reputational damage, and financial ruin. Clients, too, are left unprotected, risking inadequate recourse in the event of an issue.

Moreover, being uninsured places a hard cap on the level of work a security consultant can secure. High-value clients and larger organizations demand insurance coverage as a prerequisite for engagement, making it nearly impossible to grow or sustain a business without it. Simply put, operating without insurance in the security consulting industry is a high-risk gamble that no serious entrepreneur can afford.

An Overview of the Insurance Landscape

The insurance needs of security consultants are unique. Unlike other service-based businesses, security consulting often involves high-stakes situations, from armed protection to advising on critical infrastructure. These scenarios introduce various risks that standard business insurance policies may not cover. For this reason, you can't get the insurance you need from State Farm or Geico. You will have to gather quotes from "off-market" vendors.

Key Factors That Make Security Consulting Insurance Different:

Armed vs. Unarmed Services: Armed security work carries significantly higher liability due to the potential for bodily harm or property damage. Policies must account for the presence and use of firearms, often requiring additional premiums or specialized coverage.

Risk Scenarios: Security consultants may face claims related to negligence, breach of contract, or failure to identify or mitigate risks effectively. These situations demand comprehensive coverage tailored to the industry.

High Client Expectations: Clients in sectors like corporate security or executive protection expect consultants to carry sufficient coverage to handle complex claims.

General Business Liability and Errors and Omissions (E&O) Insurance

General Business Liability Insurance: This is the minimum insurance you should have as a security consultant. The industry standard is a $1M policy with the ability to add your client or primary contractor as an additional insured on your policy. This is standard industry practice. This foundational policy covers claims related to bodily injury, property damage, and general risks associated with running a business. For example, general liability insurance would cover medical costs and legal fees if a client is injured during a site walkthrough.

Errors and Omissions (E&O) Insurance: This is particularly critical for security consultants. It protects against claims of professional negligence, oversight, or failure to deliver promised results.

Example: A consultant advises a company on access control systems, but a subsequent breach occurs due to overlooked vulnerabilities. Without E&O coverage, the consultant could be held liable for damages.

Why It's Important: E&O insurance reassures clients that consultants have safeguards to address mistakes or unforeseen outcomes, making it essential for building trust and securing high-value contracts.

Security Driving Insurance

Driving is a significant aspect of many security consulting roles, particularly in executive protection or site assessments. Specialized driving insurance ensures that consultants are covered in high-risk driving scenarios.

Commercial Driving Insurance:

- Covers vehicles used for business purposes, particularly when transporting clients or valuable assets.
- Essential for consultants providing security chauffeur services or conducting site visits.

Flightline/FBO Driving Insurance:

- Tailored for consultants operating near airports or flight operations, such as private terminals (Fixed Base Operators or FBOs).
- Covers unique risks associated with driving on airport property, including potential damages to aircraft or ground equipment.

Why It's Important: Standard auto insurance often excludes commercial use or high-risk environments, exposing consultants without specialized coverage.

Insurance Issues for Overseas Operations

Operating internationally introduces additional risks that require specialized insurance policies. Without proper coverage, consultants may face unmanageable costs in a crisis.

Medical Evacuation Insurance:

What It Covers: Emergency evacuation in cases of injury, illness, or civil unrest. Services like Global Rescue and International SOS (ISOS) coordinate evacuations and provide medical care.

Example Scenario: A consultant falls ill while conducting a risk assessment in a remote area. Medical evacuation insurance ensures swift transportation to a medical facility.

Kidnap and Ransom (K&R) Insurance:

What It Covers: Financial protection in the event of a kidnapping, including ransom payments, negotiation services, and post-incident counseling.

Example Scenario: A consultant advising on infrastructure security in a politically unstable region is kidnapped. K&R insurance provides the resources to navigate and resolve the situation safely.

Why It's Important: International operations often involve heightened risks, making medical evacuation and K&R insurance indispensable for consultants working abroad.

Insurance Issues with Employees vs. 1099 Independent Contractors

The employment structure of a security consulting business has significant implications for insurance coverage.

Employees:

Employers are typically required to provide workers' compensation insurance, covering on-the-job injuries or illnesses.

Liability for employees' actions often falls on the employer, necessitating robust general liability and E&O policies.

Key Takeaway: If you have W2 employees, they will be covered by your company's general liability policy and other insurance. This will increase your premiums, and any claim against any of your employees will influence your premiums or your ability to renew your policy.

1099 Independent Contractors:

Contractors are generally responsible for their own insurance. However, consultants hiring contractors should verify coverage to avoid liability exposure.

Many clients require contractors to carry specific policies, such as general liability or professional liability insurance, as a condition of their contracts.

Key Takeaway. As an Independent Security Consultant hired to work a contract with either a client or as a sub-contractor, you will be required to come to the table with your own insurance. The contract will dictate the minimum level of coverage. Industry standards will dictate that you normally will have to add your client or prime contractor as an additional insured on your insurance. In turn – if you hire any 1099 Independent Contractors to assist you with a given job, it will be your responsibility to set the minimum level of insurance that they come to the table with, have them add *you* as an additional insured on their policy, as well as verify their Certificate of Insurance (COI) and Certificate of Good Standing.

Why It's Important: Understanding employee and contractor coverage differences ensures that consultants remain compliant and protected against potential claims.

Insurance as a Cornerstone of Success

Insurance is not just a safety net – it's a vital component of running a sustainable and credible security consulting business. By securing the right coverage, consultants protect themselves, their clients, and their reputations while gaining access to higher-value contracts and long-term growth. Proper insurance is the key to building a resilient and trustworthy business in an industry where risk is inherent. The critical thing to remember here is that insurance is a complex (and expensive) issue. Find a mentor and get advice. But then, go and do your homework. Make phone calls and have long talks with the insurance brokers. Clearly articulate your anticipated needs and describe the operations you intend to conduct in detail. DO NOT try to side-step or hold something back to save money. Bite the bullet and be honest. Even if nothing ever happens, there is a significant likelihood that your policy will be reviewed for accuracy by a prime contractor or a client's legal counsel. When that happens, you want to have your ducks in a row.

Chapter 5 Wrap-Up: Credibility and Trust – Your Keys to the Security Consulting Kingdom

Congratulations! You've just conquered Chapter 5, and what a chapter it's been. If your brain feels a little like a tangled security camera feed right now, that's okay – this was the deep dive into what makes a security consultant not just good but *great*. So, let's take a moment to untangle those wires and recap everything we've covered.

The Importance of Continuing Education

We started with the undeniable truth: the world doesn't stand still, and neither should you. In this business, resting on yesterday's knowledge is like showing up to a high-tech security job with a VCR.

Continuing education is your weapon against irrelevance, sharpening your skills as threats evolve and technologies advance. Whether it's diving into cybersecurity trends, brushing up on emotional intelligence, or mastering a new skill on LinkedIn Learning, lifelong learning keeps you sharp, adaptable, and ready for anything.

Becoming a Thought Leader in Security Consulting

Next, we tackled how to move from being a good consultant to *the* consultant everyone turns to for advice. From writing blogs and publishing articles to speaking at industry events, building your voice in security consulting is about visibility and credibility. Bonus points if your peers share your work – it's like having a team of cheerleaders vouching for your expertise. The takeaway? The more you share your knowledge, the more you solidify your spot as a trusted authority.

Essential Certifications for Security Consultants

Credentials, baby! Nothing screams "I know my stuff," like a lineup of certifications from respected organizations. We walked through the likes of ASIS, FEMA, ISC², and others, unpacking the who, what, and why of certifications like the CPP, CISSP, and many more. Certifications are not just letters to flaunt after your name – they're doors to credibility, high-profile clients, and industry recognition. Choose the ones that align with your niche and let them speak volumes about your expertise.

Government and Regulatory Requirements

Oh, the patchwork of rules and licenses! We discussed how navigating state and local licensing requirements can feel like threading a needle while riding a roller coaster. But it's worth it! Being licensed in at least one jurisdiction boosts your professionalism and opens opportunities. On the federal side, we touched on regulations like FISMA and ITAR, which keep you in the good graces of Uncle Sam. And remember: research, research, research – your compliance strategy depends on it.

International Regulatory Requirements

Venturing beyond U.S. borders? Buckle up because the rules can get even trickier. Some countries welcome foreign security consultants, while others might toss you out. We discussed resources like the U.S.

Embassy, OSAC, and ASIS networks to help you navigate the international maze. *Pro Tip*: don't risk working without understanding the local laws – it's not worth the potential PNG stamp on your passport (or an extended stay in a foreign prison).

Industry Standards and Best Practices

In an industry where official regulations are patchy at best, the standards set by organizations like ASIS and BEPP are your guiding stars. They fill the gap by offering consistent frameworks for professionalism and quality. Whether it's enterprise risk management or executive protection, aligning with these standards elevates your game and reassures clients that you're playing by the best possible rules.

ISO Standards

We geeked out on ISO, the global guru of standards that touch everything from risk management (ISO 31000) to cybersecurity (ISO 27001) to quality management (ISO 9001:2015). While not mandatory, ISO standards scream credibility and open doors to corporate and government clients. They're your ticket to competing on a global scale and setting your business apart in a crowded marketplace.

Insurance Issues for the Private Contractor

Finally, we tackled the oh-so-sexy topic of insurance. (No, really, it's more exciting than you think.) From general liability to Errors and Omissions (E&O) and even kidnap and ransom insurance, we learned why being insured isn't just smart – it's essential. Without it, you're like a tightrope walker without a safety net. And if you're aiming for serious, sustainable growth in this industry, insurance is non-negotiable.

Wrapping It All Together

Here's the big picture: establishing credibility and trust isn't a one-time task – it's a journey. It's about staying educated, getting certified, sharing your knowledge, playing by the rules, and protecting yourself with the proper safeguards. It might seem like a lot, but each step brings you closer to becoming the kind of security consultant clients trust implicitly.

So, give yourself a pat on the back. You've made it through a dense, data-packed chapter, and now you're armed with the tools to stand tall in a competitive industry. Next up is Chapter 6, where we'll delve into market research and business planning – because knowing your audience and crafting a killer strategy are the next steps in building your empire. Let's keep going; you've got this!

6

Market Research and Business Planning

"If you don't know where you're going, any road will get you there."

— Lewis Carroll

But "any road" doesn't work when you're trying to build a thriving security consulting business. You need a clear destination and a detailed map to get there. And that's precisely what Chapter 6 is all about understanding your market and crafting a business plan that sets you up for long-term success.

Here's a statistic to set the stage: According to a study by CB Insights, 42% of startups fail because there's no market need for their product or service. Let that sink in for a second. Nearly half of businesses fail because they didn't do their homework. But you're smarter than that, and this chapter will guide you through the critical steps to ensure your business has a strong foundation.

Market Research: Understanding the Landscape

Market research is the compass guiding your business decisions, helping you navigate the vast and often overwhelming landscape of the security consulting industry. It's the process of peeling back the layers of your market to understand who your clients are, what they need, who your competitors are, and where your services fit in. If done right, market research becomes the bedrock of your business strategy. If ignored, it's like building a house on rickety stilts – one good gust of wind, and you're sunk.

This section will closely examine the four essential components of market research for a security consulting start-up: identifying your ideal client, analyzing competitors, assessing market demand, and evaluating pricing trends. By the end of this section, you'll have the tools to understand the market and position your business to thrive.

Identify Your Ideal Client

Let's start with a universal truth: your business cannot – and should not – serve everyone. A one-size-fits-all approach may sound appealing, but it dilutes your expertise, muddles your marketing, and frustrates potential clients. Instead, focus on identifying your *ideal client* – the specific group of people or businesses that benefit most from your services and are willing to pay for them.

What Does It Mean to Identify Your Ideal Client?

Identifying your ideal client is the process of defining who you serve best. This isn't just a demographic exercise; it's about understanding their needs, goals, and pain points so you can offer solutions that feel tailor-made.

How to Identify Your Ideal Client

Demographic Profiling: Start with the basics. Are your clients small business owners, corporate executives, or government agencies? What industries are they in? What's their average budget for security services?

Example: If you specialize in physical security assessments, your ideal clients might be small-to-medium-sized businesses in retail or manufacturing. They're likely concerned about theft, compliance, and workplace safety.

Understand Their Pain Points: Ask yourself: What keeps these clients up at night? Is it the fear of a data breach? Concerns about employee safety? Regulatory compliance headaches? The more specific you can get, the better.

Example: A high-net-worth individual may worry about estate security and cyber threats targeting their family, while a school district might prioritize active shooter preparedness and perimeter control.

Define Their Goals: Clients don't just want problems solved – they want peace of mind, efficiency, and tangible results. Identifying their goals helps you align your services with their vision of success.

Conduct Interviews or Surveys: If you're starting from scratch, reach out to people in your target market. Ask open-ended questions about their challenges, needs, and expectations for a security consultant.

Example: "What's the biggest security challenge your organization has faced in the past year?" Their answers can provide invaluable insights.

Pro Tip: Keep refining your ideal client profile. As your business grows and you gain experience, revisit this exercise to ensure it still aligns with your services and goals.

Analyzing Competitors

If identifying your ideal client is about understanding your audience, analyzing competitors is about understanding the other players in the game. This next part is important, so write it down: *Competition isn't your enemy – it's your teacher. It shows you what works, what doesn't, and where the opportunities are.*

What Is Competitor Analysis?

Competitor analysis involves researching and evaluating businesses that offer similar services to yours. It's about discovering who they are, what they do well, and where they fall short so you can carve out your unique space in the market.

How to Conduct a Competitor Analysis

Identify Your Competitors: Look for direct competitors (businesses offering the same services in your niche) and indirect competitors (businesses offering complementary services). Use Google searches, industry directories, and social media to find them.

Example: If your niche is drone surveillance, a direct competitor might be a drone security firm, while an indirect competitor could be a general security consultant who occasionally offers drone services.

Evaluate Their Offerings: Study their service menus. What do they offer? What don't they offer? Are there gaps you can fill?

Example: A competitor might provide physical security assessments but needs to pay more attention to cybersecurity. If you have expertise in both, that's your differentiator.

Analyze Their Branding and Messaging: How do they position themselves? Are they targeting high-end clients or budget-conscious ones? Is their branding professional or casual?

Example: If your competitor's messaging emphasizes speed and convenience, you could differentiate yourself by focusing on thoroughness and long-term results.

Examine Their Client Reviews: Read client testimonials and online reviews. What are clients praising? What are they criticizing?

Example: If multiple reviews mention poor communication, you can highlight your commitment to responsive, transparent communication in your marketing.

Spy on Their Marketing: Follow competitors on social media, subscribe to their newsletters, and monitor their SEO strategies. Pay attention to what gets engagement.

Example: If a competitor's blog post about workplace violence prevention goes viral, consider creating your own content on the topic to capture audience interest.

Pro Tip: Don't copy your competitors – learn from them. Use their strengths as inspiration and their weaknesses as opportunities.

Assessing Market Demand

Market demand is the lifeblood of your business. Without it, even the most innovative services will struggle to gain traction. Assessing market demand ensures that there's a need for your services and that clients are willing to pay for them.

Market demand refers to the level of interest and willingness to pay for your services within a specific market.

How to Assess Market Demand

Research Industry Trends: Use tools like Google Trends, industry publications, and reports from organizations like ASIS International to identify emerging needs and opportunities.

Example: If there's a surge in articles about cybersecurity breaches, that's a strong indicator of growing demand for cybersecurity consulting.

Conduct Surveys and Focus Groups: Reach out to potential clients in your target market. Ask about their security concerns, budgets, and willingness to invest in consulting services.

Example: "If you had to prioritize one area of security improvement, what would it be?" Responses can guide your service offerings.

Analyze Market Size and Growth: Look for data on how much money is being spent on security services in your region or niche.

Example: If reports show a 15% annual growth rate in demand for drone surveillance, that's a niche worth exploring.

Test the Waters: Consider offering a limited-time promotion or pilot program to gauge interest. Monitor how many leads you generate and how many convert to paying clients.

Pro Tip: Market demand isn't static – it evolves with technology, regulations, and client needs. Keep an eye on trends and be ready to pivot.

Evaluating Pricing Trends

Your pricing strategy isn't just about covering costs – it's about communicating value. Price too low, and clients may question your quality. Price too high, and you risk scaring them off.

Evaluating pricing trends helps you find the sweet spot.

Pricing trends refer to your industry and region's standard rates and pricing structures.

How to Evaluate Pricing Trends

Research Competitor Pricing: Gather data on what competitors charge for similar services. Pay attention to how they structure their pricing – hourly rates, flat fees, or retainers.

Example: If competitors charge $100–$150 per hour for physical security assessments, consider where your expertise fits within that range.

Consider Your Costs and Value: Calculate your costs, including time, tools, and certifications, and ensure your pricing reflects the value you provide.

Example: If you offer advanced certifications or cutting-edge technology, clients may be willing to pay a premium.

Test Different Models: Experiment with pricing packages like tiered service levels or retainer agreements. Monitor which models generate the most interest.

Example: Offer a basic cybersecurity audit for $500 and a premium audit with ongoing support for $1,500.

Adjust for Market Conditions: Consider factors like location, industry norms, and client budgets when setting prices.

Example: Urban clients may expect higher prices than rural ones due to higher operating costs.

Pro Tip: Always tie your pricing to value. Clients are more likely to invest when they see clear, tangible benefits.

Pro Tip 2: Understand your value. Although this seems like an "uh, duh" statement, it is one of the greatest things you will struggle with. You need to wind the bid or secure the contract, but you can't cut your pricing so low that you are limited to the quality that your brand stands for. There will constantly be this "push-pull" of needing to stay competitively priced ("gotta win that bid!"), with understanding your worth. Conversely, don't overestimate your worth and price yourself out of the market. Pricing is one of the hardest things to get right, and I constantly struggle with it.

What's the "So What?" of all of this?

Market research is your secret weapon for building a business that's not only viable but also thriving. By identifying your ideal client, analyzing competitors, assessing demand, and evaluating pricing trends, you lay the groundwork for strategic, data-driven decisions that set you apart. Take the time to dig deep now, and your future self (and clients) will thank you. Next, we'll tackle how to turn all this research into a killer business plan.

Writing an Effective Business Plan for a Security Consulting Business

When launching a security consulting business, your business plan is more than a formality – it's your North Star. It guides your actions, clarifies your purpose, and convinces clients and investors that you're not just winging it. Think of it as your business's résumé, combined with a pathway, peppered with a splash of ambition.

Many entrepreneurs skip this critical step because it requires a lot of research, study, thinking, and writing. If you're thinking about not writing a business plan, remember the statistics we started this chapter with and reconsider. If you ever think you may want to get a business loan or secure investor funding, you'll need a good business plan anyway.

A solid business plan answers three big questions: Where are you now? Where do you want to go? And how are you going to get there? In this section, we'll break down the key components of your business plan and how to write each one with clarity and purpose.

Section 1: Mission, Vision, and Strategic Goals

The mission and vision sections define your purpose and long-term aspirations, while strategic goals break down the steps you'll take to achieve them. Think of this as the soul of your business plan – it's where you communicate your "why."

Mission Statement: Your mission statement is your business's purpose boiled down to one or two sentences. It should explain:

- What you do.
- Who you serve.
- Why your work matters.

Example Mission Statement: *"We provide tailored security consulting services to small businesses, helping them protect their assets, comply with regulations, and operate confidently in a rapidly changing world."*

How to Craft It:

Start with Why: Think about why you're passionate about security consulting.

Focus on Impact: What positive change do you want to bring to your clients?

Be Specific: Avoid generic statements like "We provide the best services." Instead, highlight what sets you apart.

Vision Statement: Your vision statement paints a picture of your business's future. It's aspirational and forward-looking, showing where you want to be in 5, 10, or even 20 years.

Example Vision Statement: *"To be the trusted partner for security solutions, empowering businesses to thrive globally in a safe and secure environment."*

How to Craft It:

Imagine the Future: What will success look like for your business?

Think Big: Don't be afraid to dream boldly – but keep it grounded in reality.

Focus on Legacy: Consider the long-term impact you want your business to have.

Strategic Goals: Strategic goals bridge the gap between your mission and vision. They should be **SMART**: **S**pecific, **M**easurable, **A**chievable, **R**elevant, and **T**ime-bound.

Example Strategic Goals:

- Secure 20 new clients within the first year of operations.
- Achieve a 95% client retention rate by the end of year two.
- Launch a blog with 50 high-value articles within 18 months to establish thought leadership.

How to Craft It:

Break Down Your Vision: What smaller milestones must you achieve to reach your vision?

Focus on Outcomes: Align goals with measurable results, not just activities.

Set Deadlines: Tie each goal to a specific timeframe to maintain momentum.

Pro Tip: Write this section with passion – it's your chance to show why you care about what you're building. Avoid jargon and make it meaningful. As discussed in a previous chapter, you want these goals to be "strain-able, yet attainable." If you make goals too unrealistic (e.g., "Earn $4.3M in Q1 of start-up year"), you'll turn off investor interest. So do not ignore the "A" in the SMART acronym.

Section 2: Target Market Identification

Your target market defines the specific group of people or businesses for which your services are designed. This section demonstrates that you've done your homework on your ideal clients. You've already done this in the above section. So just review your previous work (it's not cheating, I promise!).

How to Identify Your Target Market

Define Your Niche: Security consulting is a broad field. Will you specialize in physical security assessments, cybersecurity, or executive protection? Tailoring your niche narrows your focus and increases your chances of success.

Example: "Our target market is small-to-medium-sized e-commerce businesses seeking cybersecurity consulting to prevent data breaches."

Segment Your Audience: Group potential clients based on common characteristics, such as:

- Industry: Retail, manufacturing, finance, etc.
- Size: Small businesses, large corporations, government agencies.
- Location: Local, national, or international.

Understand Their Needs: Use surveys, interviews, or market data to uncover your target clients' challenges.

Example: "Many small e-commerce businesses lack the resources for an in-house cybersecurity team, making them vulnerable to phishing attacks and payment fraud."

Validate Your Market: Research how many businesses fit your criteria and whether they can afford your services. Tools like industry reports and census data can help.

Pro Tip: Be as specific as possible. A well-defined target market helps you focus your resources and craft a compelling value proposition.

Section 3: Competitor Analysis in the Security Sector

Again, you've already done the hard work on this in the previous section of this chapter. Competitor analysis identifies your competitors' strengths and weaknesses, helping you position yourself in the market.

How to Conduct a Competitor Analysis

Create a Competitor List: Include both direct competitors (those offering the same services) and indirect competitors (those offering complementary services).

Example:

- Direct Competitor: A local firm specializing in physical security assessments.
- Indirect Competitor: A more prominent national firm offering general security services.

Evaluate Their Services: Compare their offerings to yours. Look for gaps or areas where you can differentiate.

Example: *"Competitors lack expertise in drone surveillance for perimeter security. We will emphasize this service in our marketing."*

Assess Their Branding: Study their branding and messaging. Are they targeting high-end clients or budget-conscious ones?

Example: *"Competitor A positions itself as affordable but lacks the certifications and credentials we offer."*

Analyze Pricing: Research their pricing models to ensure your rates are competitive but reflective of your value.

Pro Tip: Don't just identify competitors – use this analysis to sharpen your focus and refine your offerings.

Section 4: Pricing and Value Proposition

This section answers the question, "What's in it for me?" from the client's perspective. Your value proposition explains why clients should choose you, and your pricing strategy justifies the cost of your services. Keep everything you analyzed in this chapter's previous section in mind. It will help make this part of your business plan easier to complete.

How to Define Your Value Proposition

Highlight Client Benefits: Focus on outcomes, not just services.

Example: "Our cybersecurity audits reduce breach risks by 40% within the first year."

Showcase Unique Features: Emphasize what sets you apart, such as certifications, experience, or technology.

Example: "We use AI-driven tools for real-time threat detection, a capability not offered by local competitors."

How to Set Pricing

Research Competitor Rates: Look at similar consultants' charges and factor in your expertise.

Example: "Local consultants charge $100–$150/hour for risk assessments. Our pricing will be $140/hour, reflecting our advanced certifications."

Consider Costs: Calculate expenses like software, travel, and marketing. Your prices must cover costs and leave room for profit.

Offer Tiers: Create packages to appeal to different budgets.

Example: "Basic: $1,000 for a physical security audit. Premium: $2,500 for an audit plus a six-month implementation plan."

Pro Tip: Use competitor pricing as a benchmark but focus on communicating value rather than competing solely on price.

Section 5: Sales and Marketing Strategies

This section details how you'll attract and retain clients. It's your playbook for turning leads into loyal customers.

How to Write It:

Lead Generation: Outline how you'll find potential clients.

Example: "We'll generate leads through LinkedIn campaigns, industry conferences, and partnerships with local business associations."

Sales Funnel: Describe how you'll move leads through the sales process – from awareness to conversion (converting a lead into a customer).

Example: "We'll engage leads with educational content, schedule discovery calls, and offer tailored proposals to close deals."

Retention Strategies: Explain how you'll keep clients coming back. How are you keeping clients engaged with regular check-ins, value-added content, loyalty discounts, and referral incentives?

Example: "We'll provide ongoing support, quarterly reviews, and discounted rates for multi-year contracts."

Pro Tip: Your sales strategy should focus on building trust and demonstrating expertise – key factors in the security industry.

Section 6: Operational Plan and Security Protocols

The operational plan details how your business will run day-to-day, while the security protocols ensure you deliver services safely and effectively.

How to Write It:

Daily Operations: Describe your workflow, including staffing, scheduling, internal and external communication, and client care/feeding.

Example: "We'll operate remotely with a small team of consultants, using project management software to streamline collaboration and CRM software to catalog issues important to our clients."

Standard Operating Procedures (SOPs): Document processes for consistency and efficiency. This is also where you would outline your Quality Management Process (QMP).

Example: "Our SOPs will cover everything from client onboarding to final project delivery, ensuring seamless execution." Or "All physical security audits follow a 10-step checklist to ensure thoroughness."

Risk Mitigation: Include protocols for handling emergencies or disruptions.

Example: "We'll establish contingency plans for client data breaches and onsite incidents, minimizing downtime and liability."

Pro Tip: A strong operational plan reassures clients that you're not just an expert – you're also organized and reliable.

Coming Full Circle

Writing a business plan might feel daunting, but it's also one of the most rewarding. This document isn't just for investors or clients – it's for you. It's your blueprint for success, your accountability partner, and your guide when things get messy (because they inevitably will).

By defining your mission, identifying your market, analyzing competitors, clarifying your value proposition, and nailing down your operations, you're setting the foundation for a business that's not only viable but poised to thrive.

Chapter 6 Wrap-Up: Putting It All Together

If Chapter 6 were a meal, it'd be a hearty stew – rich, detailed, and packed with ingredients to satisfy the hungriest entrepreneur. Market research and business planning may not sound glamorous, but they're the foundation of any successful business. Without them, you're essentially shooting in the dark, hoping to hit your target. With them? You're a strategic powerhouse armed with insights and direction that make success not just a possibility but a probability.

Let's take a moment to recap the two main courses of this chapter: *Market Research: Understanding the Landscape* and *Writing an Effective Business Plan for a Security Consulting Business*. Each subsection is built on the last, giving you the tools to understand your market, define your business, and create a growth plan. Here's a detailed review to remind you how far you've come – and why you're more than ready to take on the security consulting world.

Market Research: Understanding the Landscape

First, we tackled market research. This is where you flex your inner detective, gathering the clues that will shape your business decisions. It's not just about figuring out who your clients are – it's about understanding their problems, your competition, and the environment you'll be operating in. Let's break it down one more time:

Identify Your Ideal Client

Your business isn't for everyone – and that's a *good* thing. Narrowing your focus to a specific client type makes your marketing more effective and positions you as the go-to expert in your niche. We walked through how to define your ideal client, from demographics to pain points to goals. Remember, knowing who you serve best allows you to craft services that feel custom-made.

A business that tries to serve everyone ends up serving no one. By identifying your ideal client, you're promising to solve specific problems for a specific audience – and clients love that level of clarity.

Analyzing Competitors

The competition isn't your enemy; it's your blueprint. By studying what others are doing, you can identify gaps in the market, learn from their successes, and avoid their mistakes. Whether it's evaluating services, pricing, or branding, competitor analysis is a powerful tool to refine your approach.

Key Takeaway: Differentiation is the name of the game. Use competitor analysis to find your unique angle, whether that's offering a service they don't or marketing in a way they can't.

Assessing Market Demand

Market demand answers the critical question: "Is there a need for my services?" By researching trends, talking to potential clients, and analyzing data, you ensure that you're meeting real needs – not just solving problems you *think* exist.

No demand means no clients, which means no business. But with demand on your side, you can tailor your services to what's most needed – and most valued.

Evaluating Pricing Trends

Ah, pricing – the art of balancing your worth with market expectations. We discussed researching competitor rates, aligning pricing with your value, and experimenting with different models to find what works best.

Key Takeaway: Price isn't just a number; it's a signal. It communicates your value, your expertise, and your place in the market. Nail your pricing strategy, and you're already ahead of the game.

Final Thought on Market Research: Market research involves asking the right questions and listening to the answers. It's not a one-and-done task; it's an ongoing process that evolves as your business grows. The more you understand your market, the better equipped you are to succeed.

Writing an Effective Business Plan for a Security Consulting Business

With your market research in hand, we moved on to writing your business plan – the ultimate recipe for your business. This isn't just a document for investors or banks (though it helps there, too). It's a tool to organize your thoughts, set goals, and stay accountable. (It also enables you to secure funding!)

Mission, Vision, and Strategic Goals

We started with the soul of your business: your mission, vision, and strategic goals. Your mission is your purpose; your vision is your dream; and your strategic goals are the stepping stones to get there.

These elements ground your business in meaning and direction. They're the "why" behind everything you do and keep you focused when challenges arise.

Pro Tip: Write these sections passionately while using the acronym SMART. Clients and investors aren't just buying your services – they're buying into your story.

Target Market Identification

Building on your market research, this section focused on the specific clients you want to serve. From demographics to buyer personas, we showed you how to paint a detailed picture of your target audience.

Key Takeaway: Understanding your target market isn't just helpful – it's essential. The more precise you are about who you're serving, the more effective your marketing and services will be.

Competitor Analysis in the Security Sector

Here, we expanded on competitor analysis, digging deeper into strengths, weaknesses, and opportunities. By understanding what your competitors do well (and not so well), you can position yourself to stand out.

Your competitors are your yardstick. Knowing where you stack up gives you the confidence to highlight your unique strengths.

Pricing and Value Proposition

Pricing is more than a numbers game – it's about communicating value. We explored how to craft a compelling value proposition and set prices that reflect your expertise while remaining competitive.

Pro Tip: Don't just price for today; price for growth. Consider how your pricing strategy will support your business's long-term goals.

Sales and Marketing Strategies

Sales and marketing are the engines that drive your business forward. From lead generation to client retention, we outlined strategies to attract, convert, and keep clients.

Key Takeaway: Consistency is key. A steady stream of well-targeted marketing efforts will build your reputation and keep your pipeline full.

Operational Plan and Security Protocols

Finally, we tackled the nuts and bolts of running your business. From daily operations to emergency protocols, this section ensures you're organized, efficient, and prepared for anything.

A well-oiled machine isn't just good for business – it's good for your sanity. Detailed plans keep you focused and clients happy.

Final Thoughts on Chapter 6

If you've made it through this chapter, good job – you've just built the foundation for your business. Market research and business planning may not be the most exciting parts of entrepreneurship, but they're unquestionably the most important. These tools ensure that you're not just starting a business but starting it *right*.

Take a moment to reflect on what you've learned. You now know how to:

- Identify and understand your ideal client.
- Analyze competitors to find your unique edge.
- Gauge market demand to ensure your services are needed.
- Craft a business plan that organizes your ideas and sets you up for success.

Feeling overwhelmed? Don't be. Rome wasn't built in a day, and neither is a business. Take it step by step, and remember that every entrepreneur starts somewhere. You've got this!

Up Next: Financing your business. Because even the best plan needs funding to come to life.

7

Financing Your Security Consulting Business

"Success usually comes to those who are too busy to be looking for it."

— Henry David Thoreau

Nowhere is this more relevant than when tackling one of the biggest questions for any entrepreneur: How will I fund my business?

Launching a security consulting business presents unique financial challenges and opportunities. Whether setting up your home office, investing in certifications, or purchasing specialized equipment, understanding your start-up costs and funding options is critical. Equally important is mastering the art of managing cash flow, as even the most profitable businesses can only work if the money flows in and out efficiently.

In this chapter, we'll cover everything you need to know to get started understanding how to finance your security consulting business. Of course, it gets WAY more complicated from here. It is highly recommended that you get a good (no, scratch that) GREAT tax accountant (not just a bookkeeper) and take a few business finance classes (many are free on LinkedIn and YouTube). From calculating start-up costs to exploring funding options and creating a rock-solid budget, this chapter will ensure you're financially equipped to turn your vision into reality.

Calculating Start-Up Costs for Security Consulting

Starting a business is like building a house: you need a solid foundation before you can think about decorating. In security consulting, that foundation begins with understanding your start-up costs. For new entrepreneurs, this might feel as overwhelming as deciphering the Matrix, but don't worry – we're going to break it down step by step, brick by brick.

This section is your ultimate guide to calculating start-up costs for a security consulting business. We'll cover everything from initial investments and ongoing operational expenses to creating a financial safety net. We'll also include examples, charts, and tips to ensure you're not just guessing but making informed decisions.

Why Calculating Start-Up Costs is Important

Let's start with the obvious: you can't fund what you haven't figured out. With a clear understanding of your start-up costs, you can avoid running out of money before your business has a chance to take off. Calculating these costs helps you:

Create a Realistic Budget: Avoid unexpected expenses.

Secure Funding: Whether it's a loan, grant, or personal savings, you need a number to aim for.

Build Confidence: Knowing your numbers gives you the clarity and focus to move forward.

In short, understanding your start-up costs is the first step toward making your business a reality.

Breaking Down Start-Up Costs

Start-up costs fall into two main categories: one-time expenses and ongoing operational costs. Let's explore each category in detail.

One-Time Expenses: You'll incur upfront costs before your business officially opens its doors. One-Time expenses will include:

Business Registration and Licensing: Every business needs to be legally recognized. Depending on your location, you might need to pay for:

- Registering your business name.
- Applying for a business license.
- Obtaining security-specific licenses or certifications.
- Insurance: Security consulting isn't a low-risk industry. General liability insurance, Errors & Omissions (E&O) insurance, and specialized coverage (e.g., armed services) are essential.
- Certifications: Industry certifications establish your credibility. Whether it's CPP, PSP, or CISSP, you'll need to budget for application fees, study materials, and exam costs.
- Office Setup: A functional office is essential, even if you're starting small. Think laptops, desks, office supplies, and software subscriptions.
- Marketing Materials: From business cards to your website, initial marketing efforts require investment.

Ongoing Operational Costs: these are the expenses you'll continue to pay after your business is up and running.

- Rent and Utilities: Your costs will be minimal if you work from a home office. If you rent commercial space, factor in monthly rent, electricity, and internet.

- Software Subscriptions: Tools for project management, cybersecurity assessments, or video conferencing are essential for running your business.
- Marketing and Advertising: Keeping your brand visible requires a steady investment in advertising, social media, and content creation.
- Travel and Transportation: If your work involves site visits, factor in gas, airfare, and lodging.

Creating a Start-Up Cost Spreadsheet: A spreadsheet is your best friend when calculating start-up costs. Here's an example template to get you started. You can grow it exponentially from here.

#	Expense Category	Estimated Cost	Notes
1	Business Registration	$200	Includes LLC Registration
2	Licensing	$400	State Security License
3	Insurance	$1,200	Per year. General liability + E&O
4	Certifications	$1,500	CPP application + exam
5	Office Setup	$2,500	Laptop, furniture, software
6	Marketing Materials	$2,000	Website, ads, biz cards
	Total One-Time Costs	**$8,800**	One time
7	Rent/Utilities	$1,000	Per mo. Commercial office space
8	Software Subscriptions	$150	Per mo. Tools for Security Assess.
9	Marketing/Advertising	$500	Per mo. Social Media Ads.
10	Travel	$300	Per mo. Gas & Site Visits
	Total Ongoing Costs	**$1,950**	Per Month

Common Pitfalls to Avoid

Underestimating Costs: Many entrepreneurs forget to include hidden expenses like taxes or equipment maintenance. Always add a 10–20% buffer for surprises.

Overinvesting in Non-Essentials: Do you really need that $2,000 ergonomic chair right now? Start lean and upgrade as you grow.

Ignoring Ongoing Costs: Start-up costs are just the beginning. Ensure you can sustain your business beyond the initial investment.

The Safety Net: Building a Financial Cushion

Experts recommend saving 6–12 months' worth of expenses before launching a business. This cushion gives you breathing room to build your client base without financial stress.

Calculating start-up costs may not be glamorous, but it's an essential step in launching your security consulting business. By listing one-time and ongoing expenses, creating a detailed budget, and building a financial cushion, you're setting yourself up for success.

Funding Options Specific to Security Businesses

Funding a security consulting business isn't just about finding the money; it's about finding the *right* money. Each funding option has pros and cons, and your chosen path will depend on your unique circumstances. In this section, we'll explore five primary methods of funding a security business, giving you the tools and confidence to secure the resources you need to succeed. We'll then address *Other Money Matters* – the often-overlooked details that can make or break your financial strategy.

Self-Financing and Bootstrapping

Self-financing means using your own resources – savings, personal loans, or credit – to fund your business. Bootstrapping takes this a step further, emphasizing minimal expenses, being _uber_-frugal, and reinvesting every dollar of revenue to grow the business organically.

Why Choose This Option:

- You maintain complete control over your business.
- No debt or external obligations.

- It demonstrates commitment, which can attract future investors.

How to Self-Finance Your Business

Assess Your Savings: Review your finances to determine how much you can realistically invest. Be sure to leave enough for emergencies – your business shouldn't bankrupt your life.

Reduce Start-Up Costs: Bootstrapping means being frugal.

- Work from home instead of renting an office.
- Use free or low-cost marketing tools like Canva or social media.
- Delay non-essential purchases like premium office furniture.

Set Financial Boundaries: Decide in advance how much of your savings you're willing to invest. This will help you avoid overextending yourself.

Example: Susan, a cybersecurity consultant, started her business with $10,000 from her savings. She used $5,000 for certifications and $2,000 for marketing, keeping the rest as a safety net. By landing two clients in her first month, she reinvested her earnings into her website and software upgrades.

Pro-Tip: If you choose this option, you can list this as an initial "investment" in your business Operating Agreement. Once your business is wildly successful, your initial investment can be transferred to initial ownership shares or paid back as a shareholder dividend. Talk to your tax accountant to ensure you do it correctly.

Small Business Loans and Security Industry Grants

Loans provide capital that must be repaid with interest, while grants are essentially "free money" awarded based on specific criteria. Understand that – especially when just starting – small business loans usually require some collateral, like your home, etc. I'm not saying to bet on yourself; I'm just saying to go into it with your eyes open.

Why Choose This Option:

- Loans allow you to access larger sums upfront.
- Grants provide funding without the burden of repayment.

How to Secure Small Business Loans

Prepare Your Business Plan: Banks and lenders want to see a solid business plan that includes Market Analysis, Financial Projections, and Clear Repayment Strategies.

Check Your Credit Score: Lenders use your personal credit score to evaluate risk. A score of 650 or higher is generally preferred.

Explore Loan Options:

- Small Business Administration (SBA) Loans: These are government-backed and have lower interest rates.
- Microloans: Ideal for small businesses needing $50,000 or less.

Gather Documentation:

- Tax returns (personal and business, if applicable).
- Proof of income.
- Legal business registration documents.

How to Apply for Security Industry Grants

Research Opportunities: Look for grants tailored to security businesses, such as those offered by industry associations or government programs. Examples include DHS grants for public safety initiatives.

Understand the Requirements: Grants often have specific criteria, such as supporting a community initiative or using cutting-edge technology.

Write a Strong Proposal: Clearly outline how the funds will be used and their impact.

Example: John secured a $25,000 SBA loan to launch his physical security consulting business. The funds covered start-up costs, including certifications and marketing. His detailed business plan and substantial credit score made the process smooth.

Partnerships with Technology Providers

Tech partnerships involve collaborating with software or hardware companies that provide tools and resources in exchange for promoting their products.

Why Choose This Option:

- Reduces initial investment in technology.
- Builds relationships with industry leaders.

How to Secure Tech Partnerships

Identify Relevant Providers: Look for companies offering products aligned with your niche (e.g., cybersecurity software or surveillance equipment).

Craft a Value Proposition: Explain how promoting their product benefits them, such as access to your client base or increased visibility.

Negotiate Terms:

- Request discounted or free products.
- Offer testimonials, case studies, or product feedback in return.

Example: Maria partnered with a drone technology company for her perimeter security business. In exchange for discounted drones, she provided real-world data and referred clients to the company.

Government Contracts and Funding Opportunities

Governments at all levels often require security consulting services, providing lucrative and stable opportunities for qualified entrepreneurs.

Why Choose This Option:

- High earning potential.
- Long-term contracts build credibility.

How to Secure Government Contracts

Register with SAM: Sign up with the System for Award Management (SAM) to qualify for federal contracts.

Earn Necessary Certifications: Some contracts require specific certifications, such as CPP or PSP.

Monitor Procurement Websites: Regularly check platforms like FedBiz-Opps or your state's procurement site for opportunities.

Bid Strategically: Submit proposals that highlight your expertise and competitive pricing.

Example: James won a $50,000 contract to perform security risk assessments for local government buildings. His success came from a well-researched bid and proven track record.

Seeking Venture Capital and Private Investors

Venture capitalists and private investors provide funding in exchange for equity in your business. Think of this in terms of the famous TV shows where entrepreneurs pitch their businesses to see if they can get aggressive ocean animals to invest in them!

Why Choose This Option:

- Access to large sums of money.
- Investors often bring valuable connections and advice.

How to Attract Investors

Develop a Scalable Business Model: Investors want to see growth potential beyond local or small-scale operations.

Perfect Your Pitch: Craft a compelling pitch deck that includes:

- The problem your business solves.
- Market size and opportunity.
- Financial projections.

Network Relentlessly: Attend industry events, join networking groups, and connect with investors who specialize in security businesses.

Example: Linda secured $200,000 in funding from a venture capital firm to expand her cybersecurity consulting business internationally. Her detailed pitch deck and ambitious vision sealed the deal.

Other Money Matters

Personal Assets as Collateral: Using personal assets (like your home) can secure loans but comes with significant risk. If the business fails, you could lose your collateral.

Personal Credit Rating: A strong credit score is critical for securing loans or lines of credit. Check your score and improve it if necessary.

Separate Business Finances: Open a dedicated business bank account and credit card. Mixing personal and business finances can lead to tax issues and legal complications.

Cash Flow Management: Monitor inflows and outflows closely. Use tools like QuickBooks to track expenses and avoid cash shortages.

Emergency Fund: Keep 3–6 months' worth of expenses in reserve to weather unexpected challenges.

Tax Planning: Work with a CPA to ensure compliance and take advantage of deductions.

Legal Protections: Consider forming an LLC or corporation to protect personal assets from business liabilities. I would say this is mandatory. It is definitely expected in the security industry.

Invoice Terms: If you have the choice, set clear payment terms (e.g., Net 30) and promptly follow up on overdue invoices. We'll get more into this in Chapter 12.

Budget for Growth: Allocate funds for training, certifications, and marketing to stay competitive.

Understand Debt: Not all debt is bad. Strategic borrowing can fuel growth, but repayment terms must always be evaluated carefully.

Tip of the Iceberg: These are just the basics to keep you out of bankruptcy court for the first 12 months. Partner with a GREAT CPA (one of the few expenses you shouldn't skimp on!), get educated on the nuances of small business financing, and be stingy with your funds!

Financing your security consulting business isn't a one-size-fits-all process. You can tailor a strategy that fits your needs and goals by exploring a range of options – from bootstrapping to venture capital. Remember, financial decisions are as critical as operational ones, and a well-funded business is a step closer to becoming a thriving enterprise.

Managing Cash Flow and Budgeting for Consulting Services

"Revenue is vanity, profit is sanity, but cash flow is king." – Alan Miltz

— Alan Miltz

As a budding entrepreneur, you might assume that financial success is a given if your security consulting business is booking clients left and right. Unfortunately, the reality is far more complex. Even a wildly successful business can collapse if cash flow isn't managed effectively. Cash flow isn't just about how much money you're making; it's about *when* that money comes in and how it flows out. Mismanage this, and you could find yourself in a paradox where you're busy but broke.

This section will guide you to understanding, managing, and optimizing cash flow for your security consulting business. We'll break down concepts, from what cash flow means to actionable strategies for keeping your financial ship steady. By the end, you'll not only understand cash flow but be equipped to master it.

What Is Cash Flow?

Cash flow is the movement of money in and out of your business. Think of it as the lifeblood of your operation. When cash is flowing in (through client payments), you have the oxygen to keep your business alive. When it flows out (for expenses like rent, salaries, supplies/inventory, etc.), your ability to sustain depends on ensuring you have enough coming in to cover those costs.

Cash Flow = Cash Inflows − Cash Outflows

If your inflows exceed your outflows, you have positive cash flow. If not, you're in the dreaded negative cash flow territory. And while negative cash flow doesn't always spell disaster (sometimes it's planned during growth phases), it can quickly lead to problems if not managed carefully.

Why Cash Flow

Here's a startling fact: according to a U.S. Bank study, 82% of small business failures are due to cash flow problems.

Let that sink in. It's not a lack of customers, poor marketing, or even bad products. It's cash flow. This statistic alone highlights why understanding and managing your cash flow is non-negotiable. Here's why it's so critical:

Operational Stability: Cash flow ensures you can pay your bills, employees, and vendors on time.

Flexibility: Positive cash flow allows you to seize opportunities, such as new contracts or marketing campaigns, without hesitation.

Stress Reduction: Let's face it – nothing keeps a business owner up at night like worrying about finances. Healthy cash flow means you can sleep easy.

Understanding the Cash Flow Cycle

To manage cash flow effectively, you need to understand the cash flow cycle – how money moves through your business from start to finish.

Step 1: Generating Revenue – This is where it all begins. Revenue is generated when you provide consulting services to clients. However, revenue doesn't mean cash.

Example: You secure a $10,000 contract with a corporate client, but payment terms are Net 60. That means the revenue exists on paper, but the cash won't hit your account for 60 days from the date of invoice (you usually invoice when the job is complete).

Step 2: Incurring Costs – While waiting for revenue to arrive, you're still spending money on rent, software, travel, and more. Not to mention, the contract you won has expenses associated with it, like travel, per diem, hotel, parking, etc.

Step 3: Receiving Payments – Once the client pays, the cash finally flows in. The timing of this step is critical, as delays can create a bottleneck.

Step 4: Reinvesting or Saving – With cash in hand, you can reinvest in your business or build reserves for future needs.

The Danger of Late Payments

One of the biggest cash flow killers is late payments. In fact, 60% of small businesses report cash flow problems due to unpaid invoices. Imagine waiting 90 days for a payment while your bills are piling up – it's a nightmare scenario.

How to Combat Late Payments:

Set Clear Payment Terms: Specify payment terms upfront (e.g., Net 15 or Net 30 is ideal). If you are lucky enough to land a contract with a major company that is used to dealing with subcontractors, they will usually dictate payment terms. This is something you should *always* try to negotiate, but sometimes, it just is what it is. I've had to get a short-term loan from my bank just so I could afford to complete a contract that I had been awarded due to the payment terms being so disadvantageous to me.

Require Upfront Deposits: For larger projects, request 30–50% upfront to cover initial costs. This is SOP for our business, *especially* when working with a new client.

Incentivize Early Payments: Offer a small discount (e.g., 2%) for payments made within 10 days.

Follow Up Religiously: Use invoicing software to send due date reminders 30 days out from the due date, 15 days, 7 days, 24 hours, and especially for overdue payments.

Cash Flow Forecasting

A cash flow forecast is a projection of your inflows and outflows over a specific period. Think of it as your financial GPS, helping you anticipate challenges and plan accordingly.

List All Inflows: Include expected client payments, grants, or loans.

List All Outflows: Account for every expense, from rent to software subscriptions.

Calculate Net Cash Flow: Subtract outflows from inflows to see if you'll have a surplus or deficit.

Example Cash Flow Forecast:

Month	In-Flows	Out-Flows	Net Cash Flow
January	$10,000	$8,000	$2,000
February	$5,000	$7,000	-$2,000
March	$15,000	$6,000	$9,000

Budgeting for Consulting Services

Budgeting goes hand in hand with cash flow management. While cash flow focuses on timing, budgeting ensures you're allocating resources wisely.

How to Create a Budget:

Categorize Expenses: Divide costs into fixed (rent, insurance) and variable (marketing, travel).

Set Spending Limits: Allocate a percentage of revenue to each category.

Monitor Regularly: Review your budget monthly to identify areas of overspending or areas where saving strategies could be applied (get creative!).

Practical Strategies for Managing Cash Flow

Shorten Payment Cycles: Avoid long payment terms (e.g., Net 60). Shorter cycles mean faster cash flow.

Build a Cash Reserve: Aim for 3–6 months' worth of expenses in reserve for emergencies.

Use Invoicing Tools: Automate invoicing with tools like QuickBooks or FreshBooks to streamline payments.

Negotiate Vendor Terms: Request extended payment terms from vendors to align with your inflows.

Diversify Revenue Streams: Relying on one client or service can create instability. Explore additional offerings or markets. This is especially important if one of your primary customers has unfavorable (to you) payment terms.

Common Cash Flow Mistakes

Confusing Revenue with Cash: Just because you've booked a project doesn't mean you have the cash.

Ignoring Small Expenses: The little things add up – don't overlook subscriptions or fees.

Overestimating Sales: Be conservative in your projections to avoid overextending yourself.

Mastering Cash Flow

Managing cash flow isn't rocket science but requires vigilance and discipline. Understanding your cash flow cycle, creating accurate forecasts, and implementing innovative strategies can ensure your business stays financially healthy. Remember, a profitable business isn't necessarily cash-rich – so keep your eyes on the flow!

Chapter 7 Wrap-Up: Taking the Fear Out of Financing Your Dream

---

"Do not save what is left after spending, but spend what is left after saving." – Warren Buffett

— Warren Buffett

If there's one thing Chapter 7 has proven, it's this: mastering the financial side of your security consulting business isn't just possible – it's *empowering*. You've tackled the big question: How much money do I need to start? Where do I find it? How do I make it last? Let's break it down and celebrate how far you've come on this entrepreneurial journey.

Calculating Start-Up Costs for Security Consulting

We began with the brass tacks: figuring out how much money you need to get your business off the ground. You learned about one-time expenses like certifications, insurance, website development, and ongoing costs like marketing, software subscriptions, and rent. The goal? To take the guesswork out of start-up costs so you don't wake up one day wondering where all your money went.

Remember the magic formula: list everything, add it up, then add a buffer. With your detailed breakdown, you're no longer flying blind – you've got a clear picture of what it'll take to build your business from day one. And let's not forget the spreadsheet example we gave you; it's your new best friend.

Funding Options Specific to Security Businesses

Next, we tackled the big question: How do I pay for this?

We explored five main funding options, each tailored to fit different circumstances. From self-financing (a.k.a. the ultimate test of your savings account's resilience) to small business loans and grants, partnerships with tech providers, government contracts, and even venture capital, you now have a comprehensive menu of choices.

Here are the highlights:

Self-financing and bootstrapping: For those who want total control, with the added adrenaline rush of putting your own money on the line.

Small business loans and grants: Because sometimes you need a little help from Uncle Sam or your local bank.

Tech partnerships and government contracts: Why fund everything yourself when you can collaborate with industry giants or secure stable government work?

Venture capital: Ideal for those with big ideas and growth ambitions (and a killer pitch deck).

Remember, the key is to choose the funding option that fits your business model and comfort level. Preparation is everything, whether you're pitching to a bank, writing grant proposals, or forging tech alliances. By now, you know the documentation, pitch strategies, and legwork required to succeed in any of these paths.

Managing Cash Flow and Budgeting for Consulting Services

And finally, we dove into the lifeblood of your business: cash flow. If there's one lesson you should tattoo on your entrepreneurial brain, it's this: You can be profitable on paper and broke in real life if you don't manage your cash flow.

We covered the cash flow cycle, from generating revenue to handling expenses and reinvesting in your business. You now know how to:

- Create a cash flow forecast to predict when money will come in and go out.
- Invoice effectively to minimize late payments and cash flow gaps.
- Use budgeting tools to allocate resources wisely.

And let's not forget the practical tips: incentivizing early payments, negotiating vendor terms, and keeping an emergency cash reserve. These strategies aren't just practical – they're lifesavers.

Why the Money Side of Business Is Now Your New Expertise

Look, no one starts a business because they're dying to create cash flow spreadsheets (if you do, we salute you). But mastering the financial side of entrepreneurship is like learning to drive a car: intimidating at first but second nature once you get the hang of it.

Here's what you've accomplished in Chapter 7:

- You now know precisely how to calculate your start-up costs – no guesswork, no surprises.
- You've explored multiple funding options and understand the processes involved in securing them.
- You've demystified cash flow and budgeting, ensuring you can keep your business financially healthy even in challenging times.

Money doesn't have to be scary or overwhelming. With the tools and knowledge you now have, you're not just ready to fund your business – you're ready to *own* the financial side of it.

8

Setting Up Security Consulting Operations

"By failing to prepare, you are preparing to fail."

— Benjamin Franklin

Did you know that 60% of small businesses fail within their first five years because of poor operational planning? This statistic underscores the importance of creating a seamless and efficient operational foundation for security consultants. Operations are where your big ideas meet the day-to-day realities of running a business. From choosing the proper office setup to assembling a dream team of professionals and creating standard operating procedures, Chapter 8 is your comprehensive guide to setting up operations for your security consulting business.

Let's unpack the nuts and bolts of how to make your business run like a well-oiled machine.

Establishing a Physical or Remote Office

Where you work as a security consultant sets the tone for your business operations. Choosing the correct office setup isn't just about having a desk and chair; it's about creating a space that supports your goals, enhances productivity, and fits your budget. Whether it's a traditional brick-and-mortar office, a flexible coworking space, or the comfort of your home, each option has advantages and challenges.

Let's break down each option, analyze its pros and cons, and help you make an informed decision.

Option 1: Brick-and-Mortar Office

The traditional office space – four walls, a sign on the door, and a place where you can physically interact with clients and staff. For many, this setup represents stability and professionalism.

Advantages of a Brick-and-Mortar Office

Professional Appearance: A dedicated office space lends credibility to your business, especially when meeting with high-profile clients. Walking into a well-maintained office creates an impression of competence and stability.

Centralized Operations: A physical office provides a hub for meetings, team collaboration, and secure storage of equipment or sensitive documents.

Enhanced Security: In the security consulting industry, demonstrating your expertise starts with your own office. To impress clients, you can showcase access control systems, surveillance setups, and other cutting-edge technologies.

Client Accessibility: If your target clients are local businesses, having a nearby office can be a selling point.

Challenges of a Brick-and-Mortar Office

Cost: Renting or buying office space is expensive. You'll need to factor in rent, utilities, maintenance, and insurance.

Commitment: Leases often require long-term commitments, which may feel restrictive for a new business.

Flexibility: A physical office ties you to a location, which might not suit a business model that requires frequent travel or remote work.

Who Should Choose This Option? A brick-and-mortar office may be the best choice if your business model relies heavily on face-to-face interactions, team collaboration, or on-site equipment.

Option 2: Flex Workspaces and Coworking Locations

Flex workspaces – also known as coworking spaces – are shared office environments where professionals from various industries work side by side. Think of them as the modern, minimalist answer to the traditional office.

Advantages of Flex Workspaces

Cost Efficiency: You pay only for what you use, which is ideal for startups. Flexible plans range from hot desks to private offices, with costs significantly lower than traditional leases.

Networking Opportunities: These spaces are buzzing with entrepreneurs, freelancers, and business professionals. You never know when a casual chat at the coffee machine might lead to a valuable connection.

Scalability: As your business grows, you can upgrade to larger spaces or additional resources without the hassle of relocating.

Amenities: Flex workspaces often include high-speed internet, meeting rooms, printing services, receptionists, and communal areas.

Professional Environment Without Overhead: You gain access to a professional setting without the responsibilities of maintenance or utilities.

Challenges of Flex Workspaces

Lack of Customization: Shared spaces mean limited control over your environment, which might not align with branding or specific needs.

Privacy Concerns: Sensitive client discussions may be difficult to manage in a shared space.

Availability: Popular coworking spaces may get crowded, making securing a private room or desk harder during peak hours.

Who Should Choose This Option? Coworking spaces are an excellent choice for solo consultants or small teams looking for affordability, flexibility, and networking opportunities.

Option 3: Home Office

The home office has become popular, especially with the rise of remote work. It's a cost-effective option that offers maximum flexibility.

Advantages of a Home Office

Cost Savings: No rent, utilities, or commute expenses. Your coffee is cheaper, too.

Flexibility: Set your own hours and work in pajamas (just don't Zoom with clients dressed like that - even below the waist).

Work-Life Balance: The proximity to home life can be a perk, especially if you have family responsibilities.

Commute: Depending on your square footage, your commute to work can be measured in steps (and you don't always have to be dressed on that commute)!

Tax Benefits: Home-based businesses can deduct a portion of home-related expenses, such as utilities and internet, on your taxes.

Challenges of a Home Office

Distractions: Staying focused can be challenging. From kids to the temptation of daytime TV.

Professional Image: Meeting clients in your living room or over a noisy Zoom call might not exude the professionalism you want.

Isolation: Working from home can feel lonely and limit networking opportunities.

Storage Space: A home office might need more room for physical equipment or sensitive documents.

Who Should Choose This Option? If your business model allows for remote client interactions and you're disciplined enough to work from home, this is a practical and cost-effective choice.

Key Factors to Consider When Choosing Your Office Setup

Budget: What can you afford without overextending your resources? Start lean and upgrade as your business grows.

Business Model: Do you need a professional space or specialized equipment for client meetings?

Target Audience: Where are your clients located? Choose a setup that aligns with their needs.

Flexibility: How much freedom do you need to adapt your business?

Work-Life Balance: Consider your personal preferences. Some thrive in a home office; others need the structure of a dedicated workspace.

Making the Final Decision

There is no one-size-fits-all answer to choosing the right office setup. The best approach is to weigh the pros and cons of each option, considering your budget, goals, and personal preferences.

Remember, your office isn't just a workplace; it's a reflection of your brand and a tool for driving success.

In the end, whether it's a cozy home office, a buzzing coworking space, or a sleek downtown suite, the right environment will set the tone for your business and inspire confidence in your clients. Now, let's move on to the tools and technology that will make your office – and your business – run like a well-oiled machine!

Essential Tools and Technology for Security Assessments

Starting a security consulting company requires more than just a sharp mind and a keen eye for vulnerabilities. It requires equipping yourself with the right tools and technologies to execute assessments, manage projects, and impress your clients with professional precision. From software that simplifies budgeting to cutting-edge gadgets that enhance on-site evaluations, having the right tools can differentiate you from competitors.

Let's dig deep into the essential tools and technology every security consultant entrepreneur needs to thrive. For easy digestibility, let's break the software and tools into categories.

Financial and Budgeting Software: Managing finances can be one of the most intimidating aspects of starting a business. Without solid budgeting tools, even the most brilliant consultants can find themselves lost in a sea of invoices and expenses.

Why It's Essential: A robust financial system keeps your business afloat by ensuring accurate bookkeeping, seamless invoicing, and a clear cash flow picture.

Recommended Tools:

- QuickBooks: The industry standard for small business accounting. It handles invoicing, expense tracking, and even tax preparation.

- FreshBooks: A more user-friendly alternative with features like time tracking and project-based invoicing.
- Wave Accounting: A free option for entrepreneurs on a tight budget, offering basic accounting tools.

How to Use Financial Software: Imagine juggling multiple clients, each with unique billing terms. Financial software allows you to generate professional invoices, track payments, and set reminders to follow up on overdue accounts – all without breaking a sweat.

Pro Tip: Use these tools to create monthly cash flow reports to stay ahead of potential financial bottlenecks.

Project Management Software: Security consulting projects often involve multiple moving parts – site visits, client meetings, team coordination, and report generation. Staying organized is non-negotiable.

Why It's Essential: Project management software ensures you stay on top of deadlines, delegate tasks effectively, and provide clients with progress updates.

Recommended Tools:

- Trello: A visual tool that uses boards and cards to track tasks and deadlines.
- Asana: Ideal for more complex projects, offering Gantt charts, task assignments, and progress tracking.
- Monday.com: A customizable tool with automation options to save time on repetitive tasks.

How to Use Project Management Software: Let's say you're conducting a risk assessment for a corporate client. Use Trello to create a board for the project. Break it into cards for each step – initial consultation, site evaluation, data analysis, and report delivery. Assign deadlines and monitor progress at a glance.

Customer Relationship Management (CRM) Software:
Your clients are the lifeblood of your business, and maintaining strong relationships with them is critical for long-term success.

Why It's Essential: CRM software helps you manage client interactions, track communication history, and identify opportunities to upsell or cross-sell services.

Recommended Tools:

- HubSpot CRM: A free option with robust features like email tracking and pipeline management.
- Salesforce: A powerhouse CRM for businesses ready to scale, offering advanced analytics and integrations.
- Zoho CRM: A budget-friendly tool with features tailored to small businesses.

How to Use CRM Software: Imagine you've completed a risk assessment for a client and want to follow up with an offer for ongoing security training. Your CRM stores notes from past interactions, making it easy to craft personalized outreach.

Pro Tip: Use CRM tools to automate client reminders, ensuring you take advantage of every opportunity to follow up on leads or renew contracts.

Risk Assessment Software: Risk assessment is the backbone of security consulting. Having specialized software to analyze data and generate reports can elevate your credibility.

Why It's Essential: Risk assessment software streamlines data collection, analysis, and presentation, enabling you to focus on delivering actionable insights.

Recommended Tools:

- Resolver: Known for identifying and mitigating risks across various domains.

- ARMOR: A user-friendly tool designed specifically for security consultants.
- D3 Incident Reporting: Helps with documenting and analyzing security incidents for better decision-making.

How to Use Risk Assessment Software: Imagine you're conducting a physical security assessment for a high-net-worth client. Use ARMOR to map out vulnerabilities, assign risk levels, and suggest mitigation strategies. Generate a professional report in minutes, impressing your client with both speed and accuracy.

Surveillance Equipment

Digital Cameras: High-resolution cameras like the Canon EOS series are perfect for documenting vulnerabilities.

Drones: Tools like DJI Mavic Air allow for aerial views of properties, providing perspectives you can't get on foot.

Audio Recording Devices: Capture interviews or document observations during site assessments.

Communication Tools

Two-Way Radios: For team communication during large-scale assessments or events.

Secure Messaging Apps: Use platforms like Signal for confidential communication with clients and team members.

A wi-fi puck of some sort: Secure wi-fi is a must, especially when dealing with your client's information. Obviously, you should never trust any hotel or public wi-fi, but you should be equally cautious about trusting your client's home or work wi-fi.

Reporting Tools

Microsoft Office Suite: The gold standard for creating detailed reports and professional presentations.

Google Workspace: A collaborative alternative with cloud-based tools for real-time editing.

Lucidchart: Great for creating visual diagrams, like security workflows or emergency response plans.

Floor Plan Drawers. Great for use in physical security assessments. Look for programs like Floor Plan Creator, Planner 5D, Roomstyler, MagicPlan, CubiCasa, or SketchUp.

Data Visualization Tools

Tableau: For presenting complex data in an easy-to-understand format.

Power BI: A Microsoft tool for creating interactive dashboards and reports.

Cybersecurity Tools

Norton Security: Protects against malware and phishing attempts.

Bitdefender: Known for its lightweight yet powerful protection.

LastPass: Ensures secure storage and sharing of passwords.

Dashlane: Offers an easy-to-use interface for managing credentials.

Dropbox Business: Secure cloud storage for client data and reports.

Google Drive (Enterprise): Offers built-in encryption and seamless sharing capabilities.

Equipping your business with the right tools isn't just about efficiency – it's about credibility. Your clients will judge you based on your ability to deliver polished, professional results. By investing in the right technology, you're enhancing your workflow and signaling to clients that you take their security seriously.

And remember, tools don't have to break the bank. Start with affordable options or free trials, and upgrade as your business grows. After all, even the sharpest tools are only as effective as the hands that wield them.

Hiring Experienced Security Professionals and Consultants

"No man will make a great leader who wants to do it all himself or get all the credit for doing it."

— Andrew Carnegie

The dream of starting your own security consulting business often begins with a vision of independence. You imagine yourself as the go-to expert, seamlessly handling every project, decision, and client interaction. And for a while, you might even pull it off. But if you're following the principles laid out in this book – like niching down and delivering best-in-class service – you'll soon discover a reality that every thriving entrepreneur faces: you can't do it all alone.

Security consulting is a vast and multifaceted industry, and even if you've become a master in your niche, no one can be an expert in everything. You might specialize in physical security assessments, but what happens when a client asks for cybersecurity solutions? Or you're a whiz at risk assessments but need surveillance expertise to round out a project. This is where hiring employees or collaborating with independent consultants becomes not just a luxury but a necessity.

The Shoestring Budget Dilemma

For most entrepreneurs starting out, hiring help seems like a pipe dream. Let's be real: money is tight. Between investing in startup costs, marketing, and maintaining cash flow, the idea of paying someone else can feel overwhelming. Yet, paradoxically, hiring the right people – whether as employees or independent contractors – can often make the difference between stagnation and scalability.

Think of it like this: If you're spreading yourself too thin, trying to master every element of the business, the quality of your core offering – the thing that sets you apart – will suffer. Clients don't hire security consultants to get a mediocre jack-of-all-trades; they hire experts to solve specific problems. Your ability to bring in complementary expertise when needed allows you to stay laser-focused on what you do best, ensuring clients receive top-notch service every time.

Why Expertise?

Picture this: You're a client looking for a comprehensive security overhaul. You meet Consultant A, who claims they can handle everything – physical security, cybersecurity, investigations, and disaster planning. Then there's Consultant B, who specializes in physical security assessments but brings in a vetted cybersecurity partner for network audits. Who do you trust more?

Chances are, you'll pick Consultant B. Why? Because they're honest about their strengths and know when to call in reinforcements. Clients value transparency and trust consultants who deliver specialized expertise over those who try to do it all. Partnering with other professionals – whether as employees or independent consultants – allows you to position yourself as the orchestrator of a symphony, ensuring every note is played perfectly, even if you're not the one holding the instrument.

The Niching-Down Effect

Earlier in this book, we emphasized the importance of niching down to establish yourself as the go-to expert in a specific area of security consulting. But niching down doesn't mean limiting your potential – it means amplifying your credibility. When clients see you as a leader in one niche, they'll trust you to assemble the right team for projects that go beyond your core expertise.

Take, for example, a security consultant specializing in ultra-high-networth (UHNW) estate management. A UHNW client might request a risk assessment for their property but also need cybersecurity solutions to protect their digital assets. Rather than trying to become a cybersecurity expert overnight, you can partner with a seasoned cybersecurity consultant to deliver a comprehensive solution. This approach strengthens your reputation as a trusted advisor while allowing you to provide a broader range of services.

Scaling Without Diluting Your Brand

One of the greatest fears entrepreneurs face when hiring or collaborating is the potential dilution of their brand. After all, your business is your baby, and trusting someone else with your clients feels like handing over the keys to your prized possession. But here's the thing: bringing in the right people doesn't dilute your brand – it enhances it.

Imagine this: You're running a successful consulting business with a stellar reputation for physical security. A large client approaches you with a lucrative contract, but it involves components outside your expertise. Instead of saying no – or worse, overpromising and underdelivering – you hire or partner with a vetted expert in that area. Not only do you secure the contract, but you also impress the client with your ability to deliver a seamless solution. Your brand isn't weakened; your commitment to excellence strengthens it.

An Entrepreneurial Anecdote

Early in my career, I landed a major client who needed a comprehensive security overhaul for their corporate headquarters. I was confident in my ability to handle the physical security assessment, but I knew the project also required detailed cybersecurity expertise to combat a legitimate, nation-state ransomware threat. At the time, I wrestled with the idea of hiring a contractor. Would it cost too much? Would I lose control of the client relationship? Would the contractor deliver to my standards?

Ultimately, I decided to partner with a well-known cybersecurity consultant, and it was one of the best decisions I ever made. Not only did the client rave about the holistic approach, but they also referred me to others, impressed by my ability to assemble the perfect team. That project taught me a valuable lesson: being an expert doesn't mean going it alone – it means knowing when to bring in reinforcements.

Setting the Stage for Success

Hiring experienced security professionals – employees or independent contractors – isn't just about filling gaps; it's about building a foundation for sustainable growth. As you continue reading, we'll dive deeper into the nuances of W2 employees versus 1099 contractors, explore the legal and operational considerations, and provide actionable strategies to assemble a team that complements your vision.

For now, remember this: You don't have to be everything to everyone. Focus on being exceptional in your niche, and don't hesitate to bring in others who can help you elevate your services. After all, even the Lone Ranger had Tonto.

The Difference Between W2 Employees and 1099 Independent Contractors

Starting a business, especially one as nuanced as security consulting, brings with it a lot of decisions, and one of the biggest is how to grow your team. Do you bring on W2 employees who work under your direct oversight and payroll, or do you go the route of 1099 independent contractors, engaging external experts for specific tasks? Getting this choice wrong isn't just a matter of inefficiency – it could lead to legal headaches, financial strain, or even the collapse of client relationships. So, let's get into the nitty-gritty of what separates W2 employees from 1099 independent contractors and how to decide which is best for your business.

W2 Employees: The Backbone of Stability

A W2 employee is someone hired directly by your company. They're part of your team, work under your control, and are compensated with wages or a salary. You withhold payroll taxes and might offer additional benefits like health insurance or retirement plans. In many cases, the employer (you) is also responsible for things like workman's compensation and unemployment insurance. A W2 employee can either be hired on a full-time or part-time basis, with varying legal and financial obligations associated with each option. Employees could be hired on an hourly or salary basis. You will also fall under state and federal legal guidelines on minimum wage and overtime issues.

Advantages:

Control and Consistency: With W2 employees, you dictate how and when they perform their work. They can be trained to follow your specific processes and align with your brand.

Example: If you specialize in corporate security assessments, a W2 employee can be trained in your unique methodology, ensuring consistency across all client projects.

Long-Term Commitment: Employees often develop a sense of loyalty and investment in your company's success, making them ideal for building a cohesive team.

Scalability of Expertise: W2 employees can grow with your business. With the proper training, they can take on more responsibility and deepen their expertise.

Disadvantages:

Cost: Employees are expensive. Beyond salaries, you'll pay for benefits, payroll taxes, insurance, and more. For a small startup, this can be a significant burden.

Example: If you hire someone at a $60,000 annual salary, additional costs could push their total compensation closer to $80,000.

Administrative Burden: Managing payroll, compliance, and HR-related tasks adds a layer of complexity to your operations.

Flexibility Constraints: W2 employees are most valuable for ongoing, consistent work. If your workload fluctuates or you need expertise outside your core offerings, this model may not be ideal.

1099 Independent Contractors: The Flexibility Factor

Independent contractors are self-employed professionals who provide services to your company on a project-by-project basis. They work under a contract and are responsible for their own taxes and benefits. They can be contracted on an hourly, daily, or per-job (also referred to as "upon delivery") basis.

Advantages:

Specialized Expertise: Contractors bring niche skills to your team.

Example: A technical surveillance countermeasures (TSCM) consultant with advanced certifications and expensive equipment can handle a specific client's need, leaving you free to focus on your core services.

Cost Efficiency: You pay contractors only for the work they do – no benefits, no payroll taxes, no overhead.

Scalability and Flexibility: Contractors are ideal for short-term projects or fluctuating workloads. You can scale your team up or down as needed without long-term commitments.

Example: If a client requests drone surveillance for a one-time project, you can hire a contractor with that expertise rather than investing in training an employee.

Disadvantages:

Limited Control: Contractors have more autonomy in how they complete their work, which means you can't micromanage the process.

Example: A contractor may deliver excellent results but in a way that aligns differently with your company's style or methodology.

Lack of Exclusivity: Contractors often work with multiple clients, including your competitors. This can lead to conflicts of interest or divided attention.

No Long-Term Investment: Contractors aren't invested in your company's success. Once their project is done, they move on.

Brand Confusion: Legally, independent contractors are not allowed to represent your brand in terms of business cards, invoicing, uniforms, etc. A client hires you to complete a job but now sees two different brands completing the tasks.

Legal Distinctions: Why You Need to Get It Right

The IRS takes the classification of workers seriously. Misclassifying a W2 employee as a 1099 contractor, or vice versa, can result in hefty penalties, back taxes, and lawsuits. Here are the key factors that determine worker classification:

Behavioral Control: If you control how, when, and where workers perform their tasks, they're likely a W2 employee.

Financial Control: Reimbursing expenses or providing tools and equipment leans toward a W2 relationship. Contractors typically provide their own resources.

Relationship Nature: If the relationship is ongoing and integral to your business, it suggests an employee relationship.

Pro Tip: Consult a labor attorney to review your worker classifications and contracts to ensure compliance.

Choosing the Right Path for Your Business

The choice between W2 and 1099 isn't an either-or scenario. Many successful businesses combine both to balance control, cost, and expertise.

When to Choose W2 Employees:

- You need consistent, ongoing support.
- You value long-term loyalty and investment in your company's success.
- You're prepared to handle the costs and administrative requirements.

When to Choose 1099 Contractors:

- You need specialized expertise for short-term or irregular projects.
- You want to scale your team quickly without long-term commitments.
- You're working with a tight budget and need cost-effective solutions.

Comparison Chart W2 vs 1099: Feature

Feature	W2 Employees	1099 Contractors
Control	High	Low
Cost	Higher (salary + benefits + overtime)	Lower (no benefits, temporary)
Flexibility	Low	High
Scalability	Limited	Excellent
Loyalty	Strong	Limited until nurtured
Legal Complexity	Moderate	High risk of misclassification
Training/Onboarding	Extensive	Minimal
Cont. Ed and Cert. Sponsorship	High	None
Tax Requirements	High (payroll + unemployment + workman's compensation)	Limited (report to IRS)
Client-Facing Issues	Low	Potential for brand confusion or inconsistent quality

Understanding the difference between W2 employees and 1099 contractors is crucial for building a strong team while protecting your business from legal and financial risks. Take the time to evaluate your needs, project demands, and long-term goals. Remember, the right mix of employees and contractors can elevate your security consulting business from good to exceptional.

Identifying and Forging Mutually Beneficial Strategic Partnerships

In the world of security consulting, you're not just selling services – you're selling trust, expertise, and reliability. And while it's tempting to think you can single-handedly offer a one-stop shop for every client's needs, the reality is that no single consultant or company can do it all. This is where the magic of strategic partnerships comes into play.

Strategic partnerships are about building alliances with other professionals or companies whose expertise complements yours. It's not just about filling gaps in your service offerings; it's about creating a network of trusted allies who elevate your brand and help you better serve your clients. Done correctly, these partnerships can lead to increased revenue, a stellar reputation, and the ability to tackle larger and more complex projects.

But let's be clear: not all partnerships are created equal. Choosing the wrong partner can harm your reputation, alienate your clients, and leave you with more problems than solutions. That's why vetting, proposing, and maintaining partnerships require strategic thinking, clear communication, and a dash of humility.

Why Strategic Partnerships Matter

Imagine this: You've built a strong reputation as a physical security consultant specializing in corporate risk assessments. A client loves your work and asks if you can also handle cybersecurity. You could decline the request, potentially losing the client to someone who can offer both services. Or you could confidently say, "Absolutely. I'll bring in a trusted cybersecurity partner to ensure we meet your needs."

The second option retains your client and enhances your value proposition. By aligning yourself with experts in complementary fields, you position your business as a comprehensive solutions provider – without stretching yourself too thin or faking expertise.

The Vetting Process: How to Choose the Right Partner

Before reaching out to potential partners, take a step back and think critically about what you're looking for. Not every skilled professional or successful company will be the right fit. Here are the key factors to consider when vetting a potential partner:

Alignment of Values: Do their values and business practices align with yours? A partnership isn't just about skill sets; it's about shared values and priorities. If integrity and professionalism are central to your brand, partnering with a company that cuts corners or delivers subpar work could damage your reputation.

Another value critical in the security consulting sector is client confidentiality. How does your potential partner handle this? Search their social media and website. Ask around. If they are loose-lipped or quick to disclose to you the identity of their clients or jump on the rumor train, walk away.

A third critical value that we always try to assess is whether they are fiscally prudent. Unfortunately, you seldom get to ascertain this until it's too late. But you can start getting indications of it during the bid creation process (hang on, we'll get there!). If your potential partner is invoicing for unnecessary expenses, creating redundant or frivolous services, or not looking for cost-saving measures for the client, this should be a big red flag.

Finally, you should try to assess the level of professionalism that they hold. This industry is full of ego-driven jerks who have ILS (inflated-lat-syndrome) and think that they can do no wrong. Unfortunately, you must weed through the chaff to find the kernels. How do they treat you in conversations? Do they interrupt? Are they dismissive? Do they exaggerate to try and impress? These are indicators of much bigger hidden dangers and warning signs you want to avoid. Instead, search out those humble, quiet professionals with an understated confidence and a willingness to enter an equally beneficial relationship.

Reputation: What do others in the industry say about this person or company? A quick Google search, client testimonials, and even informal conversations with industry peers can reveal much. Yes, security companies end up on sites like Yelp and the Better Business Bureau; you can check these to see if there have been any complaints or compliments. Finally, quite a few "Security Fail" social media pages out there will highlight the bad companies in this industry. Take any post with a grain of salt because much of what you will read will either be trolling or venting and is rarely fully vetted.

Pro Tip: Check if they're active members of professional organizations like ASIS International or have certifications relevant to their expertise.

Complementary Expertise: Your ideal partner should offer services or skills that you don't – but that your clients might need. For example, if you focus on physical security, look for partners specializing in cybersecurity, emergency planning, or training programs. If you pick a partner whose area of expertise is similar to yours (or close enough that the client can't tell the difference), you run the risk of brand confusion or the client switching providers.

Track Record: Have they delivered consistent results in the past? A proven track record speaks volumes about their reliability and expertise. Look at their website and social media to see what kind of services they've provided. Are they similar to your requirements? Do they list client testimonials? Do you have any trusted agents that have worked on projects with them in the past? Do you feel comfortable reaching out to them?

Pro Tip: It is accepted as standard practice in this industry that you must do your due diligence. Expect that your potential partner will conduct the same due diligence on you. That is why it is so important to have a robust QMP that handles client, employee, and subcontractor issues before they become permanent beefs that can affect future business.

Capacity and Availability: Are they equipped to handle the demands of your projects? The best partner in the world won't be much help if they're already overcommitted.

Communication Style: How prompt are they to return a missed call? An email? Do they only communicate through emojis and acronyms? How is their spelling, grammar, articulation, and professional speech? Would you be embarrassed if they had to speak or deliver a report to your client?

Legal and Financial Stability: Are they licensed to perform the service you need in the location where you need it performed? Do they have industry-recognized training, education, and certification? What is their Dun & Bradstreet (DNB) credit rating? While not a firm indicator of trouble, if your potential partner says they need 100% of the contract cost paid up front, this could spell danger as a sign of financial instability. On the other hand, it could be situational or an indication of how they bid on contracts with unknown partners/clients.

Shared Vision: Do they share the long-term vision, purpose, and goals for this partnership? Do they approach the contract with a "one and done" or "wait and see" attitude, or are they communicating a willingness to pursue endeavors together on a long-term basis?

Making Contact: Approaching Potential Partners

Once you've identified potential partners, the next step is reaching out. This process can feel intimidating, especially if you're new to the industry, but remember: partnerships are mutually beneficial. You're not begging for help – you're offering an opportunity for collaboration that benefits both parties.

How to Approach a Potential Partner

Start with Research: Learn as much as possible about their business, recent projects, and expertise. This shows that you're serious and thoughtful.

Craft a Compelling Proposal: When reaching out, clearly articulate why you believe the partnership would be beneficial. Focus on how your combined strengths can better serve clients.

Example Email Template: Hi [Name], I've admired your work in [specific area], and I believe our expertise in [your location] complements what you offer. I'd love to discuss how we could collaborate to deliver exceptional solutions for our clients.

Showcase Your Value: Be prepared to share examples of your work, client testimonials, and your unique value proposition.

Be Transparent About Expectations: Outline how you envision the partnership working, including roles, responsibilities, and compensation.

Building the Partnership: Communication is Key

Despite what you see in the movies, no one operates on "a word and a handshake" any longer. Additionally, a great partnership isn't built overnight. It requires clear communication, mutual respect, trust, a willingness to adapt, and a healthy dose of humility. Here's how to set the foundation for success:

Define Roles and Responsibilities: Clearly outline who will handle what. Ambiguity can lead to misunderstandings and frustration.

Create a Partnership Agreement: A written agreement is essential. It should cover deliverables, payment terms, confidentiality, and dispute resolution.

Establish Regular Check-Ins: Communication is the lifeblood of any partnership. Schedule regular meetings to discuss progress, address challenges, and ensure everyone is on the same page.

Being a Good Partner

Partnerships are a two-way street. You need to be a great partner to attract and retain great collaborators. This means:

- Delivering on your promises.
- Respecting their time and expertise.
- Being transparent about challenges or changes.
- Promoting their work and celebrating their successes.

Checklist: Evaluating a Potential Partner: Criteria

Criteria	Questions to Ask Yourself
Values Alignment	• Do they share my commitment to professionalism, excellence, and confidentiality? • Are they fiscally prudent?
Reputation	• What do clients and the industry say about them? • What do previous employees, subcontractors, and vendors say about them?
Complimentary Expertise	• Do their skills and services fill gaps in my offerings? • Will the client be able to tell the difference between the services and expertise that I bring to the table and what they do?
Track Record (Proven Performance)	• Can they demonstrate consistent, high-quality results? • Are there client testimonials that I can access?
Capacity & Availability	• Do they have the time and resources to take on your projections?
Communication Style	• Are they responsive, clear, articulate, and professional in their communication? • Would I trust them if they had to communicate (verbally or in writing) with my client?
Legal and Financial Stability	• Are they financially stable and legally compliant (Sec of State Cert., Insurance, D&B rating, Certifications, Licensing, etc.)?
Shared Vision	• Do they share your long-term goals and vision for the partnership?

Strategic partnerships can be a game-changer for your security consulting business, but they require careful planning and execution. By vetting potential partners, communicating expectations clearly, and nurturing the relationship, you'll build a network of allies who elevate your brand and help you deliver unparalleled service. Remember: The best partnerships aren't just transactional – they're transformative. So, choose wisely and collaborate intentionally. After all, the right partner can turn a good business into a great one.

Developing Effective Standard Operating Procedures (SOPs) and Risk Mitigation Plans

Startups in the security consulting industry often launch with ambition, expertise, and a desire to make a difference. But without a clear way forward, even the most talented entrepreneurs can quickly find themselves in chaos. That's where Standard Operating Procedures (SOPs) and Risk Mitigation Plans come into play. They aren't just bureaucratic paperwork – they're the foundation of consistency, efficiency, and trustworthiness in your business.

Let's explore why SOPs and risk mitigation are crucial, how to create them, and what they can look like for your business.

Why SOPs Are Essential for Security Consulting

At their core, SOPs are about standardization – establishing how things are done in your company to ensure consistency, quality, and accountability. For a security consulting entrepreneur, they can mean the difference between a well-oiled machine and a chaotic operation.

Here's why they matter:

Consistency: SOPs ensure every task is done the same way every time, regardless of who's doing it. This is crucial for building trust with clients.

Example: Imagine a client requests a risk assessment report. With an SOP for report writing, every consultant on your team will deliver a document that meets your company's standards – no surprises, no inconsistencies.

Efficiency: SOPs reduce guesswork. When employees or contractors know exactly how to perform a task, they spend less time figuring it out and more time getting it done.

Example: An SOP for invoicing ensures that billing is consistent, clear, and timely, reducing payment delays and disputes.

Training: SOPs serve as training manuals for new hires or contractors. They help you onboard people quickly and effectively without reinventing the wheel. In many cases, state or federal agencies inspect policies on required mandatory training. I have even had a potential partner vendor ask me for a list of my mandatory training events and my policy governing training.

Accountability: Clear procedures make it easy to identify where things went wrong if a problem arises. This transparency builds trust within your team and with your clients.

Key Areas for SOP Development

Every business will have unique needs, but here are some critical areas where SOPs are invaluable for security consulting entrepreneurs:

Administrative Operations

Invoicing and Billing Procedures: How and when clients are billed, what payment methods are accepted, and how late payments are handled.

Client Onboarding: A step-by-step process for bringing new clients into your system, including contracts, initial consultations, and data collection.

New Talent Onboarding: A step-by-step process for hiring new employees or the necessary forms/documents for a new vendor/subcontractor.

Internal Communications: Guidelines for team communication, including email etiquette, meeting protocols, OPSEC, and escalation paths for urgent issues.

Service Delivery

Report Writing Standards: Templates and guidelines for risk assessments, security plans, and incident reports to ensure consistency and professionalism.

Client Interaction Policies: How to handle consultations, presentations, and follow-ups.

Specialized Security Operations

Pre-Travel Security Checklists: A comprehensive list of preparations for consultants traveling to high-risk areas, including gear checks, itinerary sharing, and emergency contacts.

Hostile Termination Consultation Checklists: Procedures for advising clients on safely handling employee terminations that could escalate into conflicts.

Escalation of Force Policies: Clear guidelines on when and how to use force in security operations, ensuring compliance with legal and ethical standards.

Use of Lethal Force Policies: Detailed protocols for situations involving firearms or other lethal measures developed in consultation with legal experts.

Risk Mitigation Plans

Crisis Management Protocols: What to do during a data breach, physical security incident, or other emergencies.

Contingency Plans: Backup strategies for service disruptions, such as replacing a contractor who's unable to fulfill their role.

Creating Effective SOPs

Developing SOPs isn't just about writing down processes; it's about creating clear, actionable documents tailored to your business needs. Here's how to approach this critical task:

Step 1: **Map Out Your Processes.** Start by identifying all the core functions of your business – administrative tasks, client-facing services, and specialized security operations. For each function, ask yourself:

- What steps are involved?
- Who is responsible for each step?
- What tools or resources are required?

Example: If you're creating an SOP for invoicing:

- Generate an invoice within three business days of project completion.
- Send the invoice via email to the client using standardized templates.
- Follow up on unpaid invoices after 14 days with a polite reminder.

Step 2: **Write in Plain Language.** Your SOPs should be easy to understand, even for someone new to your business. Avoid jargon and break complex tasks into smaller steps.

Example: For a pre-travel security checklist:

- Verify that passports and visas are valid for the destination.
- Share itinerary details with a designated contact.
- Pack emergency medical supplies and communication devices.
- Confirm local security arrangements, such as hotel safety protocols.

Step 3: **Incorporate Visuals.** Use flowcharts, diagrams, or checklists to make your SOPs more accessible. Visuals help convey information quickly and can be particularly useful for complex processes.

Step 4: **Test and Revise.** No SOP is perfect on the first try. Have your team follow the procedures and provide feedback on clarity, usability, and gaps. Revise as necessary to ensure the document is practical.

Step 5: **Regular Updates.** Security consulting is a dynamic field.

Regularly review and update your SOPs to reflect changes in technology, regulations, or your business model.

The Role of Risk Mitigation Plans

While SOPs focus on standardizing operations, risk mitigation plans address potential threats and outline strategies to minimize their impact. These plans are critical for protecting your business, clients, and reputation.

Developing a Risk Mitigation Plan

Step 1: **Identify Risks.** Consider your business's unique risks, from physical threats to cyberattacks to reputational damage.

Example: A cybersecurity consulting firm might identify risks such as data breaches, phishing attacks, or software vulnerabilities.

Step 2: **Assess Impact.** For each risk, evaluate the potential impact on your business and clients.

Example: A data breach could lead to financial losses, client dissatisfaction, and legal repercussions.

Step 3: **Develop Strategies.** Create specific actions to mitigate each risk. These might include:

- Implementing robust cybersecurity measures.
- Training staff on emergency response protocols.
- Establishing communication plans for crises.

Step 4: **Assign Responsibilities.** Clearly define who is responsible for implementing and managing each strategy.

Step 5: **Regular Drills and Updates.** Test your risk mitigation plans through simulations and update them based on lessons learned.

A Quick Checklist for Developing SOPs and Risk Mitigation Plans

Task	Completed?
Identify core business functions and operations	☐
Map out detailed steps for each process	☐
Write SOPs in plain, actionable language	☐
Incorporate visuals for clarity	☐
Test and revise SOPs with your team	☐
Identify potential risks to your business	☐
Develop strategies to mitigate those risks	☐
Assign responsibilities for risk management	☐
Schedule periodic reviews and updates	☐

SOPs and risk mitigation plans are the backbone of a professional, reliable security consulting business. They provide structure, consistency, and a sense of preparedness that clients will notice and appreciate. By investing the time to develop these documents thoughtfully, you're not just protecting your business – you're setting it up for sustainable growth and long-term success. So grab that energy drink, gather your team, and start writing. Your future self (and your clients) will thank you.

Chapter 8 Wrap-Up: Building the Foundation of a Thriving Security Consulting Business

Chapter 8 has been a journey, hasn't it? We've built a roadmap for structuring your security consulting operations, ensuring you're prepared to hit the ground running and equipped to run at full speed. Let's recap the core components of this chapter, one brick at a time, so you can see how they fit into the larger structure of your business.

Establishing a Physical or Remote Office

Every business needs a home, but that "home" doesn't have to come with a monthly lease that rivals your mortgage. We started this chapter by exploring the pros and cons of physical office spaces, flex workspaces, and remote offices. The key takeaway? Your choice should align with your business needs and client expectations, but it should also be realistic for your budget.

Physical offices can give your business credibility, especially when serving corporate clients who expect a professional setting. But they also come with hefty costs, from rent to utilities.

On the other hand, flexible workspaces offer a middle ground – a professional address without the full commitment of a lease.

And let's not forget remote offices. Thanks to technology, you can manage a successful business from the comfort of your living room, provided you maintain professionalism in your communications and client interactions.

This section reinforced the idea that your "office" is less about location and more about functionality. You're on the right track if it supports your goals and reflects your brand.

Essential Tools and Technology for Security Assessments

Once you've decided where you'll operate, the next step is deciding how you'll operate. And in today's world, tools and technology are your best friends. This section broke down the essential tools every security consultant needs to streamline operations and enhance service delivery, from financial software like QuickBooks to project management platforms like Trello or Asana. We delved into:

Risk assessment software that ensures your analyses are thorough and data-driven.

Customer relationship management (CRM) tools that help you track client interactions and nurture relationships.

Budgeting and financial tools to keep your business's finances in check.

The message here was clear: Technology isn't a luxury; it's a necessity. The right tools can save you time, reduce errors, and – most importantly – make you look like the rock star consultant you are.

Hiring Experienced Security Professionals and Consultants

Let's face it – no one's an expert in everything. Hiring the right people is crucial for any security consulting business. But this isn't just about finding someone with the right credentials; it's about understanding your needs and balancing the advantages and disadvantages of W2 employees versus 1099 independent contractors.

W2 employees bring stability and allow you to build a cohesive team, but they also come with costs like benefits and payroll taxes.

1099 contractors, meanwhile, offer flexibility and can fill specialized roles on an as-needed basis, but managing them requires careful attention to IRS regulations.

This section didn't just teach you the technical differences; it encouraged you to think strategically about what kind of workforce will help you achieve your goals. Whether you're building a team or partnering with other experts, your success hinges on the people you choose to work with.

Identifying and Forging Mutually Beneficial Strategic Partnerships

This might be one of the most exciting parts of running a security consulting business. Strategic partnerships allow you to expand your services, tap into new markets, and enhance your reputation – all without doing everything yourself.

We discussed how to vet potential partners, approach them with compelling proposals, and maintain these relationships for mutual success. Whether it's a cybersecurity expert who complements your physical security services or a marketing guru who helps amplify your brand, partnerships can open doors you didn't even know existed.

We also emphasized the importance of being a good partner yourself. Trust, communication, and respect are the cornerstones of any successful collaboration. After all, your partnerships will reflect your brand as much as your solo work.

Developing Effective Standard Operating Procedures (SOPs) and Risk Mitigation Plans

Ah, the crown jewel of operational efficiency – SOPs. While they may not sound glamorous, they're critical. This section guided you through creating SOPs for administrative tasks and security operations, ensuring consistency and quality in every aspect of your business.

We also explored risk mitigation plans, which prepare your business for the "what ifs" that could derail even the best-laid plans. From data breaches to client disputes, having a plan in place means you're not scrambling in the heat of the moment.

SOPs help streamline operations, train new hires, and deliver consistent client experiences.

Risk mitigation plans protect your business and clients from unforeseen challenges.

Both are living documents that should evolve as your business grows and the industry changes.

Putting It All Together

By now, you should feel like a master architect, ready to build a business that's not just functional but resilient and adaptable. Each subsection of this chapter added a crucial piece to your operational foundation:

- You've chosen an office setup that aligns with your goals and budget.

- You've equipped yourself with tools and technology to stay efficient and competitive.
- You've learned how to hire and collaborate with the right people.
- You've established partnerships that expand your capabilities.
- You've developed SOPs and risk mitigation plans to keep your business running smoothly, no matter what challenges arise.

Running a security consulting business isn't just about expertise in your niche; it's about creating systems and relationships that allow you to deliver that expertise effectively. With these tools and strategies, you're well on your way to doing just that.

As we close this chapter, take a moment to reflect on how far you've come. Starting a business is challenging, but the effort you're putting in now will pay dividends in the future. Stay focused, stay flexible, and remember: The security industry needs professionals who are committed to excellence like you.

Now, let's take all this operational wisdom and move forward into the next chapter – because if there's one thing we've learned, it's that there's always more to build.

9

Marketing Your Security Consulting Services

"Doing business without advertising is like winking at someone in
the dark. You know what you are doing, but nobody else does."

— Stuart H. Britt

Businesses that invest in strategic marketing are 60% more likely
to see substantial revenue growth within their first two years.
Yet, many entrepreneurs underestimate how crucial marketing
is to the success of their business, especially in specialized fields like
security consulting.

In this chapter, we'll explain everything you need to know about
marketing your security consulting services through digital avenues,
traditional methods, or creating a sustainable marketing budget. From
optimizing your LinkedIn presence to crafting a solid SEO strategy and
engaging directly with your local community, this chapter will arm you

with tools and techniques to make your business visible, credible, and irresistible to your ideal clients.

Introduction to Digital Marketing

Let's face it: for most new entrepreneurs, the phrase "digital marketing" feels about as approachable as quantum physics. You know it's important, you know everyone's talking about it, but where do you begin? Here's the good news: digital marketing is easier and cheaper than you might think. It's about using online platforms to tell your story, attract clients, and grow your business. And yes, you can do it without breaking the bank. Before we look at the platforms themselves, let's get comfortable with the basics.

Marketing vs. Sales: Two Sides of the Same Coin

First things first: marketing and sales are not the same things. Think of them as cousins rather than twins. Marketing is about creating awareness and generating interest – it's the party invitation. On the other hand, sales is about closing the deal – it's convincing someone to RSVP and show up.

Here's a relatable analogy: Imagine you're hosting a dinner party. Marketing is the beautifully designed invitation you send out, complete with mouthwatering descriptions of the food and ambiance. Sales is your follow-up call to Aunt Marge to ensure she is, in fact, bringing her famous pie. Without marketing, Aunt Marge might not even know there's a party. Without sales, you might end up pie-less. Both are critical, but each serves a distinct role.

In the world of security consulting, marketing ensures potential clients know who you are and what you can do. Sales ensure they sign the contract.

Free Marketing: The Budget-Savvy Entrepreneur's Friend

Contrary to popular belief, you don't need to take out a second mortgage to run an effective marketing campaign. Many digital tools are either free or cost very little to use. Social media platforms like LinkedIn, Facebook, and Twitter offer incredible opportunities to showcase your expertise, share valuable insights, and connect with potential clients – all without spending a dime.

Email marketing tools, like Mailchimp or Constant Contact, allow you to build mailing lists and send out professional newsletters for free (or nearly free, depending on the size of your list). As your business grows, you can expand into paid options, like Facebook Ads or Google Ads, to amplify your reach.

Consider this: free marketing allows you to build credibility and a loyal following, while paid marketing enables you to scale that effort. The key is knowing when and how to use each.

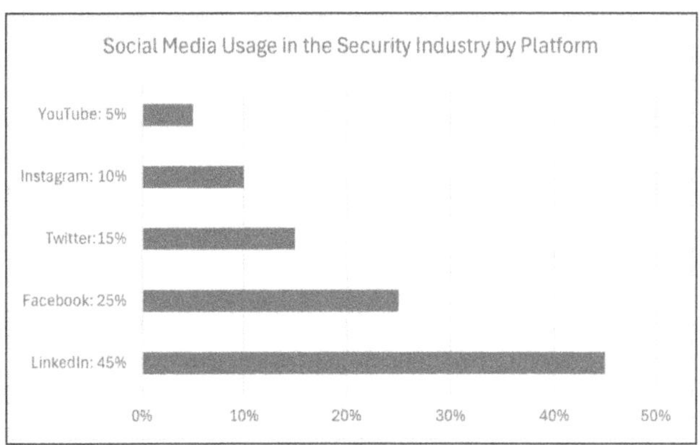

Anecdote: Free Marketing in Action

Let me tell you about my friend Eric. He started a small security consulting business out of his garage. With zero dollars for marketing, he began writing LinkedIn posts about common security risks businesses overlook. One post went semi-viral, catching the attention of a local

CEO who was so impressed he hired Dave on the spot. Fast forward a year, and Dave now runs a thriving business, still relying primarily on free marketing tools to maintain a strong online presence.

Effectiveness of Free vs. Paid Marketing

Free marketing isn't just a stepping stone; it's a foundation. Here's a quick look at how free and paid strategies compare in terms of effectiveness:

Free Marketing: Great for building trust, establishing authority, and engaging with your audience. It's slower but highly impactful for long-term credibility.

Paid Marketing: Excellent for targeting specific demographics, launching campaigns quickly, and scaling efforts. It's faster but requires a budget.

Social Media Usage in the Security Industry

Different platforms serve different purposes, and knowing where your audience spends their time is half the battle. Here's a breakdown of social media usage by security firms:

LinkedIn leads the pack as the go-to platform for professional networking and thought leadership. Facebook comes in strong for community engagement and local outreach, while Twitter and Instagram excel at sharing quick tips and visual content. Although less frequently used, YouTube is a hidden gem for creating credibility through in-depth content like webinars and training videos.

The Takeaway: Digital marketing doesn't have to be daunting or expensive. It's about creating a presence where your ideal clients already spend their time, whether that's on LinkedIn, Facebook, or in their inbox. As we move through the following subcategories, we'll explore each platform in detail so you can create a strategy that works for your business, budget, and goals.

Ready to take your first steps into the world of digital marketing? Let's look closer at LinkedIn, where your professional network is just waiting to meet you.

LinkedIn Networking and Marketing

LinkedIn: the professional's playground, a digital conference room open 24/7 where thought leaders share wisdom, opportunities are born, and yes, occasionally, someone posts an inappropriate meme and learns the hard way that LinkedIn isn't Instagram. If you're looking to market your security consulting services, LinkedIn is not just another social media platform – it's a goldmine for building connections, establishing credibility, and landing clients.

Unlike other social platforms, LinkedIn is built for business. Its users are not there to scroll aimlessly; they're actively looking for insights, opportunities, and expertise. With over 930 million users globally, including CEOs, managers, and decision-makers, it's the perfect stage for security consultants to showcase their value. Your audience isn't just hanging out; they're engaging, learning, and searching for solutions to their problems.

The LinkedIn Basics: Two Pages, One Goal

To make LinkedIn work for you, you need two key assets: a polished personal profile and a professional company page. Each serves a unique purpose and complements the other.

Your Personal LinkedIn Page

Think of your personal profile as your digital business card – only better because it doesn't get lost in someone's desk drawer. This is where you highlight your expertise, share your professional journey, and build your personal brand.

When setting up your profile, ensure the basics are covered:

Professional Headshot: No selfies, no vacation pics, no 'tacti-cool' poses with guns, no blurry images. This is your first impression – make it count.

Headline: Go beyond "Owner at ABC Security Consulting." Use a headline that conveys your value, like "Helping Businesses Strengthen Security & Minimize Risks Through Tailored Consulting Solutions."

Summary Section: Tell your story. Why did you start your consulting firm? What problems do you solve? Use this space to connect emotionally with your audience.

Remember, LinkedIn is a professional platform, so keep your posts appropriate. Share insights, articles, and updates that add value. Save your gym selfies and political rants for other platforms (if at all).

Your Company LinkedIn Page

Your company page is where your brand lives. It's the hub for sharing your services, company culture, and thought leadership. Make it visually appealing with a professional logo, a banner that reflects your brand, and a succinct but compelling "About" section. Regular updates are key – think articles, videos, case studies, and testimonials demonstrating your expertise and success stories.

Free LinkedIn Marketing Strategies: Big Impact, Small Budget

Marketing doesn't always mean spending money. LinkedIn offers a host of free tools and strategies that can yield significant results if used consistently.

Consistent Content Posting: Share content that aligns with your audience's interests and pain points. For example, a post titled "5 Common Security Gaps Small Businesses Overlook" can resonate deeply. Use a mix of articles, infographics, and short videos to keep your feed diverse and engaging.

Engagement with Industry Peers: Building relationships isn't just about posting; it's about engaging. Comment thoughtfully on others' posts, participate in discussions, and share insights. It's like networking at a conference but without the awkward small talk.

Leverage LinkedIn Groups: Join groups relevant to your niche, such as "Corporate Security Professionals" or "Cybersecurity Experts." Be active – answer questions, share your expertise, and establish yourself as a go-to resource.

Showcase Testimonials and Case Studies: Nothing builds trust like proof. Share testimonials from happy clients or post about a project where your expertise made a tangible difference. For example, "How We Helped a Mid-Sized Business Reduce Security Incidents by 40%."

Collaborate with Influencers: Connect with influencers in your niche and explore collaborations. For example, co-authoring a post or co-hosting a webinar can dramatically expand your reach.

Paid LinkedIn Marketing: Expanding Your Reach

When you're ready to invest, LinkedIn's paid marketing tools allow you to laser-focus on your ideal clients. Here's how to make the most of them:

LinkedIn offers various ad formats, including Sponsored Content, Text Ads, and Message Ads. Each serves a different purpose, from driving website traffic to generating leads.

Targeting Your Audience

One of LinkedIn's biggest strengths is its precise targeting capabilities. You can filter by job title, industry, company size, geography, etc. For instance, if you specialize in cybersecurity, you might target IT managers in mid-sized companies in the finance sector.

Crafting Effective Ads

A great LinkedIn ad has three key ingredients:

Attention-Grabbing Headline: For example, "Is Your Business Prepared for the Next Cyber Threat?"

Engaging Visuals: Use high-quality images or videos that are professional and relevant.

Clear Call-to-Action: Whether it's downloading a whitepaper or booking a free consultation, make what you want the audience to do obvious.

Case Study: A LinkedIn Ad That Worked

A security consultant specializing in event security ran a Sponsored Content campaign targeting event planners in major metro areas. The ad offered a free checklist titled "10 Must-Have Security Measures for Events." The result? A 25% increase in inquiries and two major contracts secured within a month.

Checklist for Launching a LinkedIn Campaign

Optimize Personal and Company Pages: Ensure they're professional and aligned with your brand.

Define Campaign Goals: Whether it's lead generation or brand awareness, know your "why."

Identify Target Audience: Use LinkedIn's demographic tools to narrow down your ideal clients.

Plan Content Calendar: Map out the next month's articles, videos, and updates.

Set a Budget for Ads: Start small to test what works before scaling.

Engage Consistently: Build relationships by responding to comments (constructively, objectively, and unemotionally) and participating in discussions.

By blending free and paid strategies, LinkedIn can become a cornerstone of your digital marketing efforts. It's not just about broadcasting your services; it's about building genuine connections, demonstrating your expertise, and staying top-of-mind for your audience. Ready to start posting? The LinkedIn stage is set – step into the spotlight.

Facebook: Creating a Professional Presence and Maximizing Engagement

Facebook is no longer just a platform to share vacation pictures and memes; it's a digital powerhouse with over 2.9 billion active users worldwide. It represents an unparalleled opportunity for security consultants to engage with a vast audience, establish credibility, and build lasting professional relationships. However, the key to Facebook's success lies in understanding its dual role: a stage for professional outreach and a personal sandbox – both of which must be managed with care.

Separate but Equal: Personal and Business Pages

Having a distinct Facebook page for your security consulting business is critical. Your business page acts as your storefront – a professional hub where potential clients, collaborators, and partners can find information about your services, expertise, and insights. This is where you post case studies, blog posts, links to your website, share helpful security tips, and professionally interact with your audience.

On the other hand, your personal page is just that – personal. However, in today's connected world, your personal brand can often intersect with your professional reputation. Clients or partners may look you up, so it's essential to present yourself in a way that aligns with the image you want your business to convey.

The Art of Personal Page Management

Your personal page doesn't need to mimic your business page, but it should reflect your values and professionalism. Posting photos from a family barbecue? Totally fine. Sharing your political hot takes or controversial memes? Not so much. If you want a personal page where you can let loose, consider creating a second private profile with strict privacy settings. This way, you can compartmentalize your life without risking your professional reputation.

Free Marketing Strategies: Building Relationships and Credibility

Facebook offers a wealth of free tools that make it easy to market your business, even if you're working on a shoestring budget. Here's how to leverage these tools effectively:

Creating a Business Page: Your business page is your professional headquarters. Fill out every section, from the "About" tab to your contact information. Use a high-quality profile picture (like your logo) and a visually appealing cover photo that represents your brand.

Pro tip: Keep your branding consistent across platforms. If your LinkedIn page has a sleek blue-and-white theme, carry that over to your Facebook page for uniformity.

Sharing Value-Driven Content: Engage your audience with posts that provide value. Think security tips, how-to guides, or insights into recent industry trends. For example, a post like "5 Ways to Improve Your Home Security Without Breaking the Bank" could resonate with both corporate clients and individual homeowners. Also, try and make them seasonal, "3 Ways Your Black Friday Shopping Can Be Safer", etc.

Interacting with Communities: Join local business groups or industry-specific Facebook groups to engage with others in your field. Comment on discussions, answer questions, and share your expertise. Remember, you're not just selling services but building trust and relationships.

Pro Tip: There are a LOT of trolls out there. It's nearly impossible to avoid them. DO NOT ENGAGE. Even when you are 100% in the right (and you are), it does NOT pay to get in the mud. At the very minimum, ignore it. If you can't do that, acknowledge the poster's right to their opinion, thank them for the comment, and move on. In the history of social media, no one has EVER been able to convince someone else that they are right and the other is wrong. Trust me, others are watching to see how you handle conflict resolution and de-escalation, two essential qualities of a security consultant.

Paid Marketing Strategies: Amplifying Your Reach

Facebook's paid advertising options can significantly expand your reach when your budget allows. Here's how to get started:

Defining Your Target Audience: Facebook ads are powerful because they let you zero in on your ideal audience. You can target users based on demographics (age, gender, location), interests (home security, business management), and even behaviors (online shopping habits, frequent travelers).

For example, if you specialize in corporate security, you might target decision-makers in specific industries, like finance or tech, within a 50-mile radius of your business location.

Crafting a Compelling Ad: A great Facebook ad has three main components:

- A clear headline: Grab attention with something like, "Are Your Business Premises Really Secure?"
- Engaging visuals: Use high-quality images or videos that illustrate your services in action.
- A strong call-to-action (CTA): Encourage users to take the next step, whether it's "Learn More," "Schedule a Free Consultation," or "Download Our Security Checklist."

Tracking Performance: Use Facebook's Ads Manager to monitor metrics like click-through rates (CTR), impressions, and conversions. This data will help you refine your strategy and improve future campaigns.

Storytelling and Engagement: Bringing Your Brand to Life

People don't just want services – they want stories. Facebook is an ideal platform for sharing the narrative behind your brand.

Highlight Success Stories: Share case studies or testimonials from satisfied clients. For example, post about how your consulting services helped a local business reduce security breaches by 30%. Pair this with a before-and-after photo or a short video.

Pro Tip: After every contract, I follow up with my Program Manager or Client to ensure they found every phase of my service and products to their liking. If they are pleased (if they aren't, I ensure I fix it immediately!), I transition to request a testimonial or positive review to share publicly. I often offer to write it and send it to them for approval so I can choose what aspects I want to be highlighted (that's a Pro Tip within a Pro Tip!). I will usually put these on our website and our FB page.

Go Behind the Scenes: Post "day in the life" content to humanize your brand. A quick video showing how you conduct security assessments or prepare for a consultation can make your business more relatable.

Celebrate Milestones: Did you land a major client or receive a professional certification? Share the news! These posts not only showcase your expertise but also keep your audience engaged.

Checklist: Before You Launch Your Facebook Campaign

To wrap up this subcategory, here's a quick reference checklist to ensure your Facebook marketing efforts are on point:

Personal Page:

- Ensure your personal profile reflects professionalism.
- Lock down privacy settings for non-business-related content.

Business Page:

- Complete all sections, including "About" and contact details.

- Use high-quality visuals that align with your brand.
- Post regularly with value-driven content.

Free Marketing:

- Join and engage with relevant Facebook groups.
- Share posts that educate and inspire your audience.

Paid Marketing:

- Define your target audience using Facebook's robust tools.
- Craft ads with compelling headlines, visuals, and CTAs.
- Monitor and optimize your campaigns based on performance metrics.

When used wisely, Facebook can be a game-changer for your security consulting business. It's not just about selling – it's about connecting, educating, and building trust. By mastering both free and paid marketing strategies, you'll position yourself as a leader in your niche while reaching clients you might never have connected with otherwise.

Twitter: Building Connections in 280 Characters or Less

Twitter isn't just a platform for breaking news and viral memes; it's a digital cocktail party where professionals, industry leaders, and curious minds gather to share ideas, insights, and, yes – occasionally, argue over the best pizza topping. For security consultants, Twitter offers a fast-paced and versatile way to engage with your audience, establish authority, and stay on top of industry trends.

Unlike other platforms, Twitter thrives on immediacy. It's about being part of the conversation as it happens. And with nearly 400 million active users, it's a conversation worth joining. Whether you're sharing the latest on cybersecurity breaches or offering quick tips on physical security, Twitter allows you to position yourself as a thought leader in real-time.

Free Marketing on Twitter: Conversations That Count

If you're on a tight budget (and let's face it, most startups are), Twitter offers a variety of free tools to get your message out there. Here's how to make the most of them:

Share Industry News and Insights: Twitter is the perfect platform to share bite-sized updates on what's happening in the security world. For instance:

Example: "A recent report shows a 25% increase in cyberattacks on small businesses. Here's how to stay protected: [link] #Cybersecurity #Small-BizSecurity"

By staying on top of trends and sharing relevant news, you demonstrate that you're plugged into the pulse of the industry – a trusted source of knowledge.

Provide Quick Tips: Offer actionable advice in 280 characters or less. These can be anything from home security tips to corporate safety protocols.

Example: "Did you know? Leaving a TV on when you're out can deter burglars. Simple, yet effective. #HomeSecurity #SafetyTips"

Engage in Conversations: Search for hashtags like #SecurityConsulting, #CyberSecurity, or #WorkplaceSafety to find discussions relevant to your niche. Join in with thoughtful comments or retweets.

Example: Someone tweets, "What's the most overlooked aspect of office security?" Your reply: "People often forget about employee training. A well-informed team can prevent costly mistakes. #OfficeSafety"

Paid Advertising on Twitter: Amplify Your Message

Once you've built a baseline audience, consider scaling up with Twitter's paid options. Here's how to maximize your investment:

Promoted Tweets: These are standard tweets that you pay to push to a larger audience. Promoted tweets are great for driving traffic to a specific service or blog post.

Example: A security consultant promoting a blog post titled "Top 10 Office Security Mistakes You're Probably Making."

Targeted Advertising: Twitter's ad platform allows you to zero in on your audience using parameters like location, interests, and behaviors. For example, you could target HR professionals and facility managers in metropolitan areas if you specialize in corporate security.

Analytics and Optimization: Twitter Ads Manager provides detailed metrics like impressions, clicks, and engagement rates. Use this data to tweak your strategy and improve your ROI.

Best Practices: Tweeting With Purpose

Twitter's fast-paced environment can be both a blessing and a curse. To stand out, you'll need to follow a few golden rules:

Stay Professional, Even on Personal Accounts: Much like Facebook and LinkedIn, your personal Twitter account should reflect your professionalism. A tweet about a thrilling football game? Fine. A rant about politics? Maybe keep that in the drafts.

If you want to tweet about personal passions that might not align with your business persona, consider having a separate private account. Lock it down tight with privacy settings.

Timing Is Everything: Tweets have a short lifespan – about 15 minutes of peak visibility. Use scheduling tools like Hootsuite or Buffer to post during high-traffic times, typically mid-morning and late afternoon.

Engage Authentically: Twitter is a two-way street. Don't just broadcast – interact. Retweet peers, reply to comments, and start conversations.

Storytelling on Twitter: Share Your Journey

Twitter's character limit may seem restrictive, but it's an excellent tool for sharing snippets of your professional journey.

Share Milestones: Land a major client? Finish a significant project? Share it!

Example: "Proud to have helped [Company Name] implement a comprehensive office security plan. Success feels great! #SecurityConsulting #ClientSuccess"

Behind-the-Scenes Content: People love getting a peek behind the curtain. Post a photo or video of your team setting up a security audit or testing new tech.

Example: "Testing out the latest in drone detection technology today. The future of security is here! #SecurityTech #DroneDefense"

Checklist: Before You Launch a Twitter Marketing Campaign

Profile Setup:

- Use a professional profile picture and cover image.
- Write a concise but impactful bio that highlights your niche.

Content Strategy:

- Plan a mix of news, tips, and behind-the-scenes content.
- Schedule tweets for optimal visibility.

Engagement:

- Search relevant hashtags and join discussions.

- Reply to comments and retweets authentically.

Paid Ads:

- Define your target audience with precision.
- Create compelling tweets with strong CTAs.

Twitter's simplicity and immediacy make it a powerful tool for security consultants. By balancing free and paid strategies, engaging authentically, and staying professional, you can turn 280 characters into connections that matter. It's not just about tweeting – it's about building trust, authority, and a community that values your expertise.

Instagram: A Picture Is Worth a Thousand Clients

Instagram might not scream "security consulting" at first glance, but it's a goldmine for visual storytelling and brand building. With over 2 billion monthly active users, it's a platform where businesses can showcase their personality, expertise, and services in creative, attention-getting ways. The adage holds true: people trust what they see. For security consultants, Instagram is an opportunity to turn abstract concepts like "threat mitigation" into something tangible, relatable, and engaging.

The Basics: Setting Up Shop on Instagram

Before diving into strategy, let's ensure your presence on Instagram is as professional as your consulting services. Like other platforms, having a business and personal account is essential. Why? Because your clients don't need to know about your cat's 15-minute standoff with a paper bag (as entertaining as that might be).

Setting Up Your Business Account

Choose a Professional Username: Ideally, your company name or a variation that's easy to remember.

Optimize Your Bio: Use clear, concise language to describe what you do and who you help. Add a link to your website or a specific landing page.

Example: "We protect what matters most. Expert security solutions for businesses and families. Click below to learn more. 🔒"

Profile Picture: Use your logo for instant brand recognition.

Keeping Personal and Business Separate

If you want to share personal, potentially controversial, or overly casual content, keep it confined to a private personal account. Use Instagram's privacy settings to ensure your personal musings don't inadvertently mix with your professional persona.

Free Marketing on Instagram: Creativity Without a Price Tag

Instagram's free tools allow you to reach your audience effectively, provided you're consistent and strategic. Here are a few approaches:

Share Your Expertise Through Visuals: Instagram thrives on visuals, so leverage photos, infographics, and short videos to communicate your value.

Example: Post an infographic on the Top 5 Cybersecurity Threats of 2024 with a caption offering tips to mitigate them.

Use Stories and Reels: Instagram Stories and Reels are perfect for showcasing quick tips or behind-the-scenes moments. They're temporary (Stories disappear after 24 hours unless saved as Highlights), so they feel spontaneous and approachable.

Example Story: "Heading into a corporate security audit – here's what we're looking for!" accompanied by a photo of a checklist.

Example Reel: A 15-second demo of the latest surveillance tech.

Leverage Hashtags: Use hashtags strategically to increase discoverability.

Mix popular ones like #SecurityConsulting with niche-specific ones like #DroneDefense or #CyberRisk.

Example: "Conducting a risk assessment for an UHNW client. Details matter. #SecurityConsulting #EstateSecurity #RiskManagement"

Paid Advertising on Instagram: Leveling Up

Once you've established a solid presence, it's time to consider Instagram's paid options for targeted advertising.

Sponsored Posts: Boost your best-performing organic posts to reach a wider audience.

Example: If your post on office security tips performs well, turn it into a sponsored ad targeting HR managers and office admins.

Story Ads: These full-screen ads appear seamlessly between user Stories. Use them to promote services, events, or blog posts.

Example Story Ad: "Is your office prepared for the unexpected? Swipe up for a free security consultation."

Carousel Ads: These allow you to showcase multiple images or videos in a single ad. Perfect for highlighting the range of your services.

Example Carousel Ad: Frame 1: Corporate Security Solutions. Frame 2: Risk Assessments. Frame 3: Security Training.

What to Post: Inspiring and Informing Your Audience

Instagram is the place to showcase what you do and how you do it. Here's what works:

Client Success Stories: Showcase anonymized case studies or testimonials with visuals that illustrate the impact of your work.

Example Post: A blurred-out image of a corporate office with the caption: "We helped secure this workspace, protecting their most valuable assets. Ask us how! #ClientSuccess #SecurityConsulting"

Quick Tips: Create bite-sized advice posts, like:

Example Post: "Heading out of town? Use timers on your lights to deter potential intruders. #HomeSecurityTips"

Educational Content: Share posts that educate your audience about the latest trends or threats.

Example Post: A graphic showing the rise of ransomware attacks with a caption explaining how businesses can stay protected.

Checklist: Instagram Success at a Glance

Professional Profile:

- The bio is straightforward and includes a call-to-action link.
- The profile picture is recognizable and professional.

Content Plan:

- Include a mix of visuals, videos, and infographics.
- Use Stories and Reels for quick, engaging updates.

Engagement:

- Respond to comments and DMs promptly.
- Engage with industry peers and related businesses.
- Hashtag Strategy: Research and use a mix of popular and niche hashtags.

Ad Campaigns:

- Define your audience by interests, behaviors, and demographics.
- Create visually compelling, informative ads with clear CTAs.

Instagram offers security consultants an unparalleled opportunity to connect, inform, and inspire in a highly visual and engaging way. By combining free strategies with paid options and maintaining a professional yet personable tone, you'll transform your feed into a dynamic showcase of your expertise. Now, grab your camera (or smartphone) and start snapping – your audience is waiting!

YouTube: Lights, Camera, Security Consulting!

Let's face it – YouTube is often their first stop when people want answers or need to learn something. As the second-largest search engine (right after Google) with 2.6 billion monthly active users, it's a goldmine for security consultants to educate, engage, and build trust with potential clients. Whether you're explaining the intricacies of a risk assessment or showcasing the latest in surveillance tech, YouTube is your stage, and the world is your audience.

Setting Up Your YouTube Channel

Before you hit "record," let's prepare your digital stage. A polished, professional channel is the foundation for all your video efforts.

- Create a Branded Channel
- Use your company name for consistency.
- Add a professional profile picture (typically your logo) and a visually appealing banner that reflects your brand.
- About Section: Your "About" section is your elevator pitch to the world. Be concise but impactful:

Example: "At [Your Company Name], we specialize in [Your Niche], delivering cutting-edge security solutions for [Your Target Audience]. Subscribe for expert tips, industry insights, and practical advice to protect what matters most."

Channel Trailer: Create a short video (under 2 minutes) introducing your business, services, and the value viewers can expect from your channel.

Free Strategies: Building an Audience Without Breaking the Bank

YouTube thrives on consistency and value. Here's how to leverage its free features:

Educational Content: Establish yourself as an authority by sharing practical advice and insights.

Example Video: "5 Steps to Conduct a Basic Home Security Audit". Use simple visuals and actionable tips that viewers can immediately apply.

Demonstration Videos: Showcase your expertise through walkthroughs and tutorials.

Example Video: A hands-on demonstration of setting up a wireless security camera system.

Client Success Stories: With permission, share anonymized case studies to illustrate the impact of your work.

Example Video: "How We Secured a Fortune 500 Office in 48 Hours" (with lots of blurred-out visuals, of course).

Behind-the-Scenes Content: People love to see the human side of businesses. Share your process or introduce your team.

Example Video: A day in the life of a security consultant.

Q&A Sessions: Answer common questions about your services or industry trends. This builds trust and engagement.

Example Video: "What's the Difference Between Surveillance and Counter-Surveillance?"

Paid YouTube Advertising: Amplify Your Reach

Skippable In-Stream Ads: These ads play before or during videos and can be skipped after five seconds. They're great for introducing your brand to a broader audience.

Example Ad: "Is your business ready for the unexpected? Learn how we can help secure your future."

Non-Skippable In-Stream Ads: These ads force viewers to watch for up to 15 seconds. Use this format for concise, high-impact messaging.

Example Ad: "15 seconds to peace of mind. Here's how we protect what matters most."

Discovery Ads: These ads appear alongside YouTube search results or related videos. Perfect for targeting viewers searching for security-related content.

Example Ad: A thumbnail titled, "5 Tips to Secure Your Small Business" with a compelling description.

Bumper Ads: Six-second, non-skippable ads that reinforce brand awareness.

Example Ad: "Secure your home in six seconds – call us today!"

What to Post: Tailoring Your Content for Maximum Impact

Industry Insights: Break down complex topics into digestible, viewer-friendly videos.

Example Video: "What Are the Top Security Threats in 2024?"

Product Reviews and Recommendations: Position yourself as a trusted advisor by reviewing tools and technologies.

Example Video: "Our Top 3 Picks for Business Surveillance Systems in 2024."

Event Coverage: If you attend industry events, share highlights with your audience.

Example Video: "Top Takeaways from the Global Security Expo."

Community Engagement: Highlight partnerships or give back to your community.

Example Video: "How We Partnered with Local Schools to Improve Campus Safety."

Thought Leadership: Host discussions or interviews with other experts in your niche.

Example Video: "Cybersecurity Trends: An Expert Panel Discussion."

Best Practices for Security Consultants on YouTube

Optimize Your Titles and Descriptions

- Include keywords for searchability.
- Add timestamps for longer videos to help viewers navigate.

Example Title: "10 Security Tips for Small Businesses (2024 Edition)"

Use Eye-Catching Thumbnails: Thumbnails are the first impression your video makes. Keep them clean, professional, and enticing.

Example: A split-screen thumbnail showing "Before" and "After" results of a security upgrade.

Engage with Comments: Responding to viewer comments builds community and trust. Plus, it boosts your video's ranking in YouTube's algorithm.

Consistency is Key: Stick to a posting schedule, whether weekly, bi-weekly, or monthly. Let your audience know when to expect new content.

Analyze and Adapt: Use YouTube Analytics to track which videos perform best and adjust your strategy accordingly.

Checklist: YouTube Success for Security Consultants

Channel Setup: Professional branding with a clear bio and channel trailer.

Content Plan: A mix of educational, demonstrative, and engaging content.

SEO Optimization: Keywords in titles, descriptions, and tags.

Engagement: Respond to comments and encourage interaction.

Advertising Strategy: Targeted ads tailored to your niche audience.

YouTube isn't just a platform for funny cat videos or makeup tutorials; it's a powerhouse for building your brand, establishing authority, and reaching your target audience in a dynamic and engaging way. Committing to consistent, high-quality content can turn your channel into a magnet for new clients and collaborators. Ready to hit record? The world is waiting to hear what you have to say.

SEO for Security Services Websites

Search Engine Optimization (SEO) might sound like something techies in Silicon Valley whisper over their vegan kale salads, but in reality, it's a game-changer for any business operating in today's digital age. SEO is the practice of optimizing your website to improve its visibility in search engine results. In simpler terms, it's about ensuring your website appears on the first page of Google (or Bing, if you're feeling quirky) when someone searches for your services.

For security consultants, SEO is particularly crucial. Why? Because clients rarely stroll into your office asking about surveillance camera placement or emergency response plans. Instead, they search online for phrases like "corporate security consulting," "risk management experts," or "best security consultants near me." If your website isn't optimized to pop up during these searches, you're losing potential business before you even get a chance to make your pitch.

Breaking Down SEO: The Foundations

Keywords are Key: At the heart of SEO lies keyword optimization. Keywords are the words and phrases people type into search engines. Identifying the right ones is like finding the secret handshake to a private club. For security consultants, effective keywords might include "event security planning," "residential security assessment," or "cybersecurity consultant for small businesses."

To find these golden nuggets, tools like Google Keyword Planner, Ahrefs, and SEMrush are your best friends. They'll show you which terms are most searched and least competitive, giving you a fighting chance to rank higher.

Content is King: Once you know your keywords, you need content that includes them naturally. Emphasis on "naturally." Stuffing keywords into every sentence like a turkey on Thanksgiving will only make your site look spammy. Instead, write helpful, engaging blogs, service pages, and FAQs that genuinely answer potential clients' questions.

Backlinks: The Votes of Confidence: Imagine SEO as a popularity contest. Backlinks are votes from other websites saying, "This site is legit!" The more quality backlinks you have, the more search engines trust your site. Consider writing guest blogs for industry websites or collaborating with partners who will link back to your site.

Technical SEO: Think of this as the nuts and bolts of your site. Is it mobile-friendly? Does it load faster than your grandmother's internet in 1997? Technical SEO ensures your website functions smoothly and offers a great user experience, which search engines prioritize.

Why SEO is Perfect for Security Consultants

As much as we hate to admit it, security consulting isn't a flashy industry. You're not selling the latest iPhone or a trending TikTok gadget. Your clients are typically serious and professional and often need your expertise urgently. SEO allows you to position yourself as a trusted authority, even before the first handshake.

Take this example: Imagine you specialize in cybersecurity for small businesses. A bakery owner who just experienced a data breach isn't scrolling Instagram for memes – they're Googling "how to secure my business after a cyber-attack." A well-optimized site puts your expertise front and center, helping you convert desperate searches into paying clients.

Free vs. Paid SEO Tools

Here's the good news: you don't need a Ph.D. in computer science or a Fortune 500 budget to make SEO work for you. There are plenty of free tools to help you get started:

- Google Analytics: Tracks your website's performance and user behavior.
- Google Search Console: Identifies issues affecting your search engine rankings.
- Ubersuggest: Offers keyword suggestions and competitive analysis.

Investing in paid tools like SEMrush or Ahrefs can offer deeper insights and advanced features to supercharge your SEO efforts as your business grows.

Avoiding Common SEO Pitfalls: SEO is a long game. If someone promises to get you on the first page of Google overnight, they're either lying or using "black hat" techniques that could get your site penalized. Patience and persistence are key.

Focusing solely on aesthetics: This is another common mistake. A beautifully designed website is useless if it's invisible to your audience. Always prioritize functionality and optimization alongside visual appeal.

Beyond SEO, The Bigger Picture:

SEO isn't just about getting clicks; it's about converting those clicks into loyal clients. Once potential clients land on your site, your content should guide them seamlessly toward acting – whether filling out a contact form, booking a consultation, or downloading a free resource.

Visualizing SEO Success: Imagine your SEO strategy as a well-oiled machine. Keywords are the fuel, content is the engine, and technical SEO is the framework that holds it all together. When every component works harmoniously, your website becomes a powerful magnet for attracting and converting leads.

Why SEO Deserves Your Attention

If you've made it this far, you now know more about SEO than 90% of your competitors. Remember, SEO isn't a one-and-done task; it's an ongoing effort that evolves alongside search engine algorithms and market trends. Investing time in SEO today ensures that your security consulting business has a steady stream of potential clients tomorrow. It's like planting a tree – nurture it well, and it will grow into a towering asset for your business.

Now, let's move on to the next frontier of digital marketing: email campaigns. But first, let's celebrate your new SEO savvy with your favorite energy and a high five. You've earned it!

Targeted Email Campaigns: Making Every Click Count

In the vast digital marketing arena, few tools match a well-orchestrated email campaign's cost-effectiveness and direct reach. It's the digital equivalent of slipping a handwritten note into someone's mailbox –

personal, deliberate, and, when done right, extraordinarily effective. Let's dissect the art and science of targeted email campaigns to equip you with the know-how to use them for your security consulting business.

What Is a Targeted Email Campaign?

At its core, a targeted email campaign is a strategic approach to sending tailored messages to specific groups of people. Unlike mass emails that scream, "Hello, I'm generic!" targeted campaigns are precise, addressing the recipient's unique needs, preferences, or behaviors. Think of it as a sniper shot of marketing rather than a shotgun blast.

The beauty of email campaigns lies in their ability to nurture leads, build trust, and convert prospects into clients. For security consultants, this means sharing insights about your niche, showcasing your services, or offering solutions to potential client's pain points – all while staying top-of-mind in their inboxes.

Why Are Targeted Email Campaigns Beneficial?

Cost-Effective Marketing: Emails are inexpensive compared to other forms of advertising. You can reach hundreds (or thousands) of potential clients with minimal investment.

Personalized Engagement: Emails that feel personal often outperform generic messages. Addressing your recipient by name and tailoring content to their interests fosters connection and trust.

High ROI: According to the Data & Marketing Association, the average ROI for email marketing is $42 for every $1 spent. That's a return even the savviest Wall Street investor would envy.

Trackable and Measurable: Email platforms allow you to track open rates, click-through rates, and conversions. This data helps refine your strategy over time.

How Do Targeted Email Campaigns Work?

Effective campaigns rely on three critical components: a solid email list, relevant content, and an easy way to measure success.

Building Your Email List:

- Start by compiling a database of potential clients. Leverage your existing network, ask for referrals, or use sign-up forms on your website.
- Offer a value proposition, such as a free eBook on risk management or a complimentary security consultation, to encourage sign-ups.
- Remember to comply with GDPR and CAN-SPAM regulations. No one likes unsolicited emails, and legal penalties are not worth the risk.

Segmenting Your Audience: Divide your list based on factors like industry, company size, or service needs. For instance, CEOs of small businesses might appreciate tips on budget-friendly security solutions, while large corporations may prefer insights on scalable risk management systems.

Crafting Irresistible Content:

- Headlines are crucial. A subject line like "Are Your Security Protocols Up to Par?" piques curiosity without resorting to clickbait.
- Keep the body concise but informative. Use bullet points or short paragraphs for readability.

Services to Help You Master Email Campaigns

Whether you're on a shoestring budget or ready to splurge, there's an email marketing service for you:

Free Options:

- Mailchimp: Ideal for beginners, offering up to 500 contacts on their free plan.
- HubSpot: A robust CRM platform with a generous free tier.
- MailerLite: Excellent for startups, featuring drag-and-drop editors and automation.

Paid Platforms:

- Constant Contact: Known for its user-friendly interface and real-time analytics.
- ActiveCampaign: Great for automation enthusiasts, with features like lead scoring and advanced segmentation.
- Klaviyo: Perfect for businesses wanting deep analytics and powerful integrations.

A Checklist for Successful Email Campaigns

Before you hit "send," run through this quick list:

Is the Subject Line Engaging? Your subject line is your first impression – make it count.

Have You Segmented Your List? Targeted content yields better results.

Does the Email Look Professional? Double-check spelling, grammar, formatting, and mobile responsiveness.

Is There a Clear Call-to-Action (CTA)? Tell readers what to do next, whether it's scheduling a consultation or downloading your latest guide.

Have You Tested the Email? Send test emails to your colleagues and ensure everything works as intended.

Targeted email campaigns are your golden ticket to building meaningful relationships with potential clients. Done correctly, they're not just a marketing tactic but a bridge to trust, credibility, and long-term partnerships. Start small, experiment, and refine your strategy over time. With patience and persistence, your emails won't just sit unopened – they'll spark conversations and opportunities.

Traditional Marketing Techniques for the Security Consultant

Marketing, as we've delved into already, is the oxygen of any business, and traditional methods remain as relevant as ever, especially for a niche industry like security consulting. In a world dominated by digital platforms, there's something refreshingly personal and effective about handing a polished brochure to a potential client or shaking hands at an industry event. But here's the catch: while traditional marketing can be incredibly impactful, it's also where budgets can disappear faster than donuts in a break room.

It's vital to approach traditional marketing with the same scrutiny as digital strategies. Unlike Facebook ads or email campaigns, traditional marketing often demands more upfront investment with outcomes that are harder to measure. That's why you, as a security entrepreneur, need a laser-focused approach to ensure every dollar delivers value.

Print Materials and Brochures

There's a tactile magic to holding a high-quality brochure in your hands. For many security consultants, print materials are the first impression of their brand – and we all know how much first impressions count.

Brochures and other print materials can convey professionalism and provide a tangible takeaway. Whether left behind after a meeting or handed out at a trade show, these materials serve as silent ambassadors for your brand.

Your print materials should:

Highlight Your Expertise: Include a brief section on your niche and services.

Showcase Testimonials: Real-world success stories build trust.

Include Contact Information: Make it ridiculously easy to reach you.

Invest in high-quality paper and printing. Remember, if it looks cheap, it screams, "I don't take my business seriously."

A Tip on Distribution: Think strategically about where to leave your brochures. Industry conferences, law enforcement offices (with permission), or professional associations are excellent spots.

Industry Conferences and Speaking Engagements

Conferences are not just places to listen and learn – they're prime opportunities to showcase your expertise and rub shoulders with potential clients.

The ROI of Presence: Simply attending a conference with your name tag isn't enough. Aim to get on stage as a speaker if you want to stand out. Sharing insights on your niche can position you as a thought leader and magnetize clients toward you.

Tips for Success:

Research the Audience: Tailor your content to the attendees.

Prepare a Killer Elevator Pitch: You'll meet countless people; make your intro count.

Follow-up: After the conference, connect on LinkedIn or send a follow-up email.

Don't forget to bring plenty of business cards (yes, they're still relevant) and leave them with everyone you meet. You never know which contact could turn into a contract.

Networking with Law Enforcement and Corporate Clients

The security consulting field thrives on relationships, and networking with law enforcement and corporate clients can open doors to lucrative opportunities.

Law enforcement professionals often have insider knowledge of businesses that might need your services. Similarly, corporate security teams frequently outsource projects requiring specialized expertise. Establishing rapport with these groups is essential.

Attend Local Events: Many police departments host community events that are great networking opportunities.

Offer Value First: Provide insights or offer assistance before pitching your services.

Maintain Professionalism: Always respect the boundaries of law enforcement and corporate professionals – they value credibility and integrity.

A Word of Caution: ROI in Traditional Marketing: It's tempting to throw money at every ad opportunity, but traditional marketing can be a money pit if not executed strategically. Newspaper ads are great for a local bakery but can fall flat for security consultants targeting corporate clients. Continually evaluate the cost vs. potential return and track outcomes wherever possible.

Traditional marketing techniques add a personal touch that complements your digital strategies. Done right, they can amplify your brand, build trust, and secure clients. However, approach these methods with caution and precision to avoid unnecessary expenses.

To round off this section, here's a quick checklist for assessing the effectiveness of traditional marketing campaigns:

Checklist: Assessing Traditional Marketing Campaigns

Does this campaign target your ideal client?

Is the message clear, concise, and compelling?

Have you defined measurable goals for success (e.g., new leads, increased awareness)?

Does the cost justify the potential return?

Have you allocated resources for follow-up with leads generated by the campaign?

Traditional marketing isn't about choosing one technique over another – it's about crafting a balanced strategy that blends digital savviness with old-school relationship building. Together, these approaches will ensure you stand out in the crowded security consulting field.

Creating a Marketing Budget for a Security Business

Crafting a marketing budget is like mapping a financial blueprint directly tied to your security consulting business's growth and sustainability. Without it, you risk over- or under-spending, which can be disastrous for a startup. A well-thought-out marketing budget ensures that every dollar you spend aligns with your strategic goals and provides measurable returns. Let's dig deep into the art and science of creating a marketing budget specifically tailored for security consulting businesses. This could get a bit intimidating for those who are not so inclined to math and formulas. Just breath. We'll get through it together.

What Percentage of the Budget Should Be Allocated to Marketing?

A general rule of thumb for most small businesses is to allocate 7–8% of gross revenue to marketing. However, this figure can range from 10–20% for startups since you're in the growth and client acquisition phase. This is especially true for a niche business like security consulting, where building credibility and trust is paramount.

Example: If your anticipated gross revenue is $100,000, allocate $10,000–$20,000 to marketing efforts in the first year. This might sound steep but think of it as an investment in visibility and lead generation.

Understanding Customer Acquisition Costs (CAC)

Your Customer Acquisition Cost (CAC) is the total cost associated with acquiring a new client. Knowing this figure helps you evaluate whether your marketing strategies are efficient. To calculate CAC, use this formula:

CAC=Total Marketing and Sales Spend divided by the Number of New Clients Acquired

Example: If you spent $10,000 on marketing last quarter and acquired ten new clients, your CAC is $1,000 per client.

Tracking CAC ensures you're spending wisely. If your CAC is higher than the lifetime value (LTV) of a client, your marketing approach needs recalibration.

Evaluating ROI on Marketing Expenditures

Return on Investment (ROI) is the key metric determining whether your marketing efforts are paying off. Calculate it using:

ROI= (Revenue from Marketing Efforts minus the amount you spent on Marketing) divided by the amount you spent on marketing

Example: If you spent $5,000 on a campaign that generated $15,000 in revenue, the ROI is:

ROI = (15,000–5,000) divided by 5,000 = 2 or 200%

A positive ROI indicates your campaigns are working, while a negative ROI suggests adjustments are needed.

Key Marketing Channels to Budget For: In this chapter, we've discussed all kinds of digital and traditional marketing techniques. So, how do you decide how much of your marketing budget should be allocated to the different methods? Here's a suggestion:

Digital Advertising (40–50%): Includes SEO, PPC campaigns, and social media ads. Digital platforms provide measurable results, making them a priority for many security businesses.

Content Marketing (20–30%): Blogs, eBooks, and educational videos position you as a thought leader in the industry.

Networking and Events (15–20%): Conferences, trade shows, and speaking engagements are excellent for building credibility and generating leads.

Traditional Marketing (10–15%): Print materials, direct mail campaigns, and local ads may have a smaller footprint but can still yield results, especially for local clients.

Practical Steps to Create Your Marketing Budget

Set Clear Goals: Are you aiming to increase brand awareness, generate leads, or improve client retention? Your goals dictate your spending priorities.

Analyze Competitors: Study competitors' marketing strategies and budget allocations to benchmark your efforts.

Evaluate Marketing Tools: Invest in CRM software, analytics tools, and automated email marketing platforms like HubSpot or MailChimp. These tools often have tiered pricing, allowing flexibility for startups.

Plan for Flexibility: Set aside 10–15% of your marketing budget for unforeseen opportunities or experimental campaigns.

Common Mistakes to Avoid

Underestimating Costs: Thinking social media is "free" often leads to under-budgeting. While creating a profile is free, effective campaigns usually require paid boosts.

Ignoring ROI: Focusing on vanity metrics (e.g., likes or followers) instead of conversion metrics can drain your budget.

One-Size-Fits-All Budgeting: Every business is unique. Customize your budget based on your specific goals and market.

Checklist for Crafting Your Marketing Budget

Determine Your Revenue Goals: Define how much you aim to earn in the next quarter/year.

Track Past Spending: If applicable, review what worked and what didn't in previous campaigns.

Research Costs: From ad spending to event sponsorships, ensure your estimates are accurate.

Set Priorities: Focus on high-ROI activities before diversifying.

Monitor and Adjust: Revisit your budget monthly or quarterly to adjust based on performance.

Creating a marketing budget might not sound as thrilling as crafting a dynamic LinkedIn post or filming a YouTube demo, but it's the backbone of your marketing strategy. It ensures you're spending strategically, tracking progress, and driving your business forward. Remember, marketing is not an expense – it's an investment. By treating it as such and sticking to a well-planned budget, you're setting your security consulting business up for long-term success. Now, let's get those spreadsheets ready!

Chapter 9 Wrap-Up: Marketing Your Security Consulting Services

As we bring Chapter 9 to a close, let's take a moment to reflect on everything we've learned about marketing your security consulting services. This chapter has been a masterclass in understanding the power of digital and traditional marketing, and we've laid out practical strategies for creating a marketing budget tailored to your business needs.

Digital Marketing for Security Consultants

We kicked things off by exploring the vast digital landscape. Starting with LinkedIn, we discussed the platform's professional environment and the importance of creating polished profiles for yourself and your business. LinkedIn isn't just a virtual resume – it's a networking powerhouse that lets you position yourself as an expert while building a community of like-minded professionals.

From there, we dove into Facebook, emphasizing its versatility for both personal and business branding. We explored creating engaging posts, sharing valuable content, and the delicate balance between professional and personal personas.

Next up was Twitter, where brevity reigns supreme. Whether sharing breaking industry news, quick insights, or engaging in trending discussions, Twitter allows you to showcase your expertise in real-time.

Instagram brought a visual element to the table, focusing on imagery, client success stories, and bite-sized video content. Its appeal lies in humanizing your brand and making your services relatable to potential clients.

The heavy hitter, YouTube, was a gateway to more comprehensive content like webinars, how-to videos, and security demonstrations. It's the ultimate tool for building credibility through detailed, engaging, and value-packed video content.

We wrapped up with SEO for Security Services Websites and Targeted Email Campaigns, where we delved into the mechanics of optimizing your online presence and the power of personalized email outreach. Both strategies focus on making your business accessible to the right audience and staying top of mind with prospective clients.

Traditional Marketing Techniques

In the second section of the chapter, we took a step back from the digital world and examined Traditional Marketing Techniques. Print materials like brochures, though often overlooked, were highlighted for their ability to leave a tangible impression. Industry conferences and speaking engagements emerged as prime opportunities for real-world networking and demonstrating your expertise. Finally, we stressed the importance of building relationships with law enforcement and corporate clients, offering actionable tips to create partnerships that can lead to consistent business opportunities.

Creating a Marketing Budget for a Security Business

Finally, we tackled the often-intimidating task of Creating a Marketing Budget. Starting with a breakdown of typical marketing costs, we walked through how to calculate customer acquisition costs and assess the ROI of your campaigns. By identifying fixed and variable marketing expenses, we established a framework to ensure your spending aligns with your business goals.

We emphasized that marketing budgets aren't static; they evolve alongside your business. Starting with free or low-cost strategies allows for gradual scaling as you reinvest profits into more robust campaigns. We also discussed the importance of tracking and analyzing marketing efforts to refine strategies and ensure your dollars are working as hard as you are.

The Big Picture

Marketing can be a daunting aspect of running a business, especially if you're new to the game. However, this chapter proved that it's entirely possible to approach marketing with confidence and a clear plan. From leveraging free tools like social media to understanding when and where to spend on traditional marketing techniques, the strategies outlined here are designed to make marketing manageable, effective, and even enjoyable.

Remember, marketing isn't just about promoting your services; it's about building trust, demonstrating value, and connecting with your audience in meaningful ways. By mastering both digital and traditional marketing techniques, you're not just selling services – you're establishing your brand as a trusted authority in the security consulting industry.

Now, review your notes and start crafting your marketing strategy. The world of security consulting is waiting for your expertise, and your next client might be just a tweet, email, or handshake away. Let's get to work!

Unlock the Power of Generosity

"The best way to find yourself is to lose yourself in the service of others." - Mahatma Gandhi

People who give without expecting anything in return lead richer lives — not just in success, but in fulfillment. Let's create that ripple effect together.

Would you help someone just like you — thinking about starting a security consulting business but unsure where to begin?

My mission is to make launching and running a successful security consulting business practical and achievable for anyone willing to learn and hustle.

But to reach more aspiring entrepreneurs, I need your help.

Most people choose books based on reviews. That's why I'm asking *YOU* to lend a hand by leaving a review for **Security, LLC:**

Your review could be the reason...

...one more small business secures its first client.

...one more entrepreneur builds a future for their family.

...one more team member finds meaningful work.

...one more dream transforms into a reality.

It's simple:

- Scan the QR code or visit this link: www.amazon.com/review/review-your-purchases/?asin=B0DQ6579KP
- Share what you loved about the book and how it helped you.

It takes just a moment, but your words could change someone's entire entrepreneurial journey.

If you believe in paying it forward, you're my kind of person.

Thank you and stay safe out there!

Meb West, CPP

Author, Security Consultant, and Fellow Entrepreneur.

10

Sales and Customer Relationship Management (CRM)

"You can't build a reputation on what you are going to do."

— Henry Ford

Acquiring a new client can cost five times as much as retaining an existing one. Yet, statistics show that increasing client retention by just 5% can boost profits by anywhere from 25% to 95%. In security consulting, relationships aren't just meaningful; they're everything.

Sales and client relationship management might not be the first thing that comes to mind when you think of security consulting. After all, you're a security expert, not a door-to-door vacuum salesperson. But the truth is, no matter how advanced your skills are or how cutting-edge your security solutions might be, your success ultimately hinges on one thing: your ability to build, maintain, and grow a client base.

If marketing is the strategy to get potential clients to notice you, sales is the art of turning that interest into action. And once you have the client, relationship management ensures they stay loyal, satisfied, and eager to refer your services to others. In this chapter, we'll examine the twin engines of business growth: sales and client relationships.

We'll start with the fundamentals of building a client base from scratch – a daunting but entirely achievable task. From there, we'll explore the nuances of crafting compelling proposals, pricing your services flexibly, and handling client expectations (even in a crisis).

And, of course, we'll touch on the all-important role of technology, like customer relationship management (CRM) systems, to keep your operations seamless and professional.

Sales doesn't have to feel like a sleazy pitch, and relationship management isn't about endless handshakes and schmoozing. With the right approach, it's about authenticity, value, and creating a mutually beneficial dynamic that ensures your clients feel secure – both in the services you provide and in their decision to work with you.

Let's build the foundation for – not just a successful business – but a thriving community of clients who know, trust, and respect you as their go-to security consultant.

Building a Client Base from Scratch

Starting a business in security consulting can feel like being a contestant in a scavenger hunt where the map has been set on fire. One of the biggest hurdles is figuring out how to attract your first clients – without looking desperate or inexperienced. The good news? Building a client base is a challenge every entrepreneur faces, and with the right approach, it's completely doable.

This section is your comprehensive guide to creating a client base from scratch. We'll delve into lead generation tactics, referral programs, the intricacies of creating a sales funnel, and the art of leveraging testimonials and case studies. Let's unpack each piece step by step.

Lead Generation Tactics for Security Consultants

Generating leads – the potential clients who will eventually pay for your expertise – is the backbone of your sales process. Here's how to master it.

Networking, The Original Social Media: Networking is a tried-and-true tactic for getting your foot in the door. For security consultants, networking often happens in two key places:

Industry Events: Think ASIS International conferences or specialized workshops on workplace violence prevention.

Local Business Groups: Chambers of commerce, small business meetups, or even community events can be goldmines for leads.

When attending events, have a goal: meet three new people who could be potential clients or referral sources. Always follow up with a personalized email or LinkedIn connection request.

Example: Imagine attending a cybersecurity seminar and meeting an IT manager concerned about physical data center security. By sharing insights and offering a free consultation, you've just created a warm lead.

Digital Networking: LinkedIn isn't just for job hunters – it's a lead generation machine. Post insightful content related to your niche, comment on industry discussions, and use LinkedIn's search functions to connect with decision-makers in your target market.

Cold Outreach: Personalized Over Generic - Cold outreach doesn't have to be scary. The trick is to make it personal and relevant. Research your prospect and tailor your message.

Example Email: *"Hi [Name], I noticed your company recently expanded its operations in [City]. Congratulations! With growth often comes new security challenges. I'd love to chat about how I helped another company in your industry reduce theft by 40% last year."*

Referral Programs and Rewarding Client Loyalty

Word-of-mouth is king in security consulting. If someone trusts you with their safety, they will likely tell others. A referral program formalizes and incentivizes this process.

Designing an Irresistible Referral Program: Keep it simple. Offer existing clients tangible rewards, like discounted services or gift cards, for every successful referral. Make sure to communicate this program clearly, perhaps through an email or during client meetings.

Example: A corporate client refers you to another company. Once the new company signs a contract, the referring client gets a $500 discount on their next service package.

Retaining Loyalty with Added Value: Long-term clients are your bread and butter. Small gestures like thank-you notes, loyalty discounts, or even sending them a book you think they'd enjoy can go a long way in maintaining strong relationships.

Developing a Sales Process for Security Consulting

A sales process is your roadmap for turning a curious prospect into a paying client. Without one, you're flying blind.

Define the Stages: Every sales process has stages. Here's an example tailored for security consulting:

Awareness: The client becomes aware of your services (via networking, online content, etc.).

Interest: The client shows interest, perhaps requesting more information.

Evaluation: The client assesses whether your services meet their needs.

Purchase: The client signs a contract.

Tools to Stay Organized: CRM (Customer Relationship Management) tools like HubSpot or Zoho help you track where each prospect is in your sales pipeline. It's like having a digital, magical Rolodex.

Creating a Sales Funnel

A sales funnel is like a relationship flowchart, showing how clients move from discovering you to hiring you. Let's break it down.

Top of Funnel (TOFU): Awareness – Attract potential clients with blog posts, social media content, or webinars. For example, a webinar on *"Top 5 Security Risks for Remote Workforces"* positions you as an expert and brings new leads into your funnel.

Middle of Funnel (MOFU): Consideration, Nurturing Leads – Keep your leads engaged with tailored content, like case studies or free assessments. Personalized follow-ups are critical here.

Bottom of Funnel (BOFU): Decision, Closing the Deal – At this stage, eliminate objections. Offer clear proposals and highlight testimonials from similar clients.

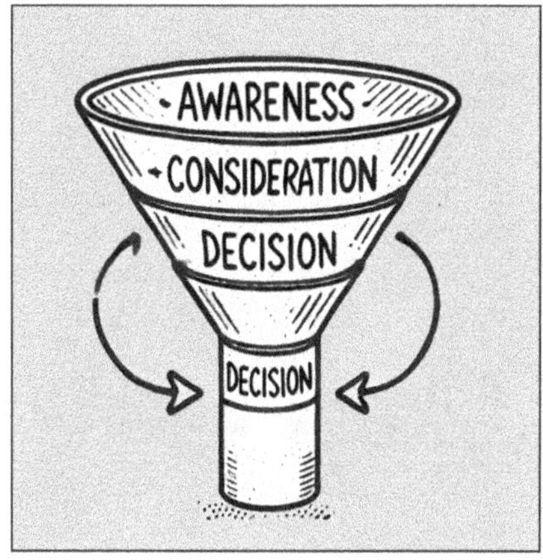

Leveraging Case Studies and Testimonials

People trust other people, especially in an industry as sensitive as security consulting. Case studies and testimonials lend credibility to your business.

Crafting a Powerful Case Study: Structure your case study around three elements:

The Challenge: What problem did the client face?

Your Solution: What did you do to address it?

The Results: How did your efforts improve the client's situation?

Example: For a retail client, your case study might highlight how your recommendations reduced shoplifting incidents by 50% within six months.

Gathering Testimonials: After completing a successful project, ask your client for feedback. Guide them by asking specific questions, like:

- *What particular benefits did you gain from our services?*
- *Would you recommend us to others? If so, why?*

Checklist: Building a Client Base

Networking:

- Attend one industry event per month.
- Join three local business groups or online communities.

Digital Presence:

- Publish two LinkedIn posts monthly.
- Share client success stories (with permission).

Referral Program:

- Design a simple program with clear rewards.
- Promote it through email campaigns or client meetings.

Sales Process: Define each stage and use CRM tools to track progress.

Sales Funnel:

- Create a free resource to attract TOFU leads.
- Schedule personalized follow-ups for MOFU prospects.

Case Studies and Testimonials:

- Write one new case study every quarter.
- Collect five client testimonials for your website.

Building a client base isn't just about finding clients; it's about creating a foundation for long-term success. By combining strategic networking, thoughtful referral programs, a structured sales process, and powerful storytelling through testimonials, you'll set yourself up for sustainable growth. And remember: every security consulting giant started exactly where you are now – with zero clients and a lot of determination.

Writing Effective Proposals

For any security consulting entrepreneur, the ability to write an effective proposal is one of the most critical skills to master. Whether responding to a formal Request for Proposal (RFP) from a company or government agency, or drafting a tailored bid for a private client, the process of proposal writing can determine whether you land that lucrative contract or watch it slip into the hands of your competitors.

This section will break down the art and science of proposal writing into two subcategories: an overview of the RFP process and the general components of a bid proposal. By the end, you'll have a comprehensive guide to crafting compelling proposals that set you apart from the crowd.

Overview of Proposal Writing and the Request for Proposal (RFP) Process

When a potential client issues an RFP, they are essentially broadcasting, "We have a problem, and we need someone to solve it." Your job as a security consultant is to convince them that you are the best person to do so. But where do you find these RFPs, and how do you determine if they are worth pursuing?

Where to Find RFP Opportunities: RFPs are typically found in public and private domains. Here are some excellent sources to start your search:

Government Portals: Platforms like SAM.gov in the United States list federal contracting opportunities. State and local governments also have their own procurement websites.

Private Sector Aggregators: Websites such as RFP Database, BidNet, and GovWin compile RFPs across various industries for a fee.

Industry-Specific Platforms: Associations like ASIS International or industry conferences often share security-specific opportunities.

LinkedIn: As you follow and regularly engage with various companies and influencers, you can be made aware of current or impending RFP opportunities.

Networking: Attending industry events and word-of-mouth recommendations can sometimes lead to direct RFP invitations.

Assessing RFP Suitability

Not all RFPs are created equal. Before dedicating time and resources, ask yourself these questions:

Do I meet the requirements? Review mandatory qualifications. If an RFP requires five years of experience in cyber risk management and you specialize in physical security, it might not be worth your effort.

Pro Tip: If the primary focus of the RFP is outside your wheelhouse, move on. But if you're missing just one-or-two of the mandatory requirements of the RFP, it's not a showstopper. Be honest. Clearly state any gaps in your current menu of services or capabilities and your plan to bridge that gap (strategic partnership, pursue the license/certification, etc.)

Do I have the bandwidth? Proposals take time. If you're swamped with other projects, consider whether you can meet the submission deadline without compromising quality.

Is the potential contract worth it? Calculate the return on investment (ROI). A low-paying contract requiring high upfront costs may not be worthwhile.

RFP Submission and Review Process

The RFP process typically follows a standard timeline:

Announcement: The RFP is published with a submission deadline.

Question Period: Vendors can submit clarifying questions about the RFP's scope or requirements.

Submission Deadline: Proposals must be submitted by this date.

Review: The client evaluates submissions, often narrowing down to a shortlist.

Interviews/Demos: Shortlisted vendors may present their capabilities in person or virtually.

Award Announcement: The winning vendor is notified and begins contract negotiations.

Sample RFP Timeline

Here's a hypothetical timeline for a security consulting RFP:

- Week 1: RFP issued.
- Week 2: Vendor questions submitted.
- Week 3: Answers to vendor questions published.
- Week 4: Proposals due.
- Weeks 5–6: Review and shortlisting.
- Week 7: Interviews and final selection.
- Week 8: Contract award announced.

Understanding this timeline will help you manage expectations and allocate resources effectively.

General Components of a Bid Proposal

A well-structured bid proposal tells a story: who you are, what you offer, and why the client should choose you. Each component plays a specific role in that narrative.

1. Letter from the Owner – This introductory letter is your chance to set the tone. Keep it professional yet personable, briefly explaining why you're excited to bid and how your expertise aligns with the client's needs.

2. Cover Page – Think of this as your proposal's handshake. Include:

- Proposal title.
- Client name.
- Submission date.
- Your company logo and contact information.

3. Company Introduction – Here's your chance to shine. Provide a concise overview of your company, its mission, and why it's uniquely positioned to be the vendor of choice for completing the project. Highlight any relevant certifications or accolades.

4. General Scope of Work – This section outlines the problem the client wants to solve and your proposed approach. Avoid jargon and focus on how your solution meets their specific needs.

5. Specified Task List – Break down the project into specific tasks or milestones. For example:

- Conduct initial risk assessment.
- Develop site-specific security protocols.
- Train onsite personnel.

Providing granular details demonstrates your expertise and thoughtfulness.

6. Manpower/Key Personnel - Describe the personnel required for the project. Be specific:

- Company POC for this contract.
- (If different) Project Manager
- Key Leader or Shift Supervisor
- Number of consultants.
- Required expertise (e.g., cybersecurity, physical security).
- Expected hours per consultant.

7. Timeline – Map out the project's phases, from kickoff to completion. A Gantt chart or milestone calendar can be helpful here.

8. Operational Security (OPSEC) Measures – Clients value discretion. Detail how you'll protect sensitive information through data encryption, NDAs, or secure communication channels.

9. Past Periods of Performance - Show, don't tell. That means that – unless you have permission – do not disclose proprietary or private information from other clients. Not only would it probably violate previous NDAs, but it also signals to your prospective new client that you don't value discretion. If you do have permission to share client-specific information, state so. Highlight similar projects you've completed successfully. Include:

- Project description.
- Client feedback (Any relevant client testimonials or reviews go here).
- Tangible results.

10. Pricing Structure - Transparency is key. Break down costs into:

Fee for Services: Hourly rates, daily rates, or flat fees. This doesn't need to be specific. You will include as a lump sum payroll, overhead, profit margin, etc. Clients don't (shouldn't) need to know the specifics, just the all-in amount.

Estimated Expenses: Travel, equipment, etc.

Explain how you'll handle over/under budgeting and outline payment terms, including penalties for late payments.

11. Bid Acceptance Signature Sheet - End with a formal section where the client can sign to indicate acceptance. Ensure it includes all necessary legal language.

Proposal writing might seem daunting, but it's also your golden ticket to landing clients. By mastering the RFP process and creating detailed, compelling proposals, you're not just bidding for contracts – you're building credibility and trust. With practice, you'll find that writing a winning proposal isn't just an art; it's a powerful business strategy.

How to Create a Flexible Pricing Structure for Your Services

Pricing your services as a security consultant is both an art and a science. It requires balancing your value, market demand, and operational costs while ensuring your rates are competitive yet profitable. A flexible pricing structure can help you adapt to various clients and situations, setting the stage for long-term success.

This section dives into the nuances of crafting a pricing model, covering essential methods like hourly and daily rates, flat fees, subscription models, retainers, and the critical considerations of location and threat level. By the end, you'll be equipped to develop a pricing strategy that aligns with your expertise and the unique needs of your clients.

Introduction to Developing a Pricing Structure

Before we get into the details, let's address a critical point: no universal "perfect" pricing model exists. What works for one consultant might not suit another. Your pricing structure should reflect:

- The type of services you provide.
- Your level of expertise.
- The market demand for those services.
- Your operational costs and desired profit margin.

Remember, pricing is as much about perception as it is about math. Undervalue yourself, and clients might question your competency. Overprice, and you risk scaring potential clients away. The goal is to strike a balance that communicates value while remaining competitive.

Hourly Rates

Hourly rates are the bread and butter of many consultants. They're straightforward, easy to calculate, and give clients a clear sense of what they're paying for. However, setting your hourly rate is more complex than pulling a number out of thin air.

How to Determine Your Hourly Rate

Calculate Your Overhead: Include costs like office space, software subscriptions, insurance, and marketing.

Account for Non-Billable Hours: Remember that not every hour you work is billable. Administrative tasks, marketing, and professional development time should factor into your rate.

Benchmark Against the Market: Research what other consultants in your niche charge. Websites like Glassdoor, Payscale, and industry-specific forums can provide insights.

Example: A security consultant specializing in cybersecurity might charge $200/hour for penetration testing, while a generalist conducting risk assessments might charge $100/hour.

Pros and Cons

Pros: Transparent and straightforward. Allows clients to scale services up or down based on budget.

Cons: Can lead to "nickel-and-dime" perceptions. Doesn't incentivize efficiency.

Daily Rates

Daily rates are ideal for projects that require a consultant to be onsite or engaged intensively for a short period. This model often suits training workshops, physical security assessments, or high-level consultations. Any job requiring the consultant's availability for more than 8 hours of day, over weekends and holidays, is typically cheaper to price at a daily rate to avoid overtime and weekend/holiday pay rates.

How to Structure Daily Rates

Base Your Rate on Hourly Calculations: Multiply your hourly rate by the number of hours you're willing to work in a day (typically 8).

Consider Value-Added Services: Clients paying for a full day expect more than just hours. Include extras like post-assessment reports or follow-up consultations in your pricing.

Example: A consultant conducting an overseas security advance assessment in preparation for an executive's arrival may charge out at a $1,200/day rate, plus expenses.

Flat Fees

Flat fees work best for clearly defined projects with predictable scopes and deliverables. This pricing model provides clients with upfront clarity and reduces the "scope creep" risk for consultants.

Examples of when to Use Flat Fees

- Security audits.
- Drafting Standard Operating Procedures (SOPs).
- Conducting vulnerability assessments.

How to Calculate Flat Fees

- Estimate the total hours required for the project.
- Add a buffer for unforeseen complications.
- Include fixed costs like travel or materials.

Example: A flat fee for a comprehensive security assessment of a corporate headquarters might be $15,000, covering interviews, onsite evaluations, and a final report.

Subscription Models

Subscription models involve charging clients a recurring fee for ongoing services. This approach is gaining traction in the security industry, particularly for services like continuous monitoring, cybersecurity, and consulting retainers.

Benefits of Subscription Models

- Predictable revenue streams for the consultant.
- Consistent support and peace of mind for the client.

Example: A subscription package might include monthly cybersecurity audits, threat intelligence reports, and 24/7 incident response for $3,000/month.

Retainers

Retainers are similar to subscription models but are typically tied to a set number of monthly hours or deliverables. This model is popular for clients who need regular access to your expertise but don't want to hire a full-time employee.

Setting Up a Retainer

Define the Scope: Clearly outline what's included in the retainer.

Track Hours or Deliverables: Use project management software to ensure transparency.

Example: A security consultant might offer a retainer of $4,000/month for 40 hours of advisory services, with additional hours billed at a discounted rate.

Adjusting for Location and Threat Level

Not all jobs are created equal. The same project will command different rates depending on:

Location: A consulting gig in Manhattan will cost more than one in rural Alabama, reflecting the higher cost of living and doing business.

Threat Level: Projects in high-risk environments or involving significant client threats warrant higher rates to compensate for increased danger and insurance costs.

Using an objective, third-party system to determine locational risk ratings.

It is important that your clients can see that you are not marketing on fear and just increasing your prices because someone said the boogie man is especially prevalent in a particular area. Additionally, there are a lot of differing opinions when it comes to determining when an area is "dangerous." It is essential, therefore, to find an objective, unassociated source that specializes in giving quantifiable risk ratings that you can base your prices on. It is important that this source updates its information regularly and relies on a wide variety of factors to determine an overall risk rating.

There are many of these sources out there. For example, the Fragile States Index (https://fragilestatesindex.org) lists every country in the world. It assigns them a 0-100 risk rating based on crime, terrorism, political risk, civil disturbance, medical/pandemic, etc. Using this third-party rating (which is updated at least quarterly), a company can set pricing structures (as an example) for areas with a risk rating of 90-100, 80-89, 70-79, 60-69, etc. This allows your clients to see an objective review of why the fee for services may change, depending on where they are operating and alleviate you of the suspicion that you are arbitrarily inflating your rates.

Determining What the Market Will Bear

Research Local Rates: Websites like Salary.com or Thumbtack can provide regional pricing insights.

Consult Peers: Join forums or professional associations to discuss market trends.

Example: A risk assessment for a high-net-worth individual in a conflict zone like Kabul might be billed out at a rate of $1,2000 per day plus expenses, while a similar assessment in a suburban U.S. town might cost $850 per day. Similarly, a job in New York, NY would probably be billed out at a higher rate than the same job in Rifle, CO.

Creating a flexible pricing structure isn't just about numbers – it's about understanding your value, market, and client's needs. Whether you're charging by the hour, day, or project, your pricing strategy should reflect your expertise and the unique challenges of each job. By mastering the art of flexible pricing, you'll secure profitable contracts and build long-lasting client relationships.

Building Long-Term Relationships with Clients

Building a client base is one thing; keeping those clients long-term is another entirely. In the security consulting business, long-term client relationships are the bedrock of stability and growth. Your expertise in assessing risks, designing protocols, and enhancing safety might land you the contract. Still, how you treat your clients beyond the scope of your work will keep them coming back – and (most importantly) spreading the word about your services.

This section explores the art of cultivating meaningful, long-term client relationships by delving into key elements like exceeding expectations, maintaining integrity, and the underestimated power of the "little things." Let's break it down.

Exceeding Expectations: The Golden Rule of Client Retention

There's a saying in business: "Under-promise and over-deliver." This approach can transform a one-time contract into a decades-long partnership in security consulting.

When a client hires you, they expect a job well done. That's the baseline. What they don't expect – and what sets you apart – is the extra effort you put in to ensure their experience is nothing short of exceptional. This could mean completing a project ahead of schedule, providing additional insights outside the agreed scope, or offering post-project follow-ups free of charge.

Example: Suppose a corporate client hires you to conduct a physical security assessment of their headquarters. Instead of merely submitting a report, you also include a brief executive summary for their board members, a prioritized action list, and a 30-minute debriefing session to answer questions. These extras may take little effort but leave a lasting impression.

Transparency and Honesty: The Pillars of Trust

In the security business, trust is non-negotiable. Clients need to know they can rely on your discretion, judgment, and advice without questioning your motives. Transparency and honesty are your greatest tools in establishing and maintaining that trust.

Be Upfront About Challenges. If an obstacle arises, whether it's a delay in delivering results or the discovery of an issue you're unqualified to handle, communicate it immediately. Clients value candor over perfection.

Own Your Mistakes. Mistakes happen, even in the best-run operations. How you handle them can strengthen or destroy a client relationship. Take ownership, offer solutions, and commit to preventing similar errors in the future.

Remain Discreet

Integrity might sound like a buzzword, but it's the quiet, consistent backbone of client retention in security consulting. It's demonstrated in the choices you make when no one is watching and the unwavering commitment to doing what's right.

Protecting Client Confidentiality. In security consulting, you're often privy to sensitive information. Never compromise a client's privacy or use their data for your gain. A reputation for discretion is a priceless asset. Decide now, at all costs, that you will treat *everything* to do with your client, the family, the company, and the job with the utmost privacy and discretion. This includes protection from accidental exposure or (God forbid) intentional exposure to "boost your credibility" (more like "feed your ego"). Unfortunately, this is an all-too-common occurrence in the security industry, and the professionals (and your future clients) are watching.

Putting the Client's Needs First. This doesn't mean giving in to every demand but prioritizing their best interests, even if it means advising against a service that would make you more money.

The Little Things That Make a Big Difference

Beyond exceeding expectations and maintaining integrity, the "little things" you do for your clients can outsize their perception of you and your business. These thoughtful gestures may have nothing to do with why you were retained, but they show clients that you see them as more than just a paycheck.

Example 1: Remembering Personal Milestones. If your client mentions their birthday during a meeting, jot it down. A simple "Happy Birthday" email or card can make them feel valued.

Example 2: Supporting Their Charitable Efforts. If your client's company hosts a charity run, sponsor a team, or participate. It's a small act that demonstrates genuine interest in their priorities.

Example 3: Celebrating Successes. Send a congratulatory note or gift if a client achieves a significant milestone – like opening a new office or hitting a financial target. It's a thoughtful way to acknowledge their achievements. This is why I always follow my clients and their company on social media.

Example 4: Being Available. Little things aren't always about physical gestures. Sometimes, it's as simple as being available for a quick call or email, even when the project is over. A client who knows they can count on you will be more likely to return when new needs arise. If I find out that a past client is experiencing trouble (weather event, labor strike, a workplace violence incident, etc.), I'll reach out to just let them know that I saw the news and am available if they need to talk.

Communication: The Lifeline of Client Relationships

Effective communication is the glue that holds long-term relationships together. It's not just about talking; it's about active listening, timely updates, and clarity.

Stay in Regular Contact. Don't let months go by without touching base. Whether it's a quarterly newsletter, an email check-in, or a friendly call, staying connected keeps you at the top of their mind.

Use Technology Wisely. CRM systems can help you track client interactions and preferences, ensuring personalized communication. Tools like Slack or Microsoft Teams can streamline ongoing collaborations.

Long-term relationships are about more than just securing repeat business – they're about building a network of advocates who will vouch for you in the industry. These clients can provide referrals, testimonials, and credibility, which are invaluable for growth. A satisfied corporate client might recommend you to another division or a partner company, opening doors you didn't even know existed.

Practical Tips for Building Long-Term Client Relationships

Deliver Results Consistently: Meet or exceed expectations on every project.

Show Gratitude: Send thank-you notes or small tokens of appreciation after a project's completion.

Be Proactive: Anticipate client needs and offer solutions before they ask.

Solicit Feedback: Actively seek client input on how you can improve your services.

Invest in Relationships: Attend client events, invite them to lunch, or simply get to know them better.

In security consulting, your ability to build and sustain long-term relationships is as critical as your technical expertise. By exceeding expectations, maintaining integrity, and focusing on the little things, you can transform clients into loyal advocates who return for repeat business and spread the word about your exceptional services.

Remember: The job you do might bring clients in, but the relationships you build will keep them.

Handling Client Feedback and Adjusting Services

Client feedback is a gift – sometimes wrapped in shiny paper with a bow, other times in crumpled newspaper held together by duct tape. Whether positive or negative, feedback is your opportunity to refine your services, strengthen relationships, and build a reputation as a consultant who listens and delivers. Handling feedback well and adjusting your services accordingly is an art that can make or break your success as a security consultant.

In this section, we'll review the nuances of receiving and responding to client feedback, the delicate process of adjusting your services mid-contract, and the fine line between flexibility and scope creep.

Why Feedback Is Important

Picture you're driving a car without side mirrors or a rearview mirror. You might make some progress, but you'd have no idea how well you're navigating the road – or what's catching up behind you. Feedback is your consulting mirror, reflecting how your services are perceived, what's working, and what's not.

Clients want to feel heard, valued, and understood. How you handle their feedback – especially the negative kind – demonstrates your professionalism, builds trust, and shows your commitment to excellence. Ignoring feedback, on the other hand, can damage relationships and your reputation.

Receiving Feedback: The Good, the Bad, and the Ugly

The Good. Positive feedback is like a pat on the back – it feels great, reinforces your confidence, and clarifies what you're doing well. But don't let it lull you into complacency. Instead, use it as a guide to double down on your strengths.

Example:

- If a client raves about your prompt communication, make it a cornerstone of your brand.
- If they're impressed by your security recommendations, consider developing case studies based on those successes.

The Bad. Harmful feedback stings, but it's often the most valuable. A dissatisfied client is essentially handing you a blueprint for improvement. The key is to separate emotions from facts and approach the feedback with curiosity rather than defensiveness.

Example: If a client says, "Your team missed key vulnerabilities in our physical security assessment," dig deeper. Ask questions to understand their perspective, review your process, and identify areas for improvement.

The Ugly. Sometimes feedback comes in hot – angry emails, terse phone calls, or public criticism. These moments test your composure and professionalism. The best approach? Acknowledge their frustration, listen actively, and focus on finding a solution rather than assigning blame.

Responding to Feedback: The Five-Step Formula

Step 1: Acknowledge. Start by thanking the client for their feedback, regardless of its tone. A simple "Thank you for bringing this to my attention" sets a collaborative tone.

Step 2: Clarify. Ask open-ended questions to understand their concerns fully. This shows you're taking their input seriously.

Step 3: Analyze. Determine whether the feedback is valid, a misunderstanding, or an unrealistic expectation. Consult your records, revisit the scope of work, and get input from your team if necessary.

Step 4: Resolve. Propose a solution that addresses their concerns. Be clear about what you can and cannot do and manage their expectations.

Step 5: Follow Up. After implementing changes, check in with the client to ensure their satisfaction.

Adjusting Services Mid-Contract

No matter how well you plan, there will be times when a client's needs evolve mid-project. Perhaps they've realized a new security threat or their priorities have shifted due to unforeseen circumstances. Or (more likely) the dreaded "scope creep" will rear its ugly head as it often does. Adjusting your services to meet these needs is part of being a flexible and client-focused consultant.

Identifying the Need for Adjustment. Pay close attention to client feedback, changing circumstances, or emerging challenges. If a corporate client suddenly expands their operations to a new site, their initial security assessment may no longer cover their needs. Recognizing these shifts early allows you to propose adjustments proactively.

Negotiating the Scope. Scope creep is the bane of many consultants. While flexibility is essential, you must protect yourself from doing more work than initially agreed upon without appropriate compensation.

Acknowledge the Change: Confirm with the client that their needs have evolved and explain how it impacts the original scope.

Propose a Revised Scope: Outline the additional tasks, timelines, and costs associated with meeting their new requirements.

Document Everything: Update the contract or create a change order document detailing the revised scope, terms, and costs. Both parties should sign off before proceeding.

Example: Envision you're hired to conduct a risk assessment for a local hospital. Midway through, the hospital's board decides to add three satellite clinics to the project. Instead of absorbing this work into the original agreement, you propose an addendum to the contract detailing the additional hours, personnel, and costs required. By addressing the change professionally, you maintain the relationship while protecting your business.

Balancing Flexibility and Professional Boundaries

It's tempting to go above and beyond for your clients, but there's a fine line between exceptional service and allowing your business to be taken advantage of. Remember:

Set Clear Boundaries: Define the scope of work and stick to it unless a renegotiation occurs.

Value Your Time: Your expertise is your product. Don't undervalue it by consistently giving away work for free.

Learn to Say No: Politely declining unreasonable requests can earn respect and protect your reputation.

Handling Feedback in Crisis Situations

In high-stakes security consulting, crises can amplify client dissatisfaction. Whether it's a data breach, a physical security incident, or an operational hiccup, your response to feedback during a crisis is critical.

Stay Calm: Clients look to you for guidance and reassurance. A composed demeanor can help de-escalate tensions.

Take Ownership: If the crisis stems from your team's oversight, own it. Then, outline the steps you're taking to resolve the issue.

Communicate Frequently: Keep clients updated at every stage of the resolution process. Silence breeds distrust.

Turning Feedback into Opportunities

Feedback isn't just a tool for improvement – it's also a marketing asset. Positive testimonials and case studies can showcase your expertise and attract new clients. Meanwhile, addressing negative feedback effectively can demonstrate your commitment to client satisfaction.

Example: Leveraging Positive Feedback. If a client praises your risk mitigation strategies, ask for a testimonial or permission to use their case as a study. Highlighting real-world successes adds credibility to your services.

Practical Tips for Handling Feedback

Create Feedback Channels: Make it easy for clients to share their thoughts through surveys, emails, or scheduled check-ins.

Be Proactive: Don't wait for clients to voice concerns. Regularly ask for input on how you can improve.

Track Feedback Trends: Use CRM tools to document feedback and identify recurring themes.

Invest in Training: Equip your team with conflict resolution and customer service skills.

Handling client feedback is both an art and a science. By approaching it with openness, professionalism, and a willingness to adapt, you can turn even the most challenging situations into opportunities for growth. Remember, it's not about being perfect – it's about showing clients that you're committed to meeting their needs and delivering exceptional service.

Adjusting your services in response to feedback is part of the job, but setting boundaries and renegotiating scope, when necessary, ensures that your flexibility doesn't come at the expense of your business. Done right, feedback isn't just a tool for improvement – it's the foundation for long-term client relationships and a thriving security consulting business.

Managing a Client's Expectations in a Crisis

Crisis management is where the rubber meets the road in security consulting. It's not just about having the right tools or the best plans – it's about guiding clients through their darkest moments with confidence, clarity, and compassion. Whether you've been hired specifically to address a crisis, find yourself in the middle of one while on retainer, or are called back to address a disaster post-contract, managing client expectations is as much an art as it is a science.

In this subsection, we'll explore the nuances of handling each scenario. Along the way, we'll equip you with strategies to maintain professionalism, communicate effectively, and leave your client feeling like they've hired the best.

Crisis Scenario 1: Hired to Resolve the Crisis

Imagine this: a corporation experiences a significant data breach and is scrambling to contain the fallout. Enter you – their hired savior. Being brought in mid-crisis is both a compliment and a challenge. The client is already in a heightened emotional state, which means their expectations may be unrealistic, their patience thin, and their demands urgent.

What to Do First

Assess the Situation: Before promising solutions, take time to understand the scope and nature of the crisis. Ask pointed questions to get to the root of the problem.

Example: If it's a physical breach, you'll need to know how the perimeter was compromised. If it's a data issue, identify the entry point of the breach.

Set Realistic Expectations: Clients may expect miracles, but you need to align their expectations with what's feasible. Be honest about timelines and outcomes.

Pro Tip: Use analogies to simplify complex scenarios. "Think of this like patching a leaky boat. The priority is stopping the water; rebuilding the boat comes later."

Balancing Urgency with Efficacy. When clients are panicking, there's a natural push for speed. While it's essential to act swiftly, cutting corners can worsen the situation. Emphasize that while you'll move as fast as possible, thoroughness is non-negotiable.

Communication is Key. Provide frequent updates – even if the update is, "We're still analyzing data." Silence breeds anxiety, and anxious clients are more challenging to manage.

Crisis Scenario 2: Crisis Hits While You're on Retainer

You've been working with a client for months, conducting security assessments and developing preventive strategies. Then, out of the blue, disaster strikes – a workplace shooting, a natural disaster, or a critical system failure. In this case, your value isn't just in what you do but in how you respond.

Having a crisis response plan in place before anything happens is ideal. If your retainer includes crafting contingency plans, revisit those documents with the client immediately. Show them you've prepared for this moment, and they'll feel reassured.

Calming Frayed Nerves. Clients in this scenario often feel betrayed by their preparedness – or lack thereof – which is why they hired you to begin with. It's your job to remind them that no plan is foolproof, but recovery is always possible. Use phrases like:

- "We anticipated this as a potential risk, and here's how we can address it."
- "While this wasn't preventable, our response will minimize its impact."

Stepping Into the Leadership Role. During a crisis, clients often look for someone to take charge. Be that person. Show confidence in your recommendations and take the lead in coordinating efforts.

Crisis Scenario 3: Post-Job Crisis

You've done your work, wrapped up the project, and moved on to the next client. Then your phone rings – it's a former client, desperate for your help. A crisis has struck, and they're turning to you as their trusted expert.

The Delicate Balance. In this scenario, you're navigating uncharted waters. The previous contract likely doesn't cover crisis management, so you'll need to establish new terms before proceeding. However, you must also demonstrate empathy and urgency to maintain the client relationship.

Steps to Take

Express Empathy: Acknowledge their distress and assure them that you'll help.

Example: "I'm so sorry this happened. Let's figure out how we can resolve this together."

Revisit the Scope of Work: Politely explain that additional work requires new terms. Frame this as ensuring the best possible outcome.

Act Swiftly: Even as you renegotiate terms, offer preliminary guidance to show your commitment.

Key Principles for Managing Expectations

Regardless of the scenario, some principles remain universal.

Honesty Above All. Clients can forgive delays, but they won't forgive dishonesty. If a solution will take longer than they'd like, be upfront. Sugarcoating or overpromising sets you up for failure.

Consistent Communication. Establish a cadence for updates – daily, hourly, or as progress occurs. Use a mix of written reports, calls, and face-to-face meetings to keep them informed.

Empathy and Compassion. Crisis situations are deeply personal for clients. Acknowledging their feelings and validating their concerns go a long way in building trust.

Stay Solutions-Oriented. Clients hire you to solve problems, not dwell on them. While analyzing what went wrong is important, focus most of your energy on actionable solutions.

Navigating Scope Creep in a Crisis

It's easy for crises to expand the original scope of work. While you want to be helpful, it's crucial to protect your business by setting boundaries.

How to Identify Scope Creep

- Requests that deviate from the original contract.
- Clients expecting 24/7 availability without additional compensation.
- Additional tasks that require hiring extra personnel or equipment.

How to Address It

Acknowledge Their Needs: Show empathy for their situation.

Propose Adjustments: Clearly outline how additional work impacts costs and timelines.

Document Changes: Always update the contract to reflect new terms.

The Importance of Post-Crisis Reflection

Once the dust settles, schedule a debrief with the client. Discuss what went well, what could have been better, and how to prevent similar crises in the future. This strengthens your relationship and positions you as a forward-thinking consultant.

Example. Let's say you're hired to secure a corporate event. Midway through, a power outage causes chaos. Your initial job was to manage access points and guest lists, but now you're coordinating emergency lighting, crowd control, and media inquiries. By staying calm, communicating frequently, and proposing new terms for expanded responsibilities, you save the day – and secure a long-term client.

Checklist: Managing Client Expectations in a Crisis

- Understand the nature and scope of the crisis.
- Communicate frequently and transparently.
- Align client expectations with realistic outcomes.
- Take ownership where applicable.
- Address scope creep professionally.
- Document all changes to the scope of work.
- Conduct a post-crisis debrief and follow-up.

Managing client expectations in a crisis isn't just about solving the problem – it's about guiding the client through a stressful situation with professionalism, empathy, and expertise. You can turn even the most challenging moments into opportunities to strengthen your reputation and client relationships by maintaining clear communication, staying solution-focused, and setting boundaries when necessary. Done right, your response to a crisis can leave a lasting impression – and ensure that your clients keep coming back.

Utilizing CRM Systems to Track Client Data and Engagements

In the realm of security consulting, where relationships can make or break your business, a Customer Relationship Management (CRM) system isn't just a tool – it's your secret weapon. It's like having a personal assistant who remembers every conversation you've ever had, tracks every email you've ever sent, and can predict what your clients need before they even ask. That's CRM in a nutshell. It's not just about data; it's about leveraging it to create meaningful, lasting relationships with your clients.

Let's start at the very beginning. CRM stands for Customer Relationship Management, which is both a philosophy and a software solution. At its core, CRM is about putting the client at the center of your business. It's about understanding their needs, preferences, and behaviors to build stronger, more productive relationships.

From a practical standpoint, CRM software is a centralized system that allows you to store, track, and analyze every interaction with your clients. Think of it as your digital Rolodex on steroids. But instead of just names and phone numbers, it tracks emails, meetings, phone calls, proposals, contracts, and even your client's favorite coffee order (because I've heard somewhere that sometimes, it's the little things that matter).

If you're wondering whether CRM is worth the investment for a security consulting business, consider this: a CRM system isn't just about making your life easier; it's about delivering exceptional service. In a business built on trust and relationships, a well-implemented CRM can mean the difference between being a one-time hire and a trusted long-term partner.

Enhanced Client Experience. Clients want to feel valued. They want to know that you understand their unique needs and can anticipate their challenges. CRM systems allow you to personalize your interactions, ensuring every communication feels intentional and meaningful.

Streamlined Operations. From tracking leads to managing contracts, CRM systems automate many administrative tasks that can take up your time. This frees you to focus on what you do best – providing expert security consulting services.

Data-Driven Decisions. By analyzing client data, you can identify trends, predict future needs, and tailor your services to meet market demands better. In other words, CRM turns raw data into actionable insights.

The Tools of the Trade

There are plenty of CRM platforms to choose from, but the right one for your business will depend on your specific needs, budget, and technical expertise. Here are a few popular options:

HubSpot. Known for its user-friendly interface, HubSpot offers a free CRM perfect for small businesses. It includes tools for contact management, email tracking, and pipeline management. You can upgrade to paid plans with more advanced features as your business grows.

Salesforce. Salesforce is the gold standard in CRM, offering robust tools for managing client relationships, tracking sales, and analyzing data. While it's more expensive, its scalability makes it an excellent choice for businesses with big ambitions.

Zoho CRM. Zoho is a cost-effective option with features like workflow automation, analytics, and social media integration. It's particularly well-suited for small to mid-sized businesses.

Pipedrive. If you're focused on sales and lead management, Pipedrive offers a straightforward, intuitive platform that helps you stay organized and close deals more efficiently.

How CRM Enhances Operations

Now that we know what CRM is and the tools available, let's explore how it can revolutionize your business operations.

Lead Management. Without a CRM system, tracking leads can feel like juggling flaming torches – one wrong move, and you've lost an opportunity. A CRM ensures every lead is logged, categorized, and nurtured through the sales funnel.

Example: A potential client downloads a whitepaper from your website. Your CRM automatically records their contact information and triggers a follow-up email, keeping the lead warm without you lifting a finger.

Task Automation. Forget sticky notes and email threads. With a CRM, you can automate repetitive tasks like sending follow-up emails, scheduling appointments, and generating reports.

Example: After completing a site assessment, your CRM can automatically send the client a detailed report, a feedback form, and a testimonial request.

Client Communication. CRM systems centralize all client communications, ensuring nothing falls through the cracks. You'll have everything you need to maintain consistent, professional communication, from email templates to call logs.

Example: A client asks for an update on their project. Instead of scrambling to piece together information, you can pull up their file and provide a comprehensive update on the spot.

Reporting and Analytics. Data is power, and CRM systems give you the tools to wield it effectively. CRM software provides the insights you need to make informed decisions, from tracking sales performance to analyzing client retention rates.

Example: If your CRM shows that most of your new clients come from LinkedIn, you can allocate more resources to that platform.

Implementing CRM in Your Business

Implementing a CRM system can feel daunting, but it doesn't have to be. Here's a step-by-step guide to getting started:

Step 1: Define Your Needs. Before choosing a CRM platform, identify what you want to achieve. Are you focused on lead generation? Client retention? Data analysis? Knowing your priorities will help you select the right tool.

Step 2: Choose a Platform. Compare CRM platforms based on features, pricing, and scalability. Many offer free trials, so don't hesitate to test a few before committing.

Step 3: Train Your Team. Even the best CRM system is useless if your team doesn't know how to use it. Invest in training to ensure everyone understands how to navigate the platform and maximize its features.

Step 4: Start Small. You don't have to use every feature from day one. Start with the basics – like contact management and email tracking – and gradually explore more advanced tools as you become comfortable.

In the fast-paced world of security consulting, a CRM system isn't just a luxury – it's a necessity. By centralizing your data, automating tasks, and providing actionable insights, CRM software allows you to deliver exceptional service, build lasting relationships, and confidently scale your business. Whether you're a one-person operation or a growing team, investing in CRM is one of the smartest decisions you can make. So, what are you waiting for? It's time to embrace the power of CRM and take your business to the next level.

Being a Good Partner with Clients from Other Security Consultants

In the security consulting world, collaboration isn't just an occasional necessity – it's a cornerstone of the industry. No one consultant or firm can be everywhere at once or be an expert in every niche. Often, you'll find yourself hosting another consultant's client, whether because the client is traveling to your area or because your niche expertise is critical to a broader project. How you handle these situations speaks volumes about your professionalism, reliability, and ability to work within the industry ecosystem.

It's important to approach these scenarios with the mindset that, in this moment, you're not just representing yourself – you're representing the originating consultant as well. This means treating their client with the same care, respect, and dedication as you would your own. Let's discuss the nuances of being a good partner when working with someone else's client.

Understanding the Nature of the Relationship

When working with another consultant's client, the dynamic differs from a direct client relationship. In this case, you're not the primary point of contact, nor are you necessarily the one who secured the contract. Your role is to support the originating consultant and their client by delivering top-notch service within the defined scope of work.

Think of this as a temporary joint venture. Your goal is to meet the client's needs while maintaining the trust and integrity of your relationship with the originating consultant. This requires open communication, strict adherence to the project scope, and an unwavering commitment to professionalism.

The Importance of Communication

Clear and transparent communication is vital when working with another consultant's client. Start by having an in-depth conversation with the originating consultant to understand:

- The client's needs and expectations.
- The scope of your involvement.
- Any sensitivities or potential issues to be aware of.
- The agreed-upon boundaries for communication with the client.

For example, if a high-profile corporate client is traveling to your city for a conference and the originating consultant wants you to pick him up at the airport and facilitate his few days in town. He might want you to provide the service but direct all follow-up questions or additional requests back to them. Respect these boundaries to maintain trust.

Similarly, keep the originating consultant updated on all progress and potential challenges. They shouldn't have to chase you for information – be proactive and thorough in your updates.

Treating the Client as Your Own

While you're not the primary consultant in this arrangement, the client should never feel like they're being handed off or treated as a second-tier priority. From the client's perspective, your service is an extension of the originating consultant's brand. If you fail to deliver, it reflects poorly on them and you.

Here are a few tips to ensure the client feels valued:

Deliver Exceptional Service. Go above and beyond within the agreed scope of work. If you're conducting a security audit, make it the most thorough and insightful audit they've ever received.

Be Professional and Personable. Engage with the client as if they were your own, balancing professionalism with a friendly, approachable demeanor.

Respect Boundaries. Don't overstep by trying to sell additional services directly to the client unless explicitly agreed upon by the originating consultant. If the client speaks of the original consultant or their work, remain neutral and focused on the service you are providing.

Navigating Regional or Niche Expertise

One of the most common scenarios in which you'll work with another consultant's client is when your expertise or geographic location makes you the best person for the job. For instance:

- A corporate client might need specialized risk assessments for their executive team in a high-threat environment where you're the regional expert.
- A consultant specializing in cybersecurity might bring you in to handle physical security measures as part of a larger project.

In these situations, your expertise is why you were brought on board. However, it's crucial to remember that your role is to complement the originating consultant's work, not overshadow it. Be collaborative, not competitive. Share your insights and recommendations in a way that enhances the overall project without undermining the originating consultant's leadership.

The Art of Hosting Clients

If the client is traveling to your geographic area, your role extends beyond providing your core services. You're essentially their host, and how you handle this responsibility can leave a lasting impression.

Key Considerations for Hosting Clients

Logistics: Assist with practical arrangements like transportation, accommodations, and local recommendations. For example, if a client is in town for a threat assessment, ensure they have safe and reliable transportation to and from your office.

Cultural Sensitivity: Be mindful of cultural differences, especially if the client is from another country. This could include dietary preferences, communication styles, or even how you greet them.

Personal Touches: Small gestures, like welcoming them with a handwritten note or providing a local guidebook, can make a big difference.

Building Trust with the Originating Consultant

Your relationship with the originating consultant is as important as your relationship with their client. Here are a few ways to strengthen this partnership:

Respect Non-Compete Agreements: If you've agreed not to solicit their client for future work, honor that commitment. Trust takes years to build and seconds to destroy. Even if there is no non-compete agreement, NEVER try to undercut the originating consultant or "scoop" the client. When people do this, the word gets around quickly. Those that do will not be in the industry long.

Be Transparent: Share any challenges, changes, or updates in real time. Surprises are rarely welcome in the consulting world.

Deliver Consistently: The originating consultant trusted you enough to involve you in their client's project. Validate that trust by delivering exceptional results.

Checklist for Being a Good Partner with Clients from Other Consultants

Understand the Scope: Clarify your role, responsibilities, and boundaries with the originating consultant.

Communicate Effectively: Provide regular updates and address any challenges proactively.

Deliver Exceptional Service: Treat the client as your own, exceeding expectations wherever possible.

Respect Agreements: Honor any non-compete clauses or other contractual terms.

Be Collaborative: Work in harmony with the originating consultant to achieve the best outcome for the client.

In the collaborative world of security consulting, how you handle another consultant's client can define your reputation within the industry. You can build strong relationships with the originating consultant and their client by prioritizing clear communication, exceptional service, and professional integrity. Remember, every interaction is an opportunity to showcase your expertise and reliability, paving the way for future partnerships and opportunities.

Chapter 10 Wrap-Up: Sales and Client Relationship Management

"If you don't take care of your customer, someone else will."

— Edwards Deming

Chapter 10 has deeply examined the intricacies of sales and client relationship management for security consultants. As we've explored, sales isn't just about making the pitch – it's about building lasting relationships, solving client problems, and positioning yourself as a trusted expert in your niche. Whether it's generating leads, crafting compelling proposals, or navigating the murky waters of client feedback, this chapter has equipped you with the tools and knowledge to effectively manage the "people side" of your business. Let's recap.

Building a Client Base from Scratch

Sales might feel intimidating at first, especially when starting from zero. But as we discussed, building a client base is less about flashy marketing campaigns and more about consistent, strategic efforts. Lead generation tactics form the foundation, such as attending industry events, networking on platforms like LinkedIn, and even creating high-value content like blog posts and webinars.

We also explored how referral programs are golden. Clients who trust you enough to recommend you to others aren't just boosting your sales – they're endorsing your brand. Rewarding their loyalty (think discounts, thank-you gifts, or shoutouts) strengthens the relationship.

The sales funnel also came into play, breaking down the journey from awareness to purchase. Understanding this process is crucial for engaging clients at every stage. And leveraging testimonials or case studies? That's where you turn satisfied clients into your most effective sales team. Nothing says "trust me" like a glowing review.

Writing Effective Proposals

Proposals are your chance to stand out from the competition and clarify your value proposition. In this section, we detailed the art of responding to Requests for Proposals (RFPs). Knowing where to find them and evaluating whether they align with your services ensures you're targeting the right opportunities.

The anatomy of a bid proposal was another key highlight. From crafting a compelling introduction to breaking down operational plans, pricing structures, and key personnel, every element plays a role in winning the client's trust. The emphasis here was on clarity, professionalism, and tailoring each proposal to the client's specific needs. We even discussed creating realistic timelines for RFP responses and contract awards, keeping you one step ahead.

How to Create a Flexible Pricing Structure for Your Services

Pricing is both an art and a science. Hourly rates, daily rates, flat fees, subscription models, and retainers each have their place, depending on the project's scope and complexity. For instance, an hourly rate might work best for short-term assessments, while retainers are ideal for long-term advisory roles.

Adjusting your rates based on location and threat level was another critical consideration. What the market will bear in New York City might vastly differ from Mobile, Alabama. Similarly, high-threat environments demand higher compensation to reflect the added risk and expertise required.

Building Long-Term Relationships with Clients

The work doesn't end when the project does. In fact, it's just beginning. Long-term client relationships are built on trust, transparency, and consistently exceeding expectations. We delved into the "little things" that matter – like remembering birthdays or supporting causes your clients care about.

The key takeaway? It's not just about the security services you provide; it's about the overall experience. Be proactive, stay communicative, and make your clients feel valued, even when you're not actively working on a project together.

Handling Client Feedback and Adjusting Services

Feedback can be a gift, even when it stings. This section covered the delicate balance of addressing client concerns without getting defensive. Whether it's positive praise or constructive criticism, handling feedback professionally and promptly can turn a potentially negative situation into an opportunity for growth.

Adjusting services mid-contract requires finesse. Scope creep is real, and knowing when to renegotiate terms ensures you're meeting client needs without compromising your bottom line. The ability to pivot while maintaining clear boundaries is a hallmark of a great consultant.

Managing a Client's Expectations in a Crisis

Crises are a defining moment for any security consultant. Whether you're brought in after a crisis erupts, hired proactively to prevent one, or in the thick of it with an existing client, managing expectations is paramount. We emphasized the importance of clear communication, swift action, and maintaining a calm, confident demeanor.

Every crisis is unique, but the principles remain the same: keep the client informed, set realistic expectations, and always have a contingency plan. It's during these moments that your expertise and professionalism will shine – or falter. With the tools from this chapter, you'll be well-prepared to navigate these challenges.

Utilizing CRM Systems to Track Client Data and Engagements

If you're still tracking client interactions on sticky notes, it's time to embrace the digital age. CRM (Customer Relationship Management) systems are game changers for organizing client information, tracking engagements, and streamlining follow-ups.

In this section, we explored the functionalities of CRM tools, from automating reminders to analyzing client behavior. We also provided a roadmap for choosing the right CRM platform, highlighting both free and paid options. The big takeaway? A good CRM system doesn't just keep you organized – it enhances your client relationships and drives repeat business.

Being a Good Partner with Clients from Other Security Consultants

Collaboration is key in the security industry. When entrusted with someone else's client, you're not just representing yourself – you're representing the originating consultant. This section emphasized the importance of clear communication, respecting boundaries, and delivering exceptional service.

We also explored the nuances of hosting clients in your geographic area or lending your niche expertise to a larger project. When handled well, these opportunities can strengthen professional relationships and open doors for future collaborations.

Final Thoughts on Chapter 10

Sales and client relationship management might initially feel overwhelming, but they're the lifeblood of any successful security consulting business. This chapter provided a comprehensive roadmap for building and maintaining strong client relationships, from generating leads to handling crises.

If there's one thing to remember, it's this: the consulting part of the job is just the beginning. How you engage with clients – before, during, and after a project – is what truly sets you apart. By applying the principles and strategies outlined in this chapter, you'll not only build a thriving business but also a reputation that clients and peers can trust.

11

Navigating Business Growth in the Security Sector

"The art of progress is to preserve order amid change and to preserve change amid order."

— Alfred North Whitehead

O r, as a more modern twist might put it: "Growth is great, but don't let your success turn into chaos with a company logo on it."

Setting the Stage: The Growth Trajectory in the Security Sector

Did you know that the global private security market is projected to reach $257 billion by 2028? Yes, you read that right. This industry is growing like a controlled explosion – intense, powerful, and potentially overwhelming if you don't handle it properly. The question for you isn't whether the security sector will grow (because it most certainly will) but how you can ensure that your business grows with it.

This chapter is your road map to sustainable growth in your security consulting business. We'll delve into how to scale your operations, reach new clients, embrace emerging technologies, and, most importantly, plan for growth in a way that doesn't leave you in over your head. Think of this as your guide to growing smart, not just big.

Scaling Security Operations: Adding More Services

Growth is an exciting milestone for any entrepreneur. It's the moment your business starts to feel less like a scrappy start-up and more like a fully-fledged operation with momentum. But like any good thing, growth has its challenges and scaling too soon or too fast can derail even the most promising ventures. This section focuses on one specific method of growth: adding more services to your core business model. While it may seem like an obvious way to expand, the decision to add services should never be taken lightly.

Let's first discuss how you, as an entrepreneur, can recognize when it's time to grow your business and why adding services is a strategy that requires both caution and ambition.

Recognizing the Right Time to Scale

Before we move into adding services, let's address the million-dollar question: how do you know it's time to scale? Growth isn't just about wanting more revenue; it's about being prepared for more complexity. There are several telltale signs that your business might be ready to scale:

Overwhelming Demand: If clients are knocking on your door faster than you can answer, it might be time to grow. Maybe you're turning down work because your team or resources are stretched thin.

Market Opportunity: Has a new trend, client need, or regulatory change created a gap in the market? Scaling to meet those demands could be a golden opportunity.

Stable Foundations: If your current services are running smoothly – think consistent revenue, happy clients, and efficient operations – you have a sturdy foundation to build on.

Clear Financial Health: Growth costs money, and you'll need a solid financial buffer to scale successfully. If your budget can't support growth, it's time to pump the brakes.

Vision Alignment: Growth should align with your long-term vision. Adding services or expanding for the sake of "doing more" often results in a lack of focus and diluted brand identity.

Ways to Scale: Adding Services as a Growth Model

Scaling can take many forms, from entering new geographic markets to expanding your target audience. However, adding services to your core offerings is one of the most accessible and impactful ways to grow. It's also fraught with potential pitfalls if approached recklessly.

Why Adding Services Is a Logical Step

Adding services is a natural extension of your business. Once you've carved out a niche and built credibility, offering complementary services can enhance your value to clients. For example, if your security consulting business specializes in risk assessments, adding incident response planning might feel like a seamless next step. Not only does this increase your revenue streams, but it also deepens client trust by offering more comprehensive solutions.

The Risks of Adding Too Much, Too Quickly

Let's address the elephant in the room: growing too fast can be disastrous. Adding too many services at once can stretch your resources, confuse your clients, and dilute your brand. Consider if you start as a high-end cybersecurity consultant and then decide to add physical security, training services, and drone surveillance – all within six months. Without the proper infrastructure, this ambitious growth could leave you juggling too many balls and dropping most of them.

Factors to Consider Before Adding Services

When deciding whether to add new services, it's essential to evaluate several key factors:

Client Demand: Are your clients asking for this service? Adding a new offering should solve a specific problem or meet an identified need.

Example: A client consistently asks for security awareness training after you complete a physical security assessment. This might indicate an untapped demand.

Operational Capacity: Do you have the infrastructure, personnel, and expertise to deliver this service effectively? Scaling services should maintain the quality of your core offerings.

Market Research: Investigate whether competitors are already offering this service. If so, what's your differentiator? If not, why not? There may be a barrier you haven't considered.

Alignment with Core Business: Does the new service align with your mission and brand? Expanding into unrelated areas might need to be clarified for your clients and dilute your reputation.

Financial Viability: Can you afford to invest in the necessary resources to add this service? Consider the costs of training, hiring, marketing, and equipment.

Scalability: Once you add the service, can you scale it? Starting small is fine, but the ultimate goal should be to grow the offering sustainably.

Practical Steps to Adding Services

Start with a Pilot Program: Test the waters before diving in headfirst. Offer the new service to a select group of clients, gather feedback, and tweak your approach.

Example: A security consultant specializing in VIP protection pilots a travel security advisory service for high-net-worth clients traveling internationally.

Train Your Team: Adding services often requires new expertise. Invest in training or hiring subject matter experts to ensure you can deliver the new service at a high standard.

Communicate Clearly: Inform your clients about your new offerings through newsletters, social media, and personalized outreach. Explain how the new services complement your existing ones.

Adjust Marketing Strategies: Highlight the benefits of your new services on your website and marketing materials. Consider creating case studies or testimonials to showcase the value.

Monitor Performance: Set metrics to measure the success of your new service. Track client satisfaction, revenue generated, and operational efficiency.

Examples of Service Expansion

To bring this concept to life, let's explore a few examples:

Example 1: Cybersecurity Consultant Adds Incident Response Services. A cybersecurity consultant might start by offering risk assessments. Over time, they notice clients struggling with breach response. Adding an incident response service fills this gap and increases client retention.

Example 2: Physical Security Consultant Adds Training Programs. A consultant specializing in physical security assessments might add employee training programs to teach clients how to implement recommendations effectively.

Example 3: Surveillance Expert Adds Drone Technology Services. A consultant with expertise in surveillance might expand into drone surveillance for large-scale industrial facilities, offering cutting-edge solutions.

Avoiding Dilution of Your Brand

Adding services should enhance your brand, not dilute it. Here are a few ways to stay focused:

Stick to Your Niche: If your brand is built around being a specialist, avoid branching into unrelated areas.

Deliver Excellence: Never compromise on quality, even if it means growing more slowly.

Client-Centered Growth: Focus on services that genuinely add value to your clients rather than chasing trends.

Adding services is an exciting opportunity to grow your security consulting business. However, it requires careful planning, strategic decision-making, and a commitment to maintaining the quality and integrity of your brand. Growth, after all, should amplify your reputation, not compromise it.

Expanding Your Client Base and Target Markets

Expanding your client base and breaking into new target markets is like planting seeds for a bountiful harvest: it requires strategy, timing, and care. For a security consulting business, this growth step is as much about solidifying your brand as it is about identifying opportunities to serve a wider audience. If you're thinking about scaling by adding clients or entering new markets, it's essential to understand that this move is not just about finding more people to serve – it's about finding the right people to serve.

Let's jump into the process of expanding your client base and target markets. This journey requires a deep understanding of who your ideal clients are, where they are, and what value you can bring to them.

Why Expand Your Client Base?

Before exploring how to expand, let's tackle the *why*. Maybe your business has hit a plateau, or your current market feels oversaturated. Perhaps you're seeking a more diverse revenue stream to mitigate risks or looking to serve clients who better align with your expertise and services. Whatever the reason, expanding your client base is about more than just financial growth – it's about creating stability, building relationships, and increasing your impact.

But here's the kicker: growth doesn't mean taking on every opportunity that comes your way. Just because you can serve someone doesn't mean you should. The goal is to attract the clients and markets that align with your skills, values, and business goals.

Understanding Your Current Client Base

Before you expand, you need to understand your starting point. Ask yourself:

Who are my current clients? Analyze their demographics, industries, and pain points. What do they have in common? Why did they choose your services?

What am I doing well? Identify what clients appreciate about your services. Is it your responsiveness, technical expertise, or ability to adapt to unique challenges?

Where am I falling short? Growth often reveals gaps. Recognizing areas for improvement now will save headaches later.

Are there untapped opportunities within my existing client base? Sometimes, the most straightforward growth strategy is expanding the services you offer to your current clients.

Identifying New Target Markets

Once you have a firm grasp of your current situation, it's time to look outward. Target markets are specific groups of people or organizations most likely to benefit from your services. Expanding into new markets involves identifying these groups and tailoring your approach to meet their needs.

How to Identify New Markets:

Research Industry Trends: Stay updated on trends within the security industry. For example, as cybersecurity threats increase, businesses in sectors like finance and healthcare are investing heavily in protection measures. Is there a niche within these industries you could serve?

Example: A security consultant specializing in physical security might expand into cyber-physical systems for industries like utilities or manufacturing.

Leverage Your Expertise: Identify industries or markets where your current skills are in high demand. If you've worked extensively in corporate security, consider branching into executive protection or crisis management for ultra-high-net-worth individuals.

Network and Collaborate: Sometimes, opportunities are just a handshake away. Attend industry events, join associations, and connect with professionals who can provide insights into new markets.

Look at Geographic Expansion: If your business operates in a specific region, consider expanding to nearby cities or states. Research these areas' regulatory requirements and client demographics to ensure a smooth transition.

Analyze Competitors: Who are your competitors serving, and what gaps are they leaving behind? Filling these voids can give you an edge.

The Importance of Value Proposition

Expanding your client base isn't just about finding new customers; it's about convincing them that you're the best choice. This is where your value proposition comes into play. Your value proposition is the unique promise of value that you deliver to clients. It's what sets you apart from the competition.

When entering a new market, your value proposition may need to evolve. For example, if you've focused on small businesses but want to target larger corporations, your messaging should shift to emphasize scalability, expertise, and proven results.

Practical Steps for Expanding Your Client Base

Leverage Referrals: Word-of-mouth referrals are one of the easiest ways to grow your client base. Encourage satisfied clients to recommend your services to their peers. Offer incentives like discounts on future services for successful referrals. *Example:* A corporate client refers your consulting firm to another department within the same company. You secure a new contract without spending a dime on marketing.

Develop Strategic Partnerships: Partnering with complementary businesses can introduce you to new clients. For example, teaming up with an IT company can help you tap into their client base while offering a comprehensive cybersecurity and physical security service package.

Use Digital Marketing: Leverage platforms like LinkedIn and industry-specific forums to connect with potential clients. Tailor your messaging to address the pain points of your target audience.

Offer Free Workshops or Webinars: Hosting educational sessions can showcase your expertise while attracting potential clients. For example, a webinar on "How to Prevent Workplace Violence" could generate leads from HR departments.

Attend Industry Events: Conferences and trade shows are gold mines for networking. Bring plenty of business cards, polish your elevator pitch, and follow up with every connection you make.

Practical Steps for Expanding into New Target Markets

Start Small: Test the waters with a pilot program before fully committing to a new market. This minimizes risk while providing valuable insights.

Tailor Your Services: One size does not fit all. Adapt your offerings to meet the specific needs of your new market. *Example:* If you're expanding into the healthcare sector, consider compliance requirements like HIPAA when developing your services.

Hire Local Experts: When entering a new region, partnering with local experts can help you navigate cultural, legal, and logistical challenges.

Invest in Market-Specific Marketing: Create marketing campaigns tailored to the preferences and concerns of your new audience. Highlight testimonials and case studies that resonate with them.

Monitor Results: Track key performance indicators (KPIs) like client acquisition costs, conversion rates, and customer satisfaction to assess the success of your expansion efforts.

Overcoming Challenges in Expansion

No growth strategy is without its challenges. Here are a few common obstacles and how to overcome them:

Breaking Into Established Markets: Entering a market dominated by competitors can be challenging. Differentiate yourself by emphasizing your niche expertise and delivering unparalleled service.

Cultural Differences: Understanding local customs and business practices is crucial to expanding internationally. Invest time in cultural training to avoid missteps.

Resource Constraints: Growth often requires significant time, money, and personnel. Plan your budget carefully and prioritize scalable strategies.

Anecdote: Learning the Hard Way

Let's say you're a security consultant specializing in risk assessments for mid-sized businesses. After hearing about the lucrative healthcare sector, you decide to expand into this market. You secure a meeting with a hospital administrator but quickly realize you're unprepared to address their specific concerns about compliance, patient safety, and regulatory issues.

The lesson? Research, preparation, and adaptability are critical when expanding your client base or target markets. By learning from missteps and continually refining your approach, you can set yourself up for long-term success.

Expanding your client base and target markets is an exciting opportunity for growth. By understanding your current clients, identifying new opportunities, and delivering exceptional value, you can build a business that's both scalable and sustainable.

Exploring New Technologies in Security Consulting

Picture the security industry as a race car. Over the years, the track has remained somewhat the same – companies protecting assets, individuals ensuring safety – but the car has gone from a basic vehicle to a high-tech machine powered by artificial intelligence (AI), drones, and advanced cyber tools. If you're an entrepreneur in security consulting, the question isn't whether you'll adopt new technology but *when* and *how* to integrate these innovations into your business model.

Let's explore what it means to harness cutting-edge technologies in security consulting and why doing so is critical for staying competitive and delivering unparalleled value to your clients.

The Ever-Evolving Security Landscape

The security industry is transforming at a pace that rivals Silicon Valley. Emerging threats, from ransomware to drone attacks, have forced the industry to innovate continuously. This shift has created a dual challenge for security consultants: staying informed about technological advancements and determining which innovations align with their business goals.

Technologies like AI, the Internet of Things (IoT), and drone defense systems are no longer optional luxuries; they're fast becoming essential components of a comprehensive security strategy. But here's the catch: jumping into new technologies without a clear plan is like buying a Indianapolis race car without knowing how to drive a stick. Let's take a closer look at how to navigate this process.

Assessing the Need for New Technology

Before diving into the latest gadget or software, ask yourself:

Does this technology solve a client's pain point? Clients hire you to make their lives easier or their assets safer. If the tech you're considering doesn't address a specific need, it's not worth the investment.

Example: If you serve corporate clients worried about insider threats, leveraging AI to monitor suspicious patterns in digital communications might be a game-changer.

Is it scalable for your business? Some technologies come with hefty price tags and steep learning curves. Ensure the investment makes sense for your current scale and potential growth.

Will it set you apart from competitors? Suppose everyone in your niche is adopting a particular technology. In that case, you may need to follow suit to stay relevant – or you might identify an underutilized innovation that gives you an edge.

Key Technologies Reshaping Security Consulting

Artificial Intelligence (AI): AI is like having a tireless assistant who never sleeps. From predictive analytics to automated surveillance, AI helps security consultants identify risks faster and more accurately than ever.

Practical Applications:

- Predicting potential breaches based on patterns in historical data.
- Automating tasks like camera monitoring to free up human resources.
- Enhancing threat detection in cybersecurity systems.

Example: A retail chain might hire you to prevent theft. Integrating AI-powered facial recognition software into their surveillance system lets you identify repeat offenders or detect suspicious behavior in real time.

Internet of Things (IoT): IoT refers to interconnected devices that share data to improve efficiency. For security consultants, IoT represents a goldmine of real-time information.

Practical Applications:

- Smart locks and access control systems.
- IoT-enabled cameras that provide live feeds accessible from anywhere.
- Environmental monitoring for sensitive areas like data centers.

Example: You're consulting for a museum housing priceless artifacts. IoT sensors can monitor temperature, humidity, and even vibrations to protect exhibits from environmental damage or tampering.

Drones and Anti-Drone Technology: Drones have become both a tool and a threat to security. While drones are invaluable for monitoring large areas, malicious actors can also weaponize them.

Practical Applications:

- Conducting aerial surveillance for events or sprawling properties.
- Inspecting hard-to-reach infrastructure like pipelines or rooftops.
- Deploying anti-drone systems to protect against unauthorized intrusions.

Example: A private estate hires you to bolster its perimeter security. By incorporating drone surveillance and anti-drone measures, you create a robust solution that outperforms traditional ground-based systems.

Cybersecurity and Ransomware Defense: The rise of cyberattacks has blurred the lines between physical and digital security. For security consultants, this means offering solutions that protect both realms.

Practical Applications:

- Implementing firewalls and intrusion detection systems.
- Educating clients about phishing and ransomware threats.
- Developing incident response plans for cyber breaches.

Example: A mid-sized business contracts you to improve its security. By providing cybersecurity training for employees and deploying advanced threat detection software, you help prevent a potential ransomware attack.

Advanced Analytics: Data is the new oil, and advanced analytics is the refinery. By leveraging data from multiple sources, consultants can make more informed decisions.

Practical Applications:

- Risk assessments based on historical incident data.
- Predictive models for staffing security personnel during high-risk periods.
- Tailoring services based on client-specific trends.

Example: After analyzing incident patterns for a hotel chain, you recommend deploying additional personnel during peak tourism seasons, reducing theft and improving guest safety.

Implementation Strategies

Adopting new technology isn't just about purchasing tools – it's about seamlessly integrating them into your operations. Here's how to do it:

Start Small: Test new technologies on a pilot basis to assess their effectiveness. For example, if you're considering AI-powered cameras, try them at a single location before scaling up.

Train Your Team: Even the best technology is useless without knowledgeable operators. Invest in training programs to ensure your team can use the tools effectively.

Collaborate with Experts: Partner with technology providers or consultants specializing in implementation. Their expertise can save you time and resources.

Monitor ROI: Continuously evaluate the performance of your technology investments. Are they delivering measurable benefits like reduced risks, improved efficiency, or higher client satisfaction?

Avoiding Pitfalls

While technology offers immense potential, it's not without risks. Here are common pitfalls to avoid:

Overloading Your Plate: Adopting too many technologies at once can overwhelm your team and dilute your focus. Prioritize tools that align with your immediate needs.

Ignoring Privacy Concerns: Facial recognition has ethical and legal implications. Ensure your solutions comply with regulations and respect client privacy.

Underestimating Costs: Beyond the initial purchase price, consider ongoing expenses like maintenance, upgrades, and training.

Anecdote: The Tale of Too Much Tech

Visualize a security consultant named Alex who decides to "go big or go home" by investing in every shiny new gadget on the market. Alex installs drones, AI systems, and IoT devices without a clear strategy. The result? A tangled mess of incompatible tools, frustrated clients, and ballooning costs.

The lesson? Technology is a means to an end, not an end in itself. By taking a measured, thoughtful approach, you can avoid Alex's fate and build a tech-savvy business that thrives. Bottom line, don't be an "Alex" …trust me.

Staying Ahead of the Curve

The security industry's technology revolution isn't slowing down. To stay competitive, you'll need to:

Stay Informed: Regularly read industry publications, attend tech conferences, and participate in webinars.

Engage with Innovators: Build relationships with tech companies and early adopters in your field.

Adapt Quickly: Be prepared to pivot your strategies as new technologies emerge.

Exploring new technologies in security consulting is both an opportunity and a responsibility. By embracing innovation, you can deliver cutting-edge solutions that set your business apart. But remember, the goal isn't just to adopt technology – it's to use it wisely, efficiently, and ethically.

Now that we've tackled scaling through technology, shall we move on to the final subsection, *Developing a Sustainable Growth Plan?*

Developing a Sustainable Growth Plan

Sustainable growth isn't about sprinting to success but pacing yourself to win the marathon. For a security consulting entrepreneur, growth is not just about scaling services, expanding markets, or jumping into the latest tech; it's about ensuring your business remains stable, adaptable, and profitable over the long haul. Without a sustainable plan, even the most promising business can buckle under the weight of hasty decisions and unchecked ambition. So, how do you grow your security consulting business in a way that is strategic, intentional, and built to last?

The Big Picture: What Does Sustainable Growth Mean?

Sustainable growth is about achieving expansion without compromising your business's brand, quality of service, integrity, or operational health. It means balancing opportunity with capacity – taking on new clients or services without overwhelming your resources. Think of it like upgrading a home. You wouldn't tear down all the walls and double the size overnight. Instead, you'd renovate room by room, ensuring everything remains functional during the process.

In security consulting, this concept is critical. Scaling too quickly can dilute your expertise, stretch your team too thin, or result in client dissatisfaction. Conversely, scaling too slowly might allow competitors to take the lead. The trick is finding the sweet spot, and that's where a sustainable growth plan comes into play.

The Growth Readiness Checklist: Are You Ready to Scale?

Is your foundation solid?

- Do you have efficient processes and Standard Operating Procedures (SOPs) in place?
- Are your current clients happy and loyal?
- Is your team equipped to handle more work or larger contracts?

Do you have the financial bandwidth? Growth often requires upfront investment, whether for hiring, training, technology, or marketing. Ensure you have sufficient reserves or access to funding.

Do you have a clear vision? Growth for the sake of growth is a recipe for disaster. Have a clear idea of why you're scaling and what success looks like.

Example: Let's say there's a security consultant named Lisa. Lisa's business is thriving, and she's considering expanding into cybersecurity. However, she noticed that her current operations lacked standardized training for new hires. Before scaling, Lisa creates a robust onboarding process to ensure her expansion keeps existing services intact.

Milestones and Checkpoints: Measuring Growth Responsibly

Just as travelers need signposts to ensure they're on the right path, entrepreneurs need milestones to gauge whether their growth trajectory is sustainable. Here are some key checkpoints:

Revenue Benchmarks: Monitor your revenue growth month over month. Are you consistently meeting targets? Sustainable growth should come with steady profitability, not wild fluctuations.

Client Satisfaction Scores: Regularly gather client feedback to ensure quality hasn't slipped. Remember, retaining clients is often more profitable than acquiring new ones.

Team Capacity Assessments: Periodically review your team's workload. Are they managing the demands comfortably, or is burnout looming?

Cash Flow Stability: Ensure your inflow consistently exceeds your outflow. Even a booming business can crash if cash flow isn't well managed.

Example: A security firm grows its client base by 20% in six months but notices an uptick in customer complaints. Upon review, the owner realizes the team is overextended. The solution? Temporarily pause new client acquisition and focus on hiring and training before resuming expansion.

Creating a Roadmap for Measured Growth

A sustainable growth plan isn't just about lofty goals – it's about mapping out the practical steps to achieve them. Here's how to structure your roadmap:

Step 1: Set SMART Goals. We've covered the acronym SMART earlier when we talked about making personal goals, so you should be familiar with the concept. It applies to sustainable growth as well. Your growth goals should be Specific, Measurable, Achievable, Relevant, and Time-bound. For example:

- Specific: Expand into cybersecurity consulting.
- Measurable: Secure three new cybersecurity clients in six months.
- Achievable: Build on existing technical expertise within your team.
- Relevant: Aligns with the increasing demand for cybersecurity services.
- Time-bound: Launch by Q3 of the fiscal year.

Step 2: Identify Resources and Gaps. Growth often requires additional resources, whether that's technology, staff, or capital. Conduct a gap analysis to determine what you need to achieve your goals.

Example: If you want to offer drone surveillance, do you have certified operators or a training plan in place?

Step 3: Develop an Action Plan. Break your goals into actionable steps. For instance:

- Researching market demand and competition.
- Training staff or hiring specialists.
- Achieve necessary credentials, certifications, and licenses.
- Develop a rebranding strategy for all online presence and print materials
- Develop marketing and launch strategy
- Set pricing structures
- Marketing the new service to existing and potential clients.

Step 4: Monitor Progress and Adjust. Growth is rarely linear. Regularly review your progress and be willing to pivot if needed. If a new service isn't gaining traction, reassess your strategy or market approach.

Avoiding the Pitfalls of Rapid Growth

Overextension. Adding too many services too quickly can overwhelm your team and dilute your expertise. Prioritize depth over breadth.

Example: Instead of launching three new services simultaneously, focus on one and establish it as a market leader before expanding further.

Neglecting Core Clients. In the rush to grow, it's easy to take existing clients for granted. However, these clients are your foundation. Keep them happy by maintaining the same level of service they expect.

Financial Overreach. Expanding without sufficient financial planning can strain cash flow. Ensure you have a financial cushion to weather the initial costs of scaling.

Anecdote: The Tale of Two Entrepreneurs

Let's compare two security consultants, Mark and Sarah. Both decide to grow their businesses.

Mark's Approach: Mark launches three new services simultaneously without much planning. Within six months, his team is overwhelmed, clients are dissatisfied, and his business faces financial strain.

Sarah's Approach: Sarah starts with one new service – cybersecurity. She trains her team, pilots the service with a few clients, and gradually scales as demand grows. Within a year, Sarah's business is thriving, with happy clients and a strong reputation.

The lesson? Measured, intentional growth beats hasty expansion every time.

Balancing Growth and Sustainability

Sustainable growth isn't about playing it safe – it's about playing it smart. By pacing yourself, prioritizing quality, and continuously assessing your progress, you can expand your security consulting business to benefit both your clients and your bottom line.

As you wrap up this chapter on navigating business growth, remember that growth is not just about getting bigger; it's about getting better. Whether adding services, exploring new markets, or adopting cutting-edge technologies, every step should be rooted in a clear, sustainable strategy.

Chapter 11 Wrap-Up: Navigating Business Growth in the Security Sector

As we close the chapter on navigating business growth, let's take a moment to reflect on the concepts we've explored and the strategies we've laid out. This chapter was a roadmap for entrepreneurs ready to take their security consulting business to the next level. It provided guidance on scaling operations, expanding client bases, embracing new technologies, and developing sustainable growth plans. Whether you're just starting or are a seasoned consultant looking to level up, these lessons are designed to set you on a path to sustainable success.

Scaling Security Operations: Adding More Services

Scaling is the heartbeat of growth, and one of the most accessible ways to achieve it is by adding more services to your portfolio. This section emphasized the importance of timing and planning. Growth for the sake of growth often leads to chaos. Instead, you must evaluate your current capacity, market demand, and operational readiness before leaping into new offerings.

We explored the critical balance of diversifying your services while staying true to your brand. Diluting your expertise by taking on too much too quickly can confuse your clients and exhaust your resources. Instead, consider how additional services align with your niche and whether they genuinely meet the needs of your current and future clientele.

Example Highlight: Remember the hypothetical consultant who specialized in corporate security assessments but added cybersecurity services after carefully analyzing market demand? That strategic move not only enhanced their value proposition but also attracted new clients while retaining existing ones. The lesson? Growth should amplify your brand, not detract from it.

Expanding Your Client Base and Target Markets

Growth isn't just about doing more; it's about reaching more. Expanding your client base and tapping into new target markets is a cornerstone of long-term success. But how do you do this effectively? This section outlined actionable strategies, from networking and partnerships to leveraging technology and market research.

We discussed the importance of understanding your ideal client in any new market. Who are they? What are their pain points? How does your expertise solve their problems? Tailoring your approach to meet these specific needs ensures your expansion efforts are both effective and profitable.

We also delved into strategic partnerships as a means of market entry. Collaborating with established entities in a new market can lend your business credibility and open doors that might otherwise remain closed. Partnerships aren't just about pooling resources but leveraging mutual strengths to create value.

Humorous Takeaway: Expanding into a new market without research is like throwing a surprise party for someone you've never met. Sure, they might love cake, but what if they're gluten-free and hate surprises? Do your homework.

Exploring New Technologies in Security Consulting

The security industry is undergoing a near-constant technological revolution, and staying ahead of the curve is non-negotiable. This section explored the transformative impact of technologies like Artificial Intelligence, the Internet of Things, drones, anti-drone measures, and advanced cybersecurity protocols. These tools aren't just nice to have for security consultants – they're becoming industry standards.

We also emphasized the importance of discernment when adopting new technologies. Not every shiny gadget or cutting-edge software will be a fit for your business or your clients. The key is aligning technological investments with your expertise, client needs, and long-term strategy.

Practical Anecdote: Picture a consultant investing heavily in drone surveillance technology only to discover their primary client base – houses of worship – rarely requires such services. The takeaway? Tech investments should be data-driven and client-focused.

Finally, we encouraged you to stay curious and committed to lifelong learning. The world of technology moves fast, and keeping pace ensures you remain relevant and competitive in the eyes of your clients.

Developing a Sustainable Growth Plan

All the strategies in the world are meaningless without a solid plan to sustain them. This section served as the blueprint for achieving measured, intentional growth. We emphasized the importance of balancing ambition with practicality, ensuring that every step forward is grounded in preparation and capacity.

Key takeaways included setting SMART goals, conducting regular capacity assessments, and leveraging milestones as checkpoints. Sustainable growth isn't about being cautious – it's about being strategic. By pacing your expansion, maintaining quality, and continuously evaluating your trajectory, you ensure that your business remains resilient and adaptable.

Example Highlight: Consider the consultant who expanded into three new markets simultaneously without ensuring their team was equipped to handle the increased workload. The result? Burnout, dissatisfied clients, and a damaged reputation. Contrast that with the consultant who piloted one new service at a time, refined their approach, and scaled only when ready. The difference? Success that was built to last, designed that way from the start.

Let's Review

Growth is exhilarating, but it's also daunting. This chapter aimed to demystify the process, breaking it into actionable steps that empower you to scale your business confidently and sustainably. Every strategy we discussed was rooted in intentionality and client-centricity, from adding services to exploring new markets and adopting cutting-edge technologies.

Let's not forget the human side of growth. At its core, scaling a business is about building relationships – relationships with your clients, your team, your partners, and even yourself. Growth is as much an internal journey as it is an external one. It requires self-awareness, adaptability, and an unwavering commitment to your vision.

As you close this chapter, remember growth isn't a destination. It's a journey. It is a journey that, when approached with care, strategy, and a touch of humor, leads to a business that's not only bigger but also better. So, take a beat, relax, revisit your growth plan, and confidently step forward. The next level of your security consulting business is waiting for you.

12

Financial Management for a Security Consulting Business

"Beware of little expenses. A small leak will sink a great ship."

— Benjamin Franklin

Money management may not be the most glamorous part of running a security consulting business, but it's undoubtedly one of the most important. The security industry is full of stories about brilliant operators with exceptional expertise who failed simply because they couldn't keep their financial house in order. Whether it's understanding profit margins, managing cash flow, or preparing for the inevitable economic ebbs and flows, financial literacy is the backbone of any thriving business.

According to the Small Business Administration, poor cash flow management accounts for 82% of small business failures. That's not a typo – 82%! If that statistic doesn't motivate you to roll up your sleeves and get into the nitty-gritty of financial management, nothing will.

This chapter is your guide to mastering the numbers side of your security consulting business. You don't need to be a CPA, but you do need to know enough to make informed decisions, avoid pitfalls, and position your business for long-term success. And if you're already sweating at the thought of spreadsheets, relax – we're going to break it all down into manageable chunks with a bit of humor to lighten the load.

Reading Financial Statements and Security Industry Metrics

Managing a security consulting business requires more than just expertise in risk assessments, physical security, or cybersecurity – it demands financial literacy. Many entrepreneurs shy away from the "numbers side" of their business, thinking it's too complex or better left to accountants. But understanding financial statements and industry metrics is not just a "nice to have" – it's essential to staying afloat, growing strategically, and ensuring your efforts translate into profitability.

In this section, we'll demystify financial statements, explore budgeting for essential resources, and tackle key concepts like cash flow, payment terms, and strategies to handle them effectively. Consider this as your personal crash course in financial management for security consulting.

Profit and Loss for Consulting Firms: The Roadmap to Profitability

The profit and loss (P&L) statement, also called an income statement, is a snapshot of your business's financial performance over a specific period. It's essentially your business's report card. The P&L shows your revenue, expenses, and the all-important bottom line – profit.

For a security consulting business, the P&L might include categories such as:

Revenue: Consulting fees, retainer payments, and project-based income.

Cost of Goods Sold (COGS): Direct costs like equipment purchased for clients or subcontractor wages.

Operating Expenses: Overheads such as office rent, software subscriptions, and travel costs.

Net Profit (or Loss): Revenue minus expenses and COGS.

Practical Application: Let's pretend you just wrapped up a large corporate security audit project that brought in $50,000 in revenue. Your expenses included $15,000 for temporary contractors, $5,000 in software tools, and $3,000 in travel costs. Your P&L for that project would look like this:

- Revenue: $50,000
- Expenses: $23,000
- Net Profit: $27,000

A solid P&L gives you insights into whether you're pricing your services correctly and where you can trim unnecessary expenses.

Budgeting for Security Equipment and Training: Investing Wisely

Budgeting isn't just about keeping track of expenses – it's about planning for the future. Investing in state-of-the-art equipment and ongoing training can be the difference between staying relevant and becoming obsolete for security consultants.

Key Considerations for Security Equipment:

High-priority tools: Risk assessment software, GPS trackers, and surveillance devices.

Quality vs. Cost: While buying the cheapest tools is tempting, low-quality equipment can backfire, costing you more in replacements and client dissatisfaction.

Maintenance Costs: Factor in regular calibration and software updates.

Budgeting for Training:

Certifications: Staying certified in areas like risk management or cybersecurity adds credibility to your brand.

Workshops and Conferences: Budget for attending industry events to network and stay updated.

Employee Development: If you have a team, their training is as important as yours.

Practical Tip: Allocate a percentage of your annual revenue – say, 10% – for professional development and equipment. For instance, if you earn $150,000 annually, set aside $15,000 specifically for this purpose.

Understanding Cash Flow and Cash Flow Management: The Lifeline of Your Business

Cash flow is the movement of money in and out of your business. Positive cash flow means you have more money coming in than going out, while negative cash flow means the opposite.

Even profitable businesses can go bankrupt if their cash flow is poorly managed. For example, if you've invoiced a client for $25,000 but their payment isn't due for 90 days, you might struggle to pay immediate expenses like rent or subcontractors.

Practical Tips for Managing Cash Flow

Forecast Regularly: Use tools like QuickBooks or Wave to predict cash flow for the next quarter.

Invoice Promptly: The sooner you send invoices, the sooner you get paid.

Negotiate Terms with Vendors: Extend your payment deadlines to align with client payments.

Example Scenario: You've taken on a project with a $40,000 budget, but 75% of that will only be paid upon project completion. To manage cash flow, you negotiate with your software vendor to delay your $5,000 payment until after payment of the final invoice is received.

Understanding Payment Terms: Net+30, 60, 90, etc.

Payment terms dictate how long your clients have to pay your invoice. Terms like Net+30, Net+60, or Net+90 indicate payment deadlines of 30, 60, or 90 days, respectively.

Long payment terms can choke your cash flow, especially if you're a small business. However, offering flexible terms can make your business more attractive to larger clients. As we discussed earlier, when you get into business with a large corporate client or an established firm, you may not have a choice and will have to accept whatever payment terms the client dictates. You should always try negotiating more favorable terms, but this can be difficult. If it's impossible to negotiate a shorter payment term, try to devise alternative solutions to limit the financial impact of waiting 30, 60, or 90 days to get paid.

Strategies to Assist with Client Payment Terms:

Deposit for Services: Require an upfront payment (e.g., 25%-50%) to cover immediate costs. Negotiate a mid-point payment and a final payment due on deliverable acceptance. If the project will go on for any length of time, negotiate a monthly or semi-monthly partial payment.

Cover payroll upfront and invoice for operational expenses: The most important thing is to ensure your guys can put food on the table. The business can wait a few weeks.

Late Fees: Include penalties for overdue invoices to encourage timely payments.

Pro Tip: As a last resort (and if it's a big client that you don't want to lose to unfavorable payment terms), you can consider getting a short-term loan to bridge the gap between making the necessary expenditures to cover the execution of the operations and when you can get a deposit in accounts receivable.

Example Scenario: You're consulting for a high-net-worth client who insists on Net+90 terms. To safeguard your cash flow, you negotiate a 30% upfront deposit, a 30% mid-project payment, and the remaining 40% upon completion.

Practical Implementation: A Comprehensive Financial Plan

Now that we've covered the fundamentals, let's create a checklist to ensure you're on top of your financial management:

Maintain a Detailed P&L Statement: Review monthly to assess profitability.

Budget for Growth: Include equipment upgrades and training expenses.

Track Cash Flow: Use accounting software to avoid surprises.

Set Clear Payment Terms: Negotiate terms that balance client convenience with your financial stability.

Anecdote to Reinforce the Point: Consider Alex, a small security consultant who landed a $75,000 project with a Net+60 payment term. Eager to impress, Alex forgot to account for the two-month gap between invoicing and payment. This oversight forced him to dip into personal savings to cover operational costs, teaching him a valuable lesson about cash flow management.

By mastering financial statements and understanding industry metrics, you'll keep your business afloat and set the foundation for strategic growth. Let your P&L guide your decisions, your budgeting pave the way for innovation, and your cash flow keeps you agile and prepared for anything the industry throws your way.

Managing Profit Margins and Cost Efficiency

When running a security consulting business, profit margins are your lifeline. A substantial profit margin doesn't just mean your business is healthy – it means you're prepared for the unexpected, ready for growth, and confident in your pricing strategy. However, keeping those margins intact is an art form that requires careful planning, wise decision-making, and a constant eye on efficiency.

Let's start with the basics: profit margin is the percentage of revenue that remains as profit after deducting all expenses. If you bring in $100,000 in revenue and spend $80,000 on operating costs, your profit margin is 20%. Simple, right? Not quite. Remember, we are considering your company as if it is its own person. So, profit margin is something we calculate for the company, not for you as an individual. As we calculate a profit margin, one of the deductions you will take away will be the expense of salary (yours and your employees). In the security consulting world, managing profit margins isn't just about reducing costs – it's about delivering value to your clients without bleeding cash.

Security consulting has unique challenges when it comes to profit margins. On one hand, clients expect top-tier expertise, technology, and services, which often come with high costs. On the other, the competitive market pressures you to keep prices attractive. Striking the right balance is like walking a tightrope with a stack of plates – you need focus, finesse, and maybe a touch of luck.

Understanding Fixed and Variable Costs

Before we get into managing costs, let's distinguish between fixed and variable expenses. Fixed costs stay constant regardless of how much business you do, such as office rent, software subscriptions, and insurance. Variable costs, on the other hand, fluctuate with the volume of work, like subcontractor wages, travel expenses, and equipment procurement.

Practical Tip: Aim to minimize fixed costs to safeguard your profit margins. For instance, consider coworking spaces or remote work arrangements instead of leasing a full-time office space. Keep variable costs flexible by outsourcing non-core services only when needed.

Cost Efficiency: The Subtle Art of Doing More with Less

Cost efficiency isn't about cutting corners – it's about maximizing value for every dollar spent. Here are some key strategies:

Automate Where Possible: Use technology to streamline repetitive tasks. For example, invest in a robust CRM system to manage client data and automate follow-ups, freeing up your time for higher-value activities.

Negotiate Contracts: Don't settle for sticker prices for software subscriptions or equipment purchases. Vendors often offer discounts for longer commitments or larger orders.

Optimize Manpower: Match your staffing model to the project's needs. For short-term or specialized tasks, opt for 1099 contractors instead of hiring full-time employees.

Anecdote: Meet Sam, a security consultant specializing in corporate risk assessments. By replacing his old travel policy with virtual site visits for initial consultations, he saved 25% on travel expenses. He increased his profit margin by 5%, while clients appreciated the faster turnaround times.

The Importance of Tracking Profit Margins Regularly

Profit margins aren't a "set-it-and-forget-it" metric. Regularly reviewing them helps you spot trends, identify inefficiencies, and adapt to market changes. For instance, if your profit margins are shrinking despite steady revenue, it's a red flag that your expenses are creeping up.

Practical Implementation: Set up a monthly review process to analyze:

- Revenue vs. Expenses
- Profit margins per project
- High-cost areas that need optimization

Pricing Strategy and Its Impact on Margins

Your pricing structure plays a critical role in maintaining healthy profit margins. If your prices are too low, you risk undermining your profitability. Too high, and you risk losing clients to competitors.

Practical Tip for Pricing: Base your pricing on the value you provide, not just your costs. For example, if your specialized training program reduces a client's risk exposure by 30%, price it to reflect that value, not just your expenses.

Avoiding the Trap of Over-Servicing

It's tempting to go above and beyond for every client, but over-servicing can erode your profit margins. Yes, offering those "extra niceties". But don't go overboard. Offering too many freebies or spending excessive time on low-revenue projects is a fast track to burnout.

Practical Guidance: Set clear boundaries on what's included in your services. For instance, instead of offering unlimited consultations, limit them to a set number per project phase.

Anecdote: Imagine a consultant who spent 20 extra hours on a $5,000 project to "wow" a client, only to realize later that his hourly rate for that job ended up being below minimum wage. Lesson learned: wow them within reason.

Tools to Boost Cost Efficiency

Accounting Software: Use tools like QuickBooks or FreshBooks to track expenses and revenue in real-time.

Project Management Tools: Platforms like Trello or Asana can streamline workflows and reduce time wastage.

Outsourcing Platforms: Websites like Upwork or Fiverr allow you to find skilled freelancers for specialized tasks, saving you the cost of a full-time hire.

Monitoring Industry Benchmarks

Staying competitive requires knowing how your profit margins stack up against industry benchmarks. Security consulting firms often aim for profit margins of 15%-20%, but this can vary based on specialization and market conditions.

Practical Tip: Join industry associations or attend conferences to network and gain insights into peer performance. This information can guide your cost management and pricing strategies.

Building a Culture of Cost Consciousness

Finally, managing profit margins isn't just a financial exercise – it's a mindset. Foster a culture of cost-consciousness within your team. Encourage employees to identify and implement cost-saving measures, from using energy-efficient equipment to rethinking travel policies.

Managing profit margins and cost efficiency isn't about being stingy – it's about ensuring the long-term sustainability of your business. By understanding your costs, strategically pricing, and optimizing operations, you'll protect your bottom line and deliver exceptional value to your clients. And remember: every dollar saved is a dollar you can reinvest into growth, innovation, or (even better) a much-needed vacation.

Understanding Security Industry-Specific Tax Considerations

Taxes: the ultimate double-edged sword of running a business. You want to reduce your profit margin to as little as possible to limit your tax liability, but you got into this business to make as much money as possible. Trying to keep up with tax laws on your own can feel like a never-ending series of puzzles designed by someone who never wanted you to win. For security consultants, the stakes are even higher, as our industry has unique nuances that make navigating tax obligations a little more complex than the average business. But don't worry – while this chapter offers a solid foundation, the golden rule here is simple: always consult a Certified Public Accountant (CPA) or tax professional to get official, personalized advice.

The Basics of Business Taxes: Where It All Starts

Before diving into the security-specific aspects, let's cover the basics. As a business owner, you'll deal with several categories of taxes, including but not limited to:

Income Tax: Based on the profit your business earns.

Self-Employment Tax: Covers Social Security and Medicare contributions for sole proprietors and independent consultants.

Sales Tax: Applicable if you're selling physical products like security equipment.

Payroll Taxes: If you have employees, you'll handle federal, state, and possibly local payroll taxes.

For security consultants, the income tax and self-employment tax categories often take center stage. Understanding how these work and determining available deductions can significantly reduce your tax liability.

Security Industry-Specific Deductions

Now comes the good news: the security industry offers a variety of tax-deductible expenses. Here are some categories to consider:

Training and Certification Costs: Whether you're earning your Certified Protection Professional (CPP) credential or training in drone surveillance, these costs are typically deductible as business expenses.

Equipment and Supplies: From surveillance cameras to secure communication devices, the tools of your trade can often be written off. Even mundane items like office supplies count.

Travel Expenses: Expenses like airfare, lodging, and meals can be deductible if your work involves travel – whether to a client site or an industry conference. Just ensure the trip is directly related to your business.

Example: Imagine you attend a security conference in Las Vegas, where you learn about the latest cybersecurity tools. Not only can you deduct the conference registration fee but also your flight, hotel stay, and even 50% of your meals. But remember, the IRS frowns on turning these trips into extended vacations, so keep those receipts and records clear.

Insurance Premiums: Professional liability insurance, equipment coverage, and even some health insurance premiums can be written off.

Home Office Deduction: If you operate out of your home, you may qualify for a deduction based on the square footage used exclusively for your business.

Pro Tip: Make sure that you separate per-diem, travel, lodging, and mileage from the rest of the income. This income is usually not taxable (check with your tax professional).

Tax Classifications for Security Consultants

The structure of your business affects your tax obligations significantly. Here's how the most common setups impact taxes:

Sole Proprietorships and Single-Member LLCs: Your business income is reported on your personal tax return, and you'll pay self-employment taxes. This simplicity is appealing to many solo consultants.

Partnerships and Multi-Member LLCs: Partnerships file a separate return but pass income through to the partners, who then report it on their personal tax returns. The advantage? Flexibility. The drawback? Complexity.

S-Corporations and C-Corporations: S-Corps allow income to pass through to the owner(s), avoiding double taxation, while C-Corps are taxed as separate entities. S-Corps often appeal to consultants with growing teams.

1099 Independent Contractors: If you're working as a contractor, you're responsible for tracking and paying self-employment taxes, as clients don't withhold taxes for you.

Practical Tip: Choose your structure based on your long-term business goals. Consulting a CPA to weigh the pros and cons of each structure against your revenue projections is worth the investment. Know the possibility of structuring your company as an LLC, taxed as an S-Corp.

Pro Tip: If you work as a 1099 independent contractor, understand that you must set money aside for taxes. The 1099 effective tax rate can be as high as 35%. A good CPA can reduce that tax rate significantly. A good CPA, while expensive in the short term, will often save you exponentially more money in the long run. It is money well spent.

Tax Compliance in the Security Industry

Security consultants often deal with multiple jurisdictions, especially if their work involves crossing state or national borders. This complicates tax compliance but isn't insurmountable with proper planning.

Multi-State Taxation: If you provide services in multiple states, you may owe taxes in each one. Keep detailed records of where income is earned to simplify reporting.

International Tax Considerations: Operating abroad introduces foreign tax obligations. Tools like the Foreign Earned Income Exclusion can help reduce your U.S. tax liability for overseas income.

Example: A consultant providing security training in Europe might owe value-added tax (VAT) in the host country. Partnering with local experts ensures you stay compliant while minimizing unexpected costs.

Payment Terms and Tax Timing

Understanding how your client's payment terms affect taxes is critical. For example, clients who pay on a Net 60 or Net 90 basis could delay your income recognition, impacting when you owe taxes.

Cash vs. Accrual Accounting: Cash accounting recognizes income when it's received, while accrual accounting recognizes it when earned. Choose the method that aligns with your cash flow and tax planning strategy.

Estimated Quarterly Taxes: Self-employed consultants must pay taxes quarterly. Underestimating these payments can lead to penalties, so track income diligently and consult your CPA for projections. Practical Tip: Set aside 25% -30 % of each payment received in a dedicated tax account. This ensures you're never scrambling when payments are due.

Avoiding Common Tax Pitfalls

Mixing Business and Personal Finances: Keep separate accounts for business and personal transactions to simplify tax reporting and avoid IRS scrutiny.

Misclassifying Employees and Contractors: The IRS has strict criteria for distinguishing between W2 employees and 1099 contractors. Misclassification can result in hefty penalties.

Neglecting Record-Keeping: Save all receipts, invoices, and tax-related documents for at least three years. Cloud-based tools like QuickBooks can make this painless.

Leveraging Tax Professionals: Finally, don't hesitate to bring in reinforcements. CPAs, enrolled agents, and tax attorneys can help you navigate the complexities of the security industry while ensuring compliance.

Practical Tip: Look for tax professionals specializing in small businesses or the security sector. Their insights can save you more than the cost of their fees.

Understanding taxes isn't just about compliance – it's about strategy. By knowing which deductions apply, choosing the proper structure, and staying organized, you can turn taxes into a manageable part of your business operations. And with a trusted CPA by your side, you'll confidently navigate even the most complex scenarios.

Financial Planning for Long-Term Stability

Running a security consulting business is more than just protecting people and property; it's also about preserving the longevity of your company. While financial planning might not have the adrenaline rush of neutralizing a threat, it's just as critical to survival. In this section, we'll explore how to keep your business financially stable for the long haul. Whether you're bracing for an economic storm, branching out into new revenue streams, or learning to pivot when the unexpected happens, financial stability is your shield against the uncertainties of the business world.

Handling Economic Downturns: Riding Out the Storm

Economic downturns are as inevitable as rainy days. Just as you wouldn't leave your house without an umbrella when the forecast is grim, you shouldn't run your business without a plan to weather financial storms. Preparing for downturns is especially critical for security consultants, whose services might be considered discretionary in lean times.

Building a Financial Cushion

The first rule of surviving an economic downturn is having a financial cushion. Experts recommend maintaining a reserve fund covering at least three to six months of operating expenses. This safety net allows you to keep the lights on, pay your team, and maintain essential services even if revenues take a hit.

Example: Let's say you run a small security consulting firm specializing in corporate risk assessments. Suddenly, a recession hits, and half your clients tighten their budgets. If you've saved three months' worth of expenses, you can keep your team employed while strategizing how to replace lost revenue.

Streamlining Operations

Economic downturns are an excellent time to evaluate your expenses. Identify areas where you can cut costs without sacrificing the quality of your services. This might include renegotiating vendor contracts, automating routine tasks, or finding more cost-effective software solutions.

Practical Tip: If using multiple software tools for CRM, invoicing, and scheduling, consider an all-in-one platform like Zoho or Freshworks. Consolidation can save you money and streamline your operations.

Retaining Your Client Base

During a downturn, client retention is crucial. Reach out to your existing clients and reinforce the value you bring. Offering temporary discounts, flexible payment terms, or bundled services can help you maintain their loyalty.

Diversifying Revenue Streams: Don't Put All Your Eggs in One Basket

One of the best ways to ensure long-term stability is by diversifying your income. Relying on a single revenue stream is risky, especially in the ever-evolving security industry.

Expanding Your Offerings

If you specialize in physical security assessments, consider adding complementary services like cybersecurity consulting or employee safety training. Diversifying your services allows you to attract more clients and reduces dependency on any single offering.

Example: A security consultant focusing on event security could expand into offering post-event risk analysis or emergency response planning. These services not only add value but also provide additional income streams.

Leveraging Technology for Passive Income

Consider using technology to generate passive income. Creating online courses, eBooks, or subscription-based access to industry insights can provide steady revenue without requiring constant effort.

Example: An experienced security consultant could create a webinar series on best practices for corporate security. Charge participants a fee to attend, and you've created a scalable income source that doesn't depend on one-on-one client interactions.

Partnering for New Opportunities

Strategic partnerships can open doors to new revenue streams. Collaborate with technology providers, insurance companies, or HR firms to offer bundled services. These partnerships not only expand your offerings but also enhance your credibility.

Financial Resilience and Adaptability: Staying Agile in the Face of Change

If there's one certainty in the security industry, it's that nothing stays the same for long. Financial resilience and adaptability are about preparing for change and pivoting quickly when necessary.

Monitoring Industry Trends

Stay informed about trends that could impact your business. Whether it's new technology, regulatory changes, or shifting client needs, understanding these trends allows you to adapt proactively rather than reactively.

Practical Tip: Subscribe to industry publications like *Security Management* or attend conferences to keep your finger on the pulse. The more you know, the better equipped you'll be to navigate change.

Building a Flexible Cost Structure

Flexibility isn't just for yoga – it's also a vital trait for financial management. Consider variable cost structures that can adjust with your workload. For example, hire contractors for short-term projects rather than full-time employees to keep overhead low.

Example: During a surge in demand for event security services, you could temporarily hire independent contractors. This allows you to scale up without committing to long-term payroll expenses.

Planning for the Worst

While no one likes to dwell on worst-case scenarios, planning for them is essential. Create a contingency plan that outlines how your business will respond to various challenges, from losing a major client to dealing with a cyberattack.

Combining Strategies for Long-Term Success

Financial stability isn't about adopting one strategy but integrating multiple approaches into a cohesive plan. Save for a rainy day, diversify your income, and stay agile in the face of change. By doing so, you'll survive economic challenges and thrive despite them.

Practical Checklist for Financial Stability:

Build a Reserve Fund: Save three to six months of operating expenses.

Diversify Revenue Streams: Explore new services, technology, and partnerships.

Monitor Industry Trends: Stay informed and adaptable.

Streamline Costs: Regularly review expenses for potential savings.

Create a Contingency Plan: Know how to respond to worst-case scenarios.

Financial planning isn't glamorous, but it's the bedrock of a successful security consulting business. With a mix of foresight, adaptability, and strategic thinking, you can ensure your business remains stable and resilient, no matter what challenges arise.

Chapter 12 Wrap-Up

Managing the financial health of a security consulting business may not be as glamorous as safeguarding clients or implementing high-tech security solutions, but it's just as critical. Without a strong financial foundation, even the best consulting firm can falter. In this chapter, we've explored the vital aspects of financial management, from understanding financial statements to planning for long-term stability. Let's revisit the key lessons to ensure you're ready to take the reins of your business finances confidently.

Reading Financial Statements and Security Industry Metrics: Knowing the Numbers

We began by diving into the fundamentals of financial literacy, discussing how to read financial statements and understand industry-specific metrics. The trio of financial statements – Profit and Loss (P&L), Cash Flow, and the Balance Sheet – serve as your business's health report. We learned how to interpret these documents to gauge profitability, manage resources, and plan for the future.

Understanding security industry metrics is equally essential. Whether tracking the cost of security equipment or the return on investment (ROI) of specialized training programs, these insights empower you to make informed decisions. We emphasized the importance of monitoring cash flow, highlighting that even profitable businesses can struggle without a steady inflow of funds. Remember, "Revenue is vanity, profit is sanity, but cash flow is king."

We also tackled the often-confusing world of payment terms – Net 30, Net 60, and beyond – and shared strategies to encourage timely payments, like requesting deposits and instituting late fees. These measures can ensure your financial stability while maintaining healthy client relationships.

Key Takeaway: Mastering financial statements and metrics is like learning a new language. Once fluent, you'll navigate your business finances with ease and confidence.

Managing Profit Margins and Cost Efficiency: The Balancing Act

Next, we explored the delicate dance of managing profit margins and maintaining cost efficiency. Keeping a close eye on margins is non-negotiable in the security consulting industry, where operating costs can be unpredictable. We outlined strategies for cutting unnecessary expenses, streamlining operations, and leveraging technology to boost efficiency.

We also emphasized the importance of pricing services correctly to maintain healthy margins. It's not just about what you charge – it's about ensuring that the price reflects the value you bring to your clients. Real-life examples illustrated how seemingly minor adjustments, like negotiating vendor contracts or optimizing team schedules, can significantly impact your bottom line.

Key Takeaway: Profit margins are the heartbeat of your business. Keep them strong by managing costs wisely and valuing your services appropriately.

Understanding Security Industry-Specific Tax Considerations: Keeping Uncle Sam Happy

Taxes may not be the most exciting topic, but they're a reality every entrepreneur must face. This section uncovered the nuances of tax considerations specific to the security industry. We covered everything from deductions for equipment and training expenses to understanding the implications of travel-related costs.

We stressed the importance of working with a certified tax professional to navigate the complex tax landscape. While this book provides a solid foundation, professional guidance is invaluable for avoiding pitfalls and maximizing tax benefits. Remember, an ounce of prevention is worth a pound of IRS audits.

Additionally, we touched on regional and international tax nuances, particularly for consultants operating across borders. Knowing when to charge sales tax, how to handle client reimbursements, and the implications of employing contractors versus full-time staff are all crucial considerations.

Key Takeaway: When it comes to taxes, ignorance is not bliss. Equip yourself with knowledge, but don't hesitate to seek professional advice to keep your business compliant and profitable.

Financial Planning for Long-Term Stability: Building Resilience

Finally, we wrapped up the chapter by focusing on financial planning for long-term stability. This is where your business goes from surviving to thriving. We discussed the importance of preparing for economic downturns by building a financial cushion and diversifying revenue streams. Flexibility and adaptability were recurring themes – whether that means adjusting services to meet new demands or pivoting to embrace emerging technologies.

We also explored the role of resilience in financial planning. Challenges are inevitable, but your ability to adapt and maintain stability sets your business apart. Strategic milestones and regular financial health reviews can keep you on track and alert you to potential problems before they escalate.

Key Takeaway: Sustainable growth isn't just about expanding your business – it's about ensuring it can withstand challenges and adapt to changes over time.

The Road Ahead

As we conclude this chapter, take a moment to appreciate the progress you've made. Financial management might not be your favorite aspect of running a security consulting business, but it's one of the most important. By mastering these skills, you're setting your business up for long-term success.

Remember, the goal isn't just to stay afloat – it's to thrive. From understanding your numbers to planning for the future, every step you take strengthens your business's foundation. Financial literacy isn't just about dollars and cents; it's about empowering you to make informed, confident decisions that lead to growth and success.

As you move forward, revisit these lessons often. Financial management is an ongoing process, not a one-time task. With the right mindset and tools, you're more than capable of steering your business toward a prosperous future. Now, let's turn the page and continue building your security consulting empire!

13

Time Management for the Solo Entrepreneur

"Time is what we want most, but what we use worst."

— William Penn

Let's kick things off with a fact that might rattle your cage: The average entrepreneur spends over 20 hours a week on administrative tasks alone, according to a study by The Alternative Board. That's half a workweek spent wrestling with emails, scheduling, and other time-draining minutiae instead of growing your business.

For the solo entrepreneur, time isn't just money – it's oxygen. Every second spent inefficiently can suffocate your dreams of success. Managing time effectively isn't just about getting through the day; it's about creating a framework that lets you focus on what truly matters while keeping the wheels turning on the rest.

In this chapter, we're diving deep into the art and science of time management. Whether learning how to prioritize tasks with the precision of a laser or finding ways to automate the mundane, these strategies are tailored for the solo entrepreneur. You'll learn how to keep your business thriving without sacrificing your sanity – or your weekends. And yes, we'll also tackle the big one: balancing work and life because burnout isn't a badge of honor; it's a recipe for disaster.

Let's break it down. Time to master your time.

Prioritizing Tasks: The Eisenhower Box Method

As a solo entrepreneur in the security consulting business, time management is more than a helpful skill – it's a survival tactic. One of the most effective and widely endorsed strategies for prioritizing tasks is the Eisenhower Box Method, also known as the Eisenhower Matrix. Named after Dwight D. Eisenhower, the 34th President of the United States, this method is simple, elegant, and immensely practical. It's a system designed to help you separate the critical from the inconsequential, ensuring you're working on the right things at the right time.

The Eisenhower Box Method is a decision-making tool that divides tasks into four quadrants based on their urgency and importance:

Quadrant 1: Urgent and Important (Do it now). Tasks that require immediate attention and are critical to achieving your goals. Think of crises, last-minute client demands, or unexpected emergencies.

Quadrant 2: Not Urgent but Important (Schedule it). Tasks that are essential for long-term success but don't require immediate action. This includes strategic planning, relationship building, and skills development.

Quadrant 3: Urgent but Not Important (Delegate it). Tasks that demand immediate attention but don't significantly contribute to your goals. These are often distractions, such as non-essential emails or requests someone else could handle.

Quadrant 4: Not Urgent and Not Important (Eliminate it). Tasks that neither contribute to your goals nor require immediate action. These are the timewasters: excessive social media scrolling, unproductive meetings, or watching that fifth cat video on YouTube.

By sorting tasks into these categories, you can focus your energy on what truly matters and avoid being bogged down by what doesn't.

Why is This Method Crucial for Solo Entrepreneurs?

As a solo entrepreneur, you're the boss, the employee, the accountant, the marketer, and sometimes even the coffee-runner. You wear all the hats, which means your to-do list is never-ending. Without a method to prioritize effectively, it's easy to get caught in the weeds, spending precious hours on tasks that don't move the needle.

The Eisenhower Box Method forces you to assess each task's true value and align your efforts with your goals. This approach is particularly relevant for security consultants, where stakes can be high, and responding to the wrong thing at the wrong time can lead to client dissatisfaction or operational inefficiencies.

Practical Implementation of the Eisenhower Box Method

Start with a Brain Dump: Write down everything you need to do. Don't worry about order or priority at this stage – just get it all out. For example, your list might include:

- Responding to a client email.
- Drafting a proposal.
- Researching new surveillance technology.
- Attending a webinar.
- Scheduling a maintenance check for your equipment.

Sort Tasks into Quadrants: Now, go through your list and assign each task to a quadrant:

- Urgent and Important: Responding to a client email about an active threat.
- Not Urgent but Important: Researching new surveillance technology.
- Urgent but Not Important: Scheduling the equipment maintenance (delegate to a technician or assistant if possible).
- Not Urgent and Not Important: Watching that YouTube video on security cameras shaped like garden gnomes.

Take Action Based on the Quadrant

- Do Quadrant 1 tasks immediately. They're non-negotiable.
- Schedule Quadrant 2 tasks. Block time in your calendar to ensure these important but non-urgent tasks get the attention they deserve.
- Delegate Quadrant 3 tasks. This might mean hiring a virtual assistant or outsourcing to a colleague.
- Eliminate Quadrant 4 tasks. This requires discipline – close that YouTube tab!

Example: A Day in the Life of a Security Consultant. Imagine you're in the middle of a high-profile consulting project for a corporate client. You wake up to find your inbox flooded with messages. Without the Eisenhower Box, you might feel compelled to tackle the emails first, only to discover you've spent hours on non-critical inquiries while ignoring more pressing issues.

Using the Eisenhower Box, you instead:

- Urgent and Important: Call the client about a potential security breach.
- Not Urgent but Important: Allocate an hour in the afternoon to update your training materials.

- Urgent but Not Important: Forward equipment servicing requests to your assistant.
- Not Urgent and Not Important: Ignore the email promoting "World's Best Tactical Flashlights."

By lunchtime, you've handled the critical tasks, scheduled important ones, and delegated the rest – leaving you free to focus on strategy instead of scrambling (and maybe check out that cool tac-light!).

Benefits of the Eisenhower Box Method

Clarity. Knowing exactly where to focus your efforts reduces stress and decision fatigue.

Efficiency. You're no longer spinning your wheels on tasks that don't matter.

Proactivity. By scheduling important but non-urgent tasks, you prevent them from becoming crises later.

Discipline. Learning to delegate or eliminate tasks helps you resist the urge to micromanage or waste time.

Common Pitfalls and How to Avoid Them

Overloading Quadrant 1. If everything feels urgent and important, you're not being honest about priorities. Take a step back and reassess.

Neglecting Quadrant 2. Don't let non-urgent but important tasks slip through the cracks. This is where long-term success is built.

Reluctance to Delegate. As a solo entrepreneur, you might feel the need to do it all yourself. Remember: delegation is not a sign of weakness but of visionary leadership.

The Eisenhower Box Method is more than a productivity hack; it's a mindset shift. By categorizing your tasks, you'll gain control over your schedule, reduce stress, and ensure that your energy is spent on what truly matters. It's a game-changer for solo entrepreneurs who must balance a mountain of responsibilities without losing sight of their goals.

Now, go ahead and try it out – starting with that to-do list you've been avoiding!

Automating Routine Tasks for Efficiency

As a solo entrepreneur in the security consulting business, you have a mountain of tasks to tackle each day, ranging from client interactions to administrative duties. The truth is that many of these tasks are repetitive and time-consuming but essential for your business to run smoothly. This is where automation steps in to become your virtual assistant, helping you work smarter, not harder. By automating routine tasks, you free up your time to focus on strategic planning, client relations, and business growth.

Task automation is the process of using technology to perform repetitive tasks with minimal human intervention. This could range from sending automated invoices to scheduling social media posts or even managing client relationships through Customer Relationship Management (CRM) software.

The goal is simple: reduce manual effort, minimize errors, and maximize efficiency. Automation isn't just about cutting corners – it's about creating a workflow that allows you to scale your business without burning out.

Why Automate? The Case for Efficiency

Imagine this: You spend hours each week manually scheduling appointments, sending follow-up emails, or compiling weekly reports. Not only does this drain your energy, but it also takes time away from high-value activities like networking or closing deals. Automating these tasks can:

Save Time: Let technology handle the mundane while you focus on strategy.

Increase Accuracy: Automation reduces the risk of human error, especially in data entry or calculations.

Enhance Client Experience: Prompt, consistent communication builds trust and professionalism.

Boost Productivity: Automating routine work ensures you're not stuck doing busywork when you could be making impactful decisions.

Examples of Tasks You Can Automate

Email Responses and Campaigns: Tools like Mailchimp or HubSpot can handle everything from sending welcome emails to drip campaigns targeting potential clients. Instead of drafting individual emails, set up templates and triggers based on client behavior.

Appointment Scheduling: Forget the back-and-forth emails trying to find a mutually convenient time. Tools like Calendly or Acuity Scheduling allow clients to book directly into your calendar based on your availability.

Invoicing and Payments: Accounting software like QuickBooks or Fresh-Books can automate invoicing, send payment reminders, and even handle tax calculations.

Social Media Management: Platforms like Hootsuite or Buffer enable you to schedule posts across multiple platforms, analyze engagement, and keep your online presence consistent.

Client Follow-Ups: CRM tools such as Salesforce or Zoho can automate reminders to follow up with clients, send thank-you notes, or schedule check-ins.

Document Sharing and Signing: Use platforms like DocuSign or PandaDoc to send and collect signatures electronically, saving time and ensuring a paper trail.

How to Implement Automation in Your Business

Identify Repetitive Tasks: Begin by listing all the tasks you perform daily, weekly, or monthly. Pay attention to activities that are time-consuming or prone to errors. For instance, are you manually creating invoices or spending too much time following up on emails? These are prime candidates for automation.

Research Tools: Once you've identified tasks to automate, research tools that cater to your industry. Many platforms offer free trials, so you can test which one fits your workflow best.

Start Small: Don't overwhelm yourself by trying to automate everything at once. Begin with one or two tasks and gradually expand. For example, you might start with automating appointment scheduling and then move on to social media management.

Set Up and Customize: Take the time to customize your automation tools to reflect your brand's tone and style. For instance, personalize email templates with your logo and a friendly tone.

Monitor and Adjust: Automation isn't a "set it and forget it" solution. Regularly review your tools to ensure they're performing as expected. Use analytics to tweak campaigns or processes for better results.

Practical Example: Automating Social Media Management

Let's say you want to maintain an active presence on LinkedIn and Instagram without spending hours each week posting updates. Here's how automation could look:

Choose a Platform: Sign up for Hootsuite, which allows you to schedule posts on both LinkedIn and Instagram.

Create a Content Calendar: Plan your monthly posts, including tips, industry news, and client success stories.

Batch Content Creation: Dedicate a few hours to write captions and design graphics for all posts at once.

Schedule Posts: Upload your content to Hootsuite, set dates and times for each post, and let the tool handle the rest.

Analyze Results: Use Hootsuite's analytics to see which posts perform best and adjust your strategy accordingly.

The Pitfall of Over-Automation

While automation is powerful, it's essential to strike a balance. Over-automating can make your interactions feel robotic and impersonal. For instance:

Client Emails: While automated responses are helpful, they shouldn't replace personalized replies for complex inquiries.

Social Media Comments: Auto-generated replies to comments can backfire if they come across as tone-deaf.

The key is to use automation as a supplement, not a substitute, for genuine human interaction.

Automation is the secret weapon of solo entrepreneurs, especially in high-stakes industries like security consulting. By automating routine tasks, you can reclaim precious hours, reduce errors, and provide a seamless experience for your clients. Start small, choose tools that align with your needs, and don't be afraid to tweak as you go.

Remember, automation isn't about replacing the human touch but enhancing it. So, go ahead and automate that inbox cleanup or those pesky invoice reminders. Your future, less-stressed self will thank you.

Balancing Work-Life as a Consultant

Being a security consultant is a demanding profession. You're often juggling multiple clients, handling crises, and striving to keep your business afloat. However, amidst all this chaos, it's crucial to remember that your personal life is equally important. The work-life balance for consultants, especially solo entrepreneurs, can often feel like a mythical creature – talked about but rarely seen. But let's debunk that myth today. Achieving a healthy balance is not just possible; it's essential for long-term success and personal well-being.

Work-life balance doesn't mean splitting your time 50-50 between work and personal life. Instead, it's about prioritizing what's important in the moment. Some weeks might demand more from your business, while others allow you to focus on family or personal pursuits. The key is finding a rhythm that keeps you productive, fulfilled, and, most importantly, sane.

The Importance of Work-Life Balance in Consulting

As a security consultant, your job involves a high level of responsibility. Your recommendations can impact a company's safety, a family's peace of mind, or even an individual's life. It's easy to get caught in the trap of working long hours, constantly chasing client satisfaction, and saying yes to every opportunity.

But here's the catch: If you burn out, you won't be able to serve your clients – or yourself. A poor work-life balance leads to stress, diminished health, strained relationships, and reduced productivity. On the flip side, maintaining balance helps you:

- Stay energized and focused.
- Deliver better results to your clients.
- Foster creativity and innovation.
- Build stronger personal relationships.

Recognizing the Warning Signs of Imbalance

Before diving into solutions, let's identify some common red flags indicating your work-life balance needs adjustment:

Constant Fatigue: If you're always tired, it's a sign you're overextending yourself.

Neglected Relationships: When friends and family start commenting on your absence, it's time to take a step back.

Loss of Joy in Work: If what once excited you now feels like a burden, you may be headed for burnout.

Physical Symptoms: Headaches, insomnia, and frequent illness are your body's way of saying, "Slow down."

Strategies for Balancing Work and Life

Set Clear Boundaries. Boundaries are the cornerstone of a healthy work-life balance. Define your working hours and stick to them. If you decide to work from 9 a.m. to 6 p.m., avoid checking emails or taking client calls after hours unless it's an emergency. Inform your clients of your availability upfront to manage expectations.

Example: If a client calls you at 8 p.m. on a Friday, let it go to voicemail and respond during working hours. You're not a 24/7 hotline – unless, of course, that's part of your contract.

Embrace Delegation and Outsourcing. As a solo entrepreneur, it's tempting to wear all the hats. However, delegating or outsourcing tasks can free up valuable time for personal activities. Whether hiring a virtual assistant to manage administrative duties or using technology to automate routine tasks, delegation is a game-changer. Remember, Superman is a fictional character. You don't have to do it all.

Schedule Personal Time Like a Meeting. Treat your personal time with the same respect as a client meeting. Block off time in your calendar for exercise, hobbies, or family dinners, and honor those commitments. Think of it as an investment in your well-being.

Example: Set aside Wednesday evenings for "me time." Whether it's hitting the gym, reading a book, or binge-watching your favorite show, that time is sacred.

Learn to Say No. Every opportunity isn't worth taking. Assess whether a potential project aligns with your goals and values. If it doesn't, politely decline. Saying no to one thing often means saying yes to something more meaningful.

Use Technology Wisely. While technology can make work more efficient, it can also blur the lines between professional and personal life. Set boundaries on your tech usage. Turn off work-related notifications during personal time and avoid the temptation to "just check emails" while watching a movie with your family.

Plan Vacations and Downtime. Taking breaks isn't just a luxury – it's a necessity. Plan regular vacations or staycations to recharge. Even a long weekend away can do wonders for your mental health.

Example: Set a goal to take one week off every quarter. Use that time to relax, reflect, and return to work with renewed energy.

The Little Things Matter

Sometimes, balance isn't about grand gestures but small, intentional actions that make a big difference. Here are a few ideas:

Morning Rituals: Start your day with a routine that centers you, whether it's meditation, journaling, or that energy drink on the porch.

Gratitude Practices: End your day by listing three things you're grateful for.

Random Acts of Kindness: Whether sending a thank-you note or surprising your partner with their favorite snack, these moments enrich your life.

Balancing work and life as a consultant is a continuous journey, not a destination. It requires mindfulness, discipline, and a willingness to adapt. You can create a fulfilling and sustainable lifestyle by setting boundaries, prioritizing personal time, and embracing the power of delegation.

Remember, a well-rested, well-rounded entrepreneur is happier, more productive, and more effective. Balance isn't just good for you – it's good for your business. So, take that walk, enjoy that family dinner, and let yourself breathe. Your business will thank you for it.

Chapter 13 Wrap-Up: Time Management for the Solo Entrepreneur

Congratulations! You've made it through one of the most foundational chapters of this book. If you've ever felt like there just aren't enough hours in the day or that the chaos of running a solo consulting business might actually swallow you whole, this chapter was written for you. Time is your most valuable resource – it's the currency of your success.

Chapter 13 was all about teaching you how to manage it with grace, strategy, and a touch of humor (because, let's face it, we all need a good laugh when the to-do list starts looking like a CVS receipt).

Let's revisit what we covered and see how each piece fits into your journey toward becoming a time-management maestro.

Prioritizing Tasks: The Eisenhower Box Method

We kicked off with the timeless wisdom of President Dwight D. Eisenhower. Who knew a guy famous for military acumen would also become the poster child for time management? The Eisenhower Box is a deceptively simple yet powerful tool to help you sift through the mountain of tasks and determine what deserves your attention – and, more importantly, what doesn't.

You learned how to divide tasks into four quadrants:

- Urgent and Important: Do these right now.
- Important but Not Urgent: Schedule these for later.
- Urgent but Not Important: Delegate these if possible.

- Neither Urgent Nor Important: Eliminate these from your life entirely.

Using this method, you start seeing your work through a new lens. The goal isn't to do everything; it's to do the right things.

We also discussed real-life examples, like dealing with a high-maintenance client's constant demands (urgent but not always important) versus creating a long-term business growth strategy (important but often shoved to the back burner). Balancing these priorities is what separates the good consultants from the great ones.

Key Takeaway: The Eisenhower Box is more than a tool – it's a mindset. When you focus on importance over urgency, you're steering the ship instead of reacting to every wave.

Automating Routine Tasks for Efficiency

Next, we dove into the magical world of automation. If "Work Smarter, Not Harder" had a greatest hits album, automation would be track one. As a solo entrepreneur, your time is stretched thin, and repetitive tasks are a silent productivity killer.

We explored how automation can handle everything from sending follow-up emails to managing invoicing, freeing up precious hours for higher-value tasks. Software like Zapier, Calendly, and QuickBooks became the heroes of the day, demonstrating how technology can take over the mundane and let you focus on what you do best – delivering exceptional security consulting services.

We shared anecdotes, like how one consultant used automated scheduling to eliminate the back-and-forth emails with clients and instead spent that reclaimed time refining a proposal that landed a six-figure contract.

Key Takeaway: Automation isn't just about saving time – it's about reclaiming energy and focusing on the things that truly matter.

Balancing Work-Life as a Consultant

Finally, we tackled the holy grail of solo entrepreneurship: work-life balance. It's no secret that running your own business can feel like running a marathon that never ends. But just because the work is endless doesn't mean your energy has to be.

We discussed strategies for setting boundaries, like defining and sticking to work hours. We also explored the power of delegation and outsourcing, whether it's hiring a virtual assistant or using technology to manage the nitty-gritty details of your business.

One of the most important lessons was recognizing the value of personal time. Scheduling family dinners, taking a vacation, or even just enjoying a quiet evening at home isn't slacking – it's essential for long-term success. We reminded you that a burned-out consultant isn't much use to anyone, least of all yourself.

We also touched on the "little things" that make a big difference in building client relationships and personal well-being – things like remembering a client's birthday or supporting a cause they care about.

Key Takeaway: Work-life balance isn't about perfection but intentionality. A balanced consultant is a happy consultant – and a happy consultant runs a successful business.

The Big Picture

So, what's the overarching lesson from Chapter 13? Time management is about more than just checking off tasks or squeezing more hours out of the day. It's about creating a life and business that align with your values and goals.

The Eisenhower Box taught you how to prioritize. Automation showed you how to streamline. And work-life balance reminded you that there's more to life than work. Together, these strategies form a trifecta of time management that will serve you well as you grow your security consulting business.

Looking Ahead

As you progress, remember that time management isn't a one-and-done skill. It's a lifelong practice that evolves with your business and personal life. The strategies we've discussed are tools in your arsenal, but it's up to you to wield them effectively.

With the foundation laid in Chapter 13, you're not just ready to manage your time – you're ready to master it. Go forth and conquer your to-do list, one well-prioritized task at a time.

14

Risk Management and Adapting to Industry Changes

"It's not the strongest species that survive, nor the most intelligent, but the most responsive to change."

— Charles Darwin

A survey conducted by Deloitte revealed that 83% of organizations have experienced at least one security incident that significantly impacted their operations. Among these, 60% admitted they were unprepared to adapt to the aftermath.

Welcome to the wild, unpredictable world of security consulting, where the only constant is change. Whether adapting to technological advancements, navigating new market dynamics, or handling legal and compliance issues, the ability to manage risk and pivot quickly separates the thriving from the merely surviving.

In this chapter, we'll journey through the intricacies of risk management and adapting to the ever-shifting landscape of the security industry. By the end, you won't just know how to weather the storm – you'll be equipped to chart a course for success even in turbulent waters.

Common Challenges in Security Consulting

Security consulting is a field that demands expertise, precision, and adaptability. However, even the most seasoned consultants face a variety of challenges that can test their mettle. For new entrepreneurs, understanding and preparing for these challenges is crucial to establishing a thriving business. This section explores common challenges in security consulting and offers practical solutions to navigate them effectively.

Challenge 1: Balancing Client Expectations with Reality

The Challenge: Clients often have lofty expectations about what a security consultant can achieve. Some may expect instant solutions, while others might have unrealistic budget constraints or timelines. The issue arises when clients want Hollywood-style security measures on a shoestring budget or expect a complete overhaul of their systems overnight.

Example: A client once approached a security consultant, asking for a "foolproof" surveillance system to monitor an entire warehouse remotely. The client's budget? Barely enough to cover a few mid-range cameras and a DVR. Managing these expectations was critical to avoid damaging the client-consultant relationship.

How to Overcome It:

Clear Communication: At the start of any project, outline what's feasible within the client's budget and timeline. Transparency is key to aligning expectations.

Educational Discussions: Educate clients about the realistic capabilities and limitations of security measures.

Tiered Solutions: Offer a range of basic, intermediate, and advanced options so the client can choose based on their resources.

Challenge 2: Staying Updated with Rapid Technological Advancements

The Challenge: The security industry evolves at a breakneck pace, with new tools, software, and techniques constantly emerging. Falling behind on the latest technologies can render a consultant's advice outdated or ineffective.

Example: A consultant who failed to stay informed about drone technology missed an opportunity to advise a high-profile client on counter-drone measures, leading to a competitor winning the contract.

How to Overcome It:

Continuous Education: Attend industry conferences, webinars, and training programs to stay ahead of the curve.

Networking: Join professional organizations where peers share insights on the latest trends and tools.

Experimentation: Invest time in hands-on experience with new technologies to build expertise.

Challenge 3: Managing Legal and Regulatory Compliance

The Challenge: Security consulting involves navigating a web of legal and regulatory requirements, which vary widely depending on location and industry. Failing to comply can lead to fines, lawsuits, or reputational damage.

Example: A consultant working in multiple states overlooked a licensing requirement in one jurisdiction. This oversight resulted in the suspension of the consulting firm's operations in that area.

How to Overcome It:

Research: Before staking on a project, research all local, state, and federal regulations that apply.

Legal Counsel: Establish a relationship with a legal advisor specializing in security regulations.

Documentation: Maintain meticulous records to demonstrate compliance.

Challenge 4: Dealing with High-Stress Situations

The Challenge: Security consultants often face high-pressure scenarios, such as managing risks during crises, addressing breaches, or mitigating immediate threats. The emotional toll of such situations can lead to burnout.

Example: A consultant overseeing security for a high-net-worth individual during a publicized event faced unrelenting demands and pressure, resulting in exhaustion and strained decision-making.

How to Overcome It:

Preparation: Develop crisis management plans in advance to reduce the stress of real-time decision-making.

Self-Care: Prioritize mental and physical health by setting boundaries and taking breaks.

Delegation: Build a reliable team to share responsibilities during demanding projects.

Challenge 5: Building Trust and Credibility

The Challenge: Establishing credibility as a new consultant can be daunting. Clients may hesitate to entrust sensitive information or critical projects to someone without a proven track record.

Example: A newly established consultant struggled to secure contracts because potential clients preferred larger, more established firms.

How to Overcome It:

Certifications: Earn industry-recognized credentials to demonstrate expertise.

Networking: Leverage personal and professional networks to gain introductions and referrals.

Showcase Results: Build trust by using case studies, testimonials, and a strong portfolio.

Challenge 6: Balancing Revenue and Client Retention

The Challenge: Security consulting involves balancing profitability with maintaining strong client relationships. Overcharging can drive clients away, while undercharging can lead to financial instability.

Example: A consultant who offered low initial rates struggled to cover overhead costs and eventually had to raise prices, causing client attrition.

How to Overcome It:

Market Research: Understand industry-standard pricing and adjust rates accordingly.

Value Proposition: Emphasize the value you bring to justify your pricing.

Loyalty Programs: Offer discounts or benefits to long-term clients to encourage retention.

Challenge 7: Navigating Competitive Markets

The Challenge: The security consulting industry is highly competitive, with firms vying for a limited pool of clients. Standing out requires differentiation and strategic positioning.

Example: A consultant offering generic services found it difficult to compete with firms specializing in specific niches like cybersecurity or executive protection.

How to Overcome It:

Niche Specialization: Focus on a particular area of expertise to carve out a unique market position.

Marketing Strategy: Invest in targeted marketing efforts to reach your ideal clients.

Continuous Improvement: Regularly refine your services to stay ahead of competitors.

Challenge 8: Managing Cultural and Regional Differences

The Challenge: Working with international clients or in diverse cultural settings introduces challenges in communication, expectations, and practices.

Example: A consultant managing security for a multinational company faced misunderstandings due to differing cultural norms regarding personal space and authority.

How to Overcome It:

Cultural Awareness: Research and respect cultural differences before engaging with clients.

Clear Communication: Use simple, jargon-free language to minimize misunderstandings.

Adaptability: Be willing to adjust your approach to align with cultural expectations.

Challenge 9: Scaling Operations Responsibly

The Challenge: As a consulting firm grows, maintaining quality while expanding services or hiring new staff becomes increasingly tricky.

Example: A rapidly expanding firm experienced a decline in service quality due to insufficient training for new hires.

How to Overcome It:

Standard Operating Procedures: Develop SOPs to ensure consistency across projects.

Hiring Practices: Hire selectively and invest in comprehensive training.

Client Feedback: Regularly solicit client feedback to identify and address issues.

Every challenge in security consulting presents an opportunity for growth and improvement. By anticipating these common obstacles and implementing proactive strategies, you can confidently navigate the industry's complexities. Remember, challenges are not roadblocks but stepping stones toward building a resilient and successful security consulting business.

Adapting to Technological Advancements

Technology evolves at lightning speed, reshaping every industry in its wake, and security consulting is no exception. In fact, the security industry is often at the forefront of these changes, adapting to counter ever-more sophisticated threats. For entrepreneurs in this field, staying ahead of technological advancements isn't just a recommendation – it's a necessity.

Let's explore how you, as a new security consultant, can adapt to this ever-changing landscape.

Understanding the Importance of Technological Adaptation

First, let's tackle why adapting to new technologies is key. Imagine advising a client to install a state-of-the-art security camera system only to discover that it's already obsolete compared to newer, AI-powered alternatives. In security consulting, your reputation hinges on being informed, relevant, and forward-thinking.

Technological advancements often introduce solutions that:

- Increase efficiency (e.g., automated surveillance systems reducing manual monitoring needs),
- Improve accuracy (e.g., AI for threat detection),
- Save costs in the long run (e.g., energy-efficient systems).

Failing to embrace these changes risks rendering your advice ineffective or, worse, irrelevant. It's akin to using a flip phone in a world of smartphones – you'll survive but won't thrive.

Staying Updated: Continuous Learning and Networking

Adapting starts with awareness. Here's how to stay informed:

Industry Conferences and Expos. Attend events like ISC West or ASIS Global Security Exchange (GSX). These gatherings showcase the latest security innovations, from biometric authentication systems to counter-drone technology. Networking with industry leaders at these events also opens doors to partnerships and insider knowledge.

Subscription to Industry Publications. Magazines like *Security Management* and *SDM* often cover new technologies before they become mainstream. A quick scan of these can save you hours of online research.

Online Courses and Certifications. Platforms like LinkedIn Learning, Udemy, and Coursera offer courses on cybersecurity, AI, and even blockchain technology – tools increasingly relevant to security consulting. Certifications like Certified Information Systems Security Professional (CISSP) also keep your skills sharp. Example: Consider a consultant specializing in estate security who embraced drone surveillance after attending an industry expo. This adoption not only impressed a high-profile client but also led to referrals within a niche market.

Practical Implementation: Embracing AI and Automation

Artificial Intelligence (AI) isn't the future – it's the present. Here's how to integrate it effectively:

AI-Powered Surveillance. Smart cameras equipped with facial recognition and behavioral analysis can detect anomalies in real time. Advising clients on these systems can set you apart as a forward-thinking consultant.

Predictive Analytics, AI tools that analyze patterns to predict potential security breaches, are invaluable for high-risk clients, such as corporations handling sensitive data.

Automation Tools. Automating routine tasks like visitor logs or access control saves time and reduces human error. These solutions often come with user-friendly interfaces, making them easy to implement.

Pro Tip: When recommending AI solutions, emphasize ethical considerations, such as privacy. Clients will appreciate your nuanced understanding of technology's impact.

Adapting to Cybersecurity Needs

With increasing reliance on digital systems, cybersecurity is now inseparable from physical security. Threats like ransomware attacks, phishing, and data breaches are growing concerns.

Partnering with Cybersecurity Experts. If you lack expertise in cybersecurity, consider partnering with specialists. Collaboration ensures your clients receive comprehensive protection.

Basic Cybersecurity Training. Offer basic cybersecurity workshops as part of your services. Topics could include recognizing phishing attempts or securing Wi-Fi networks. This added value helps build long-term client relationships.

Integrated Security Systems. Recommend solutions that merge physical and digital security, such as smart locks managed through encrypted apps.

Example: A consultant working with a luxury hotel chain integrated IoT devices for guest safety. However, they also ensured the devices were secured against cyber intrusions – a holistic approach that earned client loyalty.

Embracing New Frontiers: Drones, IoT, and Biometric Systems

Let's examine some innovative technologies reshaping the industry:

Drones and Counter-Drone Systems. Drones are revolutionizing surveillance, offering aerial views of large properties. However, they also pose security risks. Anti-drone systems, such as signal jammers, are increasingly in demand. Advising on both can make you indispensable.

Internet of Things (IoT). IoT devices, like smart thermostats and locks, enhance convenience and security. However, they are vulnerable to hacking. Your ability to recommend secure IoT setups can differentiate you in a crowded market.

Biometric Security. From fingerprint scanners to retinal recognition, biometrics offer unparalleled access control. Understanding their applications and limitations is crucial for consultants advising corporate or high-net-worth clients.

Example: A security consultant helped a client adopt biometric access controls for their estate. The result? A more secure home and a delighted client who praised the consultant's tech-savviness.

Overcoming Resistance to Change

Not all clients – or consultants – embrace change readily. Fear of costs, complexity, or failure often holds people back.

Cost Concerns: Explain the long-term savings and benefits of adopting new technologies. For example, smart surveillance might have a high upfront cost but reduces ongoing staffing expenses.

Complexity: Choose user-friendly systems that minimize training requirements for your clients.

Demonstrating Value: Use case studies or live demos to show the tangible benefits of a new technology.

Example: A hesitant client was convinced to install smart cameras after a consultant showed real-time footage from a similar setup. Seeing the technology in action was the tipping point.

Adapting to technological advancements isn't just about staying competitive – it's about leading the way. Your clients rely on you to navigate an ever-changing landscape, and embracing innovation ensures you're ready to meet their needs.

Adapting to Market or Industry Shifts

Like any other, the security industry is subject to market dynamics and external pressures that can dramatically alter the landscape for consultants. From regulatory changes to economic downturns, technological disruptions, or shifting client priorities, the ability to detect and adapt to these shifts is critical. Let's break this down, step by step, so even the newest entrepreneur can identify market or industry changes and effectively pivot to remain competitive and relevant.

Recognizing When a Market or Industry Shift is Happening

Identifying an industry shift starts with staying informed. Successful security consultants consistently monitor industry trends, client demands, and global events. A market shift might be subtle, such as a slow but steady decline in demand for a specific service, or overt, like the sudden emergence of a new competitor offering groundbreaking technology. Here are some key indicators to help you spot changes early:

Economic Indicators and Client Budgets. Economic health directly affects the security sector. A recession might lead to scaled-back client budgets, while economic booms could spur investment in security upgrades. Keep an eye on macroeconomic trends and industry-specific data, like the rise in funding for cybersecurity solutions.

Evolving Regulations. New laws or industry standards often necessitate changes in how security consultants operate. For instance, shifts in privacy regulations (such as GDPR or CCPA) or requirements for security certifications can force consultants to adapt their offerings.

Technological Innovations. A new technology – whether it's AI-powered threat detection or advanced surveillance drones – can disrupt traditional security approaches. If you notice clients showing interest in a specific tool or asking competitors for services you don't yet offer, that's a clear sign to reevaluate.

Client Feedback and Behavior. A drop in client retention or fewer inquiries about specific services could signal changing priorities. Regularly engaging with clients can help you stay attuned to their needs and identify trends before they become problems.

Example: One of the most memorable market shifts in the security consulting industry was the events of 9/11. Those events changed everything about the security landscape: clients' attitudes towards security, travel security, opinions on Duty of Care issues, physical security, asset accountability, etc. Another sea-change moment for security consulting was the COVID-19 pandemic of 2020. Once again, the industry landscape changed as we focused more on remote work, public health issues affecting the private sector, supply chain security, cyber issues, the efficiencies and dangers of technology automation (like Zoom and AI), etc. Being on top of shifts in the market or threat landscape is critical for a successful security consulting business.

Adapting to Market or Industry Shifts

Once you've identified a shift, the next challenge is adapting effectively. Here are actionable strategies:

Conduct a Market Analysis. Start by digging deeper into the shift. Who is driving the change? What specific client needs are emerging? Are competitors adapting faster, and if so, how? This research provides a clear roadmap for your next steps.

Practical Implementation:

- Use tools like Google Trends to track changes in search behavior related to your services.
- Monitor competitor websites and social media to understand their focus areas.
- Attend industry webinars or conferences to hear experts discuss current and future trends.
- Diversify Your Offerings. When faced with a market shift, diversification can keep your business relevant. Introduce complementary services that address new client needs. For example, if clients are moving from on-site personnel to automated surveillance systems, offer consulting on system selection and implementation.

Example: A consultant specializing in estate security may expand into digital privacy solutions for high-net-worth clients who now prioritize protecting their online presence.

Implementation Tips:

Measured Approach. Start with pilot projects to test demand for new services.

Network. Partner with subject matter experts to build your competency in emerging fields.

Retrain Your Team. If market shifts require you to offer new services, your team must keep up. Invest in training programs, certifications, or partnerships to ensure your personnel are equipped with relevant skills.

Example: Suppose you notice a growing demand for anti-drone measures in your region. Partnering with drone technology firms and certifying your team in anti-drone tactics will position you as a leader in this niche.

Adjust Your Marketing. As your offerings evolve, so should your marketing. Update your website, create educational content about your new services, and communicate your pivot to existing and potential clients.

Example: You've added cybersecurity assessments to your repertoire. Publish blog posts or host webinars about the intersection of physical and digital security to establish thought leadership.

Build Strategic Partnerships. When faced with an industry shift you can't tackle alone, partnering with experts can help you adapt more quickly. Collaborations allow you to expand your offerings without overextending your internal resources.

Example: If you're noticing demand for advanced AI surveillance tools, collaborate with a technology provider to offer integrated solutions under your consulting umbrella.

Reassess Your Financial Plan. Adapting to industry shifts often comes with financial implications, like new equipment, software, or training costs. Revisit your financial plan to ensure it aligns with your updated strategy.

Build a Budget. Create a flexible budget that accounts for future industry disruptions.

Monitor. Use financial metrics to measure the ROI of your adaptations.

Avoiding Common Pitfalls During Adaptation

While adapting to shifts is essential, it's also fraught with risks. Here's how to avoid some common mistakes:

Overextending Your Resources. Adding too many services or expanding too quickly can dilute your brand and strain your team. Instead, focus on gradual growth that aligns with your core competencies.

Neglecting Core Services. While adapting to new trends, don't lose sight of what made your business successful. Continue to deliver exceptional service in your original niche while scaling thoughtfully.

Ignoring Client Communication. Clients appreciate transparency. If you're adapting to meet new demands, let them know how these changes will benefit them.

Example: A boutique security consultancy decides to add executive protection services. They announce the expansion through a well-crafted email campaign, explaining how their expertise in estate security translates seamlessly to personal protection.

Building an Adaptation Checklist

Stay Informed: Monitor industry news, competitor behavior, and client feedback.

Conduct Market Analysis: Identify specific client needs driving the shift.

Develop a Strategy: Decide which services to expand or modify.

Retrain Your Team: Equip your personnel with the necessary skills.

Communicate Changes: Keep clients and stakeholders informed.

Monitor Financial Health: Ensure you have the resources to implement changes sustainably.

By embracing market and industry shifts with a proactive mindset, you'll not only survive but thrive in an ever-changing security consulting landscape. Adapting isn't just about keeping pace; it's about staying ahead of the curve.

Managing Legal Issues and Compliance Risks

When running a security consulting business, the phrase "ignorance is bliss" couldn't be further from the truth – especially when it comes to legal issues and compliance risks. A small oversight can lead to massive consequences, from fines and lawsuits to a tarnished reputation. A brief search of the public domain will uncover the demise of many otherwise extremely successful security companies for failure to follow legal or regulatory mandates. Managing these challenges can seem daunting for the solo entrepreneur or fledgling security consultant, but with the right tools, guidance, and mindset, you can confidently navigate this minefield.

The Legal Minefield: Understanding the Risks

The security consulting industry is uniquely sensitive to legal and compliance issues because it directly interacts with people's safety, privacy, and property. Missteps in these areas can result in regulatory fines, civil lawsuits, or even criminal charges.

Key Areas of Legal Concern:

Licensing and Certifications: Many jurisdictions require consultants to obtain specific licenses or certifications. Operating without the proper credentials isn't just unethical – it's illegal.

Contracts and Service Agreements: Without well-drafted contracts, client misunderstandings can escalate into legal disputes.

Data Protection and Privacy Laws: Security firms often handle sensitive client information. Compliance with laws like GDPR (General Data

Protection Regulation) or CCPA (California Consumer Privacy Act) is critical.

Employment and Contractor Laws: Misclassifying employees as independent contractors or failing to adhere to labor laws can result in hefty penalties.

Negligence or Liability: You could be held liable if your recommendations or services directly lead to a client's harm or loss. Operating uninsured increases these risks exponentially.

Practical Anecdote: A small security firm was hired to install surveillance systems for a corporate client. They didn't realize the state required a low-voltage license for such work. After an anonymous tip, regulators issued a cease-and-desist order, and the firm was fined $10,000. This incident underscores the importance of understanding local regulations.

Knowing When You're Out of Your Depth

As a security consultant, your expertise is in risk assessment, planning, and execution – not law. Recognizing when you need expert legal advice is critical to safeguarding your business.

When to Seek Legal Advice

Drafting or Reviewing Contracts: A poorly worded clause could leave you vulnerable to disputes.

Navigating Licensing and Compliance: If regulations seem unclear, consulting a professional can save you from costly mistakes.

Responding to Legal Threats: Whether it's a client dispute or a regulatory inquiry, don't go it alone.

Employee or Contractor Disputes: Labor laws are complex, and even unintentional violations can have severe consequences.

Pro Tip: Develop a checklist of scenarios where you'll call in legal help. For instance:

- Entering a new market with different regulations.
- Entering a new contractual relationship with a client
- Handling a client who refuses to pay and threatens legal action.
- Expanding your business to include services like armed security, which may have additional legal requirements.
- NDA or non-compete violations from a vendor or subcontractor

Finding and Retaining Good Legal Counsel

Hiring the right legal expert is an investment in your business's future. Here's how to identify and retain someone who will truly be an asset to your company.

Know What You Need: Not all lawyers are created equal. For security consulting, you'll likely need expertise in business law, employment law, and regulatory compliance. Look for attorneys or firms with experience working with small businesses or security firms specifically.

Do Your Research: At the end of the day, *you* are ultimately responsible for choosing your legal representation. Make an informed decision.

Ask for Referrals: Other business owners in your network can recommend reliable attorneys.

Use Professional Associations: Groups like ASIS International or the International Association of Professional Security Consultants (IAPSC) often have member directories or recommendations for legal professionals familiar with the industry.

Online Reviews and Ratings: Sites like Avvo and Martindale-Hubbell provide reviews and ratings for lawyers.

Conduct Interviews: Treat hiring a lawyer like hiring an employee. Ask them:

- How familiar they are with the security industry.
- If they've worked with businesses of your size.
- How they structure their fees (hourly, retainer, flat fee).

Establish a Retainer Agreement: Many businesses opt to keep an attorney on retainer for quick consultations. This arrangement ensures you have someone who understands your business and can act swiftly when needed.

Proactively Managing Compliance

While a good lawyer can help in emergencies, it's far better (and cheaper) to prevent issues from arising in the first place. Here are steps to proactively manage compliance risks:

Stay Informed About Regulations: Subscribe to industry newsletters, attend webinars, and join professional organizations to stay current on legal and regulatory changes.

Develop a Compliance Plan: Create policies and procedures to ensure your business adheres to all applicable laws. For example:

- Document the licenses and certifications your business holds.
- Set up a system for tracking renewal deadlines.

Train Your Team: Ensure that employees and contractors understand their legal obligations. For instance, anyone handling client data should be trained on privacy laws.

Regularly Review Your Contracts: Don't use the same boilerplate contract for years. Update your agreements to reflect changes in laws or your services.

Practical Implementation Guidance

Step 1: Audit Your Current Practices

- Are your contracts clear and comprehensive?
- Are all required licenses and certifications up to date?
- Have you documented how your business complies with privacy laws?

Step 2: Identify Gaps. For example, if you discover that your data storage practices don't align with GDPR, develop a plan to address this immediately.

Step 3: Create a Legal Toolkit. Compile essential resources, including:

- A list of licenses and certifications required for your services.
- Templates for service agreements, NDAs, and subcontractor agreements.
- Contact information for your attorney.

Step 4: Schedule Regular Check-Ins. Set a quarterly or annual reminder to review your compliance practices and update as needed.

By understanding the legal landscape, knowing your limits, and surrounding yourself with the right experts, you can confidently manage legal issues and compliance risks. Remember, prevention is always cheaper – and less stressful – than damage control.

Crisis Management and Business Continuity Planning

In the unpredictable world, where crises can range from data breaches to natural disasters, the importance of robust crisis management and business continuity planning cannot be overstated. We fervently preach the concept to our clients. But the harsh reality is that most of us don't adopt the advice for our own business. For entrepreneurs, particularly those new to the field, these plans are not just "nice-to-haves" – they are business lifelines. Without them, even the most successful ventures can unravel when faced with a sudden challenge.

Defining Crisis Management and Business Continuity

Crisis Management is the process of preparing for, responding to, and recovering from unexpected and potentially catastrophic events. It involves creating protocols and strategies to mitigate the impact of crises on your business operations, reputation, and stakeholders.

Business Continuity Planning (BCP) ensures that your company can maintain critical operations or quickly resume them in the face of disruptions, whether caused by natural disasters, cyberattacks, or supply chain failures.

One final definition to throw into the mix that is often associated: Disaster Recovery (DR) usually refers to the infrastructure and systems put in place to augment, duplicate, backup, and regenerate information systems and processes for an organization or entity.

Together, these disciplines form the backbone of a resilient organization. A crisis management plan deals with the immediate chaos. In contrast, a business continuity plan ensures long-term functionality, and a disaster recovery plan ensures that your technology, databases, and software are always available to support your operations.

Developing Crisis Management Plans

Step 1: Identify Potential Crises. Start by conducting a risk assessment to pinpoint vulnerabilities. Common crises in the security consulting field might include:

- Client Incidents: A breach of data from a security system you recommended.
- Legal Issues: A lawsuit over alleged negligence in your consulting advice.

- Natural Disasters: A hurricane or wildfire affecting your operations or those of your client.
- Technology Failures: A cyberattack or system outage crippling your ability to communicate.

Practical Anecdote: Consider the 2020 COVID-19 pandemic. Many consulting firms that had no crisis plans found themselves scrambling to adapt to remote work and rapidly shifting client needs. Those with crisis plans, however, transitioned more seamlessly and maintained client trust.

Step 2: Build a Response Team. For solo entrepreneurs, this team might initially be just you. As you grow, designate team members to handle specific crisis roles:

- Communication Lead: Handles internal and external messaging.
- Operations Lead: Ensures that client services are minimally disrupted.
- Legal and Compliance Advisor: Monitors potential legal pitfalls during the crisis.

Step 3: Draft Your Plan. Outline detailed steps for handling various crisis scenarios. Include:

- Trigger Points: What constitutes a crisis, and when the plan should be activated.
- Immediate Actions: Steps to contain and assess the situation.
- Communication Strategy: Who needs to be informed, how, and when.
- Escalation Protocols: When to call in external help, like IT specialists or legal advisors.

Implementing Business Continuity Planning

While crisis management focuses on immediate reactions, business continuity ensures the long-term sustainability of your operations.

Step 1: Conduct a Business Impact Analysis (BIA). A BIA identifies which operations are critical and the potential impact of their disruption. For a security consulting firm, this might include:

- Access to client files and contracts.
- Ongoing project deadlines.
- Communication channels with clients and subcontractors.

Step 2: Develop Continuity Strategies

- Redundant Systems: Use cloud-based tools for file storage and project management to ensure accessibility even if your primary systems fail.
- Flexible Work Arrangements: If your office becomes inaccessible, ensure your team can work remotely.
- Client Communication Plans. Prepare templated messages to inform clients about disruptions and reassure them of your proactive measures.

Step 3: Test and Update Plans. Conduct mock crises, such as a simulated ransomware attack or power outage, to test your plans. Update them regularly to reflect new risks and changes in your business structure.

Knowing When to Seek External Support

No matter how well-prepared you are, some crises exceed internal capabilities. Recognizing this early can save time and resources.

IT and Cybersecurity Consultants: If you face a cyberattack or technology outage, external specialists can often resolve issues faster and more effectively than in-house resources.

Emergency Management Experts: Partnering with firms specializing in disaster recovery can provide vital expertise for natural disasters or large-scale crises.

Legal and PR Firms: In reputational crises or legal disputes, bringing in professionals can help mitigate damage and provide guidance on navigating delicate situations.

Pro Tip: Build relationships with these external resources *before* you need them. A crisis isn't the time to start vetting cybersecurity firms or searching for a PR consultant.

Practical Implementation Guidance

Start Small: If you're a solo entrepreneur, begin with a basic plan that addresses the most likely risks. For example:

- Identify backup systems for client files.
- Create an emergency contact list for clients and vendors.

Leverage Templates: Many organizations, like FEMA and the Small Business Administration (SBA), offer free templates for crisis management and business continuity plans. Adapt these to fit your unique needs.

Involve Clients: If a crisis impacts your clients directly, such as a data breach in their systems, involve them in the planning process. Sharing your strategies can build trust and reassure them of your competence.

Anecdotal Example: The Power of Preparation

A mid-sized security consulting firm in California faced a significant challenge when wildfires swept through the region, forcing the evacuation of their offices. Because they had a robust business continuity plan, the team transitioned to remote work within hours. Clients were informed promptly, and all critical operations continued without interruption. The firm's preparation saved them from financial loss and earned them new business when impressed clients referred them to others.

By understanding the importance of crisis management and business continuity planning, and implementing these strategies thoughtfully, you ensure that your business can weather any storm – literal or figurative. After all, in the security consulting world, being prepared isn't just a motto; it's a business imperative.

Chapter 14 Wrap-Up

Risks are like mosquitos at a barbecue – it is better to take preventative measures than spend your time swatting them away.

As we conclude Chapter 14, it's clear that running a security consulting business is as much about navigating challenges and adapting to change as it is about delivering stellar services. Each subsection we explored offers essential tools and insights for managing risks and staying resilient in an ever-evolving industry. Let's revisit the highlights and pull it all together.

Common Challenges in Security Consulting

We started with the realities of security consulting, delving into the common challenges entrepreneurs face. From fluctuating client demands and unpredictable crises to the complexities of building and maintaining trust, this field is not for the faint of heart.

The Takeaway: Challenges aren't just obstacles but opportunities to grow. Whether dealing with demanding clients or navigating unexpected disruptions, your ability to meet these moments with preparation and professionalism will define your success. Remember the power of adaptability, effective communication, and a solid game plan.

Adapting to Technological Advancements

Next, we examined the rapid pace of technological evolution in the security industry. Drones, artificial intelligence, cybersecurity threats – keeping pace with these advancements is no longer optional. We emphasized the importance of not just adopting new technologies but doing so thoughtfully, ensuring they align with your business strategy.

What You Can Do:

- Stay informed through industry publications and conferences.
- Build partnerships with technology providers to access cutting-edge tools.
- Train your team to maximize the potential of new tech.

Pro Tip: Don't chase every shiny object. Prioritize technologies that directly enhance your ability to serve clients and maintain operational efficiency.

Adapting to Market or Industry Shifts

Markets change, industries evolve, and successful security consultants know how to pivot when necessary. Whether it's shifting client needs, new competitors entering the market, or regulatory changes, being proactive rather than reactive is the name of the game.

Key Strategies:

- Monitor trends and patterns in your industry.
- Maintain open communication with clients to understand their evolving needs.
- Be willing to refine your services, pricing, and marketing strategies to stay competitive.

Anecdote: Remember the firm that shifted to offering cybersecurity services in response to increasing demand? Their foresight positioned them as industry leaders and significantly boosted their revenue.

Managing Legal Issues and Compliance Risks

Legal challenges and compliance risks are unavoidable in the security consulting world. From adhering to privacy laws to managing client contracts, it's a landscape fraught with potential pitfalls. This section underscored the value of having competent legal counsel and understanding the basics of compliance.

Your Toolkit for Legal Success:

- Know when to seek professional legal advice.
- Build clear, comprehensive contracts.
- Stay updated on industry-specific regulations and compliance standards.

Crisis Management and Business Continuity Planning

We wrapped up the chapter with a detailed discussion on handling crises and ensuring business continuity. Whether it's a natural disaster, a cyberattack, or an unexpected disruption in client operations, having a plan can mean the difference between bouncing back and falling apart.

Crisis Management Recap:

- Preparation is Key: Assess potential risks and develop tailored response plans.
- Communication is Critical: Keep clients and stakeholders informed during a crisis.
- Testing Builds Confidence: Regularly review and test your plans to ensure they're effective.

Business Continuity Essentials:

- Redundant systems for file storage and communication.
- Flexible work arrangements to keep your team functional.
- Pre-prepared messaging to maintain client trust.

Final Thoughts on Crises: Don't wait for a crisis to happen before you start preparing. The time you invest now could save your business in the future.

Chapter 14 was all about resilience. We delved into challenges and risks, explored the importance of staying adaptable, and laid out practical strategies to keep your business not just afloat but thriving.

The security consulting industry is demanding, dynamic, and sometimes downright daunting. But by tackling challenges head-on, embracing change, and planning for the unexpected, you can set your business on a path of sustainable growth and success.

Your Next Steps:

Reflect on your current challenges and areas where you may be reactive rather than proactive.

Begin implementing at least one new strategy for handling risks or adapting to changes.

Stay committed to continuous learning – because the moment you stop adapting is the moment you fall behind.

Encouragement as You Forge Ahead: Running a security consulting business might feel like a never-ending obstacle course, but remember, every challenge you overcome is a stepping stone to greater success. Stay flexible, stay informed, and, most importantly, stay prepared. The skills you've honed throughout this chapter will not only help you manage risks but also position you as a trusted leader in the industry.

15

Legal Considerations and Client Contracts

"The minute you read something you can't understand, you can be sure it was drawn up by a lawyer."

— Will Rogers

A survey by the Small Business Association (SBA) found that nearly 50% of small businesses face legal challenges in their first three years of operation, with contract disputes topping the list of common issues. In the world of security consulting, where trust and liability are tightly interwoven, understanding legal nuances isn't just a best practice – it's survival.

Legal considerations may not be the most exciting aspect of running a security consulting business, but they're absolutely essential. If your contracts aren't airtight, your agreements aren't clear, or your intellectual property isn't protected, you could find yourself navigating costly disputes.

Chapter 15 dives deep into the legal frameworks that underpin successful security consulting businesses. From drafting effective contracts to understanding the finer points of NDAs and non-compete agreements, this chapter will guide you through the minefield of legal considerations. Let's not just survive this minefield – let's make sure you come out unscathed and wiser for having walked it.

The Role of Legal Contracts: Shield, Compass, and Peacekeeper

Legal contracts serve three purposes: they shield you from liability, guide the relationship, and keep the peace if things go sideways. But drafting these agreements isn't as simple as pulling a template off the internet. Each clause, term, and signature serves a purpose, and understanding that purpose is crucial.

In the security industry, where stakes are often higher than in other sectors, your contracts are more than paperwork – they're your lifeline. Whether signing on a new client, partnering with a subcontractor, or ensuring sensitive information stays confidential, the documents you create and sign set the stage for a successful (or disastrous) business relationship.

Key Themes to Explore in This Chapter

Drafting Effective Client Contracts: Learn how to craft contracts that protect your interests while making clients feel valued.

Drafting 1099 Contracts and Partnership Agreements: Explore the nuances of working with independent contractors and forging partnerships.

Understanding Non-Disclosure Agreements (NDAs): Understand the importance of safeguarding sensitive information.

Understanding Non-Compete Agreements (NCAs): Discover how to maintain your competitive edge without stifling collaboration.

Legal Dispute Resolution Strategies: Equip yourself with tools to handle disputes professionally and efficiently.

By the end of this chapter, you'll not only feel confident navigating the world of legal considerations, but you'll also gain a newfound appreciation for the power of a well-worded agreement. Let's embark on this journey together, ensuring that every "i" is dotted and every "t" is crossed in your legal strategy.

Drafting Effective Client Contracts

If running a security consulting business is akin to navigating a ship through turbulent waters, a well-drafted client contract is your sturdy hull. It doesn't just keep you afloat – it ensures you're headed in the right direction, that the cargo (your services) is delivered as promised, and that both the captain (you) and the passengers (your clients) understand the rules of the voyage.

Before we get into the nuts and bolts of crafting client contracts, let's address the elephant in the room: *You need legal counsel.* Yes, this book offers valuable insights, but when crafting legally binding agreements, there's no substitute for the expertise of a qualified attorney. Think of it this way: just as you wouldn't secure a building with faulty locks, you shouldn't secure your business with shaky contracts.

What is a Client Contract?

At its core, a client contract is a legally binding agreement that outlines the scope of work, responsibilities, and expectations between you and your client. It's not just a formal handshake – it's your safeguard against misunderstandings, disputes, and liabilities.

In the security industry, where the stakes are often high, a robust client contract isn't a luxury; it's a necessity. This document protects your business, ensures clarity, and provides a reference point if disputes arise.

Let's break down the essential components of an effective client contract.

Essential Components of a Security Consulting Client Contract

Client Information and Contact Details: Include the client's full legal name, address, and primary contact information. Double-check for accuracy. An incorrect name or address can make the contract unenforceable.

Example: A contract for "Bob's Burgers, LLC" should not mistakenly list "Bob's Burger Shop."

Scope of Work: This section defines what services you will (and won't) provide. Be as specific as possible to avoid scope creep – a common pitfall in consulting. Include deliverables, timelines, and expected outcomes.

Anecdote: A consultant once agreed to "enhance security" for a client without specifying the deliverables. The client expected 24/7 monitoring and cybersecurity services, while the consultant thought it was a one-time risk assessment. A clear scope of work could have prevented the ensuing dispute.

Payment Terms: Clearly outline the pricing structure (hourly, flat fee, retainer, etc.) and payment schedule. Specify when invoices will be sent and when they're due. Address late fees, penalties, and interest rates for overdue payments.

Pro Tip: Use "Net 30" language if you expect payment within 30 days of invoicing (recommend Net+15 if you can get away with it!). Always specify whether you require a deposit to secure your services.

Termination Clause: Include conditions under which either party can terminate the contract. Outline what happens if the contract is terminated early (e.g., refunds, prorated payments, or fees).

Confidentiality and Non-Disclosure: You'll likely deal with sensitive information in security consulting. A confidentiality clause ensures that proprietary information is protected. We'll get deeper into this in just a minute.

Liability Limitations: Protect your business by limiting liability for unforeseen damages. For example, if a security breach occurs despite your recommendations, you shouldn't be held financially responsible.

Dispute Resolution: Specify how disputes will be handled (e.g., mediation, arbitration, or litigation). Many consultants prefer arbitration for its speed and cost-effectiveness.

Force Majeure: Include a clause that absolves you of liability if unforeseen events (natural disasters, pandemics, etc.) prevent you from fulfilling the contract.

Signatures: Ensure authorized representatives of both parties sign the contract. An unsigned contract is as useful as a lifeboat with a hole in it.

Practical Steps to Draft a Client Contract

Start with a Template: Use industry-standard templates as a starting point. Websites like LawDepot or Rocket Lawyer can provide a good foundation.

Customize for Your Business: Tailor the template to reflect the unique aspects of your business and the services you offer.

Use Clear Language: Avoid jargon and legalese. Your client should be able to read and understand the contract without needing a translator.

Example: Instead of "Party A agrees to indemnify Party B for any and all liabilities," write, "The client agrees to cover any costs or damages arising from their failure to follow our recommendations."

Consult an Attorney: Before finalizing your contract, have it reviewed by an attorney familiar with the security industry. This step ensures your bases are covered.

Communicate with Your Client: Walk your client through the contract to address any questions or concerns. This proactive approach builds trust and reduces the likelihood of disputes later.

Common Mistakes to Avoid

Using Ambiguous Language: Words like "as soon as possible" or "reasonable effort" are open to interpretation. Instead, specify exact timelines and deliverables.

Failing to Include a Termination Clause: Without a clear exit strategy, you could find yourself stuck in a problematic agreement.

Overlooking Confidentiality: In the security industry, confidentiality isn't optional. Ensure this clause is robust and enforceable. Don't worry, we're going to cover this soon, I promise!

Drafting effective client contracts may seem daunting initially, but with careful attention to detail and a commitment to clarity, you'll set the foundation for professional and profitable client relationships. Next, we'll explore how to create similar effective contracts and partnerships for 1099 contractors. Let's keep the momentum going!

Drafting Effective 1099 Contracts and Partnership Agreements

Collaboration is often the name of the game when it comes to building a successful security consulting business. Whether hiring a subcontractor for a specialized task or forming a partnership with another firm, effective contracts are the glue that holds professional relationships together. Let's discuss the nitty-gritty of drafting agreements that protect your business and pave the way for productive and harmonious partnerships.

The Role of 1099 Contractors and Partners in Your Business

First things first, let's distinguish between the two main players in this section:

1099 Contractors: These are independent professionals or small businesses that you hire for specific projects or tasks. They operate independently, provide their own tools, and are responsible for their own taxes. In the security industry, this could include cybersecurity experts, personal protection specialists, or technology consultants.

Business Partners: Partnerships are typically more integrated and strategic than 1099 contracts. You might partner with a technology provider to offer state-of-the-art surveillance equipment or a training firm to provide specialized courses for clients.

Both roles are crucial, but the contracts governing these relationships have different nuances. Let's start with the 1099 contractor agreements.

Drafting 1099 Contractor Agreements

A well-drafted 1099 contract isn't just about protecting your business; it's also about setting clear expectations. Here's what a comprehensive 1099 contract should include:

Scope of Work: Define the Job: Clearly outline what the contractor is responsible for. Vague descriptions like "assist with security operations" leave room for confusion. Instead, specify tasks, deliverables, and deadlines.

Example: "Conduct a cybersecurity vulnerability assessment of the client's network and deliver a detailed report within 14 days."

Payment Terms: Include the rate of pay (hourly, per project, or milestone-based), the payment schedule, and how expenses will be handled. Specify whether the contractor is required to provide invoices.

Pro Tip: Avoid ambiguity. Instead of saying, "payment will be made promptly," write, "payment will be issued within ten business days of receiving an invoice."

Independent Contractor Status: Emphasize that the contractor is not an employee. Include language stating they are responsible for their own taxes, insurance, and benefits. This protects you from misclassification claims.

Confidentiality and Intellectual Property: If the contractor will have access to sensitive information, include a confidentiality clause. Specify who owns the work they produce – this is particularly important for intellectual property like software or training materials.

Termination Clause: Define the conditions under which either party can terminate the contract. Include what happens if the contractor doesn't deliver on time or doesn't meet quality standards.

Example: "The contract may be terminated with 14 days' written notice by either party or immediately for breach of contract."

Liability and Insurance: If the contractor's work involves risk (e.g., physical security services), require them to carry their own liability insurance and provide proof of coverage.

Drafting Partnership Agreements

A partnership agreement is more complex than a 1099 contractor agreement because it involves shared risks, responsibilities, and often profits. Here's how to create an agreement that sets the stage for a successful partnership:

Purpose of the Partnership: Start by defining why you're partnering. Is it to expand your service offerings, access new markets, or share resources? Be specific.

Example: "This partnership aims to jointly deliver cybersecurity training programs to corporate clients in the northeastern United States."

Roles and Responsibilities: Outline what each party will bring to the table. For example, one partner might provide training materials while the other handles client acquisition and logistics.

Revenue Sharing and Expenses: Clearly specify how revenue and expenses will be shared. For example, "Net profits will be divided 60/40, with Partner A receiving 60% and Partner B receiving 40%."

Decision-Making and Dispute Resolution: Include a process for making decisions, especially in areas where there may be disagreements. Decide in advance how disputes will be resolved (e.g., mediation, arbitration, or legal proceedings).

Duration and Termination: Define the duration of the partnership and how it can be dissolved. Address what happens to shared resources, intellectual property, and ongoing projects if the partnership ends.

Non-Compete and Exclusivity: If applicable, include clauses preventing either party from competing directly with the partnership or forming similar partnerships with competitors during the agreement's term.

Common Mistakes to Avoid

Failing to Customize Contracts. Using a generic template might save time, but it won't account for the unique nuances of your business or the specific role of the contractor or partner.

Overlooking Local Laws. Contract laws vary by jurisdiction. Ensure your agreements comply with local regulations.

Ignoring Intellectual Property Rights. If the contractor or partner creates proprietary materials, ensure the agreement specifies who owns the rights to them.

Neglecting Regular Updates. Business relationships evolve. Periodically review and update your contracts to reflect any changes in scope, responsibilities, or payment terms.

Practical Implementation Guidance

Use a Lawyer: Even if you draft the initial contract yourself, have it reviewed by a lawyer specializing in business law.

Communicate Clearly: Walk the contractor or partner through the agreement to ensure mutual understanding. Misunderstandings are often the root of disputes.

Keep Records: Store signed contracts securely and digitally for easy access. This is crucial in case of disputes or audits.

Drafting effective 1099 contracts and partnership agreements requires a blend of legal savvy, attention to detail, and clear communication. With these tools in your arsenal, you can build strong, productive professional relationships while safeguarding your business interests. Next, we'll explore the world of NDAs and NCAs to ensure your secrets stay secret.

Understanding Non-Disclosure Agreements (NDAs)

Non-Disclosure Agreements, or NDAs, are the unsung heroes of the business world. They quietly ensure that sensitive information stays confidential, protecting businesses from potential leaks that could jeopardize their competitive edge, reputation, or even survival. For entrepreneurs in the security consulting industry, NDAs are particularly vital due to the nature of the work, which often involves access to highly sensitive client information. Whether you're working with clients, contractors, or partners, understanding NDAs is non-negotiable.

At its core, an NDA is a legally binding contract that obligates one or more parties to keep specific information confidential. It's a straightforward concept, but the devil is in the details. NDAs define what information is considered confidential, the obligations of the receiving party, and the penalties for breaching the agreement.

There are two primary types of NDAs:

Unilateral NDAs: These are one-way agreements where one party discloses confidential information to another party who agrees to keep it secret. For example, a security consultant might disclose a proprietary risk assessment methodology to a contractor.

Mutual NDAs: These are two-way agreements where both parties share confidential information with each other and agree to maintain secrecy. This is common in partnerships or joint ventures.

Key Components of an NDA

You need to understand its key components to draft or review an NDA effectively. Let's break them down:

Definition of Confidential Information. This section specifies what constitutes confidential information. It might include client data, business plans, methodologies, trade secrets, or any other proprietary information.

Pro Tip: Be specific. If the definition is too vague, it could lead to disputes over what information is actually protected.

Exclusions from Confidentiality. Not all information qualifies as confidential. Common exclusions include:

- Publicly available information.
- Information the receiving party already knew before signing the NDA.
- Information obtained legally from another source.

Example: If a competitor independently develops the same idea, it's not protected by your NDA.

Obligations of the Receiving Party. This section outlines how the receiving party must handle confidential information. Common obligations include:

- Not sharing the information with unauthorized parties.
- Using the information only for the agreed purpose.
- Implementing reasonable security measures to protect the information.

Term of the Agreement. NDAs typically specify how long the confidentiality obligations last. This could range from one year to perpetuity, depending on the nature of the information.

Remedies for Breach. This section outlines the consequences of breaking the NDA, including monetary damages, injunctions, or other legal actions.

Governing Law and Jurisdiction. NDAs specify which jurisdiction's laws govern the agreement and where disputes will be resolved.

When Should You Use an NDA?

NDAs are indispensable in a variety of business scenarios, particularly in the security consulting industry:

Client Relationships. Clients often share sensitive information about their vulnerabilities, security protocols, and personnel. An NDA reassures them that this information will remain confidential.

Contractor Agreements. When working with 1099 contractors or vendors, an NDA ensures that your proprietary methods and client information are protected.

Partnerships. When collaborating with other firms, NDAs protect the exchange of sensitive information, such as financial details or strategic plans.

Employee Agreements. NDAs are often included in employment contracts to protect intellectual property and trade secrets.

Practical Implementation Guidance

Drafting an NDA

- Use Templates Wisely: While NDA templates are readily available online, they should be tailored to your specific needs. A one-size-fits-all approach can leave gaps.
- Seek Legal Counsel: Have a lawyer review your NDA to ensure it complies with local laws and adequately protects your interests.

Negotiating an NDA

- Be prepared for pushback. Some parties may balk at overly restrictive NDAs, so clarify why each clause is necessary.
- Be open to reasonable modifications. Flexibility can help build trust without compromising protection.

Storing and Enforcing NDAs

- Keep signed NDAs organized and easily accessible. Digital storage solutions with secure access controls are ideal.
- Monitor compliance. If you suspect a breach, consult legal counsel immediately to assess your options.

Common Pitfalls to Avoid

Overusing NDAs. Not every interaction requires an NDA. Overusing them can make you seem paranoid or overly litigious.

Example: Asking a potential client to sign an NDA before an initial consultation might deter them.

Failing to Specify the Scope. Vague NDAs can lead to misunderstandings and disputes. Clearly define what information is protected and for how long.

Neglecting to Update NDAs. As your business evolves, your NDAs may need to be updated to reflect new types of confidential information or changes in the law.

NDAs are more than just paperwork; they're a critical tool for protecting your business, clients, and reputation. By understanding their components, using them wisely, and enforcing them diligently, you can ensure that your confidential information remains just that – confidential. Next, we'll tackle non-compete agreements, the cousin to NDAs that ensures fair play in competitive industries.

Understanding Non-Compete Agreements (NCA's)

Non-Compete Agreements (NCAs) are both a shield and a sword in business, especially in industries as competitive and sensitive as security consulting. They protect businesses from unfair competition by ensuring that key personnel or collaborators don't take your proprietary methods, trade secrets, or client base and turn them against you. At the same time, if mishandled, NCAs can backfire, creating legal headaches and damaging relationships.

For security consultants, where trust, discretion, and specialized knowledge are paramount, understanding NCAs is essential. Let's get into the nuts and bolts of NCAs so you can wield them effectively and responsibly.

A Non-Compete Agreement is a legally binding contract that restricts an individual or entity from engaging in activities that compete with the business during or after their association. This can include working for a competitor, starting a competing company, or poaching clients.

Key Purposes of an NCA:

Protect Trade Secrets. Safeguard proprietary information like methodologies, client lists, or strategic plans.

Retain Competitive Advantage. Prevent key personnel from transferring valuable knowledge to competitors.

Secure Client Relationships. Ensure clients don't follow former employees or contractors to competing firms.

Components of a Strong NCA

Scope of Restriction. This defines what activities the restricted party is prohibited from engaging in. The scope should be reasonable and specific, such as barring work for direct competitors or preventing solicitation of existing clients.

Example: If you run a cybersecurity consulting firm, the NCA might restrict former employees from providing cybersecurity services to your current client base.

Geographic Limitations. The agreement must specify the geographic area where the restrictions apply. For local businesses, this might be within a city or state. For global firms, it could span multiple countries.

Pro Tip: Overly broad geographic restrictions may not hold up in court, so tailor them to your market area.

Duration of Restriction. The timeframe during which the restrictions are enforceable must be reasonable. Typical durations range from six months to two years.

Caution: Courts often strike down NCAs with excessively long durations as unfair.

Consideration. In legal terms, consideration refers to what the restricted party gets in exchange for agreeing to the NCA. This could be monetary compensation, employment benefits, or access to proprietary resources.

Definitions and Terms. Clearly define all relevant terms, such as "competitor," "client," and "confidential information," to avoid ambiguity.

Remedies for Breach. Outline the consequences of violating the agreement, such as financial penalties, injunctions, or other legal actions.

Governing Law. Specify which jurisdiction's laws will apply to the agreement. This is particularly important for businesses operating in multiple states or countries.

Practical Implementation Guidance

Drafting an NCA

- Use Legal Templates as Starting Points: Plenty of templates are available online, but remember that no template is a perfect fit. Tailor it to your business's unique needs.
- Seek Legal Counsel: Consult an attorney to ensure the NCA complies with local laws and is enforceable. Laws governing NCAs vary significantly by jurisdiction.

Negotiating an NCA

- Communicate Clearly: Explain to employees or contractors why the NCA is necessary and how it benefits both parties.
- Be Open to Feedback: Address concerns about overly restrictive clauses. A fair agreement fosters goodwill and reduces the likelihood of disputes.

Enforcing an NCA

- Monitor Compliance: Keep track of where former employees or contractors go after leaving your business.
- Act Swiftly in Case of Breach: Consult legal counsel immediately to evaluate your options, whether negotiating a resolution or pursuing legal action.

Things to Watch Out For

Overreach: NCAs that are too broad in scope, geography, or duration may be deemed unenforceable.

Example: Prohibiting a former contractor from working in the entire security industry for five years is likely to be considered unreasonable.

Jurisdictional Variability: Some states, like California, heavily restrict the use of NCAs. Always understand local laws before implementing one.

Reputation Risks: Overly aggressive use of NCAs can harm your reputation and discourage top talent from joining your team.

Example: A Security Consultant's NCA in Action

Imagine you've hired a 1099 contractor to assist with a large corporate risk assessment. The contractor gains access to your proprietary assessment tools and develops relationships with your clients as part of their work.

To protect your business, you include an NCA in their contract. The agreement restricts the contractor from providing similar services to your client base within a 50-mile radius for one year after the engagement ends. In exchange, you offer a premium pay rate and access to valuable training resources.

When the project concludes, you monitor the contractor's compliance with the NCA. Six months later, you discover they've started offering similar services to one of your clients. You consult your attorney, who helps you negotiate a resolution that protects your business interests while avoiding a drawn-out legal battle.

Balancing Fairness and Protection

NCAs are most effective when they balance protecting your business and being fair to the other party. Here are some tips to achieve that balance:

Be Transparent:　Clearly explain the purpose of the NCA and its terms during the hiring or contracting process.

Offer Value:　Provide something of value in return for signing the NCA, whether it's higher pay, access to resources, or career development opportunities.

Avoid One-Size-Fits-All:　Tailor each NCA to the specific role and circumstances of the individual.

Non-Compete Agreements are powerful tools for safeguarding your business but require careful planning and execution. By understanding their components, tailoring them to your needs, and enforcing them judiciously, you can protect your business while maintaining positive relationships with your team and partners. Next, we'll explore legal dispute resolution strategies – because even the best-laid plans sometimes go awry.

Legal Dispute Resolution Strategies

Legal disputes are a bit like unexpected flat tires in the business world. Nobody sets out hoping to have one, but sooner or later, it happens. For security consultants who deal with sensitive information, high-stakes operations, and demanding clients, the potential for disputes is ever-present. Contracts can be misunderstood, services may be misinterpreted, or unforeseen circumstances might lead to dissatisfaction.

Let's navigate the toolkit of dispute resolution strategies so you can keep the wheels turning, avoid unnecessary drama, and maintain your business integrity.

Legal dispute resolution refers to the processes and strategies employed to resolve disagreements or conflicts between two parties, often without needing to escalate to court. These strategies range from informal negotiations to formal legal proceedings.

Key Methods of Dispute Resolution

- Negotiation
- Mediation
- Arbitration
- Litigation

Each method has its own set of strengths, challenges, and ideal use cases. Let's unpack them.

Negotiation: Keeping It in the Family

Definition: Negotiation is an informal process where both parties work together to find a mutually agreeable solution. Think of it as a business version of a family meeting.

How It Works:

- Both parties discuss the issue without involving third parties.
- Goals are set, and compromises are explored.
- Agreements can be verbal or formalized in writing.

What to Watch Out For:

- Power imbalances can lead to one party dominating the discussion.
- Without documentation, verbal agreements can later lead to "he said, she said" scenarios.

Example: A client disputes an invoice, claiming they didn't approve certain hours billed. Instead of escalating, you meet with the client, show your records, and offer a discount as a goodwill gesture. Problem solved, relationship preserved.

Implementation Guidance:

- Always remain professional, even if the other party becomes heated.
- Document the outcome of negotiations to prevent future misunderstandings.
- Use negotiation as a first step before considering more formal methods.

Mediation: The Neutral Third Party

Definition: Mediation involves a neutral third party (the mediator) who facilitates discussions between disputing parties to help them reach a resolution.

How It Works:

- The mediator doesn't make decisions but guides both parties toward a solution.
- Mediation sessions are typically confidential.

What to Watch Out For:

- Mediation isn't binding, so either party can walk away.
- Success depends on both parties being willing to compromise.

Example: A subcontractor claims they were underpaid for work performed, but you believe their claim is baseless. To avoid tarnishing your reputation, you agree to mediation. The mediator helps both sides review the contract and clarify misunderstandings, leading to a resolution.

Implementation Guidance:

- Choose a mediator experienced in security consulting or your industry.
- Prepare all relevant documentation and evidence beforehand.
- Approach mediation with an open mind and a willingness to compromise.

Arbitration: The Courtroom Lite

Definition: Arbitration is a more formal process where a neutral arbitrator hears both sides and makes a binding decision. It's often used when contracts specify it as a dispute resolution method.

How It Works:

- Both parties present evidence and arguments.
- The arbitrator evaluates the case and issues a binding decision.
- Arbitration is less expensive and quicker than litigation but more formal than mediation.

What to Watch Out For:

- Decisions are binding, so there's no appeal.
- Arbitration fees can still be substantial.

Example: Your client claims your security assessment didn't deliver the promised results, but you believe you fulfilled the contract. Arbitration allows both parties to present their case without the drawn-out timeline of a lawsuit. The arbitrator rules in your favor, saving you months of courtroom drama.

Implementation Guidance:

- Ensure your contracts include an arbitration clause if you prefer this method.
- Understand that arbitration can be a double-edged sword – it's final.
- Hire a lawyer to represent your case if the stakes are high.

Litigation: The Last Resort

Definition: Litigation involves resolving disputes in court. It's the most formal and structured process, requiring legal representation and adhering to court rules.

How It Works:

- A lawsuit is filed, and the case is heard by a judge or jury.
- Evidence, witnesses, and legal arguments are presented.
- A binding verdict is issued.

What to Watch Out For:

- Litigation is costly and time-consuming.
- Public trials can damage reputations.

Example: A former employee breaches their non-compete agreement by poaching clients. Negotiation, mediation, and arbitration fail. You file a lawsuit, and the court orders the employee to cease their activities and pay damages.

Implementation Guidance:

- Use litigation only when other methods fail, or the stakes are too high.
- Work with an attorney experienced in your field.

- Be prepared for a lengthy and potentially expensive process.

Additional Tips for Effective Dispute Resolution

Stay Professional: No matter how heated things get, professionalism builds credibility and can sway outcomes in your favor.

Invest in Preventative Measures: Clear contracts, detailed records, and transparent communication can prevent many disputes before they start.

Know When to Call in the Experts: If a dispute involves complex legal, technical, or financial issues, hire an expert. Don't wing it.

Disputes are a natural part of business, especially in high-stakes industries like security consulting. Understanding and implementing these resolution strategies allows you to navigate conflicts effectively, protect your business, and maintain professional relationships. Next, we'll wrap up the chapter by tying together these legal insights into a cohesive strategy for your security consulting business.

Chapter 15 Wrap-Up

Legal considerations and client contracts are the backbone of any security consulting business. They're the delicate threads that keep operations running smoothly, protect relationships, and ensure you stay on the right side of the law. In Chapter 15, we examined the vital components of legal and contractual obligations, equipping you with the tools to navigate the often-daunting world of legalities. Now, let's bring it all together, highlighting the key takeaways from each subsection.

Drafting Effective Client Contracts: The Art of Mutual Understanding

We kicked off the chapter by dissecting the intricacies of client contracts. These agreements are not just paperwork – they're the foundation of every professional relationship. A well-drafted client contract sets clear expectations, defines deliverables, and outlines the scope of work, ensuring everyone is on the same page.

We emphasized the importance of using precise language to avoid ambiguity. Whether it's specifying payment terms, laying out timelines, or detailing deliverables, clarity is king. Anecdotes from the field illustrated how vague contracts have led to disputes, reinforcing why thoroughness is key.

Advice: Work closely with legal counsel to tailor your contracts to your business needs. Off-the-shelf templates can be a starting point, but they rarely cover the unique complexities of the security consulting industry. Contracts that reflect your specific services protect your business and instill confidence in your clients.

Drafting Effective 1099 Contracts and Partnership Agreements: A Balancing Act

Navigating relationships with subcontractors and partners adds another layer of complexity. This section delved into the essentials of drafting 1099 contracts and partnership agreements, focusing on building strong, fair, and legally sound collaborations.

We explored the delicate balance of maintaining your brand's integrity while partnering with other professionals. Whether you're hiring a subcontractor for their niche expertise or entering a joint venture, the contracts governing these relationships must be rock-solid. Including clauses like performance expectations, payment schedules, and dispute resolution mechanisms ensures that partnerships run smoothly.

Advice: Always include clear non-disclosure and non-compete clauses where appropriate (and legal). These protect proprietary methods and client relationships, safeguarding your hard-earned reputation.

Understanding Non-Disclosure Agreements (NDAs): Guarding the Vault

In the high-stakes world of security consulting, information is currency. NDAs act as the vault doors, protecting sensitive client and business data. We unpacked the components of an effective NDA, from the definition of confidential information to the duration of the agreement.

Anecdotes demonstrated the fallout of inadequate NDAs, like when a competitor gained access to sensitive strategies because of a poorly drafted agreement. These cautionary tales underscored the importance of robust, enforceable NDAs.

Advice: Ensure all employees, subcontractors, and partners sign NDAs as part of your onboarding process. And remember, an NDA isn't a one-size-fits-all document – customize it to the scope of each relationship to ensure it's legally enforceable.

Understanding Non-Compete Agreements (NCAs): Protecting Your Turf

Non-compete agreements are often a double-edged sword. On one hand, they protect your business from unfair competition; on the other, they can stifle professional growth if not crafted judiciously. In this section, we explored how to draft NCAs that strike the right balance.

We clarified the key components of an NCA, including duration, geographic scope, and the specific activities it prohibits. Practical examples highlighted when NCAs are appropriate and how to avoid common pitfalls, such as overly restrictive terms that might not hold up in court.

Advice: Work with legal counsel to ensure your NCAs comply with local laws and industry standards. Remember, an NCA should protect your business without being unnecessarily punitive.

Legal Dispute Resolution Strategies: Keeping the Peace

No matter how meticulous your contracts are, disputes can still arise. This section equipped you with a toolkit of strategies to handle legal disputes, from informal negotiations to formal litigation. Each method was dissected to show its strengths and ideal use cases.

We illustrated how negotiation can often resolve disputes quickly and amicably, while mediation and arbitration provide more structured alternatives. For those rare cases where litigation is unavoidable, we offered guidance on how to prepare and minimize its impact on your business.

Advice: Prevention is the best medicine. Clear contracts, open communication, and proactive problem-solving can reduce the likelihood of disputes. However, when disputes arise, having a structured resolution plan can save time, money, and relationships.

Bringing It All Together

Contracts and legal strategies may not be the most glamorous aspects of running a security consulting business, but they're among the most critical. They're the guardrails that keep your business on track, ensuring that you can focus on delivering exceptional service without getting bogged down by avoidable legal woes.

This chapter provided a comprehensive roadmap for navigating these complexities. From crafting airtight client and subcontractor agreements to protecting sensitive information and resolving disputes, you now have the tools to safeguard your business's interests. The emphasis on seeking professional legal counsel cannot be overstated. While this book offers guidance, there's no substitute for personalized advice from a qualified attorney.

With the knowledge from this chapter, you're better prepared to handle the myriad of legal and contractual challenges that come your way. As you move forward, remember that your contracts are living documents – they should evolve as your business grows.

16

Long-Term Success and Exit Strategies

"The best way to predict the future is to create it."

— Peter Drucker

According to a study by Exit Planning Institute, over 70% of business owners don't have a formal exit strategy, yet nearly 50% plan to leave their business within the next decade. The lesson? Even the most successful companies need a clear plan for the future.

Welcome to the final chapter of your journey in building a thriving security consulting business. At this point, you've mastered the art of starting, running, and growing your enterprise. But the true mark of a successful entrepreneur lies in their ability to think beyond the present – to plan for longevity, legacy, and eventual transition. This chapter guides you in crafting a future-proof blueprint for long-term success and navigating the complex process of exiting the business on your terms.

Think of this chapter as a security plan for your business's future, complete with proactive strategies and contingency measures. Whether your goal is to build a legacy, pass the baton to the next generation, or prepare for a merger or sale, the key is thoughtful preparation. And just as you've learned to adapt to industry changes and client demands, this chapter will help you adjust your business to the next stage of its lifecycle.

Let's explore how to build a sustainable future, give back to the community, and plan for a successful exit when the time comes.

Setting the Stage for Long-Term Success

Just as in security consulting, where anticipating threats and opportunities is vital, planning for the future of your business requires foresight, adaptability, and strategic thinking. This chapter focuses on six essential components:

Building a Legacy in the Security Consulting Business. Ensuring your business stands the test of time and becomes a model for excellence in the industry.

Giving Back to the Security Community. Contributing to the growth of the field and mentoring the next generation of professionals.

The Art of Continuous Improvement. Keeping your business dynamic and relevant through constant learning and innovation.

Succession Planning and Leadership Development. Identifying and nurturing future leaders to carry the torch.

Preparing for Business Sale or Merger. Positioning your business as an attractive prospect for buyers or partners.

Exit Strategies for Security Professionals. Crafting a plan that aligns with your personal and professional goals.

This chapter is about more than just leaving – it's about leaving a legacy. Whether you plan to step away in five years or fifty, the steps you take now will shape how your business evolves and thrives in your absence. As always, we'll sprinkle in humor, practical tips, and a touch of storytelling to keep things engaging.

Building a Legacy in the Security Consulting Business

Building a legacy is about crafting a narrative that outlives your tenure in the business. It's not just about creating a successful security consulting firm; it's about creating a meaningful impact, influencing the industry, and leaving a positive imprint on clients, employees, and the community. A legacy is people's story about you and your business long after you've stepped away.

A legacy in business is the culmination of your values, achievements, and influence. In the security consulting industry, this can mean:

Professional Excellence: Becoming a trusted name synonymous with quality and reliability.

Mentorship and Leadership: Developing the next generation of security professionals.

Innovation: Introducing new methodologies or technologies that redefine industry standards.

Community Impact: Giving back through education, charity, or advocacy.

A legacy isn't built overnight. It's an intentional, ongoing process woven into every decision, relationship, and milestone.

Laying the Foundation for a Legacy

Define Your Legacy Goals. Ask yourself: What do you want to be remembered for? Do you want to revolutionize risk assessments? Mentor the next generation? Be a thought leader in corporate security? Pinpointing your aspirations will guide your efforts.

Embed Core Values in Your Business Practices. Your values shape your legacy. Whether it's integrity, innovation, or client commitment, ensure these principles shine through in your operations, from employee training to client interactions.

Consistency Over Time. A legacy isn't built in a day or even a year. It's a product of consistent action and decisions over time. Stick to your principles even during challenges to solidify your reputation.

Practical Steps to Building a Legacy

Establish a Unique Brand Identity. Your brand is your business's personality and one of the most visible aspects of your legacy. A strong brand resonates with clients and colleagues alike.

Example: A security consultant known for cutting-edge cyber solutions will leave a legacy as an innovator, while one who excels in community safety might be remembered as a humanitarian.

Invest in Relationships. Building a network of strong, genuine relationships amplifies your impact. Cultivate relationships with clients, employees, peers, and industry organizations. Relationships ensure your influence and values carry on.

Anecdote: Consider Alex, a security consultant who spent years mentoring young professionals. When he retired, his mentees carried forward his methodologies, embedding his legacy into their practices.

Give Back to the Industry. Sharing your knowledge through speaking engagements, publishing thought leadership content, or creating educational resources helps secure your place as an industry leader.

Implementation Tip: Host free webinars for small businesses on improving security practices. This not only builds goodwill but also reinforces your expertise.

Encourage Employee Development. Your team is a reflection of your leadership. Empowering employees to grow, innovate, and succeed ensures that your values and vision endure beyond your direct involvement.

Example: If you prioritize diversity and inclusivity in hiring, your company may become known as a trailblazer in creating equitable opportunities within the security sector.

Document and Share Best Practices. Codify your methodologies and operational standards. Share these with your team, clients, and the industry to ensure your approach continues to influence others.

Example: Publishing a guide on conducting risk assessments could position you as a thought leader and extend your reach long after retirement.

Overcoming Challenges in Building a Legacy

Imposter Syndrome. Many entrepreneurs worry they haven't achieved enough to leave a legacy. Remember, a legacy isn't about perfection; it's about impact.

Balancing Profit with Purpose. It's easy to focus solely on the bottom line. However, a lasting legacy often prioritizes purpose alongside profit. Finding this balance is key to long-term success.

Staying Relevant. A legacy can become stagnant if you fail to adapt. Commit to continuous learning and innovation to remain impactful in an evolving industry.

The ROI of a Legacy

While a legacy may seem intangible, its benefits are concrete:

Client Loyalty: A business rooted in strong values attracts and retains loyal clients.

Industry Recognition: Your contributions position you as a leader, opening doors to new opportunities.

Sustainability: A legacy-driven business is better equipped to thrive through transitions.

Building a legacy in the security consulting business isn't just a noble endeavor – it's a smart one. It requires vision, commitment, and action, but the rewards are immeasurable. A strong legacy ensures your influence endures, your business thrives, and your story continues to inspire.

Remember, every decision you make today shapes the legacy you'll leave tomorrow. So, ask yourself: What will your story be? Then, start writing it – one action at a time.

Giving Back to the Security Community

Giving back to the security community isn't just a matter of goodwill – it's a vital way to foster professional growth, enhance your reputation, and contribute to an industry that has given so much to you. For entrepreneurs in the security consulting field, giving back creates opportunities to influence the next generation, support peers, and elevate standards across the industry.

But what does it mean to "give back," and how can you do it effectively? Let's explore.

At its core, giving back is about creating a positive ripple effect. By investing in the industry, you strengthen its foundation and contribute to its evolution. Here's why it's crucial:

Building a Better Industry: Sharing knowledge and resources ensures that others can build upon your successes, ultimately raising the bar for everyone.

Establishing Credibility: A consultant who gives back is seen as a leader. It signals confidence, expertise, and a genuine commitment to the profession.

Networking Opportunities: Contributing to the community puts you in contact with like-minded professionals, potential collaborators, and even future clients.

Personal Fulfillment: There's an undeniable satisfaction in knowing your work has positively impacted others, whether through mentorship, volunteering, or financial support.

Practical Ways to Give Back

Mentoring Emerging Professionals

What It Looks Like: Taking young professionals or newcomers under your wing, offering guidance, and sharing your experiences.

Why Bother: Security consulting can be an intimidating field for beginners. A mentor can provide valuable insights, helping mentees avoid pitfalls and find their niche.

How to Do It: Join mentorship programs offered by professional organizations like ASIS International or host informal sessions with junior consultants.

Anecdote: Consider the story of Mark, a senior consultant who mentored a recent graduate, Lisa. With Mark's advice, Lisa developed her niche in cybersecurity, eventually becoming a recognized expert in the field.

Speaking at Industry Events

What It Looks Like: Sharing your expertise at conferences, webinars, or local meetups.

Why Bother: Speaking engagements position you as a thought leader while providing valuable knowledge to attendees.

How to Do It: Start with smaller local events and build up to larger conferences. Ensure your presentations are informative, engaging, and actionable.

Implementation Tip: Tailor your talks to your niche. For example, if you specialize in executive protection, focus on emerging trends in that area.

Supporting Security Education and Training

What It Looks Like: Funding scholarships, donating equipment, or volunteering to teach courses.

Why Bother: Education is the backbone of professional growth. Your contributions can shape the careers of future security professionals.

How to Do It: Partner with colleges, training centers, or online platforms to provide resources or host workshops.

Example: Imagine donating a small fund to a local college's security studies program, enabling underprivileged students to enroll in advanced certifications.

Creating Open-Access Resources

What It Looks Like: Publishing free eBooks, guides, or blogs to share your insights.

Why Bother: Not everyone has the means to access premium resources. Open-access materials democratize knowledge and enhance industry standards.

How to Do It: Identify common pain points within the industry and create content that addresses them. For instance, write a guide on conducting threat assessments or managing corporate security risks.

Implementation Tip: Use platforms like LinkedIn, Medium, or your company website to distribute these resources widely.

Volunteering Your Expertise

What It Looks Like: Offering pro bono consulting services to non-profits, women's shelters, schools, community organizations, etc.

Why Bother: Many organizations operate with limited budgets but could greatly benefit from professional security advice.

How to Do It: Identify local organizations that align with your values and offer your services for a specific project or period.

Anecdote: A security consultant helped a local women's shelter implement a robust security plan after a series of threats. The consultant's actions protected the residents and elevated the consultant's standing in the community.

Advocating for Industry Standards

What It Looks Like: Participating in task forces or committees that shape security protocols and certifications.

Why Bother: Active participation in standard-setting ensures that the industry continues to evolve fairly, effectively, and inclusively.

How to Do It: Join organizations like the International Association of Professional Security Consultants (IAPSC) or the Overseas Security Advisory Council (OSAC). Participate in working groups to develop industry guidelines.

Implementation Tip: Share your experiences from the field to ensure standards remain practical and relevant.

Common Challenges in Giving Back

Balancing Time and Resources. Many entrepreneurs struggle to find time for community contributions amidst their workload. Prioritize initiatives that align with your values and are feasible within your schedule.

Overextending Yourself. It's tempting to say "yes" to every opportunity. However, overcommitting can dilute your efforts and lead to burnout. Focus on a few impactful activities rather than spreading yourself too thin.

Navigating Criticism. Public contributions may occasionally attract naysayers. Stay focused on your goals, and remember that meaningful work often invites scrutiny.

Building a Culture of Giving Back

Giving back shouldn't be a solo endeavor. By fostering a culture of generosity within your organization, you multiply your impact.

Involve Your Team: Encourage employees to participate in volunteering, mentorship, or advocacy efforts. Create programs that reward their contributions.

Highlight Your Impact: Share stories of your initiatives with clients and peers. This not only inspires others but also reinforces your commitment to the industry.

Make It Sustainable: Incorporate giving back into your business model. Allocate a percentage of profits or dedicate specific hours each month to community work.

The Ripple Effect

When you give back to the security community, the benefits extend far beyond your immediate efforts. You inspire others to follow suit, strengthen the industry as a whole, and leave a meaningful and enduring legacy.

Whether mentoring a rising star, speaking at a conference, or donating to a training program, every contribution counts. Giving back isn't just about what you do today – it's about the future you help shape for tomorrow.

So, where will you start? Maybe it's as simple as offering advice to a newcomer or writing that long-overdue blog post. Whatever your path, know that your efforts will make a difference. And isn't that the ultimate reward?

The Art of Continuous Improvement

Continuous improvement is the lifeblood of success, especially in a dynamic and high-stakes field such as security consulting. Staying stagnant is not an option in an industry that demands adaptability, foresight, and perpetual learning. But what does it mean to improve continuously? More importantly, how does one cultivate a mindset and practice of steady growth, day after day, year after year?

At its core, continuous improvement is a commitment – one small, deliberate step at a time. It's not about massive leaps (although those are welcome when they happen). Instead, it's about consistent progress.

Why Continuous Improvement Is Key

Staying Relevant: Technology, threats, and client needs evolve rapidly. Continuous improvement ensures you're not left behind.

Building Credibility: Clients trust consultants who stay ahead of industry trends. Showing you're invested in self-improvement builds confidence.

Personal Satisfaction: Progress feels good. Knowing you're better today than you were yesterday fosters motivation and pride in your work.

The Pitfalls of Complacency

A lack of growth leads to outdated knowledge, reduced competitiveness, and potential irrelevance. No one wants to hire a consultant who is still touting the "best practices" of 1995 in a world of artificial intelligence and drone technology.

Strategies for Continuous Improvement

Embrace Lifelong Learning. Learning doesn't stop when you get your first client – or your fiftieth. Lifelong learning is a habit, not a phase.

Formal Education: Pursue certifications and advanced degrees. Programs like Certified Protection Professional (CPP) or Master of Business Administration (MBA) can significantly enhance your expertise.

Online Courses: Platforms like LinkedIn Learning, Udemy, and

Coursera offer affordable courses on niche topics like cybersecurity, threat analysis, and even business strategy.

Reading: Subscribe to industry journals, blogs, and publications. Books by thought leaders can also provide fresh perspectives.

Example: Jane, a consultant specializing in corporate security, realized her clients were increasingly concerned about cyber threats. Instead of ignoring the trend, she enrolled in an online cybersecurity certification program. Within six months, she expanded her services and doubled her client base.

Solicit Feedback and Act on It: Feedback is a goldmine for improvement, but it's only valuable if you act on it.

Ask Clients: Create formal feedback loops, such as post-project surveys or quarterly check-ins.

Peer Reviews: Regularly engage with industry peers to evaluate your performance and offer constructive criticism.

Self-Assessment: Reflect on each project. What went well? What could have been better?

Implementation Tip: Maintain a "lessons learned" journal. After every project, jot down what you'll do differently next time. Over time, this becomes a personal map for growth.

Experiment and Innovate. Playing it safe is fine for certain tasks, but innovation often requires stepping outside your comfort zone.

Test New Tools: Stay open to emerging technologies, whether using AI for threat assessment or integrating advanced risk management software.

Pilot New Services: Offer beta versions of new services to select clients. Their feedback will help refine your approach.

Example: A consultant experimenting with drone technology for perimeter security piloted the service with a long-term client. The feedback led to a full-scale service rollout that quickly became a cornerstone of his business.

Network Like a Pro. Improvement isn't just about what you know – it's also about who you know.

Join Professional Organizations: Groups like ASIS International or the International Association of Professional Security Consultants provide access to conferences, webinars, and peer discussions.

Engage on Social Media: Platforms like LinkedIn are treasure troves for industry insights and opportunities to connect with other professionals.

Mentorships: Be both a mentor and a mentee. Learning flows in both directions.

Implementation Tip: Set a networking goal, like attending three industry events per year or connecting with five new professionals monthly.

The Role of Metrics in Continuous Improvement

You can't improve what you don't measure. Tracking progress ensures you're on the right path.

Define Success Metrics: Identify what "better" looks like in your context. Is it an increase in client retention? Higher earnings? Enhanced technical skills?

Monitor Progress Regularly: Use project management software or simple spreadsheets to track your development goals.

Celebrate Milestones: Improvement can be slow, so take time to acknowledge your achievements. Reward yourself for certifications earned, services launched, or client praise received.

Overcoming Common Barriers

Time Constraints: Continuous improvement requires time, but prioritization is key. Dedicate specific hours each week to learning or skill development.

Fear of Failure: Trying something new always carries risks. Embrace mistakes as learning opportunities.

Financial Limitations: Free resources, like webinars, podcasts, and community forums, can be as valuable as paid courses.

Making Continuous Improvement a Habit

Set Clear Goals: Break down your improvement journey into actionable steps.

Build a Routine: Allocate consistent time for learning and reflection.

Stay Curious: Approach every challenge with a mindset of "What can I learn from this?"

The art of continuous improvement is just that – an art. It's a blend of discipline, curiosity, and adaptability. As a security consultant, the stakes are high, but so are the rewards. By committing to steady growth, you're not just improving yourself; you're elevating your entire business and setting a standard for others to follow.

So, what's your next move? Whether it's taking a course, seeking feedback, or exploring a new tool, start small but stay consistent. After all, the best security consultants aren't born – they're continuously improved.

Succession Planing and Leadership Development

Succession planning and leadership development might sound like topics reserved for sprawling corporate entities with complex hierarchies. But even in the world of security consulting – a field often dominated by solo entrepreneurs or small teams – these concepts are critical. Why? Because building a business isn't just about today; it's about ensuring your legacy, creating continuity, and empowering the next generation of leaders to carry your vision forward.

The Dual Pillars: Succession Planning and Leadership Development

At first glance, succession planning and leadership development might seem like two separate endeavors. In reality, they're intricately linked. Succession planning focuses on preparing for the future by identifying and developing individuals to take on leadership roles. Leadership development is the process of equipping those individuals with the skills and mindset needed to thrive in those roles.

Succession Planning Defined: Succession planning is your strategy to ensure your business can continue to operate – and even flourish – when you're no longer at the helm. Whether you plan to retire, sell your business, or simply step back to focus on other ventures, having a robust plan in place mitigates chaos and ensures continuity.

Leadership Development Defined: Leadership development is about creating a culture of growth and learning. It's not just about preparing for "someday" but empowering team members to lead in the present, handle challenges, and drive the business forward.

Succession planning is often overlooked in small businesses, but its importance cannot be overstated. Without a plan, the departure of a key leader – whether through retirement, illness, or unexpected circumstances – can spell disaster.

Steps to Effective Succession Planning

Identify Key Roles and Responsibilities: Start by mapping out the essential functions in your business. Beyond your own role, consider other critical positions that drive operations, such as project managers or client relationship leads.

Evaluate Potential Successors: Look for individuals within your team – or even external hires – who demonstrate the skills, values, and potential to lead.

Implementation Tip: Create a "bench strength" assessment – a simple chart listing potential successors for key roles and their readiness level.

Develop Successors Gradually: Leadership isn't learned overnight. Provide opportunities for potential successors to shadow you, lead projects, or manage client relationships.

Document Critical Knowledge: Create a repository of essential information, from operational procedures to client histories. A secure digital document or knowledge management system ensures nothing gets lost in transition.

Establish a Timeline: Succession doesn't have to happen tomorrow; setting milestones ensures you're moving in the right direction.

The Importance of Leadership Development

Leadership development isn't just about preparing for your departure. It's about strengthening your business today. A strong leadership team fosters innovation, builds client trust, and creates a resilient organization.

Strategies for Leadership Development

Formal Training Programs: Invest in leadership training programs for your team. Topics like conflict resolution, decision-making, and strategic planning are invaluable.

Mentorship: Pair emerging leaders with seasoned mentors who can provide guidance and perspective.

Example: John, a junior consultant, was paired with a retired security director. Through regular meetings, John learned technical skills and how to handle high-pressure client interactions.

Empowerment Through Delegation: Leadership development doesn't happen in a vacuum. Empower your team by delegating meaningful responsibilities and giving them decision-making autonomy.

Anecdote: Sarah, a consultant in a growing firm, was tasked with leading a high-profile project. While she initially struggled, the experience transformed her into a confident leader, ready for more significant challenges.

Practical Considerations for Small Teams

Small teams often face unique challenges in succession planning and leadership development. With fewer people, each individual's development becomes even more critical.

Cross-Training. Ensure team members are trained in multiple roles. This not only strengthens the team but also reduces disruptions during transitions.

Leverage External Expertise. If your team is too small to cultivate leadership internally, consider bringing in external consultants or interim leaders during transitions.

Balancing Long-Term and Immediate Needs: While succession planning focuses on the future, leadership development addresses both the present and the long term. Striking a balance between these two priorities is essential.

Immediate Needs: Empower current leaders to handle challenges effectively.

Future Needs: Build a pipeline of talent ready to step up when needed.

Measuring Success: How do you know if your succession and leadership development efforts are paying off?

Employee Engagement: Are team members taking ownership of their roles and seeking growth opportunities?

Business Continuity: Are you confident the business could run smoothly without you for a month? Six months? A year?

Client Feedback: Do clients see your business as stable and well-led, regardless of who they interact with?

Succession planning and leadership development might not be the most glamorous aspects of running a security consulting business, but they're among the most important. These efforts ensure your business thrives not just under your leadership but for years – or even decades – beyond.

By embracing these strategies, you're not just building a business but creating a legacy, empowering future leaders, and securing a lasting impact in the security consulting world. So, where do you start? Begin by looking at your team, your goals, and your timeline. The future of your business depends on it.

Preparing for Business Sale or Merger

For many security consultants, the idea of selling their business or merging with another firm may seem like a distant milestone – or perhaps an unlikely one altogether. Yet, whether you plan to transition out of business in the near future or simply want to keep your options open, preparing for a sale or merger is an exercise in foresight, strategy, and understanding the value of what you've built.

Even if selling or merging isn't on your immediate horizon, laying the groundwork ensures you're ready if an opportunity arises. Consider it like maintaining a pristine car: whether you drive it for years or decide to trade it in, its value remains high because of the care you've invested.

Maximizing Business Value: A business prepared for sale is generally more efficient, better documented, and more appealing to potential buyers or partners.

Flexibility for Life Changes: Unexpected events – a health issue, family needs, or an irresistible offer – can make selling or merging suddenly relevant. Being prepared eliminates scrambling.

Strengthening the Business: The steps you take to prepare for a sale or merger often align with building a stronger, more resilient operation.

Step 1: Understand the Value of Your Business

The first step in preparing for a sale or merger is understanding what your business is worth. This isn't just about what's in the bank; it's about intangible assets, growth potential, and market positioning.

Financial Health: Ensure your financial statements are accurate and up-to-date, and paint a clear picture of profitability. Potential buyers will scrutinize cash flow, profit margins, and revenue trends.

Anecdote: One security firm discovered a discrepancy in their bookkeeping just days before a meeting with a prospective buyer. The hiccup delayed the sale by months and created unnecessary mistrust. Keeping clean books from the start avoids such pitfalls.

Client Base: A well-diversified client base reduces risk for buyers. Heavy reliance on a single client may lower your business's value.

Brand Reputation: Your reputation in the industry – built on trust, reliability, and professionalism – is a critical asset. Client testimonials, awards, and online reviews play a significant role here.

Recurring Revenue: Subscription models, retainers, or long-term client contracts can significantly boost valuation. Buyers like predictability.

Step 2: Organize Your Documentation

Selling or merging a business involves providing a detailed dossier of information to potential buyers or partners. Being organized is non-negotiable.

Financial Records: Include at least three years of tax returns, profit and loss statements, balance sheets, and cash flow analyses.

Client Contracts and Agreements: Ensure all agreements with clients, vendors, and employees are documented, signed, and easy to locate.

Standard Operating Procedures (SOPs): A well-documented set of SOPs shows that your business runs like a well-oiled machine. Buyers want to know operations won't collapse the moment you step away.

Intellectual Property: If your business has proprietary training methods, software, or systems, document these assets thoroughly.

Regulatory Compliance: A clean compliance record with industry regulations is a significant selling point. Address any outstanding issues before putting your business on the market.

Step 3: Enhance Operational Efficiency

Buyers or merger partners will look for businesses that are efficient and scalable. If you're considering a merger, demonstrating operational efficiency makes you a more attractive partner.

Streamline Processes: Examine your workflows for inefficiencies. Automate where possible to reduce human error and save time.

Develop Leadership: A business reliant entirely on you is less appealing to buyers. Cultivate a leadership team capable of managing daily operations. Anecdote: A solo consultant successfully transitioned to a sale by training her senior team to handle client interactions and strategic decisions months in advance. This preparation made the handoff seamless.

Diversify Revenue Streams: If your business relies on a single service or client type, consider adding complementary services or entering new markets.

Step 4: Build Relationships with Potential Buyers or Partners

Sometimes, the best opportunities arise from relationships cultivated over years.

Attend Industry Events: Conferences and trade shows are excellent places to network with potential buyers or merger partners.

Engage with Competitors: It may seem counterintuitive, but competitors are often the most interested in acquiring or merging with businesses in their industry.

Hire a Business Broker: A broker with experience in the security industry can help connect you with serious buyers or partners.

Step 5: Legal and Tax Considerations

Selling or merging your business has significant legal and tax implications.

Hire Experts: Retain an experienced attorney and accountant specializing in business sales. They'll guide you through due diligence, contracts, and tax strategies.

Plan for Taxes: The proceeds from a sale may be subject to capital gains tax. Understanding these implications early helps you plan accordingly.

Preparing for a Merger

Mergers differ from outright sales in that you're combining operations with another entity. While the principles are similar, mergers require additional considerations:

Cultural Alignment: Do your company values, goals, and work styles align with the potential partner?

Synergies: Identify areas where the merger creates value – such as complementary services or expanded geographic reach.

Integration Plan: Develop a process for integrating teams, systems, and operations post-merger.

Practical Tools and Tips

Use a Checklist: Create a comprehensive checklist to ensure you're covering all bases – from financial records to client communications.

Leverage Technology: Tools like virtual data rooms (VDRs) make it easy to share sensitive documents securely with potential buyers or partners.

Communicate Transparently: If you have a team, keep them informed. Sudden changes can create anxiety, so transparency helps maintain morale.

Preparing for a business sale or merger is a journey, not a sprint. It requires meticulous preparation, strategic thinking, and the ability to view your business objectively. Whether you're looking to retire, pivot to a new venture, or simply capitalize on your hard work, the key is to start planning early.

Exit Strategies for Security Professionals

As a security professional and entrepreneur, designing an exit strategy is one of the most critical yet often overlooked aspects of business planning. Whether you're planning to retire, pivot to a new industry, or simply step away from the day-to-day grind, having a clear plan for exiting your business ensures that your hard work translates into financial stability and a seamless transition. Without one, you risk losing control over your business's legacy and value.

An exit strategy is a structured plan for transferring ownership or closing your business in a way that maximizes value and minimizes disruption. It's your plan for when it's time to hand over the keys – be that to a buyer, a successor, or even to dissolve the business. A strong exit strategy answers questions such as:

- Who will take over?
- What will happen to clients and employees?
- How will you extract maximum value from the transition?

Think of it as designing your business's final chapter while ensuring the story ends on a high note.

Types of Exit Strategies for Security Professionals

Selling to a Third Party: Selling your business outright is a popular option. This can involve selling to a competitor, an investor, or another entrepreneur looking to enter the security consulting field.

Example: Imagine you've built a business specializing in corporate security assessments. A larger firm looking to expand its client base could see your company as a perfect acquisition. You can secure a competitive price by preparing your financials and client portfolio in advance.

Selling to Employees or Management (Management Buyout): A management buyout (MBO) involves selling your business to current employees or a leadership team. This ensures continuity for clients and can preserve the company culture you've worked hard to establish.

Anecdote: One security consultant transitioned ownership to his senior team over five years. By offering a phased payment plan, he ensured the business was in good hands while receiving a steady income stream post-retirement.

Succession to a Family Member or Protégé: For those with family or trusted protégés involved in the business, transferring ownership can be an attractive option. However, it's crucial to clearly outline roles and expectations to avoid familial conflicts.

Mergers: Partnering with another firm through a merger can offer the opportunity to step back while maintaining a stake in the company. This approach is often chosen when two firms see mutual benefits in combining resources and expertise.

Liquidation: While less glamorous, liquidation can be an effective strategy for businesses without a clear buyer or successor. This involves selling off assets and closing operations.

Key Considerations When Planning Your Exit

Timing Is Everything. Exiting a business at the right time can significantly impact its value. Industry trends, market conditions, and the economic climate should all factor into your decision.

Pro Tip: Avoid trying to time the market perfectly. Focus instead on ensuring your business is consistently valuable and well-documented.

Valuation of the Business. Understanding your business's worth is critical. A professional valuation considers revenue, profit margins, intellectual property, and even goodwill associated with your brand.

Client Transition Plans. Your clients are the lifeblood of your business. A detailed transition plan ensures continuity and preserves relationships, vital for maintaining your business's reputation.

Legal and Financial Planning. Work closely with legal and financial advisors to navigate the tax implications, contract obligations, and any liabilities tied to your exit.

Preparing for an Exit: Practical Steps

Start Early. The best time to prepare an exit strategy is years before you actually plan to leave. Early planning allows you to fine-tune your operations, build value, and address potential roadblocks.

Document Everything. Organized documentation builds buyer confidence and expedites the sale process.

- Financial records
- Standard operating procedures (SOPs)
- Client contracts
- Asset inventories

Strengthen Relationships. A potential buyer or successor values strong client and vendor relationships. Take proactive steps to nurture these connections.

Develop a Handoff Plan. Whether selling, merging, or passing on your business, a well-thought-out handoff plan minimizes disruptions. This includes training, knowledge transfer, and a timeline for your involvement post-transition.

Challenges and How to Overcome Them

Emotional Attachment. Many business owners struggle with letting go of the company they built from the ground up. It's important to remember that transitioning out of the business doesn't erase your legacy.

Finding the Right Buyer or Successor. Not every buyer will align with your vision or values. Patience and due diligence are key.

Client Retention Risks. Clients may feel uncertain during a transition. Clear communication and reassurance about continuity are essential.

The Role of Experts in Exit Strategies

Business Brokers: These professionals specialize in matching buyers with sellers, handling negotiations, and managing due diligence.

Financial Advisors: They help you understand the economic implications of your exit and optimize your post-sale income.

Legal Counsel: From drafting contracts to navigating regulatory hurdles, having a skilled attorney is non-negotiable.

Tips for a Seamless Transition

Communicate Early and Often. Inform employees, clients, and stakeholders about your plans well in advance. Transparency fosters *trust and reduces uncertainty.*

Maintain Operational Excellence. The period leading up to your exit should showcase your business at its best. Avoid cutting corners or making drastic changes.

Plan for Life After Exit. Consider what comes next – retirement, a new venture, or even consulting for your own industry. Having a plan helps ease the transition.

An exit strategy isn't just about leaving; it's about ensuring your hard work lives on. Whether you're ready to retire, explore new opportunities, or simply secure your business's future, having a clear and actionable plan makes all the difference.

Chapter 16 Wrap-Up: Mastering Long-Term Success and Exit Strategies

Chapter 16 has been a study of the final frontier of security consulting: ensuring your business thrives in the long term and preparing for a smooth exit when the time comes. Every topic we've covered has been designed to equip you with the tools and insights necessary to transition from a security entrepreneur to a true industry icon, from building a legacy to planning for a merger or sale. Let's revisit the key lessons and insights you've gained in this chapter.

Building a Legacy in the Security Consulting Business

Building a legacy isn't just about financial success – it's about creating something that lasts beyond your tenure. We explored how to cement your reputation as a pioneer, innovator, or trusted expert in the security industry. A legacy is about more than just clients; it's about your impact on employees, partners, and the industry itself.

Practical examples included fostering mentorship programs to groom the next generation of consultants and building a strong company culture that becomes the benchmark for competitors. Your legacy is as much about relationships as it is about results, and we've provided you with strategies to ensure both are equally stellar.

Key Takeaway: Your legacy is built on daily decisions. Make choices that align with your values and long-term vision, and the rest will follow.

Giving Back to the Security Community

The security industry has likely given you countless opportunities, so why not pay it forward? We delved into the importance of giving back, not just as a goodwill gesture but as a way to solidify your reputation as a leader and advocate.

Whether volunteering your time to educate aspiring security professionals, donating resources to community safety programs, or partnering with industry associations to develop new standards, giving back enriches your business and the industry as a whole. Anecdotes about successful consultants who built industry-wide trust by prioritizing community engagement reinforced the idea that generosity breeds goodwill – and goodwill breeds success.

Key Takeaway: Giving back doesn't detract from your business; it enhances your credibility, expands your network, and strengthens the security ecosystem.

The Art of Continuous Improvement

Complacency is the death knell of any business. We emphasized the necessity of maintaining a mindset of perpetual learning and adapting. From staying updated on the latest industry trends to investing in training for your team, continuous improvement ensures you remain at the forefront of the field.

You learned how to cultivate a feedback-rich environment where your team isn't afraid to identify areas for growth. We also discussed leveraging metrics to track performance and using those insights to make strategic adjustments. Continuous improvement isn't a one-time project; it's a mindset – and the most successful consultants embrace it.

Key Takeaway: In a rapidly evolving industry, staying the same is falling behind. Always be improving.

Succession Planning and Leadership Development

Who will carry your torch when you're ready to step away? Succession planning and leadership development are not afterthoughts – they are strategic necessities. We explored how to identify potential successors, provide them with opportunities to lead, and ensure they're ready to take the reins when the time comes.

Leadership development isn't just about teaching skills; it's about instilling values. By mentoring the next generation of leaders, you're not just ensuring your business's longevity – you're also shaping the industry's future. Anecdotes about businesses that thrived under new leadership – and those that faltered due to a lack of preparation – illustrated the importance of thoughtful succession planning.

Key Takeaway: A well-prepared successor is the best gift you can give your business and the industry.

Preparing for Business Sale or Merger

Selling your business or merging with another is a significant milestone. We discussed preparing your company for this transition by streamlining operations, documenting processes, and enhancing financial transparency.

Anecdotal examples highlighted the pitfalls of entering negotiations unprepared. You learned the importance of seeking professional advice – from business brokers to legal counsel – and how to ensure that your business's value is fully recognized. Mergers and acquisitions are about finding the right fit, and we walked you through how to identify a partner who aligns with your vision.

Key Takeaway: A business sale or merger isn't the end; it's a new beginning. Preparation ensures that it's a beginning you're proud of.

Exit Strategies for Security Professionals

An exit strategy isn't just about leaving – it's about leaving well. Whether you're planning to retire, pursue new opportunities, or simply to take a step back, having a structured plan ensures a smooth transition. We explored various exit strategies, from management buyouts to mergers, and emphasized the importance of early planning.

Anecdotes about poorly planned exits served as cautionary tales, while success stories provided inspiration. You learned practical steps for valuing your business, transitioning client relationships, and communicating your plans effectively to all stakeholders.

Key Takeaway: The best exits are planned well in advance. A thoughtful exit strategy protects your legacy and secures your future.

Chapter 16 was about looking forward – beyond the immediate challenges of running your business to the long-term considerations defining success. Whether building a legacy, giving back, fostering continuous improvement, or planning your exit, each topic was designed to help you think strategically about the future.

Remember, today's decisions shape the business you'll leave behind tomorrow. Approach each step with intentionality, and you'll not only succeed – you'll inspire others to follow in your footsteps.

Conclusion

"Success is not final, failure is not fatal: It is the courage to continue that counts."

— Winston Churchill

According to a U.S. Small Business Administration report, nearly 20% of small businesses fail in their first year, and about 50% fail by their fifth year. Yet, for those armed with knowledge and a strategic plan, the odds of long-term success increase dramatically.

As you close the final chapter of this book, take a moment to reflect on where you began. You embarked on this journey perhaps with little more than an idea and a dream of establishing yourself in the dynamic world of security consulting. Together, we've traversed the complex yet rewarding terrain of entrepreneurship, laying the groundwork for what could be a thriving enterprise.

Great job on making it to this point. If you're here, it means two things: one, you've got a dream to start your own security consulting business, and two, you're willing to invest the time and energy to do it right. Let me start by saying this loud and clear: **YOU CAN DO THIS!** This book wasn't written to make you an expert overnight but to arm you with the tools, knowledge, and confidence you need to turn that dream into a thriving reality. By now, you've walked through the chapters, laughed at a few jokes (I hope), and, most importantly, learned that entrepreneurship isn't about being fearless; it's about being prepared.

The First Step: Assessing Readiness and Building Foundations

Starting a business isn't just about having a great idea – it's about understanding if you're ready to step into a role that will challenge you in ways you never imagined. In Chapter 1, we explored the traits of successful security entrepreneurs. You don't need to be perfect, but you do need resilience, adaptability, and a knack for problem-solving.

You also assessed your readiness and took inventory of your skills. If you discovered a few gaps along the way – whether in financial management or marketing – don't sweat it. Entrepreneurship is as much about learning as it is about doing. And let's not forget the transition from employee to entrepreneur. It's a shift, yes, but it's also incredibly freeing. You're no longer just executing someone else's vision – you're building your own.

Crafting a Unique Identity and Business Model

Moving into the middle chapters, we tackled the nuts and bolts of building your security consulting business. From crafting a business model that stands out in a competitive industry to developing a brand that clients will trust, you learned how to position yourself as an expert. But the real magic? Finding your niche.

The security industry is vast, and you don't have to be all things to all people. Maybe you're a whiz at risk assessment for high-net-worth clients or an ace at cybersecurity for small businesses. Whatever your specialty, we drilled down on why focusing on your strengths and solving specific problems for specific clients is the key to standing out.

Building Credibility and Trust

In the security world, credibility is everything. Chapter 5 taught you how to earn that trust, whether through certifications, thought leadership, or building a solid reputation in your community. You learned how to navigate the maze of licensing, accreditations, and industry standards, and you clearly understood what it takes to establish yourself as a trusted expert.

Marketing and Selling Like a Pro

Marketing might not be the first thing that comes to mind when you think "security consultant," but it's the lifeblood of your business. In Chapters 9 and 10, we explored how to leverage digital platforms like LinkedIn, Facebook, and even YouTube to showcase your expertise. We also discussed traditional methods like networking and word-of-mouth referrals, emphasizing that you don't have to be a marketing guru to get results – you just have to be authentic and consistent.

Sales can feel daunting, but here's the truth: it's not about "selling" in the pushy sense. It's about solving problems and showing clients why you're the best person for the job. From lead generation to crafting proposals, we walked through the process step by step. You even learned how to develop a pricing structure that works for both you and your clients.

Managing Growth and Staying Adaptable

Growth is exciting, but it's also challenging. Whether it's scaling your operations, exploring new technologies, or adapting to market shifts, we covered how to manage growth in a sustainable and smart way. Security consulting isn't static; it's an industry that evolves with every new technology and every global event. But that's what makes it exciting. You're not just running a business – you're building a legacy in an ever-changing field.

The Financials: More Than Just Numbers

If numbers make your head spin, don't worry – you're not alone. Chapters on financial management demystified everything from reading a profit-and-loss statement to managing cash flow. We discussed the importance of keeping personal and business finances separate (seriously, don't mix them), and you now know how to plan for both the expected and the unexpected.

Handling Challenges with Grace

No business journey is without its hurdles. From legal disputes to industry changes, you learned to anticipate and handle challenges like a pro. Whether it's drafting airtight contracts, navigating compliance risks, or planning for crises, you now have a toolbox of strategies to keep your business running smoothly, no matter what comes your way.

The Bigger Picture: Building a Legacy and Planning for the Future

In the final chapters, we shifted focus to long-term success. Building a legacy in the security consulting industry isn't just about financial success – it's about making an impact. Whether through mentoring, giving back to the community, or developing the next generation of leaders, you learned how to create something that lasts beyond you.

We also covered exit strategies, because planning for the end is just as important as planning for the beginning. Whether you want to sell your business, merge with another, or simply step back while someone else takes the reins, you now understand the steps involved in making that transition seamless.

The Final Pep Talk

Bottom line: starting and running a security consulting business is absolutely achievable. Is it hard work? Sure. Will there be days when you question your sanity? Probably. But the rewards are worth every ounce of effort.

Remember, you're not alone in this journey. This book is here to guide you, and the security industry is full of professionals who started where you are now. They didn't have all the answers at the beginning and didn't need to. They just needed the drive to start and the willingness to learn along the way.

So, take a deep breath and commit...fully. No half-measures. And when you hit a bump in the road (because you will), just remember that every successful entrepreneur started as someone with a dream and a plan. Now, it's your turn.

Go make it happen.

Annex A

The Importance of Having a Corporate Social Responsibility Program (CSRP)

"Doing good is good business."

— Richard Branson

According to a 2022 report by *Porter Novelli*, 88% of consumers are more likely to support a company that leads with a clear Corporate Social Responsibility (CSR) strategy, demonstrating values that align with their own.

As the owners of a security consulting company, we are well versed in the struggles that face both the business owner in general and the plight of the service support company in the security industry. We lovingly refer to these daily challenges as "The Grind" as we face two repetitive questions every morning: 1) How will we keep the lights on today? and 2) How do we add value to both our brand and our clients, as well as make a positive impact on our local/global community? This should be an all-too-familiar sentiment among our fellow independent security practitioners.

However, I want to concentrate on a topic that seemingly has nothing to do with the finances, administration, or operational minutia that comes with running a security company. I want to review the concept of Corporate Social Responsibility (CSR).

Many people do CSR-type activities in their personal and professional spheres. Most of us in this industry are drawn to contribute to the common good; whether through volunteerism, donating our time/money/expertise, or being more ecologically minded in our operations. There is definitely a "feel good" aspect to doing these types of activities. When we donate our time, money, or efforts to a charity or cause, there is a sense that we are being "good citizens" or "contributing members of society." Most of the time, we do these types of activities, not expecting anything in return. We do "good" for good's sake. This is appropriate and how it should be.

But is there a pragmatic business approach to these activities that can benefit from our charitable efforts? It may seem counter-intuitive, but many benefits accompany these types of activities, some of which even positively impact your company's bottom line.

Our company's CSR program is constantly evolving. Our primary goal is to improve the quality of service/support we provide to those causes we choose to be involved in. But that is not the sole focus. We also keep a constant eye on improving the business case for these efforts. After all, few of us are in this game as a charity. The bottom line is that we cease to exist when we cease to make money. So, capitalizing on our altruistic endeavors only enables us to grow as a business.

Moreover, the better we can shape, define, and develop the business case of our CSR program, the more we can increase both the quality and quantity of our support to our local and global community through our CSR initiatives. The goal of our CSR program(s) is to create that win-

win relationship, building a synergy that helps both the people/organizations/causes we support and our company as a whole.

In this section, I'll outline the benefits of a well-crafted CSR program. I hope I will successfully build the case of why you should design and incorporate a CSR program into your operations, whether you're a company of one, ten, or thousands.

Let's get started, shall we?

Quantifying the Data

Intuitively, I can articulate that our CSR program brings a myriad of benefits to our company. I can (and will) point out specific examples and correlate those directly to a business impact. But we're just one company. To build a business case relevant to an audience as broad as the readership of this book, it is crucial that I rely on much broader research. Research that is quantitative and not just based on intuition or one specific example. To that end, I turned to the study of the Doughty Centre on Corporate Responsibility. They conducted a two-phase, multi-year research project of nearly 200 companies to define and quantify the benefits of social responsibility programs. Their findings match much of what we have realized in our small sphere but are based on a much wider sample pool.

The Primary Objective

As I began crafting this section, I wrestled with the fact that I don't want to lose sight of what is most important when it comes to charitable causes. The primary objective of any of these efforts is to help our fellow man, the planet, or a segment of society. As a business entity, we should look for those causes that resonate with us personally. We should examine causes that parallel our company's unique brand, values, or ethics. And then, we should do what is in our power to bring assistance to those issues.

For example, if you're a veteran-owned small business, you may feel called to assist organizations that help veterans, such as your local American Legion or VA office. If you are a K-9 company, the causes of groups that help with animal rights issues may resonate with you. Maybe you operate in an area where pollution or clean water are issues that impact your company or the community you work in, so recycling and ecological matters are important to you. If you operate in an urban environment, the issue of homelessness may be front and center. There are ample organizations out there dealing with domestic violence, school shootings, workplace violence, etc., all of which have a unique security component where you can bring value to the table. The list of causes is endless, but you get the idea.

One cannot escape the fact that there is a mutual, personal benefit to regular engagement in CSR-type activities. While we may give a small portion of our time, money, attention, or effort to a given cause or charitable organization, there is a ten-fold return on emotional investment. The ability to be something larger than ourselves and contribute to the "general good" is something that we are drawn to by our very human nature.

The important thing to emphasize right at the start is that there is an emotional and philanthropic component that should be the primary objective of any CSR program. We do it because it's the right thing to do. We do it because the cause/organization resonates with us as individuals or matches our company's goals, values, and/or ethics. We do it because – if not us – then who?

Building the Business Case

However, we want to ensure that we are able (from a business perspective) to continue or grow that support and effort to those causes that we are involved in. Central to this concept is the karma-like assurance that *"What you give will always come back for you to receive."* We must recognize that if our company cannot gain financial or intrinsic value from our CSR efforts – if, in fact, our CSR efforts come at a cost or drain on company resources – then our ability to continue that support will eventually diminish. It is, therefore, important that we craft our CSR efforts in such a way as to bring value to our company that enables growth. This growth, in turn, will increase our ability to sustain or expand our charitable efforts.

For our purposes, we will concentrate on *five core benefits* to a business engaged with social responsibility efforts. Each of these benefits brings an intrinsic or tangible value to the company that can be quantified and expressed in real dollars. Those benefits are:

- Risk Reduction & Management
- Brand Value & Reputation
- Employee/Workforce Satisfaction
- Direct Financial Impact
- Business Opportunity

Risk Reduction & Management

How ironic, that the first benefit of a well-crafted CSR program aligns with the core function of any security organization! If our altruistic efforts can contribute to reducing and managing risk, it seems a no-brainer that we would concentrate some of our efforts to this end.

A thoughtful implementation of an effective CSR program will increase the level of goodwill and enhance the reputation of the company involved. This can assist in reducing the risk of boycotts, improve local population sentiment, and minimize negative press. Given the advent of the internet and the never-blinking "news on demand" of the modern era, many companies face risk exposure from even the most casual observers with access to social media. Now, more than ever before, risk management is irrevocably linked to reputational management.

If a company's CSR efforts enhance positive community relations, they will help decrease its exposure to risk and conflict and protect its social contract (its ability to operate in its given environment).

Additionally, we all work with customers/clients who have hired us to recommend ways to mitigate risk. Therefore, one of our core obligations is to advise them on how their company can engage in CSR efforts to reduce its risk exposure. Implementing our advice only makes our job easier.

Case Study: Our company was contracted by a major oil exploration company to conduct a risk mitigation assessment of their operations as they explored entering a new market in Nigeria. Other companies in that sector were experiencing high rates of kinetic incidents, kidnappings, and poor support from the local populace. Talking with the heads of security for these companies, we learned that they had attempted to reduce their risks by conducting their own version of CSR-type activities (digging wells, building schools, etc.) with limited results. Our assessment uncovered that the efforts of our client's competitors were not addressing the negative perceptions associated with companies of this type, nor were they addressing the true grievances of the locals.

We found that oil exploration companies were seen as "foreigners" who were exploiting natural resources, destroying local commerce and agriculture, and irrevocably damaging the environment and ecosystem of the homeland of the local populace. Additionally, we understood that these types of companies significantly disrupted the local business environment, especially affecting the local farmers and fishermen. This disruption had equated to a significant unemployed population that had all the time in the world to concentrate their negative sentiment on what they perceived was the root cause of their problems.

We advised our client that successful operations in this environment were possible and their risk exposure could be significantly less than their competitors if they invested in a two-pronged CSR program. First, they had to make a very public effort to reduce the environmental impact of their operations and build a marketing and branding campaign that supported this effort. Second, they needed to develop a program whereby they not only employed members of the local populace but also created an internship/mentorship program that developed and trained local workers to assume leadership/management roles within their organization (thus reducing the "foreign" signature on the client's efforts). Five years into this program, the client has a far superior reputation and brand management program with strong local populace support, their local intelligence network is vastly superior, and (most importantly) they have had significantly fewer security-related incidents than any of the other regional operators. The money/time/effort spent by the client to develop and implement their comprehensive CSR program has positively impacted their bottom line in terms of decreasing downtime (fewer incidents to recover from), their security program is much more efficient (increased intelligence, fewer incidents, zero strikes/walk-outs), and their global reputation has improved as an example of how to operate in a high-risk area successfully.

Brand Value & Reputation

Brand value and reputation are closely linked and often thought of as two sides of the same coin. In the Doughty Centre's study, a company's reputation was cited as primarily helpful in improving the brand's value. Conversely, respondents stated that the primary way to enhance the brand's value was through improving the company's reputation through market differentiation, leading to customer attraction, employee retention, and advocacy of causes that resonated with the company's customer base.

Attracting new customers is the lifeblood of any successful business. Marketing efforts and sales departments exist with this singular focus in mind. It has been proven that a company with a strong identity in terms of values and standards helps strengthen the overall brand identity and attract customers who align with those values. This, in turn, leads to an overall increase in customer satisfaction and customer loyalty and serves as a market differentiator among like competitors.

A strong customer base and customer acquisition program has the compound benefit of attracting investors who see these factors as markers to economic success. Subsequently, a company with a strong brand, loyal customer base, and investor attraction is seen as more valuable than competitors in the same space, thus feeding back into the cycle to bring more customers...

However, the cycle begins with a strong brand/reputation based on clearly identified values. One of the most efficient ways to identify those values is through the social responsibility projects that a company is involved in. When your potential client/customer pool sees that you are not simply out to make a buck but also contribute to causes that align with their values, a bond is immediately formed. That bond separates you from competitors who offer (in their perception) identical services.

Case Study: The tagline at my company is Collaborative • Security • Solutions. We set out to build a brand based on a unified "we're in this together" approach to risk mitigation. The undercurrent of this concept is a strong sense of team and community, as we work together to solve a given problem. To that end, one of our CSR initiatives is creating and implementing a small business networking group for our local community. Humble in its origins, this community has grown to over 2,000 local businesses (from every sector and industry) focusing on mutual support, community engagement, and service projects.

Our Director of Operations facilitates this networking group. It includes quarterly networking events, fundraising activities for local families in need, and "RAK attacks" (Random Acts of Kindness) that support our local businesses and first responder networks.

The financial investment in this group has been minimal, yet we have seen a marked improvement in our brand and reputation. Surprisingly, even to us, this increase in brand value and reputation has expanded past our local community to our global clients. Our current clients love the fact that we are so involved locally. Feedback has shown us that our efforts to improve our local community resonate with them and show them that we genuinely value the collaborative approach that we advertise. This has proved itself in terms of customer loyalty, as our contract renewal rate has never declined. Our referral business has also increased. We have spent nearly nothing on marketing and customer acquisition but acquired new customers based solely on the recommendations of current clients. This has a tangible increase in our bottom line, rooted in our local community's CSR efforts.

Employee/Workforce Satisfaction

A primary cost center for any business is acquiring, training, and retaining qualified talent. Any effort to make this process more efficient adds to the bottom line. Effectively crafted CSR efforts enable a company to attract and hold on to quality employees more efficiently. This includes employee motivation, productivity, satisfaction, engagement, and loyalty. What better ambassadors does a company have than a workforce who is passionate about their employer's mission(s) – both business and philanthropic –?

The energy created between the shared values of an organization and its employees cannot be overestimated. When an employee has the opportunity to act in their jobs in a way that is consistent with their personal values and ethics, a bond is formed that surpasses the typical employer/employee relationship. An employee who is satisfied in this way is more efficient, more apt to bring new thought leadership to the table, and more willing to be an effective brand ambassador for the organization.

This concept is highlighted in the Doughty Centre's research by two stunning statistics:

- 75% of employees who consider their organizations to be paying enough attention to issues that match their core values exhibit high levels of commitment. In contrast, 52% of those working for an organization that an employee believes does NOT have matching values (or possess inadequate CSR policies) demonstrate low levels of commitment.

- In a study of 40 global companies over 3 years, we found an improvement of more than 5% in operating margin and more than 3% in net profit between the companies with high employee engagement vs. those with low employee engagement.

Case Study: At my company, we find true enjoyment with the organizations we connect with through our CSR initiatives and the work we do within those organizations. The values and ethics of our chosen CSR organizations resonate with us, engage us, and keep us motivated to do great things for those we assist locally and globally. When one is anxiously and actively involved in something greater than oneself, suddenly life goes beyond a small optic and opens up beyond a chair, a desk, a computer screen, and four walls (or whatever work situation we may find ourselves in on any given day). When we can get outside of the "office" environment and feel the difference that a small kindness can make in the lives of others, it keeps us motivated to not only keep the business' lights on but to work even harder to retain our customers, work even harder to earn the funds that our clients pay for our work, work even harder to earn customer loyalty and work even harder to market ourselves in order to find new customers. The hard work mutually benefits both the company and our CSR organizations. Basically, we work hard so we can give. We give because we enjoy these connections. If work=giving, then we are in 110%.

Direct Financial Impact

Intrinsic value is great, and it is easy to see how everything we have discussed to this point adds value to a company's bottom line, but nothing quantifies the case better than direct financial impact. This includes lower penalty payments, proactive measures that lead to direct cost savings, improvements in investor relations (that lead to bigger/better investment), increased shareholder value, and sales/business increases directly attributable to responsible business practices.

Socially responsible investment also leads to improved access to capital from VC funding and support. This is an enormous growth market. According to the Doughty Centre's research, 881 companies are now signatories of the UN-backed *Principles for Responsible Investment* (*PRI*). This indicates an increase of 30% in just 12 months and represents a whopping $22 trillion in assets under management. This is something that investors and VCs sit up and take notice of. It indicates that companies with strong CR policies will gain a competitive advantage regarding international markets and access to finance.

The Doughty Centre research further states that there is growing evidence that mainstream investors and financial analysts are paying greater attention to CSR-related issues and, more generally, to intangible assets and intellectual capital. This is likely to increase the profile of CSR issues in the financial valuation of enterprises.

CSR does not just deal with charities and causes. By definition, it also involves those actions that demonstrate a responsibility on the part of the company to do the morally and ethically "right" thing in their given market sector.

Case Study: Our company takes seriously its commitment to compliance with ISO and industry standards regarding our company's operations. Due to the lack of regulations governing the security industry, our compliance is not mandatory and strictly voluntary. We have made the financial and time investment to be ISO 9001 compliant. We ensure that we abide by relevant ASIS guidelines and standards, even though some of our competitors cut corners on these issues. We feel it is the right thing to do, and our customers seem to agree.

Several times, we have had a potential client referred to us who is attracted to our company's service by a mutual acquaintance. Despite the recommendation/referral, the question is often posed, "What separates you from your competitor?" or "I am considering several companies for this job; why should I pick you?". Not only are we able to outline some of the CSR initiatives we are involved in, but we are also able to articulate our voluntary compliance to non-mandatory standards and guidelines. Our experience has shown that this is an enormous market differentiator and, we suspect, has led to us winning competitive bids and contracts.

Business Opportunity

Adopting a deliberate CSR program can cause a company to re-think the role of their business in society, leading to a better understanding of impacts on and from issues previously seen as outside of their concern. Examples include poverty among a company's customer base, climate change affecting the supply chain, or an aging population affecting the acquisition of an effective labor workforce. Reconsidering such issues in light of what they mean to the business and how business impacts on these issues has uncovered new opportunities for all parties involved.

Re-analyzing your company and brand in this light also leads to partnerships and relationships that expand into previously unrecognized value spaces. For example, when two separate companies come together to engage in a CSR initiative that has mutual benefit, there is an aura of goodwill that can lead to further business ventures that had not existed previously.

Summary

Most of us in this industry have an inherent desire to "do something good," to be part of an effort bigger than ourselves. We can all agree on the emotional and kismet-associated benefits of philanthropy. At our company, we genuinely believe that you receive back what you put out into the universe, both from a personal and a business perspective. We enjoy engaging in altruistic activities for the joy of doing them. For the ability to make a difference and be part of our local community or a solution that resonates with us or matches our business values and ethics. We want to be involved in activities that mean something. At times, however, it isn't easy to quantify or justify spending the time, money, or effort to engage in these activities, especially when the resources required are in such short supply. There is a business case for committing these resources to socially responsible initiatives. There are benefits to security and risk mitigation, brand management, workforce satisfaction, tangible financial value, and business opportunities.

Whether you're an established business with dozens of employees and a large budget or a solo practitioner wondering how to use limited time, money, and resources to further your brand-new start-up (or anywhere in between), we hope that you gained something of value in this article and look at CSR activities as a viable way to receive a tangible return on your investment...and hey, do a little good in the world while you're at it!

Annex B
Having and Implementing a Quality Management Process (QMP)

"Quality is not an act; it is a habit."

— Aristotle

In the world of security consulting, where trust, professionalism, and precision reign supreme, this quote couldn't be more relevant. A Quality Management Process (QMP) isn't just a box to check – it's the lifeblood of a business that promises safety and security. Whether you're auditing a corporation's physical defenses or advising on cyber-threat mitigation, your clients rely on you to deliver excellence consistently. A well-structured QMP ensures you meet that standard every time.

What Is a Quality Management Process?

A QMP is a systematic approach to ensuring your services and deliverables meet or exceed client expectations. It's not just about avoiding mistakes; it's about continuously improving your processes, creating value, and building a reputation for reliability and excellence.

In the security consulting industry, a QMP could cover everything from how you onboard new clients to how you conduct post-project reviews. It's how to ensure your work isn't just good – it's great.

You might think, "I'm just starting – do I really need a QMP?" The answer is a resounding yes. Here's why:

Reputation Is Everything: In the security industry, trust is non-negotiable. A single misstep could damage your reputation and cost you clients. A QMP helps you avoid errors and ensures your work speaks for itself.

Efficiency and Consistency: Think of a QMP as the ultimate time-saver. It standardizes your processes, reducing the time spent on guesswork and increasing your capacity to take on more projects.

Client Satisfaction: A happy client is a loyal client. A QMP ensures you consistently deliver results that meet or exceed expectations, keeping your clients coming back for more.

Continuous Improvement: No matter how good you are, there's always room for growth. A QMP helps you identify areas for improvement, keeping your business competitive and innovative.

Key Components of a QMP for Security Consulting

Define Your Quality Objectives: Start with the end in mind. What does "quality" mean for your business? Is it flawless execution? Exceeding client expectations? Speedy delivery? Once you know your goals, you can build processes to achieve them.

Map Out Your Core Processes: Identify the key activities that drive your business. For a security consultant, this could include:

- Initial client consultations
- Risk assessments
- Proposal preparation
- Project implementation
- Post-project reviews

Set Standards for Each Process: What does success look like at each stage? Be specific. For instance:

Client consultations: Respond to inquiries within 24 hours.

Risk assessments: Ensure all assessments are reviewed by a senior consultant before submission.

Document Everything: Your QMP should live in a comprehensive manual. This isn't just for you – it's for your team, future hires, and even your clients. A well-documented QMP demonstrates professionalism and instills confidence.

Train Your Team: Everyone involved in your business needs to understand the QMP. Conduct regular training sessions to ensure alignment and to foster a culture of quality.

Monitor and Measure Performance: Use metrics to evaluate your performance. Are you meeting deadlines? Is client feedback positive? Regularly review these metrics and use them to refine your processes.

Continuous Improvement: A QMP isn't static. Schedule regular reviews to identify what's working, what isn't, and what needs to evolve.

Implementing a QMP: Step-by-Step

Assess Your Current Processes: Start by mapping out how you currently operate. Where are the bottlenecks? What are clients consistently happy (or unhappy) about? Use this assessment as your baseline.

Develop a Pilot Process: Choose one aspect of your business – say, client onboarding – and develop a detailed process for it. Test this process, gather feedback, and refine it.

Expand the QMP: Once you've nailed one process, expand your QMP to cover other areas of your business. Prioritize high-impact activities like project delivery and client communication.

Use Technology to Your Advantage: Tools like project management software, customer relationship management (CRM) systems, and quality assurance platforms can streamline your QMP.

Gather Feedback: Your clients and team are invaluable sources of insight. Regularly solicit their feedback and use it to improve your QMP.

Why a QMP Is Non-Negotiable

In the security consulting industry, where the stakes are high and the competition fierce, a QMP isn't just a competitive advantage – it's a survival tool. It ensures you deliver consistent, high-quality results, which is the foundation of long-term success.

But perhaps more importantly, a QMP reflects your commitment to excellence – not just to your clients but to yourself and your team. It's a statement that you're not just here to participate but to excel.

So, roll up your sleeves, embrace the process, and watch your business thrive. Because, in the end, quality isn't just an act or a habit – it's your legacy.

Annex C
The Meaning of Colors in Business Logos and Branding

"Color is a power which directly influences the soul."

— Wassily Kandinsky

Colors are not just visual stimuli; they are your brand's emotional connectors, storytellers, and silent ambassadors. In the world of security consulting – or any industry, for that matter – the colors you choose for your logo and branding aren't arbitrary. They whisper (or shout) your values, promises, and personality to your audience. The right palette can instill trust, inspire action, and create recognition. Conversely, a poor choice might send the wrong message or be quickly forgotten.

In this annex, we'll delve into the meaning of individual colors, their use in business contexts, and how strategic pairings can amplify your brand's voice. We'll also explore pitfalls to avoid and equip you with the tools to ensure your brand colors speak volumes – without saying a word.

The Psychology of Individual Colors

Red: Power, Passion, and Urgency. Red is the color of fire and blood. It conveys energy, strength, and passion. Businesses often use red to grab attention or create a sense of urgency.

Use: Red is effective for brands that want to appear bold or create excitement. Think Coca-Cola or Target. In security, it can symbolize action, warning, or alertness.

Caution: Too much red can come across as aggressive. Balance it with neutral tones to avoid overwhelming your audience.

Blue: Trust, Stability, and Professionalism. Blue is the king of corporate branding. It exudes trust, calm, and intelligence, which makes it a staple in industries where reliability is key.

Use: Security firms often lean on blue to signal trustworthiness and authority. Think of brands like IBM or LinkedIn.

Caution: Light blues can feel overly casual, while dark blues can appear overly rigid if not paired with complementary colors.

Green: Growth, Balance, and Safety. Green is associated with nature, renewal, and money. It's a versatile color that can project growth and calm simultaneously.

Use: Ideal for eco-friendly initiatives or to convey financial growth and stability.

Caution: Be mindful of the shade. Bright greens can feel playful, while darker tones suggest prestige and wealth.

Yellow: Optimism, Energy, and Caution. Yellow is the happiest color on the spectrum, representing warmth and optimism. However, it also doubles as a cautionary hue.

Use: Best for brands that want to appear approachable or inspire positivity. Think McDonald's golden arches.

Caution: Yellow's high visibility can be jarring when overused. Use it as an accent to avoid looking amateurish.

Black: Elegance, Sophistication, and Power. Black is timeless. It represents authority, elegance, and simplicity.

Use: Perfect for luxury or high-end services. Security firms can use black to convey seriousness and exclusivity.

Caution: Overuse can feel intimidating or cold. Balance with lighter tones to soften the edges.

White: Purity, Simplicity, and Clarity. White is clean, modern, and simple. It provides a neutral backdrop that amplifies other colors.

Use: Often paired with bold colors for contrast, making logos stand out. Think Apple or Tesla.

Caution: On its own, white can feel sterile. Pair it with warm or vibrant tones for balance.

Purple: Creativity, Luxury, and Wisdom. Purple has long been associated with royalty and spirituality. It's a color that conveys luxury and creative thinking.

Use: Ideal for premium services or to inspire imagination and innovation. Think Cadbury or Hallmark.

Caution: Too much purple can feel overly indulgent or eccentric. Balance it with neutral tones.

Orange: Energy, Enthusiasm, and Creativity. Orange is cheerful, bold, and full of vitality.

Use: Best for brands that want to appear dynamic and friendly. Think Fanta or Harley-Davidson.

Caution: It's easy for orange to feel brash. Tone it down with darker shades or pair it with calming colors.

Grey: Neutrality, Balance, and Sophistication. Grey is practical and timeless. It conveys balance, calm, and professionalism.

Use: Perfect for secondary or accent colors to anchor brighter tones.

Caution: Overuse can make your brand appear dull or uninspired.

Pairing and Contrasting Colors

Complementary Colors. Complementary colors sit opposite each other on the color wheel (e.g., blue and orange, red and green). These combinations create high contrast and make elements pop.

Example: A navy blue logo with orange accents can signal both trust and energy.

Analogous Colors. Analogous colors are next to each other on the color wheel (e.g., blue, green, and teal). They create harmony and are visually pleasing.

Example: A gradient of blues and greens for a security firm logo suggests balance and trustworthiness.

Triadic Colors. Triadic colors form a triangle on the color wheel (e.g., red, yellow, and blue). These combinations are vibrant and balanced.

Example: Using a dominant color like blue, with red and yellow as accents, creates a professional yet engaging aesthetic.

Monochromatic Schemes. Monochromatic schemes use different shades, tints, or tones of the same color. This approach is clean and cohesive.

Example: A brand that uses varying shades of green can signal growth and unity.

Colors to Avoid or Use Sparingly

Neon Colors. While noticeable, neon colors can feel unprofessional and are often hard to read.

Clashing Colors. Avoid combinations like red and green (unless it's Christmas) or yellow and pink, as they can confuse or repel your audience.

Overly Dark Palettes. Too much black, dark grey, or brown can make your brand feel unapproachable.

Practical Tips for Choosing Colors

Test for Accessibility: Ensure your color scheme is readable for those with visual impairments or color blindness.

Consider Cultural Associations: Colors carry different meanings across cultures. For instance, white signifies purity in Western cultures but mourning in some Eastern traditions.

Stick to a Maximum of Three Colors: Overcomplicating your palette can dilute your message. Choose one dominant color and one or two accent colors.

Let Your Colors Speak

Your logo and branding colors are your silent ambassadors, making a first impression before you've said a word. By understanding the psychology of color, leveraging smart pairings, and avoiding common pitfalls, you can create a visual identity that resonates with your audience and supports your mission.

So, take a moment to reflect: What story do you want your brand colors to tell? Because, in the end, the right palette isn't just about aesthetics – it's about building trust, evoking emotion, and leaving a lasting impression. Let your colors do the talking, and your business will stand out in all the right ways.

Annex D

Free or Inexpensive Sources for New and Veteran Entrepreneurs

"Do what you can, with what you have, where you are."

— Theodore Roosevelt

Starting or scaling a business can feel like assembling IKEA furniture without the instructions: exciting, overwhelming, and often confusing. But here's the good news – there are countless free and low-cost tools to help new and seasoned entrepreneurs navigate the complexities of business ownership. This is particularly true for veterans who bring unique skills, experiences, and networks to entrepreneurship.

Whether you're looking to organize your business, market your services, manage finances, or leverage mentorship opportunities, this annex highlights resources that can be game changers. We'll delve into the tools, programs, and platforms available, tailored for entrepreneurs of all kinds, with a special focus on veteran-specific initiatives.

BUSINESS ORGANIZATION

Starting on the right foot requires structure. These resources simplify the process from selecting a business entity to registering your company.

Free Resources:

Small Business Administration (SBA): Offers free guides, templates, and step-by-step instructions for forming and organizing your business. Their Veteran Business Outreach Centers (VBOCs) provide targeted support for veteran entrepreneurs.

IRS.gov: Allows you to obtain an EIN (Employer Identification Number) at no cost, a critical step for hiring employees and managing taxes.

Veteran-Specific Resources:

Warrior Rising: Provides veterans free access to business development courses, mentoring, and networking opportunities. Their mission focuses on helping veterans transition from the military to entrepreneurship.

Institute for Veterans and Military Families (IVMF): Through Syracuse University, IVMF offers programs like Boots to Business and the Veteran EDGE Conference, which provide business training and networking opportunities.

Inexpensive Resources:

LegalZoom: Helps entrepreneurs establish LLCs or S-Corps with easy-to-follow processes and affordable packages.

ZenBusiness: Offers comprehensive services for starting and managing a business at a lower cost than traditional legal options.

LOGO & BRANDING SERVICES

Your brand is the face of your business. These tools help create a professional identity without breaking the bank.

Free Resources:

Canva: A user-friendly platform with free templates for logos, social media posts, and marketing materials.

Hatchful by Shopify: Provides AI-generated logo designs tailored to your industry and style preferences.

Veteran-Specific Resources:

Bunker Labs: This nonprofit supports veteran entrepreneurs, including branding and marketing guidance through their Veterans in Residence program.

Patriot Boot Camp: Offers veterans workshops that include branding and messaging strategies to differentiate their businesses.

Inexpensive Resources:

Fiverr: Hire designers for as little as $5 to create logos, business cards, and other branding essentials.

99designs: This platform provides access to multiple designers for a slightly higher investment, giving you various creative options.

LEGAL RESOURCES

Understanding the legal landscape is vital for avoiding pitfalls. These resources help you manage contracts, compliance, and more.

Free Resources:

SCORE.org: Offers free mentorship from legal experts and templates for contracts, NDAs, and other essential documents.

LawDepot: Provides free trials for legal documents like partnership agreements and leases.

Veteran-Specific Resources:

Veteran Entrepreneur Portal (VEP): Through the VA, this portal connects veterans with legal resources and guides for navigating government contracts.

StreetShares Foundation: Offers funding and legal guidance tailored to veteran-owned small businesses.

Inexpensive Resources:

Rocket Lawyer: Provides affordable subscriptions for ongoing access to legal documents and advice.

UpCounsel: A marketplace for affordable, on-demand legal advice from qualified attorneys.

FINANCIAL RESOURCES

Managing cash flow, budgeting, and accessing funding are critical for business success.

Free Resources:

Wave Accounting: Free software for managing invoices, tracking expenses, and reconciling accounts.

Mint: Ideal for budgeting and expense tracking in the early stages of business development.

Veteran-Specific Resources:

Veterans Business Fund: Offers loans specifically for veteran entrepreneurs who lack the capital to start or grow their businesses.

StreetShares: A veteran-focused funding platform that provides small business loans, lines of credit, and grants.

Inexpensive Resources:

QuickBooks Online: Offers low-cost bookkeeping, payroll, and financial reporting plans.

Bench: An affordable bookkeeping service for entrepreneurs who prefer to outsource.

MARKETING & ADVERTISING RESOURCES

Reaching your audience effectively doesn't have to drain your budget. These tools make professional marketing accessible.

Free Resources:

HubSpot CRM: Provides free tools for email marketing, lead generation, and customer relationship management.

Google My Business: A free service to manage your online presence, particularly for local businesses.

Veteran-Specific Resources:

Operation Vetrepreneur: Provides free workshops on digital marketing and advertising strategies for veterans transitioning into entrepreneurship.

V-WISE (Veteran Women Igniting the Spirit of Entrepreneurship): Focuses on veteran women and offers marketing and branding courses.

Inexpensive Resources:

Mailchimp: Free for basic email campaigns, with affordable paid plans as your audience grows.

Hootsuite: Allows for affordable social media scheduling and analytics to streamline your digital marketing efforts.

MENTORSHIP PROGRAMS

Guidance from experienced mentors can fast-track your success and help you avoid costly mistakes.

Free Resources:

SCORE: Offers free one-on-one mentoring from experienced business professionals.

Veterati: A free platform connecting veterans with mentors across industries.

Veteran-Specific Resources:

American Corporate Partners (ACP): Matches veterans with corporate executives for year-long mentorships.

Boots to Business: Part of the SBA, and in partnership with Syracuse University, this program helps veterans access mentorship and business training. The Boots-to-Business program has a great Project Management prep program.

Inexpensive Resources:

Clarity.fm: Offers pay-per-minute access to mentors and industry experts.

LinkedIn Premium: Provides enhanced networking capabilities, including InMail, to connect with potential mentors.

Practical Tips for Entrepreneurs

Vet Resources Carefully: Not every free or inexpensive tool is worth your time. Read reviews and ask peers for recommendations.

Combine Tools: Maximize efficiency by integrating free tools with affordable paid options.

Leverage Your Network: Whether you're a veteran or not, tapping into your community can uncover hidden resources and opportunities.

The path to entrepreneurial success doesn't have to be paved with gold – it can be navigated with ingenuity, perseverance, and the right tools. Whether you're a veteran using your unique skills to build something meaningful or a first-time entrepreneur diving into the deep end, these resources support your journey.

Resourcefulness isn't just a trait – it's a secret talent. Use it wisely, and you'll find that success is well within reach.

Sources

INTRODUCTION

- Miltz, A. (n.d.). Revenue is vanity, profit is sanity, but cash flow is king. [Source of quote, if available.]
- Sinek, S. (2009). *Start with Why: How Great Leaders Inspire Everyone to Take Action.* Portfolio.
- Sinek, S. (2014). *Leaders Eat Last: Why Some Teams Pull Together and Others Don't.* Portfolio.
- U.S. Small Business Administration. (n.d.). *10 Steps to Start Your Business.* Retrieved from https://www.sba.gov

Chapter 1: Assessing Your Entrepreneurial Readiness

- Brown, B. (2012). *Daring Greatly: How the Courage to Be Vulnerable Transforms the Way We Live, Love, Parent, and Lead.* Gotham Books.
- Goleman, D. (1995). *Emotional Intelligence: Why It Can Matter More Than IQ.* Bantam Books.
- Kolb, D. A. (1984). *Experiential Learning: Experience as the Source of Learning and Development.* Prentice Hall.
- LinkedIn Learning. (n.d.). *Online learning platform.* Retrieved from https://www.linkedin.com/learning
- Udemy. (n.d.). *Online courses for personal and professional growth.* Retrieved from https://www.udemy.com
- Empowered Quotes » Entrepreneurship is living a few years of your life like most people won't, so that you can spend the rest of your life like most people can't. https://empoweredquotes.com/2008/12/30/entrepreneurship-is-living-a-few-years-of-your-life-like-most-people-won%E2%80%99t-so-that-you-can-spend-the-rest-of-your-life-like-most-people-can%E2%80%99t/
- Entrepreneur. (n.d.). *Self-assessment tools for business readiness.* Retrieved from https://www.entrepreneur.com
- Harvard Business Review. (2017). *Transitioning to entrepreneurship: Challenges and strategies.* Retrieved from https://hbr.org
- Forbes. (2023). *How to shift careers and start a business.* Retrieved from https://www.forbes.com

Chapter 2: Introduction to the Security Consulting Industry

- IBISWorld. (2023). *Security services industry market analysis.* Retrieved from https://www.ibisworld.com
- Allied Market Research. (2023). *Global private security services market size and forecast.* Retrieved from https://www.alliedmarketresearch.com
- ASIS International. (2023). *The role of security consultants in today's world.* Retrieved from https://www.asisonline.org
- Security Management Magazine. (2023). *Security industry insights and thought leadership.* Retrieved from https://www.asisonline.org/security-management-magazine
- Security Training Archives - Page 2 of 5 - PalAmerican Security. https://www.palamerican.com/category/security-training/page/2/
- Tips Archives - MERIDIAN REMOTE TEAMS. https://www.meridianremoteteams.com/tag/tips/

Chapter 3: Building a Unique Business Model

- Kim, W. C., & Mauborgne, R. (2005). *Blue Ocean Strategy: How to Create Uncontested Market Space and Make the Competition Irrelevant.* Harvard Business Review Press.
- Porter, M. E. (1985). *Competitive Advantage: Creating and Sustaining Superior Performance.* Free Press.
- ASIS International. (2023). *Security consulting niches and specialization opportunities.* Retrieved from https://www.asisonline.org
- OSAC. (n.d.). *Resources for international security professionals.* Retrieved from https://www.osac.gov
- The Man Who Chases Two Rabbits Catches Neither. https://wherever-i-look.com/tag/the-man-who-chases-two-rabbits-catches-neither

Chapter 4: Building Your Security Brand

- ASIS International. (2023). *Membership benefits and certifications.* Retrieved from https://www.asisonline.org
- Canva. (n.d.). *Logo design tools and resources.* Retrieved from https://www.canva.com
- International Association of Professional Security Consultants (IAPSC). (n.d.). *Best practices and networking opportunities.* Retrieved from https://www.iapsc.org

- International Protective Security Board (IPSB). (n.d.). *Industry advocacy and resources.* Retrieved from https://www.iprotectsecurityboard.org
- LegalZoom. (n.d.). *Comparing business structures.* Retrieved from https://www.legalzoom.com
- NGC Media Page Logo and Branding | NGC Construction. https://ngcgroupinc.com/ngcmedialogos/
- Pantone. (n.d.). *Color psychology and branding guidelines.* Retrieved from https://www.pantone.com
- Rocket Lawyer. (n.d.). *Choosing the right legal entity for your business.* Retrieved from https://www.rocketlawyer.com
- The Comprehensive Guide to Starting an Utah LLC in 2023 - LLCKeen. https://llckeen.com/utah-llc/
- USPTO. (n.d.). *Trademark search and registration guidance.* Retrieved from https://www.uspto.gov

Chapter 5: Establishing Credibility and Trust in Security Consulting

- Anti-Terrorism Accreditation Board (ATAB). (n.d.). *Certifications for anti-terrorism professionals.* Retrieved from https://www.atab.org
- ASIS International. (2023). *Certification programs: CPP, PSP, PCI.* Retrieved from https://www.asisonline.org
- BEPP. (n.d.). *Standards for executive protection professionals.* Retrieved from https://www.bepp.org
- FEMA. (n.d.). *Emergency management certifications.* Retrieved from https://training.fema.gov
- ISO. (n.d.). *Standards for risk management and security consulting.* Retrieved from https://www.iso.org
- ISO. (n.d.). *ISO/TC 262 and ISO/TC 292 standards.* Retrieved from https://www.iso.org
- VPS Bahamas - Vertrou Professional Services. http://www.vpsbahamas.com/

Chapter 6: Market Research and Business Planning

- SCORE. (n.d.). *Free business plan templates.* Retrieved from https://www.score.org
- Statista. (n.d.). *Market research and trends.* Retrieved from https://www.statista.com
- Google Trends. (n.d.). *Keyword and market trend analysis.* Retrieved from https://trends.google.com

- U.S. Small Business Administration. (n.d.). *Business plan writing tools and examples.* Retrieved from https://www.sba.gov
- BPlans. (n.d.). *Sample business plans.* Retrieved from https://www.bplans.com

Chapter 7: Financing Your Security Consulting Business

- (2015). Soundbites. Journal of Property Management, 80(1), 7.
- (2022). Calendar. The Enterprise, 51(45), 11-12,14.
- AngelList. (n.d.). *Venture capital and angel investment resources.* Retrieved from https://angel.co
- QuickBooks. (n.d.). *Financial management tools for small businesses.* Retrieved from https://quickbooks.intuit.com
- SAM.gov. (n.d.). *Contracting with the federal government.* Retrieved from https://sam.gov
- SBA. (n.d.). *Grants, loans, and funding options.* Retrieved from https://www.sba.gov

Chapter 8: Setting Up Security Consulting Operations

- (2015). Ed board needs better plan. The Hutchinson News, (), n/a.Resolver. (n.d.). *Risk assessment and security tools.* Retrieved from https://www.resolver.com
- American Psychological Association. (2020). *Publication manual of the American Psychological Association* (7th ed.). Washington, DC: Author.
- ASIS International. (2023). *Operational standards and guidelines.* Retrieved from https://www.asisonline.org
- Basecamp. (n.d.). *Project management and team collaboration software.* Retrieved from https://basecamp.com
- Blair, E., & Marcum, T. M. (2015). *Ethics in strategic partnerships: Best practices for mutual benefit.* Business Horizons, 58(2), 167–174. https://doi.org/10.1016/j.bushor.2014.10.002
- Chen, L. J. (2019). *Adopting technology for security assessments: A systems approach.* Journal of Applied Security Research, 14(2), 109–125. https://doi.org/10.1080/19361610.2019.1234567
- DJI. (n.d.). *Drone technology for professional use.* Retrieved from https://www.dji.com
- IRS. (n.d.). *Guidance on employment classification (W2 vs. 1099).* Retrieved from https://www.irs.gov
- Federal Motor Carrier Safety Administration (FMCSA). (n.d.). *Commercial driver's license standards.* Retrieved from https://www.fmcsa.dot.gov

- Friedman, T. L. (2005). *The world is flat: A brief history of the twenty-first century.* New York, NY: Farrar, Straus, and Giroux.
- Gantt, H. L. (1919). *Work, wages, and profits: Their influence on the cost of living.* New York, NY: Engineering Magazine.
- HubSpot. (n.d.). *Customer relationship management (CRM) tools.* Retrieved from https://www.hubspot.com
- Intuit QuickBooks. (n.d.). *Small business accounting software.* Retrieved from https://quickbooks.intuit.com
- International Organization for Standardization (ISO). (n.d.). *ISO 31000: Risk management – Principles and guidelines.* Retrieved from https://www.iso.org
- Jones, A., & Fielding, M. (2020). *Key metrics for operational success in security consulting.* Risk Analysis Review, 18(4), 23–37. https://doi.org/10.5678/risk.2020.0023
- Kaplan, R. S., & Norton, D. P. (2004). *Strategy maps: Converting intangible assets into tangible outcomes.* Boston, MA: Harvard Business Review Press.
- Lynch, T. D., & Lynch, C. E. (2017). *Security risk management: Building effective SOPs and mitigation plans.* New York, NY: Security Management Press.
- Microsoft. (n.d.). *Microsoft 365 for business: Tools for collaboration and productivity.* Retrieved from https://www.microsoft.com
- Microsoft Teams and Zoom. (n.d.). *Remote collaboration tools.* Retrieved from https://www.microsoft.com and https://www.zoom.us
- National Institute of Standards and Technology (NIST). (n.d.). *Framework for improving critical infrastructure cybersecurity.* Retrieved from https://www.nist.gov
- Porter, M. E. (1996). *What is strategy?* Harvard Business Review, 74(6), 61–78.
- Project Management Institute. (2017). *A guide to the project management body of knowledge (PMBOK guide)* (6th ed.). Newtown Square, PA: Project Management Institute.
- Smith, G. R., & Brown, H. L. (2018). *Risk and resilience in global security operations.* Journal of Security Studies, 12(3), 45–58. https://doi.org/10.1234/jss.2018.0045
- Trello. (n.d.). *Visual collaboration and project management tools.* Retrieved from https://trello.com
- U.S. Department of Labor. (n.d.). *Understanding the difference between employees and independent contractors.* Retrieved from https://www.dol.gov
- Workman, J. P. (2019). *Operational excellence in consulting: SOPs and risk management strategies.* Chicago, IL: Operations Press.

Chapter 9: Marketing Your Security Consulting Services

- Andrews, D. (2020). *The power of social media marketing*. Social Media Strategies Press.
- Baker, S. (2019). *LinkedIn mastery: Networking and branding for professionals*. Professional Networking Publishers.
- Cho, A. (2021). *Social media algorithms and organic reach: How to navigate the changes*. Digital Marketing Insights, 12(4), 45–56.
- Digital Marketing Institute. (n.d.). *What is SEO? A guide to search engine optimization*. Retrieved from https://digitalmarketinginstitute.com
- HubSpot. (n.d.). *The ultimate guide to email marketing*. Retrieved from https://hubspot.com
- Lee, T. (2018). *Content creation for YouTube: Strategies for audience growth*. New Media Horizons.
- Patel, N. (2022). *SEO simplified: A step-by-step guide for small businesses*. Content Growth Publications.
- Statista. (2023). *Social media usage among businesses worldwide*. Retrieved from https://statista.com

Chapter 10: Sales and Client Relationship Management

- Anderson, C. (2017). *Client retention strategies for consultants*. Consulting Success Journal, 14(2), 23–35.
- Brown, J., & Harris, M. (2020). *Crafting winning proposals for small businesses*. Bids & Proposals Publishing.
- CRM Magazine. (n.d.). *Choosing the right CRM for small businesses*. Retrieved from https://crm.com
- Drucker, P. (2006). *The practice of management*. Harper Business.
- HubSpot. (n.d.). *The art of sales funnel creation*. Retrieved from https://hubspot.com
- McCarthy, R. (2021). *Flexible pricing strategies for consultants*. Business Solutions Quarterly, 9(3), 50–67.
- Salesforce. (n.d.). *How CRM systems can drive small business growth*. Retrieved from https://salesforce.com
- Smith, P. (2019). *Building trust with clients through transparency*. Professional Services Journal, 11(6), 67–81.

Chapter 11: Navigating Business Growth in the Security Sector

- ASIS International. (2021). *The state of security management in 2021*. Retrieved from https://www.asisonline.org.
- ASIS International. (2023). *Guidelines for security consulting practices*. Retrieved from https://www.asisonline.org.
  - Christensen, C. M., Raynor, M. E., & McDonald, R. (2015). What is disruptive innovation? *Harvard Business Review,* 93(12), 44-53.
- Collins, J. (2001). *Good to Great: Why Some Companies Make the Leap and Others Don't.* HarperBusiness.
- Deloitte Insights. (2023). *Security industry outlook: Emerging trends in 2023.* Retrieved from https://www.deloitte.com.
  - Drucker, P. F. (1999). Managing oneself. *Harvard Business Review,* 77(2), 64-74.
- Frost & Sullivan. (2023). *Global security consulting market trends and forecasts.*
- Gartner. (2023). *Emerging technologies in security consulting.* Retrieved from https://www.gartner.com.
  - Grant, R. M. (1996). *Toward a knowledge-based theory of the firm.* Strategic Management Journal, 17(S2), 109-122.
- Harvard Business Review. (2022). *How companies scale operations effectively.* Retrieved from https://hbr.org.
  - IEEE. (2023). *AI and cybersecurity integration in the security sector.* Retrieved from https://www.ieee.org.
- International Association of Professional Security Consultants (IAPSC). (2023). *Best practices for growing a security consulting business.* Retrieved from https://www.iapsc.org.
- Kotler, P., & Keller, K. L. (2016). *Marketing management* (15th ed.). Pearson.
- McKinsey & Company. (2022). *Scaling security businesses in the digital age.* Retrieved from https://www.mckinsey.com.
  - Nejedlo, R. J. (1983). FROM TRANSFORMATION TO CREATIVE LEADERSHIP. Counselor Education and Supervision. https://doi.org/10.1002/j.1556-6978.1983.tb00582.x
- Niche Business Solutions: Maximizing Your Business Potential | Wedding Photos. https://weddingphotoss.com/28054-niche-business-solutions-maximizing-your-business-potential-59/
- Osterwalder, A., & Pigneur, Y. (2010). *Business Model Generation: A Handbook for Visionaries, Game Changers, and Challengers.* Wiley.
- Porter, M. E. (1996). What is strategy? *Harvard Business Review,* 74(6), 61-78.
- Ries, E. (2011). *The Lean Startup: How Today's Entrepreneurs Use Continuous Innovation to Create Radically Successful Businesses.* Crown Business.

- Sinek, S. (2009). *Start With Why: How Great Leaders Inspire Everyone to Take Action*. Penguin.
- Small Business Administration. (2023). *Guidelines for sustainable business growth*. Retrieved from https://www.sba.gov.
- SCORE. (2023). *Scaling for success: A guide for small businesses*. Retrieved from https://www.score.org.
  - Symantec. (2023). *Future trends in anti-drone technology*. Retrieved from https://www.symantec.com.
  - Unlock Success for Your E-Commerce Clients: Partner with Our Expert Social Media Management Agency - Drop Service News - Startup Blog. https://www.dropservicenews.com/unlock-success-for-your-e-commerce-clients-partner-with-our-expert-social-media-management-agency/
  - Unlocking the Power of Email Marketing for B2B Success. https://www.webociti.com/the-unmatched-power-of-email-marketing-for-b2b-companies/
- World Economic Forum. (2023). *The role of artificial intelligence in the security industry*. Retrieved from https://www.weforum.org.

Chapter 12: Financial Management for a Security Consulting Business

- (2016). Letters and comments, Sept. 15. Winnipeg Free Press, (), A6.
- ASIS International. (2022). *Security industry metrics: A practical guide*. ASIS Publishing.
- Atrill, P., & McLaney, E. (2021). *Accounting and finance for non-specialists* (11th ed.). Pearson Education.
- Bragg, S. M. (2019). *Business ratios and formulas: A comprehensive guide* (4th ed.). Wiley.
- FreshBooks. (2023). *Small business finance solutions*. Retrieved from https://www.freshbooks.com
- Gitman, L. J., & Zutter, C. J. (2020). *Principles of managerial finance* (15th ed.). Pearson Education.
- Goleman, D., & Boyatzis, R. (2020). *Leadership and self-deception in financial resilience*. Harvard Business Review Press.
- Grablowsky, B. J. (2020). *Small business cash flow management: Key strategies for entrepreneurs*. Entrepreneur Press.
- Henderson, M., & Josephs, R. (2022). *Diversification and risk management for small businesses*. Wiley.
- Holtzblatt, M., & Norrell, L. (2021). *Small business taxation: Understanding the essentials*. CPA Insights.
- Horngren, C. T., Sundem, G. L., Burgstahler, D., & Schatzberg, J. (2018). *Introduction to financial accounting* (12th ed.). Pearson Education.

- International Association of Security Consultants (IASC). (2022). *Guidelines for security consulting financial practices*. IASC Standards.
- Internal Revenue Service. (2023). *Tax guide for small business (Publication 334)*. U.S. Government Printing Office. Retrieved from https://www.irs.gov
- Intuit QuickBooks. (2023). *QuickBooks for small businesses*. Retrieved from https://quickbooks.intuit.com
- Johnson, L. K. (2021). *Resilience in business: Lessons for long-term stability*. Business Growth Publications.
- National Association of Tax Professionals (NATP). (2022). *Professional tax strategies for small businesses*. NATP Publications.
- National Security Institute (NSI). (2023). *Best practices for budgeting and financial planning in the security sector*. NSI Press.
- Portnoy, A. (2020). *The small business owner's guide to financial freedom*. Entrepreneur Press.
- Shepherd, D. A., & Patzelt, H. (2018). *Entrepreneurial growth: The role of resilience in navigating downturns*. Oxford University Press.
- Sutton, A. (2021). *The essential guide to managing small business finances*. Small Business Press.
- Tracy, J. A., & Barrow, T. (2020). *How to read a financial report: Wringing vital signs out of the numbers* (9th ed.). Wiley.
- Xero. (2023). *Financial planning for small businesses*. Retrieved from https://www.xero.com

Chapter 13: Time Management for the Solo Entrepreneur

- Adams, G., & Freedman, A. (2020). Effective Use of Automation in Small
- Allen, D. (2001). *Getting Things Done: The Art of Stress-Free Productivity*. Penguin Books.
- Asana. (2023). Task Management for Teams and Individuals. Retrieved from https://asana.com.
- Berkowitz, R. (2019). Time Management Practices for Independent Contractors. *Entrepreneurship Research Journal*, 9(4), 357–371.
- Businesses. *Journal of Business Strategy*, 41(3), 45–58.
- Covey, S. R. (1989). *The 7 Habits of Highly Effective People: Powerful Lessons in Personal Change*. Free Press.
- Eisenhower, D. D. (1961). Speech on Time Management and Prioritization. Eisenhower Presidential Library Archives.
- Forbes. (2021). Work-Life Balance Tips for Entrepreneurs. Retrieved from https://www.forbes.com.
- Harvard Business Review. (2019). The Eisenhower Matrix: How to Use it Effectively. Retrieved from https://hbr.org.

- How To Do a To Do List – Peggy W Barnes. https://peggywbarnes.com/how-to-do-a-to-do-list/
- HubSpot Blog. (2022). The Ultimate Guide to Time Management for Entrepreneurs. Retrieved from https://blog.hubspot.com.
- Inc.com. (2020). How to Automate Your Small Business to Save Time and Money. Retrieved from https://www.inc.com.
- McKeown, G. (2014). *Essentialism: The Disciplined Pursuit of Less*. Crown Business.
- Miller, J., & Smith, P. (2021). The Impact of Task Prioritization Techniques on Entrepreneurial Success. *Small Business Management Review*, 12(2), 65–83.
- Mind, have you been to the Eisenhower Matrix? | Laserfocus. https://www.laserfocus.io/blog/the-eisenhower-matrix
- Newport, C. (2016). *Deep Work: Rules for Focused Success in a Distracted World*. Grand Central Publishing.
- Pink, D. H. (2018). *When: The Scientific Secrets of Perfect Timing*. Riverhead Books.
- Small Business Administration (SBA). (2022). Time Management Tips for Entrepreneurs. Retrieved from https://www.sba.gov.
- Trello. (2023). Kanban Boards for Time Management. Retrieved from https://trello.com.
- U.S. Department of Labor. (2022). Understanding Work-Life Balance Statistics. Retrieved from https://www.dol.gov.
- Zapier. (2022). 50 Tasks You Can Automate Today. Retrieved from https://zapier.com.
- Zapier. (2023). Automation for Business Efficiency. Retrieved from https://zapier.com.

Chapter 14: Risk Management and Adapting to Industry Changes

- Anderson, M. (2021). *Navigating legal compliance for small businesses: A guide for entrepreneurs*. Small Business Press.
- Barton, L. (2018). *Crisis management: Preparing for the unexpected*. Harvard Business Review Press.
- Brynjolfsson, E., & McAfee, A. (2014). *The second machine age: Work, progress, and prosperity in a time of brilliant technologies*. W. W. Norton & Company.
- business continuity planning Archives - SEE Forge creators of FAT FINGER. https://fatfinger.io/tag/business-continuity-planning/
- Cambridge Centre for Risk Studies. (2020). *Global risk index 2020: A guide to managing uncertainty*. University of Cambridge.

- Cisco. (2023). 2023 *cybersecurity threat report*. Cisco Systems. Retrieved from https://www.cisco.com/c/en/us/products/security/2023-cybersecurity-report
- Deloitte Insights. (2021). *Adapting to industry shifts: A roadmap for resilience*. Deloitte. Retrieved from https://www.deloitte.com/insights
- Fisher, C., & Ury, W. (1981). *Getting to yes: Negotiating agreement without giving in*. Penguin Books.
- Harvard Business Review Staff. (2020). How to adapt your business strategy to market shifts. *Harvard Business Review*.Retrieved from https://hbr.org
- ISO. (2022). *ISO standards for business continuity and risk management*. International Organization for Standardization. Retrieved from https://www.iso.org
- It is not the strongest species that survive, nor the most intelligent, but the most responsive to change: Charles Darwin. https://www.pulsus.com/scholarly-articles/it-is-not-the-strongest-species-that-survive-nor-the-most-intelligent-but-the-most-responsive-to-change-charles-darwin.html
- Kaplan, R. S., & Mikes, A. (2012). Managing risks: A new framework. *Harvard Business Review*. Retrieved from https://hbr.org
- KPMG. (2022). *Technology transformation in the security sector: Trends and strategies*. KPMG. Retrieved from https://home.kpmg/xx/en/home/insights.html
- National Institute of Standards and Technology (NIST). (2023). *Cybersecurity framework for small businesses*. U.S. Department of Commerce. Retrieved from https://www.nist.gov
- Porter, M. E. (1980). *Competitive strategy: Techniques for analyzing industries and competitors*. Free Press.
- Rostron, R. (2019). *Adaptability: The art of navigating change*. McGraw-Hill Education.
- Strategies to Grow Your Business: Planning for Success - Technology for Learners. https://technologyforlearners.com/strategies-to-grow-your-business-planning-for-success/
- Taleb, N. N. (2010). *The black swan: The impact of the highly improbable*. Random House Trade Paperbacks.
- Taneja, H., & Manfredi, E. (2021). How to prepare for industry disruptions. *MIT Sloan Management Review*. Retrieved from https://sloanreview.mit.edu
- World Economic Forum. (2023). *The global risks report 2023*. Retrieved from https://www.weforum.org/reports

Chapter 15: Legal Considerations and Client Contracts

- American Bar Association. (n.d.). Contract drafting essentials. Retrieved from https://www.americanbar.org
- Cornell Law School. (n.d.). Non-compete agreements. Legal Information Institute. Retrieved from https://www.law.cornell.edu
- Cornell Law School. (n.d.). Non-disclosure agreements. Legal Information Institute. Retrieved from https://www.law.cornell.edu
- Effective Strategies for Small Business Owners in Legal Disputes - Norton Pelt, PLC. https://nortonpelt.com/effective-strategies-for-small-business-owners-in-legal-disputes/
- FindLaw. (n.d.). Understanding contract law basics. Retrieved from https://www.findlaw.com
- Gaille, L. (2021). 1099 contractor agreements: Key elements and best practices. Small Business Resources Weekly. Retrieved from https://www.sbrw.com
- Harvard Business Review. (2019). Building strategic partnerships: Dos and don'ts. Retrieved from https://www.hbr.org
- How to Become a Lawyer: Steps to Becoming an Attorney. https://www.enjuris.com/students/becoming-a-lawyer/
- Mergers & Acquisitions News. (2020). Legal dispute resolution techniques in small business contexts. Retrieved from https://www.ma-news.com
- Small Business Administration (SBA). (2022). Drafting and managing contracts: A guide for small businesses. Retrieved from https://www.sba.gov
- What Should Be in a Freelance Contract? - The Contract Shop®. https://thecontractshop.com/blogs/posts/what-should-be-in-a-freelance-contract

Chapter 16: Long-Term Success and Exit Strategies

- 5 Key Elements to Investigate Before Investing in a Business – Meritus Group Business Brokerage. https://meritus.group/5-elements-for-buyers-to-investigate/
- American Management Association (AMA). (2020). Succession planning and leadership development: A guide. Retrieved from https://www.amanet.org
- Beyond the Pandemic: Strategies for Startups to Thrive in the Post-COVID Era. https://www.cofi.ai/resources/beyond-the-pandemic-strategies-for-startups-to-thrive-in-the-post-covid-era
- Forbes. (2022). Selling your business: Steps to maximize value. Retrieved from https://www.forbes.com

- Harvard Business Review. (2021). Leadership pipelines: Developing talent for tomorrow. Retrieved from https://www.hbr.org
- How to Develop SOPs for Enhancing Business Agility: Your Ultimate Guide. https://www.prosulum.com/how-to-develop-sops-for-enhancing-business-agility-your-ultimate-guide/
- Inc. Magazine. (2021). Exit strategies for small businesses: Options and tips. Retrieved from https://www.inc.com
- SCORE. (n.d.). Preparing your business for sale or merger. Retrieved from https://www.score.org
- Security Industry Association (SIA). (2020). Long-term planning in the security industry. Retrieved from https://www.securityindustry.org
- The Balance. (2023). Continuous improvement strategies for entrepreneurs. Retrieved from https://www.thebalance.com
- "The best way to predict the future is to create it." - Deep Quotes Blog. https://www.deepquotes.in/quotation/the-best-way-to-predict-the-future-is-to-create-it
- The Conference Board. (2020). Building a legacy in business: Lessons from industry leaders. Retrieved from https://www.conference-board.org

- https://cl.pinterest.com/ideas/failure-is-not-fatal/927040818366/
- Why New Businesses Fail. https://www.smallbmentor.com/blog/howtoensureyourbusinessdoesntfail

General Resources Referenced Across Chapters 15 and 16

- Entrepreneur Magazine. (2021). Best practices for small business contracts. Retrieved from https://www.entrepreneur.com
- National Federation of Independent Business (NFIB). (2022). Understanding small business legal risks. Retrieved from https://www.nfib.com
- U.S. Chamber of Commerce. (2021). Legal considerations for entrepreneurs. Retrieved from https://www.uschamber.com

Annex A: The Importance of Having a Corporate Social Responsibility Program (CSRP)

- Carroll, A. B., & Shabana, K. M. (2010). The business case for corporate social responsibility: A review of concepts, research, and practice. *International Journal of Management Reviews, 12*(1), 85-105. https://doi.org/10.1111/j.1468-2370.2009.00275.x
- Kotler, P., & Lee, N. (2005). *Corporate social responsibility: Doing the most good for your company and your cause.* Wiley.
- Porter, M. E., & Kramer, M. R. (2011). Creating shared value. *Harvard Business Review, 89*(1/2), 62-77. https://hbr.org/2011/01/the-big-idea-creating-shared-value
- United Nations Global Compact. (n.d.). *Principles of corporate social responsibility.* Retrieved from https://www.unglobalcompact.org

Annex B: Having and Implementing a Quality Management Process (QMP)

- ISO. (2015). *ISO 9001:2015 - Quality management systems – Requirements.* International Organization for Standardization.
- Deming, W. E. (1986). *Out of the crisis.* MIT Press.
- Juran, J. M. (1999). *Juran's quality handbook.* McGraw-Hill.
- Crosby, P. B. (1979). *Quality is free: The art of making quality certain.* McGraw-Hill.
- American Society for Quality (ASQ). (n.d.). *What is quality management?* Retrieved from https://asq.org

Annex C: The Meaning of Colors in Business Logos and Branding

- 800+ Color Quotes to Explore Shades of Emotion and Thought in 2024. https://onlycaptions.com/color-quotes/
- Creating a Visual Identity that Resonates with Your Audience. https://www.joiebrands.com/journal/creating-a-visual-identity-that-resonates-with-your-audience

- Eiseman, L. (2006). *Color: Messages and meanings: A Pantone color resource.* Hand Books Press.
- Hynes, N. (2009). Colour and meaning in corporate logos: An empirical study. *Journal of Brand Management, 16*(8), 545-555. https://doi.org/10.1057/palgrave.bm.2550130
- Singh, S. (2006). Impact of color on marketing. *Management Decision, 44*(6), 783-789. https://doi.org/10.1108/00251740610673332
- Wheeler, A. (2017). *Designing brand identity: An essential guide for the whole branding team* (5th ed.). Wiley.

Annex D: Free or Inexpensive Sources for New and Veteran Entrepreneurs

- American Corporate Partners (ACP). (n.d.). *Veteran mentorship program.* Retrieved from https://www.acp-usa.org
- Bunker Labs. (n.d.). *Veterans in Residence.* Retrieved from https://bunkerlabs.org
- Canva. (n.d.). *Graphic design platform.* Retrieved from https://www.canva.com
- Forbes. (n.d.). *Small business trends and challenges.* Retrieved from https://www.forbes.com
- Google My Business. (n.d.). *Manage your online presence.* Retrieved from https://www.google.com/business/
- Harvard Business Review. (n.d.). *Leadership, strategy, and innovation insights.* Retrieved from https://hbr.org
- HubSpot. (n.d.). *HubSpot CRM.* Retrieved from https://www.hubspot.com
- Institute for Veterans and Military Families (IVMF). (n.d.). *Boots to Business.* Retrieved from https://ivmf.syracuse.edu
- LinkedIn Premium. (n.d.). *Networking and professional growth.* Retrieved from https://www.linkedin.com
- Mailchimp. (n.d.). *Email marketing platform.* Retrieved from https://mailchimp.com
- Mint. (n.d.). *Personal finance and budgeting app.* Retrieved from https://www.mint.com
- QuickBooks. (n.d.). *Accounting software.* Retrieved from https://quickbooks.intuit.com
- Rocket Lawyer. (n.d.). *Affordable legal services for businesses.* Retrieved from https://www.rocketlawyer.com
- SCORE. (n.d.). *Free business mentoring and resources.* Retrieved from https://www.score.org
- Security Management Magazine. (n.d.). *Industry thought leadership and*

resources. Retrieved from https://www.asisonline.org/security-management-magazine

- StreetShares. (n.d.). *Funding and mentorship for veteran entrepreneurs*. Retrieved from https://streetshares.com
- U.S. Small Business Administration (SBA). (n.d.). *Resources for small business owners*. Retrieved from https://www.sba.gov
- V-WISE: Veteran Women Igniting the Spirit of Entrepreneurship - D'Aniello Institute for Veterans and Military Families. https://ivmf.syracuse.edu/item/v-wise-veteran-women-igniting-the-spirit-of-entrepreneurship/
- Warrior Rising. (n.d.). *Empowering veterans to succeed in business*. Retrieved from https://www.warriorrising.org

Unlock the Power of Generosity

People who give without expecting anything in return lead richer lives — not just in success, but in fulfillment. Let's create that ripple effect together.

Would you help someone just like you — thinking about starting a security consulting business but unsure where to begin?

My mission is to make launching and running a successful security consulting business practical and achievable for anyone willing to learn and hustle.

But to reach more aspiring entrepreneurs, I need your help.

Most people choose books based on reviews. That's why I'm asking *YOU* to lend a hand by leaving a review for **Security, LLC: The Entrepreneur's Comprehensive Blueprint for Launching and Running a Thriving Consulting Business.**

Your review could be the reason...

...one more small business secures its first client.

...one more entrepreneur builds a future for their family.

...one more team member finds meaningful work.

...one more dream transforms into a reality.

It's simple:

1. Scan the QR code below or visit this link: www.

2. SHARE WHAT YOU LOVED ABOUT THE BOOK AND HOW IT
   HELPED YOU.

IT TAKES JUST A MOMENT, BUT YOUR WORDS COULD CHANGE SOME-
ONE'S ENTIRE ENTREPRENEURIAL JOURNEY.

IF YOU BELIEVE IN PAYING IT FORWARD, YOU'RE MY KIND OF
PERSON.

THANK YOU AND STAY SAFE OUT THERE!

MEB WEST, CPP

AUTHOR, SECURITY CONSULTANT, AND FELLOW ENTREPRENEUR.

About the Author

Meb West, CPP, CCM, CHS-III is a globally recognized security management expert, entrepreneur, and thought leader with over three decades of experience in security consulting, business development, and executive leadership. As the founder and Director of Seven Spears Security International, Meb has built a reputation for delivering innovative and actionable security strategies for clients ranging from multinational corporations to ultra-high-net-worth individuals. His approach blends tactical precision with a deep understanding of business operations, making him a sought-after advisor in the security consulting industry.

Meb's career includes distinguished service as a US Army Ranger and Senior Leader with 26 years of service specializing in Military Intelligence and Special Operations. His military expertise sharpened his ability to develop and implement complex security programs, lead cross-functional teams, and manage large-scale crisis contingency operations across the globe.

In the private sector, Meb has advised Fortune 500 companies, secured high-value assets in unstable regions, and designed enterprise-level business continuity plans. His leadership extends to serving as Vice President, Director of Training at a prominent security training academy, where he mentors future security professionals.

Meb holds a Master's Degree in Security Management and executive certifications from prestigious institutions, including Harvard Business

School, IE Business School (Madrid, Spain), and the University of Pennsylvania's Wharton School of Business. His industry credentials include certifications as a Certified Protection Professional (CPP) and Certified Continuity Manager (CCM) and numerous specialized security certifications from globally recognized organizations.

Through *Security LLC: The Entrepreneur's Comprehensive Blueprint for Launching and Running a Thriving Consulting Business*, Meb channels his passion for mentorship, guiding aspiring security entrepreneurs with practical insights, industry-specific strategies, and lessons learned from a lifetime of operational success. His mission is simple: to empower others to turn their passion for security into thriving, impactful businesses.